Anthropological Research

Skolt Lapp with Draught Reindeer Headed for Market, Sevettijarvi, Finland

Anthropological Research

THE STRUCTURE OF INQUIRY

Pertti J. Pelto
UNIVERSITY OF CONNECTICUT

Harper & Row, Publishers
NEW YORK, EVANSTON, AND LONDON

Picture Credits

Frontispiece by the author. Chapter opening pages: 1, Irma Honigmann; 21, Norman A. Chance; 47, 154, and 213, the author; 67 and 320, James Faris; 89, Gerald Berreman; 175, Gretel H. Pelto; 276, Paul Conklin; 329, John Honigmann.

Anthropological Research: THE STRUCTURE OF INQUIRY

Copyright © 1970 by **Pertti J. Pelto**

LIBRARY OF CONGRESS CATALOG CARD NUMBER: 76-101538

To Gretel, Jonathan, and Ari

Contents

Preface

When I embarked on my first major anthropological research venture—the field work for my Ph.D. dissertation—I had had no formal training in the logic and structure of social sciences research. Many of my peers have described a similar lack of methodological preparedness in the years of their doctoral candidacy. Our generation of anthropologists, trained in the 1950s, learned the descriptive and theoretical contributions of our predecessors, but not how these anthropological contributions were achieved. We were not unconcerned about how field research is carried out—in fact we were almost frantic to find out—but we were assured by our teachers that we could learn the mysteries of field work only through personal immersion in the practically undescribable but romantically alluring complexities of the field. Much of the lore about field research that we picked up informally in our graduate-student days was concerned with the gentle arts of rapport-building and role-playing in field situations. We were not so much concerned, nor were our mentors, with rules of evidence, questions of "representativeness," "validity," "reliability," and the many other related elements of scientific inquiry with which our friends in other social sciences seemed to be preoccupied. I can recall no discussion or even mention of the idea of "operationalizing variables" in those halcyon days.

As I took up my first position of teaching anthropology to a newer generation, I developed an interest in teaching research methods to graduate students. I quickly found, however, that discussions of anthropological methods were few and far between in our professional writing and that to examine many problems of the social sciences it was necessary to turn to a fairly voluminous literature in sociology and psychology, much of which had to be reinterpreted to fit the context of our cross-cultural research interests. In recent years there has been a steady increase in the amount of anthropological discussion of research methods. This accumulating literature includes many personalized accounts of field experiences that provide useful information about what anthropologists do in field research and how they collect specific types of information. There still seems to me, however, to be a serious shortage of material concerning the logical steps and requirements whereby ethnographers convert the stuff of raw observation into abstract anthropological conceptual structures. This is the domain of methodology, as contrasted with the concrete, how-to-do-it realm of field techniques.

In this book I focus my discussion on what I consider to be the essential elements of preparing and manipulating the supporting evidence from which generalizations about human behavior are derived. At some points this discussion of research logic must touch base in the relatively concrete details of specific tools of observation—e.g., informant interviewing, observing ceremonial behavior, and survey research. But my main intention is to examine the details of particular research instruments only to the minimum extent necessary for looking at how these basic observations can be systematically translated into sociocultural generalizations.

Most of the principles of research methodology that I incorporate into this book have been around in the social sciences for a long time, and they have been successfully utilized by a number of anthropologists. Thus, in writing this book I have tried to serve mainly as a compiler of methodological principles and techniques.

In general, the reader of these pages will note that my point of view is quite eclectic; I put strong emphasis on quantification and statistics, but I also feel strongly that many of the more qualitative aspects of anthropological working styles are essential to effective research. If I were to pick out some main themes of my argument, the following working principles would receive special emphasis:

1. Anthropological generalizations and more complex theoretical structures can be built up only through careful *operationalizing* of basic concepts—the building blocks of all theory.
2. Successful description and hypothesis testing depend on the judicious mixing of quantitative and qualitative research materials.

Many people helped me write this book. At various stages in its preparation portions of the manuscript were read and commented on by Harold Driver, Theodore Graves, Myles Hopper, James Jacquith, Philip Kilbride, Robert Maxwell, Raoul Naroll, Philip Newman, Richard Pollnac, Michael Robbins, Ronald Rohner, and Douglas White. I owe them all many thanks for their suggestions.

The research projects that provided much of the experience on which this book depends involved many graduate students, some of whose research contributions are discussed in the text. Of these, I am particularly grateful for the excellent field work and critical discussion of John Lozier, J. Anthony Paredes, John Poggie, Jr., Stephen Schensul, and Barbara Simon.

Over the past few years I have had innumerable conversations with anthropologists, sociologists, psychologists, and other social scientists about methodological problems. Of these people I am particularly indebted to Gerald Berreman, Fernando Cámara, Robert Flint, Luther Gerlach, Eugene Hammel, William Lambert, Luis Leñero, Frank Miller, Paul Mussen, Rafael Nuñez, John M. Roberts, Murray Straus, Arthur Wolf, and Frank Young, and many others who contributed directly and indirectly to the writing of this book. To all of these people and to those I have not mentioned, I would like to acknowledge a large debt of gratitude.

My wife, Gretel, has read all parts of this manuscript several times and has been my chief assistant, adviser, and editor. Many aspects of my treatment of methodological issues were developed in discussions with her. I have occasionally incorporated passages into this book over her objections but, for the most part, she shares fully in whatever credit and criticism may come from this work.

Among the many other people who contributed time and thought to the preparation of the manuscript I owe grateful thanks to Ellen Kinberg, who had the difficult chore of translating my drafts into cleanly typed copy.

P. J. P.

Storrs, Connecticut
January 1970

John Honigmann Interviewing Indian Informant About His Kinship System

1. Introduction

In simple, personalized terms, the essence of research methodology lies in seeking answers to the following basic questions: How can I find "true and useful information" [1] about a particular domain of phenomena in our universe? This fundamental question actually involves two closely related problems.

---

[1] I use the expression "true and useful information" in quotation marks in order to indicate that, although we generally assume the presence of a concrete, "real world," "the truth" or "the facts" about the real world are always seen and interpreted by means of our observational equipment, our conceptual categories, and our general theoretical outlook. Hence we can never establish any final "absolute truth." On the other hand, scientific information varies with regard to its degree of approximation to some postulated "absolute truth." In general, though, the truth value of our information is best measured by criteria of usefulness—in predicting and explaining our experience in the natural world. Criteria of usefulness are derivable both from theoretical domains of science and from people's practical experiences and problems.

1. How can I personally investigate some domain of phenomena in order to obtain "true and useful information"?
2. How can I know, with some assurance, what another person (researcher) means when he asserts propositions about information, and how can I judge whether I should believe him?

The first problem directs our attention to the techniques and conditions necessary for exploration of our phenomenal world. If I wish, for example, to gain some new information about stellar bodies and their behavior, it is likely that a telescope would be a handy tool in this search for "the facts." The many different domains of phenomena in our universe each require their special tools and techniques for gathering information about them. The study of bacteria and other microorganisms requires a microscope; the examination of electrical circuitry requires various meters and other devices; "getting the facts" about the anatomical characteristics of animals requires surgical techniques and tools for opening up and looking at features that are generally hidden from view.

When it comes to studying human behavior, the matter of research instruments is a little different. Most primary data in the social sciences come from three sources: directly observing human behavior; listening to and noting the contents of human speech; and examining the products of human behavior—particularly those products found in archives, records, and libraries. For example, in the study of economic behavior the significant data may be in the form of prices of goods, volume of goods (e.g., numbers of cars, bushels of wheat), costs of production, and related numerical information. Research in economics, then, may be carried out without special instruments of observation and measurement, but the researcher must be able to go to sources of already recorded information (governmental statistical records, record systems of individual manufacturing enterprises, etc.). The monetized structure of economic behavior in our society provides built-in observational units. In tribal and primitive societies without cash economies, on the other hand, economic research involves primary observations of behavior and goods; hence techniques of data collection must be quite different. In general, the social sciences differ from other scientific fields in that primary data gathering is in most cases possible without the aid of highly specialized observational instruments.

An untrained person looking into a microscope or telescope learns practically nothing from his use of the powerful instrument. Similarly, a nonspecialist presented with lists of prices, costs, and other numerical data can make little sense of this pile of economic data. Without some kind of additional experience and information, the novice has no framework and no rules for interpreting what he sees. The novice microscope user needs to acquire a conceptual framework for differentiating living from nonliving forms; he needs a set of definitions concerning types of organisms, parts of organisms, and their relationships. The novice economist is probably already equipped with at least common-sense definitions of "price," "cost," etc.; but he cannot make sense of a mass of data without some logical rules for plotting "curves," "indexes," and other relational statements. Ethnographic observations, similarly, make little sense unless the observer has a general conceptual framework for sorting out and organizing behavioral elements.

Thus, in addition to the basic tools and instruments of observation and measurement, a scientific researcher must have, at the very least, sets of procedural rules (including concepts and definitions) by which he transforms sensual evidence into generalizations about phenomena. It is one of the goals of all scientific disciplines to link together low-order generalizations, or propositions, into larger networks of propositions that will make possible the prediction and explanation of phenomena within the given domain. Such networks of propositions are generally called *theories*. The relationships among the several elements of scientific work can be diagramed as in Figure 1.

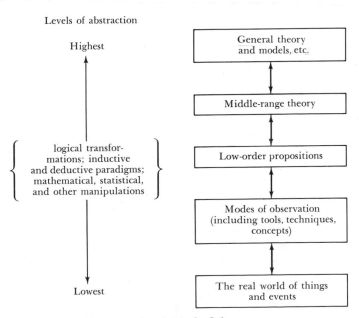

FIGURE 1. **The Domain of Methodology**

Methodology, then, refers to the structure of procedures and transformational rules whereby the scientist shifts information up and down this "ladder of abstraction" in order to produce and organize increased knowledge. At the point of primary observation, as the bacteriologist peers into his microscope, he *must* have available to him some conceptual tools—definitions of things seen and experienced—in terms of which he can give form and description to his observations. The primary descriptions, in turn, are related to more abstract propositions—to general theory about microorganisms—by a progression of logical steps which must be very clearly understood and agreed on by fellow scientists in the profession. This progression through levels of abstraction is not a one-way process, however. The bacteriologist does not select objects for observation randomly. His general, theoretical framework is a main source of ideas and predictions in terms of which particular foci of observation are selected.

Thus defined, "methodology" can be distinguished from "research techniques" in that the latter term is useful for referring to the pragmatic problems of primary data collection, while methodology denotes the "logic-in-use" involved in selecting particular observational techniques, assessing their yield of data, and relating these data to theoretical propositions. In practice, the practical problems of using particular techniques of data gathering cannot be entirely separated from the examination of their "logic-in-use." Any methodological discussion, then, must include some reference to techniques.

In Chapter 5 we will examine methodological problems related to interviewing key informants. Whole books have been written about *techniques* of interviewing, for the yield of data by this process can vary greatly depending on the skill, tactics, and other characteristics of the interviewer. On the other hand, our concern in this book will be mainly with the *logical manipulations* whereby we make use of interview data to accomplish theoretically important (and valid) results.

Let us turn to an example from anthropological research in order to illustrate this basic paradigm of research methodology. Suppose we are interested in finding out something about the cultural and social characteristics of relatively isolated, nomadic groups of hunting peoples. If we want to get first-hand information about such groups, we must, of course, arrange for a field expedition to a region where they may be found. On the other hand, there are published accounts of nomadic societies, and we can begin our methodological analysis with these materials. We could start with a systematic collection of relevant literature under the rubric *nomadic hunting societies.* Notice that our opening move—a search of the literature—is impossible without some definitions. We need at least tentative definitions of "nomadic," "hunting," and "societies." And the definitions of these concepts can make no sense unless they distinguish nomadic from nonnomadic and hunting from nonhunting in a larger domain of concepts. Since the literature we need to examine contains reports from a great many different ethnographers, *general agreement* about definitions and concepts is of great importance. Thus, even the most elementary conceptual tasks depend on some sort of larger, more abstract, theoretical system.

Having set out our tentative definitions of the research domain, we obtain a set of materials dealing with a number of hunting peoples in various parts of the world. Suppose one of the research reports about nomadic societies is Allan Holmberg's *Nomads of the Long Bow* (1969), an account of the Siriono people of eastern and northern Bolivia. As we turn to an examination of *Nomads of the Long Bow* we learn that "besides being a member of a nuclear family, every Siriono also belongs to a larger kin group, the matrilineal extended family" (p. 128). Our first problem is what Holmberg means by the expression *matrilineal extended family.* Fortunately, he provides a definition that is quite explicit: "An extended [matrilineal] family is made up of all females in a direct line of descent, plus their spouses and their unmarried children." This definition is, in effect, a *rule* for grouping information. That is, the concept *matrilineal extended family* allows Holmberg to state a number of generalizations that apply simultaneously to several different actual groups of persons. Holmberg's monograph, like all such works, is full of terminology which, in essence, permits the clustering, or abstracting, of information into shorthand form in terms of transformational rules.

We are now faced, however, with the problem of knowing how Holmberg assembled the information contained within the expression *matrilineal extended family.* From the monograph and other sources, it is clear that he lived with the Siriono for a number of months, so the possibilities for gaining the information were clearly present. Perhaps during this time he asked one of the Siriono about his kinsmen. His informant might have replied, "I, like all Siriono, belong to a matrilineal extended family, which may be defined as. . . ." Such a response is unlikely, however. It is much more likely that Holmberg's hypothetical informant would have answered with a series of statements concerning his "most important" kinsmen, or perhaps with statements about the people with whom he shared food and other items. Under further questioning, he might have told the ethnographer that "everybody" belongs in or "has" a group of kinsmen with whom food and other items are shared, and that these groups are "always the same" in that membership in them is traced through female links in a particular way.

Holmberg may also have gotten the information by direct observation. It turns out that members of the extended families "cooperate to build that portion of the dwelling which they occupy. They sometimes plant gardens in common" (*ibid.*, 128). Also, "the distribution of food rarely extends beyond the extended family." Since Holmberg lived among the Siriono and since each band lives in a communal house, we expect that he had ample opportunity to observe that certain individuals were regularly grouped together in terms of key activities.

Without asking about kin groups from the people themselves, Holmberg may have noted that whenever a certain individual A returned to the communal house with some meat he distributed it to persons B, C, D, and E, but never to any of the other persons in the band. In addition, he may have noted that A, B, C, D, and E worked together to build a portion of the communal dwelling, after which they were usually to be found in that portion of the house— sleeping, eating, or resting—if they were present in the band area. He would, of course, need verbally produced information about the presumed kinship relationships linking the persons in the observed groups.

Typically, anthropological fieldworkers combine the data from personal, eyewitness observation with information gained from informants' descriptions of behavior. Holmberg's statements about matrilineal extended families among the Siriono undoubtedly were based on both kinds of information. Unfortunately, Holmberg's description, like practically all ethnographic descriptions, rarely makes clear exactly what kinds of observations formed the basis for particular generalizations.

Like most ethnographers, Holmberg intended to collect a wide range of information about his chosen research people in order to present a "holistic" portrait of their way of life. That is, the theoretical orientation of cultural anthropology has for the most part encouraged a very eclectic view with regard to selection of relevant data. In a summarizing section, Holmberg drew together the wide range of primary observations written up in *Nomads of the Long Bow* into a series of generalizations about the Siriono. On the whole, he felt, these people are rather unsuccessful in their food quest, and they live under conditions of perennial food insecurity and hunger frustration. From another complex array of primary observations, he came to the conclusion that the Siriono are uncooperative vis à vis one another, greedy about food, uncaring about one another's welfare, and generally quarrelsome and suspicious.

From these descriptive field data Holmberg suggested a series of middle-range generalizations "for further refinement and investigation in other societies where conditions of food insecurity and hunger frustration are comparable to those found among the Siriono." The following are a sampling from his list of propositions:

1. Such societies will be characterized by a general backwardness of culture.
2. Aggression will be expressed largely in terms of food.
3. Positions of power and authority will be occupied by individuals who are the best providers of food.
4. There will be a tendency to kill, abandon, neglect, or otherwise dispose of the aged, the deformed young, and the extremely ill.
5. Prestige will be gained and status maintained largely by food-getting activities.

These middle-range theoretical propositions were advanced by Holmberg as derivatives from a very general psychophysiological theory of human behavior. Thus, the low-order descriptive generalizations about the Siriono were combined with elements from much higher levels of abstraction (general psychological theory) to form a series of potentially researchable statements concerning "societies with high food insecurity."

There are several points of methodological interest in this research example. First, it is clearly recognized by the researcher himself that the data from a single society can only be used for *suggesting* higher-order relationships; establishing more abstract theoretical propositions depends on some kind of transformation of primary descriptive data, through a process involving information from many different societies.

Also, it is important to keep in mind that the successful testing of Holmberg's research hypotheses can be carried out only if available descriptive data from other "hungry societies" contain the same kinds of observations and descriptive generalizations as those available for the Siriono. Even if such data are available, there may be some serious problems in making systematic comparisons, because of the difficulty of establishing cross-culturally usable definitions of such terms as *backwardness of culture, aggression,* and *positions of power and authority.* Even seemingly obvious concepts, such as "best providers of food" and the "extremely ill," require definition; and what is more important, for each of these basic terms in Holmberg's propositions there must be specification as to the methods of data gathering by means of which the concepts are operationalized. That is, from the variety of *possible* ways to obtain the needed comparative information, some *one* method should be selected if these cross-cultural data are to be strictly equatable.

It is instructive to note that Holmberg's propositions have not been tested in any definitive way, although *some* individual cases of other "hungry societies" have been described as providing refutations of the hypotheses. Since the Siriono data and accompanying research suggestions were originally published two decades ago (1950), why should those rather important research ideas have remained untested? The answer to this question takes us to the heart of some methodological dilemmas of contemporary anthropology. As already suggested above, cross-cultural testing of anthropological hypotheses requires standardization of research procedures in such a manner that operationally equivalent observations can be selected and compared. At the very least, research reports would have to include enough information about research procedures so that an investigator seeking to compare information from a number of societies could make informed judgments concerning the comparability of descriptive statements. Thus, Holmberg's hypotheses have remained largely untested at least partly because of the methodological difficulties involved.

In this review of Holmberg's research on the Siriono we see an illustration of the fact that the expression "true and useful information" in my original methodological question refers to a wide range of different kinds of statements, at different levels of abstraction. At a relatively low level of abstraction we have such information as: "The Siriono are frequently hungry." At the level of middle-range theory Holmberg suggests a series of propositions about societies with high "food insecurity and hunger frustration." These statements (hypotheses) relate to very general theoretical propositions such as:

The human organism is stimulated to behave by what are known as drives. . . . They are of two kinds: primary (basic or innate) and secondary (derived or acquired). The primary drives are those which result from the normal biological processes . . . such as hunger, thirst, sex, fatigue, and pain. (*Ibid.,* 244.)

There is no essential logical difference between the low-level generalizations and those at the most abstract levels. That is, description and theory are not different kinds of logical processes. The congruence of these forms is apparent in the following transformations (arranged in descending order of abstraction):

1. Noun phrase / verb phrase
2. The human organism / is stimulated by what are known as drives.

3. Societies high in food insecurity and hunger frustration / allocate prestige and status largely in terms of food-getting activities.
4. The Siriono / allocate prestige and status largely in terms of food-getting activities. "If a man is a good hunter, his status is apt to be high." (*Ibid.,* 145.)
5. Enía (brother-in-law of Chief Eantándu) / was of low status until Holmberg taught him to use a shotgun, and he began to bring in lots of game.
   "Needless to say, when I left Tibaera he / was enjoying the highest status." (*Ibid.,* 146.)

This set of transformations of data statements, based on the logical patterning of Holmberg's statements about the Siriono, suggests a series of questions for special methodological attention.

1. What kinds of primary observations of Siriono individuals are necessary and sufficient for establishing useful statements about, for example, "allocation of prestige and status"?

Closely related to this first question are the following:

2. How many observations (based on what criteria of selection) are needed to establish the generalization(s) about prestige and status?
3. How can societies characterized by high food insecurity and hunger frustration be identified and contrasted with other societies in order to test propositions about allocation of prestige and status?
4. Holmberg assumes that characteristics of the individual human organism (drives) can be transformed directly into *group,* or societal, characteristics (allocation of prestige and status). Many anthropologists (and others) would disagree, maintaining that individual organic processes and societal behavior norms represent two distinct *levels of phenomena,* so that transformations between the two levels cannot occur in the form implied by Holmberg. How can this general methodological conflict be resolved?
   Stated in more general terms, what are the rules for transformations of data *across* supposed "levels of phenomena"?
5. The informational statements in the paradigm above are highly subject to modification or even total negation) from other factors affecting human behavior. What rules and procedures can be used to express the interrelationships among a large number of interrelated factors affecting social events and processes?
6. Theoretical propositions derived from other domains and "schools" of the social sciences may be equally efficient sources of higher-order statements which can be transformed into the lower-order information about the Siriono.
   That is, a number of other kinds of statements could be substituted for some of Holmberg's statements.

How can the *most effective* general theoretical propositions (or systems of general theory) be selected from among competing alternatives?

If one became involved in actual research on Holmberg's propositions, a large number of additional methodological issues would have to be faced. However, my discussion here is intended to set out only the outlines of our problems concerning anthropological methodology. Additional details about these problems, as well as some proposed solutions to them, will be discussed in relation to specific research "cases" in later chapters.

Elements of Research Methodology

The discussion about the Siriono and about Holmberg's theoretical statements is intended as an illustration of the main elements of research methodology. These elements make up the research language, the logical framework, in terms of which anthropological investigations (and other scientific studies) are carried out. At this point it would be useful to clarify some of my assumptions about these methodological elements.

CONCEPTS AND DEFINITIONS

The language of anthropology, like that of every science, consists mainly of concepts, propositions, and theories. Concepts are the basic elements—the building blocks of anthropological research. Familiar anthropological terms, such as *family, digging stick, peasant, hunter, slash-and burn agriculture,* and *religion,* are all examples of concepts, though these examples differ considerably in degree of abstraction. The point to emphasize is that concepts are abstractions from concrete observations. The term *digging stick,* for example, is an abstraction that is intended to symbolize a variety of pointed (usually wooden) objects by means of which horticulturalists in various parts of the world carry out some of the essential acts related to crop growing. This statement (which is not a definition) is constructed from a whole string of abstract concepts. Nonetheless, the term *digging stick* is much less abstract than, for example, the term *religion,* which does not refer to a particular type of object, but rather to a domain of widely varied beliefs, objects, and actions.

Whole books in the philosophy of science have been devoted to examining the fundamental logic and relationships among scientific concepts. We will not explore this vast area of discourse here, but certain fundamental assumptions need to be made clear. First, it should be emphasized that concepts are arbitrary selections from the universe of experience. Goode and Hatt, in discussing the arbitrariness of definitions, make the following significant points:

Concepts develop from a shared experience.
Terms used to denote scientific concepts may also have meanings in other frames of reference.
A term may refer to different phenomena.
Different terms may refer to the same phenomena.
A term may have no immediate empirical referent at all.
The meaning of concepts may change.
(Goode and Hatt, 1952:44–48)

For this last point it is instructive to take an example from the physical sciences. Ernest Nagel, in his discussion of the structure of science, points out that the definition of the concept *electron* has changed as theoretical physics has developed.

What is to be an electron is stated by a theory in which the word "electron" occurs; and when the theory is altered, the meaning of the word undergoes a modification. . . . In particular, though the same word "electron" is used in prequantum theories of the electronic constitution of matter, in the Bohr theory, and in post-Bohr theories, the meaning of the word is not the same in all these theories. (Nagel, 1961:88.)

This illustrates one of the several significant ways in which theory and methodology are interwoven.

PROPOSITIONS

Propositions are statements of interrelationships among concepts. The statement "Peasants are pragmatic" is a proposition whose relative truth value depends on the effectiveness of the researcher's manipulations of the concepts *peasant* and *pragmatic*. As I have illustrated in the case of Holmberg's Siriono, propositions usually assume a two-part, subject-predicate form, in which one concept involves the definition of the given population (of objects, persons, events) about which a measurement or judgment of qualities (e.g., pragmatic, joyous, intelligent, homogeneous, well-organized, effective) is to be made.

In all cases the definitions of particular concepts as subjects of research involve explicit or implicit contrasts between the concept under consideration (e.g., peasants) and the set of all other possible subjects chosen from the same universe. Thus *peasant* is defined as a type of person (or community) having particular characteristics that contrast with *urban dwellers, hunters,* and other possible members of this particular domain of discourse (human groups categorized in a subsistence-based typology). Since the conceptual domain of *humans (people, human societies, cultures)* can be differentiated in terms of a great number of different characteristics, it follows that each anthropological researcher establishes a typology within this conceptual domain in terms of his assumptions (stated or unstated) about important or "theoretically significant" distinctions among types of *humans.* Systems of concepts (typologies and taxonomies), propositions about concepts, and the assumptions that underlie such propositions constitute theories.

THEORIES AND HYPOTHESES

Theories, as systems of interrelated concepts and propositions, can be "grand theories" which attempt to fit together in logical pattern vast areas of human behavior. On the other hand, a theoretical system can be much more modest in scope, involving only a small number of concepts and propositions.

Theories as such are never "proved." Rather, they differ with regard to their effectiveness as sources of propositions that can be tested by means of empirical research, and they also differ with regard to the numbers of empirical observations that support the propositions of which the given theoretical system is constituted. Thus, the general theoretical system usually called the "theory of biological evolution" is supported by a very large array of empirical observations, whereas in the social sciences theoretical systems of similar scope can boast of far fewer supporting empirical observations.

When an individual says, "I have a theory about that," he frequently means that he has a proposition about certain phenomena which (presumably) could be put to empirical test. Such a proposition is usually referred to as a *hypothesis.* Theoretical systems are the general sources for researchable propositions (hypotheses), and it can be argued that every hypothesis (and the concepts of which it is composed) is derived from some sort of theoretical system, even when the person presenting the hypothesis is unable to state the nature of his theoretical assumptions. If this is so, then it follows that in anthropology there is no such thing as "mere description" or concepts that are "theoryless" empirical statements.

Successful verification of propositions (hypotheses) always has implications for the theoretical system to which it relates. Each such verification helps to "build theory." This is the case even if the researcher is unaware of the set of theoretical assumptions from which his hypothesis was derived. Theories and elementary concepts are thus inextricably interrelated, and discussions about which of these "come first" are beside the point.

MODELS

The term *model* is sometimes used now simply as another synonym for the term *theoretical system*. However, Kaplan has argued that

a more defensible usage views as models only those theories which explicitly direct attention to certain resemblances between the theoretical entities and the real subject matter. With this usage in mind, models have been defined as "scientific metaphors." A metaphor, like an aphorism, condenses in a phrase a significant similarity. When the poet writes "the morn, in russet mantle clad, walks o'er the dew of yon high eastern hill," he evokes awareness of a real resemblance, and such awareness may be made to serve the purpose of science. When they do serve in this way, we are likely to conceptualize the situation as involving the use of *analogy*. The scientist recognizes similarities that have previously escaped us, and systematizes them. Electricity exhibits a "flow," there is a "current" exerting a certain pressure (the voltage), having a certain volume (the amperage), and so on. Analogies, it has been held, do more than merely lead to the formulation of theories, so that afterwards they may be removed and forgotten; they are "an utterly essential part of theories, without which theories would be completely valueless and unworthy of the name." (Kaplan, 1964:265, ending with a quote from N. Campbell.) [2]

When the essential elements and relationships in a theoretical system can be made isomorphic with a set of arithmetic notations and the tautological relationships involved in the arithmetic notations, a particularly powerful kind of model becomes possible. The logical properties of the arithmetic system can then be used to generate new propositions and hypotheses. The theory of games and probability theory are two such mathematical models that are now widely used in social sciences and related areas. Davenport (1960) has applied the game-theory model to an analysis of Jamaican fishing, and aspects of probability theory are rather widely used in all the social sciences. However, major problems are generally encountered in meeting the informational requirements of these mathematical models.

It is also useful to apply the term *model* in a more modest fashion to those theoretical systems for which scientific metaphors or analogies can be rendered in the form of diagrams, flow charts, or other pictorial and physical representations. In anthropology the standard rendering of kinship charts is a most frequently encountered type of model, but more comprehensive systems, such as the interrelationships in complex ecological interactions, can often be

[2] From *The Conduct of Inquiry* by Abraham Kaplan published by Chandler Publishing Company, San Francisco. © 1964 by Chandler Publishing Company. Reprinted by permission.

made more clear and explicit by means of some sort of pictorial representation. Figure 2 is the theoretical model in terms of which the psychologically oriented Six Cultures Project was conceptualized (Whiting, 1963).

When a set of theoretical relationships has been expressed in some kind of pictorial representation (or even in a physical structure, such as the models of molecules one often sees in general-science laboratories, or the model cities in schools of architecture), the discovery of new relationships and research directions is often facilitated. It becomes possible to "experiment" with the model itself, to see if changes in some parts of the structure force predictable modifications in other portions. Such experimentation is often greatly enhanced if at least some of the relationships among the parts of the model can be expressed in mathematical terms.

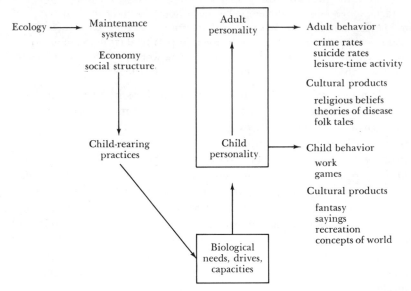

FIGURE 2. The Relation of Personality to Culture
ADAPTED FROM Whiting, 1963.

The question of the validity of particular theoretical models is an empirical one, and the conclusions derived from mathematical computations or other manipulation of models must be examined by means of research in the "real world." Some schools of social theory have been justly criticized for their nearly exclusive concentration on models, unsupported by any program of empirical research.

Assessing the Usefulness of Definitions

It has been mentioned that every concept, however concrete in appearance, implies a typology or categorization of the conceptual domain from which the particular concept is derived. Also, it is our position here that such concepts are arbitrary selections from the vast range of things and events in the universe. The anthropological literature is full of examples that illustrate the arbitrariness of concepts. For example, the categories of color which we take to be "natural" are organized differently among various human cultures. The Navaho, like many other people in the world, do not distinguish terminologically between green and blue, whereas their neighbors, the Zuñi, do not have separate words for red and orange. The Navaho and the Zuñi have different (probably implicit) theories about color as a conceptual domain, and the results are typologies which differ from the color system common in Euro-American culture.[3] It can be suggested that among Euro-Americans males and females have different theoretical systems with regard to color. At least it appears that the females in our society recognize such colors as "holiday gold," "plum," "charice," "fuchsia," "puce," "magenta," "emerald green," and "breen," which have little functional significance for most Euro-American males.

Even though we pay lip service to the idea that definitions, concepts, and typologies of phenomena are arbitrary slices from the world of experience, it goes against the grain to accept the idea that *all* definitions and typologies are equally valid. We feel intuitively that the Linnean system of classifying plants and animals is the natural and thus the right one; any other classification would be "wrong." But what distinguishes "right" or "significant" classifications from those we feel to be wrong? Abraham Kaplan, in *The Conduct of Inquiry* (1964), states the case as follows:

What makes a concept significant is that the classification it institutes is one into which things fall, as it were, of themselves. It carves at the joints, Plato said. Less metaphorically, a significant concept so groups or divides its subject matter that it can enter into many and important true propositions about the subject matter other than those which state the classification itself. Traditionally, such a concept was said to identify a "natural class" rather than an "artificial one." Its naturalness consists of this, that the attributes it chooses as the basic classification are significantly related to the attributes conceptualized elsewhere in our thinking. Things

---

[3] This does not mean that Navaho and Zuñi *perceptions* of color are necessarily different from those of Euro-Americans.

are grouped together because they resemble one another. A natural grouping is one which allows the discovery of many more, and more important, resemblances than those originally recognized. Every classification serves some purpose or other (the class-term has a use). It is artificial when we cannot do more with it than we first intended. The purpose of scientific classification is to facilitate the fulfillment of any purpose whatever, to disclose the relationships that must be taken into account no matter what.

Plainly, the significance of a concept in this sense is a matter of degree. Even an artificial classification is not wholly arbitrary if it really serves its own limited purposes. A classification of books by size and weight is not "as natural," we feel, as one based on their content. But the printer and the freight agent have claims as legitimate as the librarians. The point is that the former stand nearly alone in their interests; the librarian is joined by every reader, by everyone else who is concerned about his reading. Whether a concept is useful depends on the use we want to put it to; but there is always the additional question whether things so conceptualized will lend themselves to that use. And this is the scientific question. (Kaplan, 1964:50–51.) [4]

Inductive and Deductive Approaches

The logic-in-use of scientists is far from being a unidirectional process. Generally, scientific hunches and ideas arise somewhere in the realm of models and theories, but some researchers generate new research ideas by concentrating on the characteristics of their observational tools and techniques. Again, a relatively atheoretical observation of a set of events or things "in the real world" can provide the stimulus for a new hypothesis. Framing a hypothesis requires concentration on, and selection of, tools and techniques for the observations involved in the testing of the hypothesis. Successful testing of the hypothesis adds to a body of theory or elaboration of a model; which in turn leads to re-examination of "the real world" *and* the techniques of observation. It is unlikely that any one pattern of interaction among these elements is the highroad to successful science; on the contrary, insistence on a single mode or pathway of research work can lead to stultification of creative effort.

Sir Francis Bacon is often credited with the definitive statement of an inductive approach to scientific effort. In his *New Organon* (1620), Bacon contrasted the deductive and inductive methods and cast his ballot for the latter:

There are and can be only two ways of searching into and discovering truth. The one flies from the senses and particulars to the most general axioms, and from these principles, the truth of which it takes for settled

4 Kaplan, *op. cit.*

and immovable, proceeds to judgment and to the discovery of middle axioms. And this way is now in fashion. The other derives axioms from the senses and particulars, rising by a gradual and unbroken ascent, so that it arrives at the most general axiom last of all. This is the true way, but as yet untried. (Bacon, 1960:43.)

A generally accepted modern view of scientific procedure holds that effective theory construction depends on *both* inductive and deductive procedures. That is, solid foundations for scientific propositions often depend on a painstaking accumulation of, and generalization from, basic observations of "the real world"; but, just as often, theoretical systems provide the frame of reference and basic assumptions in terms of which relevant hypothesis-testing observations can be pursued. In any case, a random gathering of facts cannot by itself result in an increase of scientific understanding. Bacon phrased a useful simile to illustrate this aspect of science:

Those who have handled sciences have been either men of experiment or men of dogmas. The men of experiment are like the ant, they only collect and use; the reasoners resemble spiders, who make cobwebs out of their own substance. But the bee takes a middle course; it gathers its material from the flowers of the garden and of the field but transforms and digests it by a power of its own. Not unlike this is the true business of philosophy; for it neither relies solely or chiefly on the powers of the mind, nor does it take the matter which it gathers from natural history and mechanical experiments and lay it up in the memory whole, as it finds it, but lays it up in the understanding altered and digested. (Bacon, 1960:93.)

Theory, Method, and Empiricism

In our examination of the general paradigm of research methodology, the point has been made in a number of ways that atheoretical description is not logically possible—that all research is structured in terms of some sort of theoretical constructs, however implicit and unrecognized by the researcher. In spite of the ubiquitous presence of theory, anthropologists (and other researchers) vary a great deal in the extent to which they organize research in terms of explicit theoretical systems.

In the ethnographic literature there are many generalized community studies which purport to be relatively nontheoretical, "holistic" ethnographic descriptions. Often such holistic descriptions conclude with a set of theoretical generalizations that are thought of as inductively developed propositions posed as "suggestions for future theoretical research." This type of study, with or without the theoretical conclusions, may be thought of as structured in terms of a very generalized "meta-theory" of anthropology, which, I feel, has the following features:

1. A set of assumptions about "culture" as a master concept in terms of which human behavior is broadly explainable.
2. A set of assumptions about the relative homogeneity of human "cultures," which set the methodological requirements for data gathering. That is, most community studies provide no discussion about sampling techniques and representativeness of data, because the supposed uniformity or homogeneity of culture makes such a discussion unnecessary. Other monographs, on the other hand, do discuss problems of sampling and representativeness, apparently because of a somewhat different set of general assumptions about behavioral uniformities.
3. A set of assumptions about the main aspects of human behavior which are important enough to be worth at least a chapter or more in the usual monograph. Such important topics usually include: ways of obtaining food; main lines of social organization; kinds of economic relationships among the residents; family structure and household composition; and religious practices and beliefs.
4. A set of assumptions concerning the interrelationships among the various aspects of culture.
5. A set of assumptions concerning the importance of symbolic ritual and ceremonial behavior as expressions of social and cultural information.
6. Some other general, unstated assumptions concerning human behavior and values. Many of these are derived from generalized Western democratic philosophy.

In addition to this generalized meta-theory underlying all or most descriptive research, each anthropological researcher possesses a set of assumptions (often implicit) in terms of which he interprets aspects of day-to-day human behavior, and which gives some of the individual flavor of ethnographic reporting. For example, some anthropologists tend to assume that small human communities are peaceful, friendly, "genuine," and relatively not anxiety-ridden (in comparison with urban industrial societies). Other anthropologists tend to assume the opposite. Again, some anthropologists place a high value on verbal behavior as the data of most significance for anthropological research, whereas other researchers regard nonverbal behavior as more significant, relegating interview information and other verbal observations to the status of "further supporting evidence."

All anthropological researchers structure their research in terms of the general meta-theory, plus liberal amounts of (usually unanalyzed) "personal theory," plus varying amounts of explicit special anthropological theory. The special anthropological theories are quite numerous and include the following:

1. Evolutionist theory (nineteenth-century variety)
2. Neoevolutionism
3. Culture-and-personality theory (psychoanalytic)
4. Culture-and-personality theory (neobehaviorist)
5. Structural-Functionalism (several varieties)
6. Formal semantic and cognitive theory (several varieties)
7. Technoenvironmental determinism
8. Diffusionist-historicalism
9. Kulturkreise theory
10. Various combinations of the above

Plain ethnographic description in anthropological research may be understood as composed of the meta-theory plus personal theory, with little or no acknowledgment of the presence of any special theory (although each researcher's personal theory always includes a number of elements that are the same as propositions found in one or another of the explicit special theories).

Theory-oriented anthropological research, which is becoming more prevalent in the literature, generally includes careful discussion of one of the special theoretical systems, usually with little recognition of the underlying meta-theory and accompanying assumptions relatable to the individual's personal anthropological theory.

It is probably the presence of the unrecognized, or at least unexamined, meta-theory, plus the variable and unknown effects of personal theories, that has posed the most problems for anthropological research methodology. Usually the anthropologist is faced with two important "credibility gaps." Among fellow anthropologists, the assumptions relatable to the general meta-theory will for the most part be accepted without challenge, but the researcher's personal theory (his personal bias), as it influences the data gathering and presentation relevant to a particular theoretical position, leads to heated debate. Critics *outside* the membership of anthropology, particularly those in the social sciences, are often more concerned about the meta-theory of anthropology, especially those portions affecting standards of representativeness, reliability, and validity of observations.

My position is that, regardless of which special theory or theories serve as the frame of reference for particular instances of research, the main pathway to eliminating anthropological "credibility gaps" is to concentrate methodological attention at the relatively low-abstraction end of the research paradigm. That is, the most pressing problems in improving anthropological research design lie in the structure of primary data gathering—in the actual field-research operations. Once the procedures and concepts of primary anthropological description have been systematized, rigorous controlled comparisons can be developed, and theory building can then proceed on much firmer foundations.

The logic-in-use of our data-gathering operations is essentially the same as that of all scientific endeavors. Therefore, our examination of methodological principles does not depend on any one particular anthropological theory. Research examples in later chapters will represent a number of different theoretical positions, but their logical structures belong to a general scientific realm that embraces at least all those disciplines concerned with human behavior.

Methodological advances in anthropology, particularly the systematizing and operationalizing of primary data-gathering procedures, should lead to clarification and modification of anthropological meta-theory, as well as to increased control over the (probably unavoidable) effects of anthropologists' personal theories. These intended methodological changes will be put together in terms of a general attitude labeled *operationalism*. The elements of this research attitude will be examined in Chapter 3, after a brief discussion (Chapter 2) of the nature of science.

REFERENCES CITED

BACON, SIR FRANCIS
1960. *The New Organon and Related Writings.* (First published in 1620.) Indianapolis: Bobbs-Merrill.

DAVENPORT, WILLIAM
1960. "Jamaican Fishing: A Game Theory Analysis." Yale University Publications in Anthropology. Vol. 59:3–11.

GOODE, WILLIAM J., and PAUL K. HATT
1952. *Methods in Social Research.* New York: McGraw-Hill.

HOLMBERG, ALLAN R.
1969. *Nomads of the Long Bow: The Siriono of Eastern Bolivia.* (First published in 1950.) Garden City: The Natural History Press.

KAPLAN, ABRAHAM
1964. *The Conduct of Inquiry.* San Francisco: Chandler.

NAGEL, ERNEST
1961. *The Structure of Science.* New York: Harcourt, Brace & World.

WHITING, BEATRICE, ed.
1963. *Six Cultures: Studies in Child Rearing.* New York: Wiley.

Eskimo Village of Kaktovik, Alaska

2. Science and Anthropology

The paradigm of research methodology discussed in Chapter 1 is only one aspect of a much larger realm—that of general scientific scholarship. It will be useful to examine some aspects of this larger domain in order to place our methodological discussion in perspective. From this review of the nature of science it should become clear that rigorous methodological procedures ought not be considered by themselves as synonymous with "the scientific enterprise," although there are particular points at which principles of method are of central importance.

When we try to establish a useful definition of *science,* we immediately encounter the basic problem of all definitions: different people use the term in quite different ways and contexts, and it is often loaded with a considerable freight of value judgment. We have only to listen to the outpouring of claims in the mass media for "scienti-

fically proved" products to see the term's range of usage and implication. Consider also the problems raised by the following expressions: "Christian Science," "scientific haircuts given here," "library
science," and "scientific bridge-playing."

The word *science* is derived from the Latin word *scientia* (*sciens,*
the present participle of *scire,* "to know"), and *Webster's Collegiate
Dictionary* gives a series of definitions for it, including:

1. Knowledge; 2. Any department of systematized knowledge; 3. Art or
skill—chiefly humorous or sporting; as, the *science* of boxing; 4. A branch
of study concerned with observation of facts, esp. with the establishment of
verifiable general laws. . . . 5. . . . accumulated knowledge systematized
and formulated with reference to the discovery of general truths or the
operation of general laws.

A widely accepted way of defining *science* is to equate the term
with the concept of "methodological rigor." For example, after
combing a wide range of literature about science, Carlo Lastrucci
suggests that there exists something like a

consensus among authoritative writers with regard to the essential attributes or processes of science. According to such a consensus, *science may be
defined* quite accurately and functionally as: *an objective, logical, and
systematic method of analysis of phenomena, devised to permit the accumulation of reliable knowledge.* (Lastrucci, 1963:6; his italics.)

By this definition, science becomes a particular mode of investigation, rather than a body of knowledge, a quest for knowledge, or a
search for nomothetic generalizations.

Lastrucci's definition appears to imply that anyone who is not systematic or personally objective is ipso facto not part of, or contributing to, the development of science. Lastrucci appears to leave little room for the work of men who are, for example, impelled to scientific inquiry by passionate, subjective motives of nationalism or
by a fanatic desire to save lives. Also, such a definition places scientists' intuitions, theoretical speculations, and serendipitous discoveries outside the realm of scientific enterprise; or at least it shunts
these elements into a devalued limbo.

W. I. B. Beveridge, in his suggestively titled book *The Art of Scientific Investigation,* has given us rich illustrations of some apparently unsystematic and disorganized aspects of research. Strict methodological procedures seem notably lacking, for example, in the
case of von Mering and Minkowski (1889 in Strasbourg), who accidentally discovered the importance of urine-carried sugar (and related facts about diabetes) when they noticed the swarms of flies attracted to the urine of a dog from which they had removed the pan-
creas. The discovery of penicillin by Fleming appears to have been

due to the dust and dirt in his antiquated laboratory, where some colonies of staphylococci were accidentally contaminated (and killed) by a theretofore unknown substance.

One of the most striking anecdotes in Beveridge's recitation is about the pharmacologist Otto Loewi at the University of Graz. Professor Loewi awoke in the middle of the night with a brilliant idea. He reached for a pencil and paper and jotted down a few notes. On waking the next morning, he was aware of having had an inspiration during the night, but to his consternation he could not decipher his notes. During the next night, to his great joy he again awoke with the same flash of insight, which he carefully recorded before going to sleep again.

The next day he went to his laboratory and in one of the neatest, simplest, and most definite experiments in the history of biology brought proof of the chemical mediation of nerve impulses. (Beveridge, 1957:95.)

The German chemist Kekulé is described as having developed the idea of the benzene ring (which revolutionized organic chemistry) during a dream as he sat napping in front of his fireplace. He described how the atoms "flitted" before his eyes:

Long rows, variously, more closely, united; all in movement wriggling and turning like snakes. And see, what was that? One of the snakes seized its own tail and the image whirled scornfully before my eyes. As though from a flash of lightning I awoke; I occupied the rest of the night in working out the consequences of the hypothesis. . . . Let us learn to dream, gentlemen. (Quoted in Beveridge, 1957:76.)

These examples suggest that any useful definition of science should be based on the general premise that "science is whatever it is that is happening when scientists are productive." So, if we include these cases in the realm of science, our definition should be broad enough to include, at least tacitly, some nearly random scanning of phenomena (with or without microscopes, etc.); seizing upon "accidents," exceptional events, and other chance circumstances for generating new research ideas; and a fair amount of simple but inspired day (and night) dreaming. A caution should be introduced, however: these are illustrations of the unpredictable and intuitive nature of the origins of scientific ideas; processes of systematic verification of hunches and hypotheses are much more subject to objective description and codification.

Ernest Nagel alludes to the same problem when he states in *The Structure of Science:*

There are no rules of discovery and invention in science, any more than there are such rules in the arts. . . . Nor, finally, should the formula

be read as claiming that the practice of scientific method effectively eliminates every form of personal bias or source of error which might otherwise
impair the outcome of the inquiry. (Nagel, 1961:12–13.)

Thus, while the scientific method Lastrucci describes is important
in identifying *some* aspects of science, it should not, in my opinion,
be taken as synonymous with science, for that leads to a disregard of
the less systematic emotionally flavored search for ideas and theoretical insights. In the history of science there have been important
events that can only be described as wild speculation about relationships and forces and concepts, some of which may never be definable in terms of empirically observable phenomena.

Science and History

In earlier decades of this century it was fashionable to divide scholarly research into two realms: history and science. In terms of this
dichotomy, history is ideographic research, in which the aim of investigation is to give concrete descriptions of particular events,
things, and peoples, located in time and place. Science, on the other
hand, is the search for the nomothetic laws or principles that apply
to a particular domain of phenomena without regard to specific
times or locations. Thus, basic principles of chemistry and physics
are highly nomothetic, whereas descriptions of the Battle of Water-
loo or the aboriginal cultural patterns of the Mandan-Hidatsa Indians are ideographic studies.

Many anthropologists, including Radcliffe-Brown (1952), Kroeber
(1952), and Hoebel (1966) have made use of the history *vs.* science
dichotomy in discussing the nature of anthropology and its relationships with other fields of study. This dichotomy has a certain heuristic usefulness, but when it is used to characterize entire
disciplines (as Kroeber has done), it asserts a distinction between
description and theoretical work that is no longer generally accepted. Historical description has come to be recognized as a highly
selective process in which observations are ordered in terms of some
theoretical frame of reference, however implicit, even when the researcher claims that he is "only giving the facts" (cf. Nagel, 1961:
79–152; Lastrucci, 1963). Maintaining the distinction appears to be
increasingly impractical in discussions about the nature and objectives of scholarly research. Robert Brown comes to somewhat the
same kind of conclusion in his *Explanation in Social Science* when
he concludes that

in order that a theory—a set of deductively related hypotheses—may be
applied in the explanation of a particular kind of event, the theory must

be combined with existence statements of an appropriate sort. To this extent, then, historical explanation is part of every scientific one, and their earlier divorce at our hands was one of convenience and not of incompatibility. (Brown, 1963:193.)

Those who have argued that anthropology is mainly a historical or humanistic discipline, basically different from "real" science, have often taken physics and chemistry as their points of comparisons and have perhaps oversimplified their conceptualization of science. In the first place, it should be recognized that a number of respectable scientific propositions in the physical sciences involve particularistic observations. To name only one class of examples, we can note the number of scientific statements that include particularistic references to the sun, the moon, and other stellar bodies.

In general, limiting science to examples drawn from physics and chemistry produces an extremely narrow view of the scientific enterprise, for this is to ignore important areas of research in geology, biology, paleontology, and many other established disciplines that are frankly particularistic in important respects. Few people claim, for example, that the geologist is not scientific, even though his aims may be the study of particular features of the Cambrian Age, or descriptions of some glacial sequences of northern Europe.

Just as scientists in other disciplines are not always concerned solely with nomothetic generalizations, historical researchers are far from being totally idiographic. Historians and anthropologists are frequently concerned with describing human behavior in specific times and places, but it is not *in principle* impossible to find nomothetic propositions applicable to large classes of concrete historical "cases," and many writers (Toynbee, Spengler, Kroeber, and others) have generalized about broad features of "civilizations," "fall of empires," and other nomothetic topics.

Nagel, in *The Structure of Science,* lists four principal modes of explanation employed in scientific discourse: (1) *deduction* from known and lawlike principles; (2) *probabilistic statements,* in which the "explanatory premises do not formally imply their explicanda"; (3) *functional or teleological explanations,* in which statements are made about the "functions (or even dysfunctions) that a unit performs in maintaining or realizing certain traits of a system to which the unit belongs, or of stating the instrumental role an action plays in bringing about some goal" (Nagel, 1961:24); and (4) *genetic, or historical, explanations,* "which set out the major events through which some earlier system has been transformed into a later one" (p. 25). A glance at parts of biology (embryology, study of evolution, etc.) and astronomy (study of the history of our universe) reminds us that this fourth mode of explanation is not uniquely a property of those disciplines that study human history and behavior.

If we accept Nagel's four types of explanations as valid traits of science and scientific inquiry, we may suggest that different sciences exhibit different *mixtures* of these four logical models, without thereby departing from membership in the scientific community. The kinds of explanations sought by some historians, anthropologists, and others who reject the label of science are not different in kind from the types of explanations of interest to other scientists, but the traditional patterns of research and use of evidence make their pursuits *seem* radically different from those of the sciences. The logic of scholarship is the same for both, but canons of evidence are different, and it may be suggested that where the canons of evidence differ (between historical scholarship and "scientific inquiry") the use of evidence on the historical side appears to be the more questionable.

For example, much has been written by scholars in diverse fields about the so-called "national character" of the Germans, Russians, Japanese, Americans, and other large national groups. The explanations have traversed the spectrum of theoretical viewpoints from the psychological (including psychoanalytic) through the geographical, historical, and biological to complicated models of structural-functionalism. Each such study seeks to produce "truths" based on explicit and implicit propositions about character and personality formation, and each is naturalistic in that supernatural causation is not assumed. Yet some of these studies involve careful data gathering and rules of evidence, with accompanying statistics, whereas others present their arguments in a broad-brush, vividly anecdotal fashion, leaving key terms and concepts undefined, and employing verbal eloquence, rather than tightness of data-handling, as their chief means of enhancing credibility.

Science and Controlled Experiments

Some of the people who have argued that anthropology, and the social sciences generally, cannot really be scientific disciplines make much of the fact that controlled experiment is supposedly impossible in the study of human behavior. If "controlled experiment" is used to mean only those kinds of situations where *all* supposedly relevant variables are controlled and manipulated by the researcher, then we would have to agree that anthropologists cannot make use of controlled experiments in any useful sense. However, we must then ask whether all the so-called "hard sciences," rely upon controlled experiment as the principal method of research. We have already pointed out above that there are numbers of sciences that depart from the model of science offered by physics and chemistry. Geology and astronomy can again be cited as examples of scientific inquiry where the methods of observation frequently do *not* involve controlled experiment, but which nonetheless have produced reputable bodies of theory and explanation.[1]

The Problem of Cross-Cultural Comparisons

Another argument sometimes offered by the critics of a scientific anthropology runs approximately as follows:

1. You can't compare individual traits—e.g., marriage or circular dwellings among different peoples of the world, because these traits have different histories and different "cultural meanings" in different groups; hence *they are not the same type of thing.*
2. Therefore, a truly pan-human comparative study of culture and behavior is not possible.

This idea raises very serious questions for cross-cultural researchers, but the proposition is, I feel, founded on a faulty assumption. The basic flaw in the argument is in the meaning of the expression "the same type of thing." When are two items the same? Or similar? When are they different? What is meant by the statement that a cocker spaniel and a greyhound are the "same type" of animal? Are cocker spaniels and greyhounds similar? The answer to these questions suggests that membership in a particular class can be assigned in terms of a set of rules stating a particular *aspect* of resemblance —in this case involving information about genetic coding. The basis for the classification does not involve size, color, or a number of other characteristics. Now let us take the case of wings. Bats, bees, crows, and Boeing 707s all have wings. Are all of these cases of wings examples of a single category? Historically they are different, for they are not traceable to a common ancestral prototype. Yet they are all lumped together and called *wings.* If we embark on a minute description of our four cases, we can easily show that they

---

[1] It should also be pointed out that the "experimental sciences" can only claim to control all known variables. Since the presence of additional, unknown, variables is logically possible in all experimental situations, the control of variables is a matter of degree, rather than an absolute criterion for differentiating one type of research from another. In chemistry and physics it would appear that relatively high levels of control are possible; in biological sciences the problems of control are much greater; even the most strictly controlled experiments in psychology involve problems of unknown factors which may seriously influence research results. (Cf. Blalock, 1964.)

are different in structure, form of manipulation, and historical origins. Therefore, we can, if we wish, regard them as different. On the other hand, we can, as in the case of the dogs, single out some one or a few elements that they have in common, for example:

1. All four types of wings are used in the process of airborne travel.
2. They are all shaped with reference to the physical properties of the atmosphere; each presents a relatively broad, flat surface when the wings are in extended position.
3. In each case the wide, flat surface is shaped in certain ways that can be explained by referring to principles of aerodynamics.
4. In each case the wings are attached in symmetrical pairs to the central somewhat elongated body of the creature.

Clearly, then, the *wings* of bees, crows, bats, and Boeing 707s are similar in some respects, different in others. They are assignable to a single class of things—*wings*—only if we are careful to specify in what way they are considered to have the same characteristics. This is, of course, true of all phenomena to which we attach labels. No two tables are the same, no two trees are the same, and no two runs of a laboratory experiment are the same. Our only justification for lumping units under a particular label is that we are prepared to state in what respects (*in our definition*) these units are similar, at the same time accepting the proposition that in other respects these units are distinct. For comparative purposes we must, of course, be prepared to deal with the ways in which the similar units do in fact differ from each other.

Now back to our anthropological examples. In comparing several cases of *circular dwellings* we may be able to state fairly easily the definition by which we are selecting cases of similarity. The mind does not boggle at the prospect of making clear distinctions for both *circular* and *dwellings*. And we can consider *circular dwellings* to be the same kind of things, even when some of them are made of mud, others of hides and poles, and still others of snow.

With a concept such as *marriage,* however, the problem is more complex. As every elementary anthropological text makes clear, the modes of marriage, and their ceremonial accouterments are of great variety among peoples of the world, and the literature is far from clear on what could be given as a unitary definition for this class of phenomena. At this point it is useful to step over to the side of the critics for a moment to admit the possibility that no really adequate definition of marriage has so far been advanced into common usage. On the other hand, I can find no logical support for the belief that in principle it is impossible to define marriage in an acceptable, cross-culturally useful manner, even though the human behavior observable in different types of conjugal arrangements show wide divergences in manner and meaning. The nature of such a definition will depend on its fit with a particular theoretical structure.

Ernest Nagel gives an illustration from the hard sciences that suggests further extensions of this logical problem:

Consider, for example, the following purely physical phenomena: a lightning storm, the motions of a mariner's compass, the appearance of a rainbow, and the formation of an optical image in the range finder of a camera. These are undeniably quite dissimilar occurrences, incomparable on the basis of their manifest qualities; and it may not seem antecedently likely that they could be illustrations for a single set of integrally related principles. Nevertheless, as is well known, these phenomena can all be understood in terms of modern electromagnetic theory. There are, of course, different special laws for each of these phenomena; but the theory can explain all the laws, since different laws are obtained from the theory when different initial conditions, corresponding to the evident dissimilarities of the various systems, are supplied. (Nagel, 1961:462.)

Science: A Definition

From the foregoing, it appears difficult and misleading to maintain any narrow definition of science, either as a particular commitment to strict methodology or as a nomothetically oriented search for laws and basic general principles. This leads me to propose a broader, more diffuse definition:

Science is the structure and the processes of accumulation of systematic and reliable knowledge about any relatively enduring aspect of the universe, carried out by means of empirical observations, and the development of concepts and propositions for interrelating and explaining such observations.

I suggest that science includes a large component of searching, speculating, and discovering—a whole set of activities which cannot be easily codified and systematized. Serendipitous discoveries and inspired daydreaming are part of this aspect of science. The institutional organization of science—the schools, laboratories, journals, and other communications channels—are also included within the bounds of this definition. Furthermore, there are large areas of science in which complex value judgments rather than strict methodological criteria form the basis for action. The decisions about *which* topics are to be given research priorities, where the money for investigation comes from, and who shall carry out research activities are part of the institutional structure of science. A further large component of value judgment enters at the "output stage"—in the articulation to practical applications. Who shall receive the scientific information? Who will apply the knowledge, and in what situations? In some areas of science the men who call themselves scientists work actively in the practical applications end of the scientific endeavor. In other domains of research the investigators keep themselves far removed from the engineers and administrators whose job it is to apply available knowledge to concrete practical human needs and activities.

Science is a very broad spectrum of scholarly activity. No sharp lines can be drawn to differentiate the so-called hard sciences from other disciplines, and no strict methodological canons can clearly distinguish the work of the scientific Nobel Prize winners from that of a host of unknown research assistants. Science has many facets that articulate with philosophy, the performing arts, and ethical judgment. But somewhere in the middle of this conceptual domain is the matter of methodological verification—the sets of rules whereby useful knowledge can be accumulated and pyramided into a more powerful understanding of the universe.

The position taken in this book is that anthropology can usefully be considered a science. That is, to paraphrase my earlier definition, anthropology involves the accumulation of systematic and reliable knowledge about an aspect of the universe (man and his behavior), carried out by empirical observation, and the interrelating of concepts referable to empirical observations. A comparative cross-cultural study of human behavior, involving marriage, circular dwellings, and great numbers of other elements of behavior and products of behavior, is a feasible enterprise. However, we need to look closely at some reasons why progress in the accumulation of an extensive, useful body of anthropological theory appears to be extremely slow and uneven.

Anthropology and Problems of Methodology

From the point of view on the nature of science and scientific method adopted in the preceding section, all anthropologists are "doing science" whenever they are actively engaged in accumulating raw data or in putting together generalizations based on observational data in a search for systematized and reliable knowledge about human behavior. It is beyond argument that anthropologists, like all scholars, are trying to be systematic, and that they are generally favorably disposed toward reliable information rather than error and falsehood.

The conflict begins when we take up the subject of the effectiveness of particular methods of research and scholarship. It is in the area of canons of evidence and the believability of anthropological research results that we find our focus of controversy. Those outside the field who say that anthropology is not a science probably intend to say that anthropologists accept generalizations about human behavior on the basis of evidence that will not stand up to close logical scrutiny. Further, these outside critics can probably make a strong claim that anthropologists frequently present a prima-facie case for a proposition and then move on to some other area of study, leaving the generalization to be debated pro and con in a speculative manner, rather than proceeding with careful examination of empirical evidence. That is, anthropologists are lax in their theory-building habits.

One well-known instance of theoretical debate in the anthropological literature is the Oscar Lewis–Robert Redfield controversy about life in the Mexican village of Tepoztlán. Redfield had studied the community in the 1920s and described the people as living in harmony with their universe. Seventeen years later, Oscar Lewis and his associates studied the same community and reported a quite different picture. Lewis summed up the differences between the two research reports in these words:

The impression given by Redfield's study of Tepoztlán is that of a relatively homogenous, isolated, smoothly functioning and well-integrated society made up of a contented and well-adjusted people. His picture of the village has a Rousseauan quality which glosses lightly over evidence of violence, disruption, cruelty, disease, suffering and maladjustment. We are told little of poverty, economic problems, or political schisms. Throughout his study we find an emphasis upon the cooperative and unifying factors in Tepoztecan society.

Our findings, on the other hand, would emphasize the underlying individualism of Tepoztecan institutions and character, the lack of cooperation, the tensions between villages within the municipio, the schisms within the village, and the pervading quality of fear, envy and distrust. (Oscar Lewis, 1951:428–429.)

Redfield replied with an admission that

. . . Lewis established the objective truth of certain of the unpleasant features of Tepoztecan life. He has shown that more than half of the villagers did not own land at the time that he studied the community; that many were in serious want; that stealing, quarreling, and physical violence are not rare in Tepoztlán. . . . It is true that the two books describe what might almost seem to be two different peoples occupying the same town. (Redfield, 1960:134.)

He adds, however, that:

The greater part of the explanation for the difference between the two reports on this matter of Tepoztecan life and character is to be found in differences between the two investigators. . . . I think that it is simply true that . . . I looked at certain aspects of Tepoztecan life because they both interested and pleased me. (Redfield, 1960:135.)

Another instance of this sort of anthropological debate concerns the character of life among the Pueblo Indians of the Southwest. The story begins in 1934, when Ruth Benedict published her characterization of the Pueblo Indians in *Patterns of Culture*. In this work she described the Pueblos as "Appollonian"—restrained in emotions, avoiding violence, quarrels, or warfare and given to moderation in all things. Other writers, notably Laura Thompson, have given similar portraits of the integrated qualities of Pueblo culture.

This "Apollonian" ethos of the Pueblo peoples is supposedly so pervasive that alcohol has never become a problem among them. "Drunkenness is repulsive to them," Benedict wrote. "In Zuni after the early introduction of liquor, the old men voluntarily outlawed it and the rule was congenial enough to be honored" (*ibid*. 1934:82). Similarly, all types of emotional and violent display were said to be entirely inconsistent with Pueblo attitudes.

On the other hand, Esther Goldfrank and Dorothy Eggan (among others) have described some aspects of Pueblo lifeways (particularly among Zuñi and Hopi) as traumatic, violent, and repressive. (See especially Eggan, 1943; Li An-Che, 1937; Goldfrank, 1945.) In support of her argument, Esther Goldfrank offered, for example, the following quotation from H. R. Voth's observations of the Oraibi Powamu ceremony:

With the crying and screaming of the candidates, men and women mingle their voices, some encouraging them, others accusing the Katcinas of partiality, claiming that they whip some harder than others; in short, pandemonium reigns in the kiva during this exciting half hour. But the scene has not only its exciting, but also its disgusting features. As the whips are quite long, they frequently extend around the leg or hip of the little nude boys in such a manner that the points strike the pudibilia, and the author noticed on several occasions that the boys, when being placed on the sand mosaic, were warned to protect these parts, which they tried to do by either quickly freeing one hand and pushing the pudenda between the legs or by partly crossing the legs. It was also noticed on several occasions that some of the boys, probably as a result of fear and pain, involuntarily micturated and in one or two cases even defecated. (Quoted in Goldfrank, 1945.)

Concerning the Pueblo people's alleged aversion to alcohol, Barnouw (1963) gives a considerable list of evidence to the contrary, including the information that "Matilda Coxe Stevenson, whose report on Zuni was published in 1904, also described prevalent drinking, particularly around the time of the Shalako festival" (Barnouw, 1963:45). Thus, on the liquor problem, the empirical facts seem to be contrary to what was claimed by Benedict, and have been so at least since the turn of the century.

John Bennett examined the two versions of Pueblo culture and concluded:

The differences in viewpoint, therefore, cannot be explained entirely either on the basis of scientific goodness or badness, nor on the basis of publication differentials. Underneath both these factors lies what I have already suggested may be a genuine difference in value orientation and outlook in the feeling about, the reaction toward, Pueblo society and culture in the light of values in American culture, brought to the scientific situation by the anthropologist. (Bennett, 1956:211.)

According to Bennett's analysis, Thompson and Benedict stressed (and showed approval of) the organic unity and "logico-aesthetic integration" of Pueblo culture as an admirable end product, whereas Goldfrank, Eggan, and other observers have concerned themselves with the means (painful initiation and other social control mechanisms) by which the supposed integration of Pueblo life is maintained. Thus, "scientific anthropology is . . . implicated in an on-going process in our own culture, and from this level of observation, it is "nonobjective" and "culturally determined" (Bennett, 1956:212).

From the point of view of scientific method in anthropology, we can summarize the situation as follows:

1. All of the anthropologists cited appear to have been sincerely concerned with presenting "systematic, reliable information." All were trying to be scientific (in terms of our earlier definition).
2. All of the materials in these cases were derived from, or purported to be derived from, empirical observation.
3. Each of the authors attempted to set forth propositions about particular, definable communities, using terminology that implied a naturalistic and objective orientation rather than metaphysical or supernatural speculation.
4. In each case the method of the author was to present a general, unified (but somewhat vague) hypothesis about very general and abstract conditions of life in particular communities, around which he accumulated a series of sketches, anecdotes, quotations, and other bits and pieces that formed a network of evidence in favor of the hypothesis.
5. In each of these cases the necessary conditions for negation of the hypothesis were notably lacking.
6. In each of the cases, types of societies were postulated—e.g., "Apollonian," "peaceful peasants," "hostile peasants"—that were treated as real categories. The ensuing debates centered on the question of whether the particular societies conformed to the ideal types.

7. In each of the cases the main hypothesis was at such a high level of abstraction (the configuration of a culture; ethos of society) as to be for practical purposes nearly unresearchable.
8. However, none of these research ideas appear to be *in principle* unresearchable, even though serious problems of definition would be encountered before a systematic research methodology could be constructed.

Given these conditions of scholarship, it seems intrinsically likely, as Bennett observes, that the general value preferences of the anthropologists have had an important, if covert, role in shaping the directions of argument and description. Redfield openly admits this in his reply to Lewis.

The cases of Tepoztlán and the Pueblos are only the most famous of a long series of instances in which anthropologists have strongly disagreed concerning theoretical constructs and interpretation of masses of objective (or potentially objective) data. In most such debates, the language of dispute is at such a high level of abstraction (so far removed from the concrete observations themselves) that their resolution continues to be in terms of emotional and literary persuasiveness, frequently backed by the weight of "authoritative opinions" of "leading scholars," rather than in any systematic analysis of evidence.

What, then, is missing in these studies, and in contemporary anthropology, generally, that causes them to be lacking in scientific rigor? Some people will here call out "Quantification." The position taken in this book, however, is that quantification is but one aspect of a more complicated problem. In his short but excellent statement *The Scientific Approach,* Carlo Lastrucci outlines what appear to be the basic elements of the scientific method. Abstracting from his work and similar discussions, I offer the following list of essential ingredients that should be present or accounted for in any sound piece of scientific work, however intuitive the sources of the original hypotheses or propositions:

1. The problem, the aim, of the particular work should be stated, and that problem should be researchable, at least in principle. The statement of the problem may be simply a hypothesis to be tested, an event to be described, or any of a number of other possible types of research aim. (Hypothesis is here defined as "a tentative theory or supposition provisionally adopted to explain certain facts and to guide in the investigation of others.")
2. The essential elements, or terms, of the problem must be defined. Definition may involve simply identifying elements or units that are common knowledge among researchers, stating operational definitions (measurements, types of observations, etc.), or referring to previously established definitions of a particular researcher

or school of researchers. All the terms in the stated problem must relate to observable natural phenomena of the universe, however indirect the paths of abstraction involved. THE SINGLE MOST SERIOUS PROBLEM IN ANTHROPOLOGICAL RESEARCH IS THE FAILURE TO PAY CAREFUL ATTENTION TO DEFINITION OF UNITS AND VARIABLES.

3. The procedures of observation related to the essential, defined elements must be described in enough detail so that another anthropologist (or other scientist) reading his work can evaluate the adequacy of the research observations and can clearly understand what steps would be necessary to replicate the observations involved in the piece of research.

4. The step-by-step analysis of these observations must conform to the usual canons of logic employed in the sciences. The logic involved in anthropology is in principle the same as in all other scholarship.

5. Steps 2, 3, and 4 must be so constituted that it is possible to see what data would constitute a negation of the results described by the researcher. That is, the work must be falsifiable.

Some comments should be added here about this tentative model for evaluation of research works:

a. Statement No. 2 concerning definitions should not be construed to mean that all the concepts employed in anthropology (or any other science) must have direct and accessible empirical referents. Lastrucci (p. 115) lists such terms as "force," "symbiosis," "intelligence," and "social mobility" as "having no apparent empirical qualities." The anthropologist could easily add to this "culture," "evolution," "acculturation," and "personality."

b. Whatever abstract, relational terms of this sort are employed in research, the research design must nonetheless make clear to the reader just what observational procedures will be taken as evidence supporting a proposition involving the abstract concept.

c. In scientific work the aims of research and the terms employed in bringing about the aims should not be normative; that is, scientific work does not express opinions concerning the abstractly "good" or "desirable" per se. Nothing in this statement prevents the scientist from doing research concerning relationships or objective phenomena to which others may assign normative values. Thus, while the scientist does not include value statements as intrinsic to his research, he can produce generalizations that include information, such as "Safety devices (under stipulated conditions) save human lives." It is also, of course, legitimate for the scientist to observe and report the value judgments of people: "Americans value devices that save human lives."

When we look at the published works of anthropologists, we note first that there are many to which application of our "yardstick of scientific method" will be fairly difficult. Ethnographic monographs describing particular peoples and cultures generally consist of great numbers of both descriptive and analytic statements; frequently objective and "simple" descriptions are interspersed with statements referring to abstract relationships.

Here are examples from Julian Pitt-Rivers' *The People of the Sierra* (which is used here simply for illustrative purposes and does not represent as far as I know any notable departure from what is usual in such monographs). In a section on sex roles, the anthropologist tells us:

The role of women, as in all societies, centers upon the home. All work to do with the home, the care of children and clothes is theirs. Of the animals, only chickens and rabbits fall within their province. Girls sometimes may be seen pasturing goats, but this is only because the family is poor and there is no male child of the appropriate age. The matanza, the killing of the household pigs, shows a clear differentiation of the roles of the two sexes. It is something of a celebration and relatives who no longer form part of the household are often present. Some skill and experience is required in killing, and, if no member of the family possesses it, a son-in-law or uncle, known for his ability in this respect, may be invited. This would avoid having to employ a professional "matador" (meaning in this instance, "pig-killer," not bullfighter). The men prepare the *patio,* light fires to heat the water, rig up the sling, catch the pig, hold it down upon the table, and the matador cuts its throat. When the pig is dead, the men clean the hair and dirt off with scrapers, while the women serve them, pouring the boiling water on the carcass. The men then sling the animal up on its hind legs, and the matador butchers it. The role of the men ends when they have borne the meat into the house. There the women clean it and make sausages and prepare the meat in other ways. (Pitt-Rivers, 1961:85.)

Farther along:

It is not only occupation which differentiates the sexes. In recreation the same dichotomy is maintained. Women do not go into cafes but stay in their houses where they visit one another. Women do not smoke. (*Ibid.,* 87.)

To an intensely critical empiricist there may be some difficulty concerning the extent to which the above pattern of behavior actually applies to all or most of the people in the community being described, but the data given in these passages involve behavior which any normally competent anthropologist or other observer should be able to report accurately. There would seem to be no problems about the definitions of terms and the logic of explanation.

Going on to a description of "the values attaching to womanhood," Pitt-Rivers says the following.

The male social personality has been related to the concept of manliness. The feminine counterpart of the conception, which expresses the essence of womanhood, is *vergüenza,* or shame. In certain of its aspects only, for the word has, first of all, a general sense not directly related to the feminine sex, and it is this which must first be explained. (*Ibid.,* 112.)

A bit farther on:

Let me now try a definition:

Vergüenza is the regard for the moral values of society, for the rules whereby social intercourse takes place, for the opinion which others have of one. But this, not purely out of calculation. True *vergüenza* is a mode of feeling which makes one sensitive to one's reputation and thereby causes one to accept the sanctions of public opinion.

Thus a *sin vergüenza* is a person who either does not accept or who abuses the rules. And this may be either through a lack of understanding or through a lack of sensitivity. One can perceive these two aspects of it. (*Ibid.,* 113.)

Just as the official and economic relations of the family are conducted in the name of its head, the husband, who has legal responsibility for and authority over its members, so the moral standing of the family within the community derives from the *vergüenza* of the wife. The husband's manliness and the wife's *vergüenza* are complementary. Upon the conjunction of these two values the family, as a moral unity, is founded. From it the children receive their names, their social identity and their own shame. (*Ibid.,* 115.)

This time we are involved in description that is far from simple. The general subject of "the moral values of society" poses very serious problems of observation and evidence. Going to our list of elements composing scientific investigation, we can feel that the objectives of the anthropologist are relatively clear in the quoted passages. But what about the definitions of the various terms that appear in this material? We can fairly ask for more specific information about the meaning of the following expressions and statements:

1. "essence of womanhood"
2. "moral standing of the family"
3. "From it [vergüenza] the children receive their names, their social identity and their own shame."

Now each of the terms involved in these passages is in theory definable, but the anthropologist did not give us any definitions. In fact, examination of the rest of the chapter from which these statements are taken fails to produce any clear information about how the researcher arrived at them. Some statements of description in the monograph appear to depend on direct observation of behavior, others on reports of informants, while still others seem to be shaped from an analysis of language usage, as in some of the statements about *vergüenza*. In any case, in the passages above, we are given no information about how the data were obtained.

Finally, Pitt-Rivers gives us no systematic set of logical operations by which the complex relationships involving *vergüenza,* behaviors of various males and females, and the presumed "moral standing of the family" can be shown.

Examination of other chapters in *The People of the Sierra* shows us that similar questions about meanings, definitions, and research operations can be raised about dozens of statements. In this respect, this particular monograph does not differ significantly from the average ethnography, whether written by a British social anthropologist, a French structuralist, an American cultural anthropologist, or an anthropologist from any other school. Various explanations are given by anthropologists to account for this state of affairs. Probably the reactions to the problems raised above can be divided into three main categories:

1. Some anthropologists would readily admit that the passages cited above are lacking in scientific rigor, but would assert that the problem is unavoidable because the description of a community in all its aspects involves so much information that strict research operations (and the reporting of them) cannot be adopted because of time and space limitations.

2. Some anthropologists would feel that there are no serious problems posed by the above passages, since the accuracy and effectiveness of anthropological research operations depend on *building into the anthropologist* certain standard techniques of observation that result in accurate reporting, even though the processes of combined intuition-and-observation are too complicated to be included in a description of the data.

3. Some anthropologists now argue that anthropological field techniques must be more carefully structured (and described) than they have been in the past. For complex holistic community studies it is impossible (and unnecessary) to develop rigorous methods for documenting *every* piece of information that makes up a monographic description; nonetheless a *framework* of carefully operationalized evidence is necessary. Methods for the study of complex values, attitudes, and cognitive orientations must be developed that will make possible the objective, replicable testing of the hunches and intuitions of field workers. Furthermore, readily observable data such as houses and furnishings, vehicles, animals, and other material possessions, occupations, and many aspects of social relationships should be studied by means of techniques that include carefully constructed sampling procedures that can provide quantifiable bases for empirical generalizations.

A study by Mark Zborowski (1952), "Cultural Components in Responses to Pain," is interesting in terms of our methodological criteria because it satisfies some of our requirements for research rigor, yet falls short of full "credibility." In the opening sentence of his paper, Zborowski clearly states his objective to be "discovering the role of cultural patterns in attitudes toward and reactions to pain which is caused by disease and injury" (Zborowski, 1952:16).

Zborowski selected Jewish, Italian, Irish, and "Old American" patients at a New York veterans' hospital for study. The total of 103 respondents were interviewed at length (approximately two hours each), and the verbatim interview materials were examined for responses and attitudes toward pain. Type of pain experienced was controlled by limiting the research population to patients suffering from neurological diseases, mainly herniated discs and spinal lesions.

Summarizing some of his results, Zborowski tells us that both the Jewish and Italian patients

were described [by hospital staff members] as being very emotional in their responses to pain. They were described as tending to exaggerate their pain experience and being very sensitive to pain . . . the general impressions of doctors were confirmed to a great extent by the interview materials and by the observation of the patients' behavior. (*Ibid.*, 21.)

On the other hand,

while the Italian patients seemed to be mainly concerned with the immediacy of the pain experience and were disturbed by the actual pain sensation which they experienced in a given situation, the concern of patients of Jewish origin was focused mainly upon the symptomatic meaning of pain and upon the significance of pain in relation to their health, welfare, and, eventually, for the welfare of the families. (*Ibid.*, 22.)

In contrast,

there is little emphasis on emotional complaining about pain among "Old American" patients. Their complaints about pain can best be described as reporting on pain . . . . When examined by the doctor he [the "Old American"] gives the impression of trying to assume the detached role of an unemotional observer who gives the most efficient description of his state for a correct diagnosis and treatment . . . . Withdrawal from society seems to be a frequent reaction to strong pain. (*Ibid.*, 24–25.)

Zborowski appeared to be quite systematic and thorough in his interviewing, and he gives the reader information about these procedures. Can we accept his research results without qualm?

The major credibility gap in Zborowski's research occurs because he does not provide a set of rules and procedures whereby another investigator could analyze the same interview protocols and generate the same set of conclusions. Even though Zborowski uses quasi-quantified expressions, such as, "seemed *mainly* concerned with," "was focused *mainly* on," "*often* continued to display," "there is *little* emphasis on emotional complaining" (italics added), he does not indicate that these conclusions resulted from any real counting of items in the interviews. In fact, at one point he makes the claim that no quantification was necessary because the differences among the Jewish, Italian, and Old American patients are qualitative rather than quantitative (p. 20). Perhaps the differences in cultural patterns are so pervasive that *all* Jews are different from all Italians. That possibility is shattered, however, when we note his discussion of intracultural variations (*ibid.*, 26–27).

When Zborowski reports that differences in reactions to pain are related to levels of education, differences in occupation, degree of assimilation to American mainstream culture, and so on, we begin to realize that he has provided no description of how these variables are controlled in the basic research design, nor has he indicated the methods of analysis by which he examined the effects of these variables in his interview materials.

A number of other criticisms can be made concerning this particular research effort, but the problems listed above are sufficient to render the judgment "not proved" for Zborowski's materials. We are left with the feeling that his intuitions and hypotheses "make sense" and accord with other known data and hunches about Italians, Jews, and "Old Americans," but more rigorous methods of data analysis are needed in order to close the credibility gap sufficiently so that one could pronounce the hypotheses to be clearly and strongly supported by the evidence. Unlike the situation with Pitt-Rivers' *The People of the Sierra,* however, it is possible that *no new data need be collected* by Zborowski. The missing links in the chain of research are mainly in the analysis of materials, rather than in the structuring of the primary observational procedures.

Most of the criteria for satisfactory research are met in a paper by Norman Chance concerning acculturation and personality adjustment in a North Alaskan Eskimo community (Chance, 1965). The researcher set out to test the hypothesis that "those Eskimos who were found to have had relatively little contact with Western society and yet strongly identified with that society, would show more symptoms of personality maladjustment than would those Eskimos who had a greater amount of inter-cultural contact irrespective of whether they identified with Western society or not" (Chance, 1965:377). In other words, Chance suggested that a discrepancy between identification with Western culture and opportunity to actualize the identification through articulation to the dominant

White society would be associated with psychological maladjustment.

The population studied by Chance consisted of 53 residents, 31 males and 22 females, of the village of Kaktovik (over 90 percent of the adult population). Degree of identification with Western culture was empirically established in terms of (1) preference for Western games and dances, etc.; (2) preference for Western foods, i.e., canned foods, potatoes, fruits, etc.; (3) preference for Western clothing and hair styles as opposed to traditional Eskimo styles. The variable of "extent of Eskimo-White contact" was similarly operationalized in terms of several specific indicators. Personality adjustment was measured by means of the Cornell Medical Index, which is a "battery of questions designed to elicit responses concerning the respondent's past and present physical condition and family life history, as well as indicate feelings of the individual's own perception of his state of mind and health" (*ibid.*, 378). Two Eskimo "judges" were used in making the ratings for Western identification.

Chance found that Eskimo women showed markedly more signs of psychological maladjustment than did the men. Among both the male and female groups his statistics show strong support for his main hypothesis.

There are, of course, aspects of this research that can be criticized. The validity of the Cornell Medical Index as a measure of psychological adjustment among Eskimos can be questioned, though we should note that it was used only for intracultural comparisons. Chance himself notes that there are weaknesses in the statistical analysis. Furthermore, a careful analysis of the data could produce alternative hypotheses that might fit the findings as well as Chance's theoretical formulations. But a main point to be stressed here is the fact that the research operations in this project were clearly described and specified, so that the reader can form a mental image of the steps of investigation; and these research steps could be used by another investigator to replicate the research.

VALIDITY AND RELIABILITY

The problems of anthropological credibility that I have reviewed above can be looked at in relation to two important concepts that are commonly encountered in methodological discussions. "Validity" refers to the degree to which scientific observations actually measure or record what they purport to measure. For example, door-to-door interviewing about intimate details of respondents' sexual behavior might produce a corpus of answers duly recorded in interviewers' notebooks, but we would seriously doubt that the answers were an accurate representation of real behavior. Thus, spot interviewing on sensitive subjects is thought to be seriously lacking in *validity*. Our judgment about the validity of particular bodies of such data should not be overly hasty, however. Validity is a relative matter and is strongly influenced by the conceptual definitions employed, as well as by the theoretical framework to which the data are to be applied. In the example just given, the validity of the data may be high if the data are defined as "modes of public response to sensitive questions," rather than as "true" statements about actual behavior. Such a definition of terms would be useful, for example, in predicting styles of public discourse about topics of varying sensitivity—e.g., sexual topics *vs.* sports topics in the mass media.

"Reliability" is often closely related to the matter of validity, but refers to the repeatability, including intersubjective replicability, of scientific observations. If a particular set of door-to-door interviews produces approximately the same set of responses on repeated trials (and with different interviewers), we can say that the observational technique has high *reliability*, regardless of the validity of the findings.

Most anthropological field work may be characterized by its relative concern with validity, at the expense of reliability. The anthropological habit of long-term field work in small communities—employing a variety of participant observation and interviewing situations—is generally thought to produce data with a high degree of validity. The fieldworker who interviews a large number of informants concerning their kinship behavior has a number of opportunities to correct for individual informants' "mistakes" concerning the type of information sought. The detailed descriptions of behavior given in ethnographic monographs (including the ones discussed above) generally have a high level of both "face validity" and "construct validity" (defined as articulation or "fitting in with" related theoretical and conceptual domains).

The arguments between Redfield and Lewis concerning Tepoztlán were principally concerned with reliability rather than validity, though at a very general level. Lewis claimed that Redfield's "measurement" of particular dimensions were inaccurate, because they were grossly different from his own observations of the same general set of phenomena. Validity is also involved in the conflict, for Lewis argued that Redfield had not observed the phenomena that he had claimed to observe.

In the case of Pitt-Rivers' *The People of the Sierra* the questions and problems I raised refer particularly to the replicability of his materials. The replicability is in question for several reasons: most important perhaps is the lack of specification of research *operations* that another investigator could use in any attempted replication.

Definitions of key terms are lacking, and the precise modes of observation (interviewing format, selection of behavioral scenes for participant observation, etc.) are not specified by the ethnographer.

The study of cultural components in responses to pain is interesting in that, while the matter of validity is again not seriously questioned, the problem of reliability is focused on a different aspect of methodology than we found in *The People of the Sierra* and in Tepoztlán. The data-collection procedures employed by Zborowski seem quite replicable, and conducive to reliability. But he fails to make clear the transformational process whereby the data in the voluminous taped interview protocols are translated into generalizations about his research populations. Clearly some kind of content analysis was performed on the taped interviews, but this analysis was apparently intuitive and nonquantitative. There are some problems about the precise methods of obtaining the interviews, but these seem insignificant compared to the task of replicating the intuitive measurements which resulted in such statements as "there is little emphasis on emotional complaining about pain among 'Old American' patients."

The study of Eskimo psychological adjustment by Norman Chance illustrates the effects of reliability enhancement with some sacrifice of validity. Introducing quantified data-gathering devices such as the Cornell Medical Index makes replication of the research easier; hence it has a good possibility of improving the reliability of the data. (The relatively high reliability of the CMI has been documented in other areas.) On the other hand, critics of the research may raise doubts concerning the "truth" of information obtained among Eskimos by means of an instrument devised for use among literate members of modern American society.

It is somewhat surprising (and a bit disconcerting) that scientists in other disciplines often cite anthropological field data without serious reservations. The "matrilineality" of the Trobrianders, the "Apollonianism" of the Pueblos, and the "sexual freedom" of adolescent Samoans are apparently widely accepted in the scientific community. This ready acceptance of complex nonquantified ethnographic information is probably a result of the anthropological maximizing of validity, through a "multi-instrument," long-term mode of research. Whenever ethnographers have turned to more structured instruments—projective tests, for example—questions of validity have immediately been raised, both inside and outside the discipline (cf. Lindzey, 1961).

All of this taken together suggests that the holistic inclinations of anthropological researchers have a considerable methodological strength, provided that problems of replication and reliability are given more attention. There are sound methodological reasons for maintaining an eclectic "mix" of research operations—a blend of relatively nonstructured observations (high validity) plus structured interviews, tests, and other more formalized research instruments (emphasizing high reliability and replicability).

Conclusions

From the lessons of the Redfield-Lewis debates about Tepoztlán, and the disputes concerning the interpretation of Pueblo culture, it appears that anthropologists need to develop research methods that protect the researcher from his own subjective assumptions and value judgments. Contrary to some earlier opinions, training in anthropology does not rid the investigator of conscious and unconscious cultural biases, but methodological training can provide ways of minimizing the researcher's personal biases by means of systematic, objectifiable research tools.

Quantification and statistical analysis may aid significantly in objectifying anthropological research, but a most important first step toward rigorous methodology lies in careful definition of the focus of research, with specification of the empirical observations that will be used as evidence for and against the propositions to be tested.

The methodological requirements suggested above do not in the least suggest that anthropologists give up the time-tested general procedures of participant observation and informal interviewing. These traditional anthropological techniques are indispensable for identifying the significant questions, as well as for finding out how these questions can be studied in terms of the local setting. The intuitive observations of the sensitive fieldworker are essential to the general tasks of anthropological research, particularly in the discovery of significant patterns in cultural behavior. Once the anthropologist begins to lay hold of significant cultural relationships through his intuitive hunches, he needs to devise means to test and verify these hunches through systematized research routines.

The arch-empiricist Sir Francis Bacon observed:

. . . for let men please themselves as they will in admiring and almost adoring the human mind, this is certain: that as an uneven mirror distorts the rays of objects according to its own figure and section, so the mind, when it receives impressions of objects through the sense, cannot be trusted to report them truly, but in forming its notions mixes up its own nature with the nature of things. (Bacon, 1960:22.)

The task of the anthropologist is to reduce to a minimum the distortions of "this uneven mirror" by a careful definition of concepts and a specification of research operations, so that the powers and vagaries of the human mind work to his advantage—without reducing anthropological research to the level of "count 'em" mechanics.

REFERENCES CITED

BACON, SIR FRANCIS
1960. *The New Organon and Related Writings.* (First published in 1620.) Indianapolis: Bobbs-Merrill.

BARNOUW, VICTOR
1963. *Culture and Personality.* Homewood, Ill.: Dorsey.

BENEDICT, RUTH F.
1934. *Patterns of Culture.* Boston: Houghton Mifflin.

BENNETT, JOHN W.
1956. "The Interpretation of Pueblo Culture: A Question of Values." In *Personal Character and Cultural Milieu,* ed. D. G. Haring. Syracuse: Syracuse University Press, 202–217.

BEVERIDGE, W. I. B.
1957. *The Art of Scientific Investigation.* 3d ed. New York: Vintage.

BLALOCK, HUBERT M., JR.
1964. *Causal Inferences in Nonexperimental Research.* Chapel Hill: University of North Carolina Press.

BROWN, ROBERT
1963. *Explanation in Social Science.* Chicago: Aldine.

CHANCE, NORMAN
1965. "Acculturation, Self-Identification and Personality Adjustment." *American Anthropologist,* 67:372–393.

EGGAN, DOROTHY
1943. "The General Problem of Hopi Adjustment." *American Anthropologist,* 45:357–373.

GOLDFRANK, ESTHER
1945. "Socialization, Personality and the Structure of Pueblo Society." *American Anthropologist,* 47:516–539.

HOEBEL, E. A.
1966. *Anthropology.* 3d ed. New York: McGraw-Hill.

KROEBER, A. L.
1952. *The Nature of Culture.* Chicago: University of Chicago Press.

LASTRUCCI, CARLO
1963. *The Scientific Approach.* Cambridge: Schenkmann.

LEWIS, OSCAR
1951. *Life in a Mexican Village, Tepoztlán Restudied.* Urbana: University of Illinois Press.

LI AN-CHE

1937. "Zuni: Some Observations and Queries." *American Anthropologist,* 39:62–76.

LINDZEY, GARDNER

1961. *Projective Techniques and Cross-Cultural Research.* New York: Appleton-Century-Crofts.

NAGEL, ERNEST

1961. *The Structure of Science: Problems in the Logic of Scientific Explanation.* New York: Harcourt, Brace & World.

PITT-RIVERS, JULIAN

1961. *The People of the Sierra.* Chicago: University of Chicago Press. © 1954 by S. G. Phillips, Inc. Reprinted by permission.

RADCLIFFE-BROWN, A. R.

1952. *Structure and Function in Primitive Society.* London: Cohen and West.

REDFIELD, ROBERT

1960. *The Little Community/Peasant Society and Culture.* (Bound together.) Chicago: University of Chicago Press.

Webster's Collegiate Dictionary

1948. Springfield, Massachusetts: World Pub.

ZBOROWSKI, MARK

1952. "Cultural Components in Responses to Pain." *Journal of Social Issues,* 8:16–30.

"Signatures" of Chicago Street Gangs

3. Operationalism in Anthropological Research

As has been frequently pointed out, a main requirement of the scientific method is that the procedures of the researcher should be clearly (and publicly) specified, so that other scientists can understand *how* particular results were produced and can replicate the research if they should wish to do so. In *The Structure of Science* (1961), Nagel states:

If . . . theory is to be used as an instrument of explanation and prediction, it must somehow be linked with observable materials. The indispensability of such linkages has been repeatedly stressed in recent literature, and a variety of labels have been coined for them: coordinating definitions, operational definitions, semantic rules, correspondence rules, epistemic correlations, and rules of interpretation. (Nagel, 1961:93.)

47

He adds that:

> the ways in which theoretical notions are related to observational procedures are often quite complex, and there appears to be no single scheme which adequately represents all of them. (*Ibid.*, 94.)

Operationalism and Intersubjectivity

Examination of the pages of typical scientific reporting provides us with a fairly clear idea of what operationalism is all about. Descriptions of research in the pages of *Science*, for example, are full of information such as the following (all examples are from *Science*, May 12, 1967):

> Calves were lightly anesthetized with thiopental and then given continuous intravenous infusion of succinyl choline. (*Ibid.*, p. 827.)

> A hyper-transfused-polycythemic (HP) state was induced by intraperitoneal injections of 0.5 ml of washed, packed, homologous red blood cells on 3 consecutive days and again on day 5. (*Ibid.*, 832.)

> Five cocks received alcohol (9 ml/kg body weight, of 33 percent grain alcohol administered orally) and five cocks received an equal amount of water without alcohol 30 minutes before the initial exposure to newly hatched chicks. (*Ibid.*, 836.)

It is evident from these examples that the "operations," as given in scientific journals, are often set forth in highly technical codes which refer to established research procedures that are the standard practices of particular sciences. Much of undergraduate and graduate training in these sciences involves laboratory practice with the standardized operations.

All of the examples given above refer to laboratory experiments. The descriptions deal with the experimental manipulations by means of which the effects of selected variables can be observed and measured. In the sciences in which laboratory experiments are the most usual form of research, procedural descriptions such as the ones given above provide a guide or "recipe" whereby another scientist in another laboratory can repeat the experiment to see if his results agree with those reported earlier. However, in many types of research this "repeatability" of observations is not strictly possible. Behavioral scientists observing an unusual and aperiodic event—a natural disaster, riot, or a nonrepeatable ceremony such as the crowning of a particular king—cannot provide for repeatability of the observations, no matter how completely they describe the research operations. Similarly, astronomers sometimes report observations of cosmic events which are nonrecurring.

Aperiodic, nonrecurring events require accurate description just as much as do experiments—in order that other scientists may ascertain the extent to which the researcher's procedure was "objective." In such a case the main question to be asked is: "If another observer had been at the particular event, and if he had used the same techniques, would he have obtained the same results?" This is a question of "intersubjectivity." Research methods and descriptions which fail to provide sufficient operational description to satisfy the requirements of intersubjectivity are extremely common in the social sciences and are an important indicator of disciplinary immaturity.

The philosopher Herbert Feigl states the basic issue as follows:

> There are two questions with which we are (or at least *should* be) concerned in any cognitive enterprise: *"What do we mean by the words or symbols we use?"* and *"How do we know that what we assert in these "terms is true (or confirmed to some degree)?"* (Feigl, 1945:250; his italics.)

Operationalizing research procedures is not carried out simply for the edification and information of other scientists, however. The scientist tries for better and better research operations in order to generate more accurate observations, hence more effective theory building and testing. Specification of operations enhances his control of extraneous variables, increases the precision of basic measurements (or other types of observations), and provides the framework of information which permits the researcher to retrace his steps mentally in order to understand both predicted and unpredicted results.

The process of operationalizing research is in some ways analogous to using a recipe for baking a fancy cake. The "recipe" provides the following advantages:

1. It can be given to someone else, and that person can produce the same result if he follows the recipe point by point.
2. The recipe provides for accurate measurements of "variables," and makes clear which variables are the most important to measure accurately.
3. By stating a list of essential ingredients, the recipe by implication makes clear which kinds of variables are to be "controlled," or kept out of the procedures. (E.g., in beating the egg whites for a cheesecake, any oil or grease in the mixture would ruin the effort.)
4. The recipe provides a clear series of steps that can be retraced to find one's "mistake" if something goes wrong and the product turns out badly. Also, the clever baker can examine the recipe to find ways in which the procedures can be improved. Significant innovations can be made at certain points only.

5. The recipe provides explicit operational definitions for important concepts that are often left vague and undefined in ordinary discourse. (For example, "bake in a hot oven" becomes translated into "place in oven set at 450°F for 30–35 minutes.")

Our analogy is also useful for pointing out the ways in which scientific operations *are not like* cooking with recipes. The model has definite limitations. A cookbook recipe is usually used in a situation in which one wishes to produce an already known end product. This, of course, is not the case in scientific research, especially in the social sciences.

Unlike the cookbook recipe for a cake or pie, the operationalizing of research must always provide for a careful assessment of the adequacy of the end product. The "cookbooks of science" focus attention on the procedures whereby the results are examined in terms of their relevance for scientific theory.

Lest the reader misconstrue this discussion as a plea for a sterile, mechanical, "cookbook" mode of anthropological research, let me hasten to point out another element in the analogy. Expert cooks do not slavishly follow the dictates of recipes! Recipes provide general sets of guidelines, in terms of which the *chef de cuisine* experiments with new combinations and innovative procedures in the manner of a creative artist. Scientific investigation is similarly a highly creative art, as made clear by W. I. B. Beveridge (see Chapter 2). The creative scientist, like the creative cook, can be highly innovative in the production of new knowledge because he is intimately acquainted with his standard ingredients and techniques; he perhaps differs from the cook in that he uses careful procedures of verification to assess his results.

Operationalism and Operationism

From the foregoing discussion, the idea of operationalism that is essential to effective scientific advance may be defined as follows:

Operationalism is a research strategy in which primary elements (terms) of descriptions and theoretical propositions are structured, *wherever possible,* in forms which prescribe, or otherwise make intersubjectively available, the *specific acts of observation* which provide the primary transformations from "raw experience" to the language of theoretical systems. Furthermore, the strategy provides that higher-level theoretical propositions and models be constructed, whenever possible, by means of intersubjectively specified "transformational rules" which set standards of sampling, definitions, and logical fit whereby low-level descriptions and generalizations are sorted and organized.

The intention of this rather abstract statement will, I hope, become more clear as we take up some concrete examples later in this chapter.

While there is no serious disagreement concerning the proposition that any science, to be effective, must employ sets of "correspondence rules" and operational definitions, some complexity has been added to discussions of methodology by those social scientists who have insisted on a "radical empiricist" research strategy known as *operationism*. According to their thinking, concepts in theoretical systems *have no meaning independent of the particular research procedures* in which they are used. Thus, the term *intelligence* can mean only "that which is measured by a particular intelligence test," and nothing more. (By this same logic, a distance measured with a calibrated tape and a distance measured by a process of triangulation are *two different concepts* of distance.)

The attitude of strict operationism may be useful in some areas of science, but it is far too restrictive to be useful in anthropology. Insistence on fully operationalized research methods appears to arise in part from a misunderstanding of the structure of research operations in the so-called "hard" sciences. The advanced state of the mathematical and other procedures of physics has led some people to believe that the "correspondence rules" and operations of physics are clear, direct, and fully operationalized. Such, however, is not the case.

Feigl (1945) has pointed out that the various sciences have two general kinds of theoretical structures which he labels neutrally "theories of the first kind" and "theories of the second kind." Theories of the first kind are those in which the constructs "are homogeneous with the operationally defined terms in the empirical laws of the given fields." Type I theoretical systems include those of chemistry (with its elements, compounds, compounding weights, affinities, etc.), classical thermodynamics, and, in psychology, Hullian and Skinnerian behaviorism. Type II theoretical systems are made up of heterogeneous constructs for which transformational rules are often somewhat vague. Atomic theory, statistical thermodynamics, and the neurophysiological theories of Sherrington and Köhler are examples, Feigl says, of theoretical systems in which there are some "gaps," and in which hypothetical constructs or rough-and-ready transformations link one construct level with that of another.

Ernest Nagel has examined this matter of the correspondences of theoretical ideas with experimental observations in some detail. Like Feigl, he characterizes some areas of theoretical physics by saying that "rules of correspondence for connecting theoretical with experimental ideas generally receive no explicit formulation; and in actual practice the coordinations are comparatively loose and imprecise" (Nagel, 1961:99). Nagel's example is that of Niels Bohr's (in its time) relatively successful atomic theory, which was "an eclectic fusion of Planck's quantum hypothesis and ideas borrowed from classical electrodynamic theory" (Nagel, 94).

Nagel comments:

But how is the Bohr theory brought into relation with what can be observed in the laboratory? On the face of it, the electrons, their circulation in orbits, their jumps from orbits to orbits, and so on, are all conceptions that do not apply to anything manifestly observable. (*Ibid.*, 95.)

He notes that the Bohr atomic theory was usually not presented "as an abstract set of postulates, augmented by an appropriate number of rules of correspondence," but rather as a model expounded "in relatively familiar notions, so that instead of being statement-forms the postulates of the theory appear to be statements, at least part of whose content can be visually imagined" (*ibid.*, 95). As a result of this kind of theory presentation, "despite the use of a model for stating a theory, [it should be clear] that the fundamental assumptions of the theory provide only implicit definitions for the theoretical notions employed in them" (*ibid.*).

Feigl points out:

The prototype of an operational definition such as we can advance for directly measurable magnitudes should not mislead us into banishing all concepts which do not come up to this high level of methodological aspiration. Even in physics we have to define many concepts (not only highly indirectly but) sometimes only very partially. Before any theory of x-rays was developed, x-rays were simply "what you got when cathode rays impinged on metal surfaces," and "that which produced photographic images of a certain kind." Only as we advance in discovery and technique such very sketchy definitions are supplemented by fuller qualitative, quantitative, and far-flung relational characteristics. Operationism wisely understood and applied must take account and render account of the level of precision, completeness, and fruitfulness reached at the given stage of concept formation. (Feigl, 1945:256.)

These comments about operationism and the differing degrees to which theoretical terms are (or can be) operationalized may be summed up as follows:

1. It appears to be generally agreed among scientists and philosophers of science that, wherever feasible, concepts should be given meaning in terms of their relationships to other specified concepts and (particularly) in relation to methods of observation and experimentation which give them empirical content.
2. While some people have taken a position of "radical operation-

ism," insisting on full operationalizing and empirical definition of *all* scientific terms, a more widely held, and more moderate, view accepts the prospect that even in well-developed sciences there are frequently elements of terminology which are only loosely tied to empirical observations.

3. It would appear that in some cases scientific concepts have proved useful and productive even when the technology of the time offered little possibility of operationalizing the variables. In Feigl's words,

> Concepts of atomic structure were very far beyond practical testability only forty years ago. Concepts regarding the nature of cerebral memory traces are in the promissory-note stage today. Scientific research as an ongoing process involves a continuous scale of degrees of technical testability. (*Ibid.,* 253.)

4. When we survey the great welter of anthropological work that is produced without any semblance of operationalism, we can be assured that most of the anthropological enterprise would experience a drastic slowdown if *complete operationism* were to be insisted on. On the other hand, as a matter of productive moderation, it would seem highly justified to suggest that anthropologists pay considerable attention to the possibility that many or most concepts in common use should come to have operational definitions. In theory it would appear that much of the work of anthropologists is easier to operationalize than are the obscure constructs with which physiologists, for example, struggle in their laboratories.

5. The fact that anthropology is not a laboratory science in no way detracts either from the importance of, or the possibilities of, operationalizing the elements of our theoretical systems.

Operationalism in Anthropology

Judging from the examples of anthropological literature reviewed in Chapter 2, operationalism is not highly developed in anthropology. Statements of ethnographic fact are often given without any mention of the research techniques used to derive them. Just as often, the anthropologist reports in a general way that the data were gathered by means of interviewing and participant observation, but the *particular observations* on which key generalizations are based remain unreported. There are exceptions, of course. Sometimes psychological tests or specialized questionnaires are used (as in the paper by Norman Chance described in Chapter 2) to collect certain kinds of information, and these procedures provide at least minimal operational definitions of important concepts.

The ethnographer often makes some general introductory statements about his research procedures (he may make gracious acknowledgments of the invaluable help provided by his informants, etc.), but particular fact statements in the ethnography are not accompanied by information concerning *how* the fieldworker made these particular observations. Since field-work observations generally consist of complex mixtures of interviewing and "direct observation," laced with variable quantities of other more specialized procedures, it is frequently impossible to separate data that are operationalized in the form of informants' statements from those that were based on the anthropologist's direct visual observations.

Some writers have discussed the lack of scientific rigor in anthropological research as arising from a "mystique of field work." Field research in non-European cultures has been referred to as a mysterious "rite of passage," in which the most significant ethnographic information is obtained through an intuitional "experience"—a process that is basically indescribable to outsiders (including graduate students of anthropology). Morris Freilich has suggested that secretiveness concerning field-work techniques has developed because of the serious difficulties (and occasional failures) encountered in the field situation, the admission of which is not encouraged in the profession, since success in field work is thought to reflect one's personal character and professional adequacy (Freilich, 1970).

Part of the reason for the relatively carefree attitude toward operational specificity in anthropology probably stems from an earlier day when both lay and professional opinion held that most cultural "customs" (among "primitive" peoples) were clear, observable entities, requiring no concern with sampling, sophisticated interview procedures, or other specialized modes of observation. This complacency has largely disappeared, and most schools of anthropology are showing a rapidly increasing concern about methods and techniques of research. The problem then arises—what kinds of techniques, or research operations, can succeed in the complicated business of observing the day-to-day behavior of human groups? It seems clear that the time-tested techniques of interviewing and participant observation are still the mainstays of field procedure, but how can these procedures be systematized for those portions of ethnographic observation that call for stricter operationalism?

It is evident that strict operationalizing of *all* field observations would be well-nigh impossible to achieve, and would be extremely slow, cumbersome, and wasteful of effort. Many observations in field work would appear to require little in the way of procedural support. Statements about numbers of houses, usual crops grown, distance to other settlements, materials from which tools are made, locations of water, supplies, and so on would in many cases be self-evident and would not require operational definitions. Also, statements about events, such as "The weekly market was held on Saturday," "The Ravens beat the Wolves by a score of 29–17," appear to be unambiguous.

The need for operationalizing descriptive constructs in research reporting depends also on the level of use of particular types of information. Data statements that are given in a general way as part of the descriptive background of a community study may be exempted from the requirements of operationalization, but the same descriptive constructs, when they appear as central terms in general hypotheses or propositions, require more careful specification. For example, "distances to other settlements" given as approximations may be perfectly adequate as informational background to a descriptive ethnography, but the data require greater specificity when they become part of a statement such as "Rates of intervillage marriages decline sharply as the distance between settlements increases." In this statement it is important to know whether "distance" means "as the crow flies"; "along footpaths or roads"; whether it is by land or by water; whether it is measured, estimated, or extrapolated; by whom it is measured; and so on.

The more complicated, abstracted, fact-statements which fill our descriptive ethnographies pose much more serious problems of operational definition, however. From a recent anthropological journal, we culled the following:

Social atomism is evidenced by a characteristic weakness of formal organic bonds between individuals or subgroups in the kinship, economic, political, or religious fields of activity.

Feelings of hostility and repulsion—in the common forms of backbiting and evil gossip . . . are so prevalent as to form a social pattern.

The overt expression of either hostility or intimate friendship is rarely seen in [the community].

The Italian male must be *maschio* at all times.

The alignment of lineages is relevant only in certain situations, of which the most important are fighting, marriage and ritual.

Much of the struggle for headship of the lineage is played out during the dying elder's last hours.

Winter affords more leisure time than any other season of the year.

Relations between a mother and her sons are in general warm and affectionate.

In each of these ethnographic statements we can recognize two main procedural problems: (1) What kinds of behaviors or things are to be grouped together conceptually to "mean" organic bonds, feelings of hostility, backbiting, alignment of lineages, struggle for headship, leisure time, warm and affectionate relations? And (2) How does the fieldworker amass sufficient observations of these particular behaviors (and things) so that he can reasonably make such descriptive statements?

Some of the possible methodological solutions to these descriptive problems can be best examined by a review of anthropological handling of a widely used construct. For this purpose we will take the problem of *status inequality*, which is frequently a central concern in community descriptions and has received considerable attention in the methodological literature.

One of the major studies in which status inequalities are a focus of interest is Marshall Sahlins' *Social Stratification in Polynesia* (1958). He notes that:

> an egalitarian society would be one in which every individual is of equal status, a society in which no one outranks anyone. But even the most primitive societies could not be described as egalitarian in this sense. There are differences in status carrying differential privilege in every human organization. (Sahlins, 1958:1.)

The most general element in Sahlins' conception of status, therefore, is the matter of differential "privilege" in whatever terms privileges are allocated in particular societies. The various elements in terms of which privilege and prestige are allocated include economic (material) advantages, such as food, land, and other resources; political power; religious privileges and prerogatives; and social ratings of valor, bravery, patriotism, effectiveness in combat, wisdom, and other "virtues," the meanings and contents of which vary markedly from one society to another.

In spite of the differences in *contents or criteria* of stratification, Sahlins feels that comparisons can be made among societies in degree of stratification because certain general features of stratification are broadly similar in human societies. The least stratified human societies, Sahlins feels, are those such as the Australian aborigines, in which the only qualifications for higher status are those which practically every society uses to some extent, namely, age, sex, and personal characteristics.

Sahlins suggests that any society in which these universals are the only criteria of rank allocation can be designated "egalitarian," since such a society exhibits the minimum level of stratification found in human societies. Any society that has stratification beyond the theoretical minimum Sahlins refers to as a "stratified society," but he quickly notes that societies vary a good deal in the degree to which they are stratified.

One society may be considered more stratified than another if it has more status classes, restricted by principles other than the universals, or if high rank bestows greater prerogatives in economic, social, political, and ceremonial activities. Criteria for estimating stratification . . . are thus divisible into "structural"; the degree of status differentiation, and "functional"; the degree to which rank confers privilege. (*Ibid.*, 2.)

As Sahlins and numbers of other researchers have pointed out, the relative importance and extent of correlation among economic, sociopolitical, and ceremonial (and other) elements in stratification can vary from society to society, although these functional aspects of stratification tend to be highly interrelated.

Given these preliminary observations about the general definition of "social stratification," we can pass on to the problem of operationalizing the concept for given theoretical purposes. In Sahlins' own monograph the data are drawn from the available ethnographic descriptions of various Polynesian societies, and these sources usually provide information in the form of *assertions about stratification,* rather than systematic presentation of the relevant evidence.

In spite of many differences in the specific contents and forms of social stratification in the several Polynesian societies, Sahlins was able to group these ethnographic materials into four classifications for purposes of theoretical analysis. For example, his Group I (Hawaii, Tonga, Samoa, Tahiti) is characterized by the following features:

Structurally complex ranking systems, usually with three status levels; preeminent stewardship by high chiefs; severe punishments and dispossession of those who infringe chiefly decrees on land or sea use; control of communal production by high and middle levels; direct supervision of household production by chiefly and middle levels, including inspection and ability to apply secular sanctions for failure to plant; complex redistributive hierarchy of three levels; ability of chiefs to confiscate goods of others by force in some cases; divorce of upper level, and perhaps middle level, from subsistence production; large range of clothes, ornaments, etc., serving as insignia of rank; arbitrary despotism described in general statements by observers; control of socioregulatory processes by high chiefs; marked difference by status in ability to inflict secular punishments on wrongdoers including ability to kill or banish those who infringe chiefly rights; close-in marriages among chiefs strictly enforced; very complex mana-tabu system concerning upper status level; elaborate obeisance postures and other forms of respect including developed chiefs' languages and carrying of chiefs on litters, etc.; unique rites for all life crises of high chiefs, held on a spectacular scale. (*Ibid.*, 11.)

These very abstract descriptive statements, and other similar materials employed by Sahlins in his theoretical analysis, suggest some of the kinds of direct observations in terms of which these data about social stratification were obtained.

The elements from which ethnographic descriptions have been made in the area of social stratification (in Polynesia and elsewhere) include:

1. *Statements* by informants as to the existence of different, named groups in the society, accompanied by statements that such groups have differential powers and prerogatives.
2. *Statements* by informants as to differential decision-making powers of various individuals in their communities.
3. *Statements* by informants concerning the ritual meaning of ceremonial performances and rules (reflecting differential prestige).
4. *Observations* of ceremonial performances in which elements of the rituals reflect inequalities through either universalistic symbolism, or symbolic interpretations provided by members of the local community.
5. *Observations* of differences in access to the favors of supernaturals or in access to esteemed ritual performances.
6. *Observations* of differences in decision-making among different individuals in the community.
7. *Observations* of differences in possession of, or access to, scarce economic resources, e.g., land, among the populace.
8. *Observations* of differences in possession of significant (and presumably desirable) consumable goods.
9. *Observations* of inequalities in access to differentially valued occupations of the community.
10. *Observations* of inequalities of access to other scarce resources, such as sexual favors of females (and marriage partners), freedom of travel, and access to public and ceremonial places, etc.
11. *Observations* of dress, ornaments, insignia, speech, etc.
12. *Observations* of differential respect, differential behavior, etc.

Some of these general possibilities will be considered in terms of more specific observations.

As a general rule, we can say that observations by the researcher (or his agents or assistants) may be regarded as of higher value than the (essentially hearsay) evidence provided by informants' statements. "Hearsay evidence" provided by informants is much used by anthropologists, and is rendered valuable whenever independent statements of several informants can be cross-checked for reliability. Anthropologists usually (though not always) take into account the possibilities of "prejudicial interests" of given informants. The anthropologist, like the court of law, is especially suspicious of evidence against Smith introduced by his known enemy, Brown. At the same time, Smith's best friends and kinsmen are not always to be regarded as unbiased reporters of Smith's behavior either.

One of the most thoroughgoing attempts to develop systematic techniques for observing status inequalities has been the work of W. Lloyd Warner and associates. These methods have, for the most part, been developed through research on American communities, but as general techniques they appear to have a wide cross-cultural applicability.

SOCIAL RANKING BY INFORMANTS

One of Warner's methods for obtaining data on social ranking is to ask informants to name general categories of persons, and then to assign individual members of the community to these categories. Warner calls this the method of "rating by matched agreements." We have already observed that informants' opinions are not always as desirable as other forms of data, but by using a sufficiently large sample of informants and by carefully selecting one's sample operationalization in this form can be a useful procedure.

The method of ranking social *categories* by pooling the responses of a "panel" of local informants was used by Stanley Freed to obtain a ranking of castes in a village in India (Freed, 1963). Freed asked 26 males in the village of Shanti Nagar to rank all the local caste groups (their names were written on slips of paper) in a single hierarchy of prestige. Median rank scores were then calculated in order to determine the consensus of the panel. While there were interesting discrepancies among the rankings given by the informants, the results indicated a high degree of consensus in the local community.

Paul Hiebert (1967) examined the caste rankings of another village in India, using methods similar to those just described. However, in addition to the caste rankings, Hiebert also obtained rankings of a series of *individuals* in terms of their relative prestige. He found that the prestige positions of individuals were not isomorphic with the caste rankings, thus reflecting the fact that caste membership is only one of the determinants of relative prestige in Indian villages (though it is a relatively powerful factor in most cases).

Prestige ranking by informants in caste-structured communities appears to work well because the concept of a hierarchy of status is so pervasive in local social action. In other types of societies such prestige ranking may be more difficult, particularly in those communities in which there is an ideological commitment to the idea of equality and "classlessness." In American communities Warner and his associates (1960) have found that informants are quite willing and able to make status distinctions in terms of "classes" and hierarchies, even though there is thought to be a strong commitment to egalitarianism in American cultural traditions. In several different American communities, Warner has found that the status hierarchies usually are conceptualized in terms of "upper," "middle," and "lower" classes, each of which can often be subdivided into two parts. The conceptualization of class stratification in the Deep South, for example, is depicted by Warner as in Table 1.

TABLE 1. **Class Stratification in the Deep South**

Social Classes	As Seen by Upper-Class People
Upper upper	"Old aristocracy"
Lower upper	"Aristocracy, but not old"
Upper middle	"Nice respectable people"
Lower middle	"Good people, but 'nobody' "
Upper lower	Poor people
Lower lower	Poor people

ADAPTED FROM Warner *et al.* 1960:19.

In Midwestern communities, such as "Jonesville" Warner found that an "upper upper" class was typically lacking. "Such communities usually have a five-class pyramid, including an upper class, two middle, and two lower classes" (Warner *et al.,* 1960:17).

INDEX OF STATUS CHARACTERISTICS

The categories of general prestige ranking obtained by Warner and associates, as well as similar data obtained by sociologists working in the area of status inequalities, appear to be quite closely related to certain socioeconomic variables which are simultaneously "indicators" of relative social ranking *and* elements in the differential distribution of scarce resources. The most significant status indicators in American communities, Warner believes, are (1) occupation, (2) source of income, (3) house type, and (4) dwelling area. Of these variables, he considers occupation the most important and dwelling area the least important measure of status. Many social scientists use *amount* of income, rather than source of income, in their status inequality indexes. Since American society is a very highly monetized sociocultural system, it is not hard to see why aspects of monetary income, occupation (as source of income), and related fiscal variables might play a leading role in differential allocation of prestige, at the same time that the financial differentials are direct expressions of inequalities in access to scarce goods. It takes money to obtain fancy houses, and the style and relative opulence of houses are common symbolizations of differences in "social merit."

Many anthropologists have noted differences in housing styles in their various research communities, but as yet the possibility of using house style and furnishings as indicators of status gradations has not been systematically explored in non-Western ethnographic contexts. (This is surprising, since archaeologists have used these indicators with considerable success.) Frequently special domiciles, such as palaces of kings, large houses of chiefs, and the like, are mentioned in ethnographic literature as symbols of high status; on the other hand, the lowest rungs of social worth in many societies are at least partially identifiable by their housing styles, which receive labels such as "hovels," "shacks," "slums." Homelessness is often (but certainly not always) an indicator of lowest social position. The relationships of domicile to social ranking are empirical problems that require different solutions in different societies.

RATING BY SYMBOLIC PLACEMENT

Of course the status indicators suggested above are all symbolic in significant respects, even though houses, occupations, and income have their important pragmatic aspects as well. Some societies—perhaps those which seek to deny *utilitarian* differences in social status, as well as those in which social differences are pervasively salient—provide systems of relatively nonutilitarian symbols in terms of which prestige inequalities are expressed. In some communities in Mexico (particularly in the Mayan areas) a series of religious "offices" with their attendant obligations, including financial expenditures, provide the calculus in terms of which social excellence is measured. These religious offices are called *cargos.*

Frank Cancian (1965) has provided a detailed analysis of the *cargo* system of the community of Zinacantan. He presents statistical and other evidence for the prestige ranking of the various *cargos,* from the first level of *mayordomos* and *mayores* (34 different positions) to the three highly prestigious *alcaldes* (Cancian, 1965:29).

Although the *cargos* are ideologically considered equal in that "all *cargos* are in service of the saints, and all service of the saints is equally virtuous," Cancian was able to produce evidence for the close interrelationships between men's general prestige ranking and the specific *cargo* levels they had served. With this evidence as background, it becomes valid to use the data on *"cargos* served" as a direct, symbolic index of men's relative social worth in the community. Cancian also demonstrated that this indicator of relative prestige is related positively to socioeconomic status as measured in other ways. Thus, socioeconomic privileges tend to follow the lines of differential religious excellence.

Our task at this point is not to provide an exhaustive critique of studies of stratification, but to examine *status inequality* as a complex social variable that has been operationalized in several different ways. Following the leads provided by the examples above, a field worker who wishes to examine social stratification of *status inequalities* has three different strategies from which to choose. He may (1) ask his informants to rank members of the local populations in terms of relative "merit," "prestige," or "social worth"; (2) seek out objective socioeconomic indicators, such as housing style and other significant material possessions, in terms of which to differentiate people; or (3) examine important ritual events for evidence of status differences (e.g., differential roles in religious observances). The particular combination chosen for intensive work depends very much on other characteristics of the research situation.

In each of the studies described above, the fieldworker defined a *standardized information-getting system* which provided him with the socially differentiating "indicators" for a series of individuals and groups in the community. These primary data on differentiation were then organized in terms of scores, index numbers, "average ranks," or other means of analysis in order to set out the actual social positions of the research subjects. Although the precise steps have not been given in full detail here, the research procedures of Warner, Freed, Hiebert, and Cancian provide the "recipes" by means of which other researchers could go to the same communities and establish (with high degree of probability) the same social hierarchies as those described in the original monographs.

In all human societies differential prestige and privilege take manifold forms. Differences in socioeconomic status are expressed in myriad small and large symbolic events, inequalities of action, and status-revealing possessions. Many books have been written about the uncountable ways in which Americans, for example, make evident their status differences. Different schools, expensive summer camps, special license-plate numbers, titles, habits of speech, dress fashions, hair styles, body markings, and modes of entertainment (e.g., fancy parties) are part of our code of invidious distinctions.

It follows that any operational definition of social stratification represents only a *sample,* at one point in time, of the complex, multidimensional domain intended by the theoretical cover term *social stratification.* The researcher selects a small segment of behavior from this general semantic domain and announces that this segment "stands for" the general theoretical construct which carries the same label. Naturally, the researcher intends that his sampling process be "fair" or "representative."

The word *indicator* has been used here a number of times. This label, too, carries the meaning of "sampling" from the large, usually unmeasurable universe encompassed by a theoretical concept. Thus footsteps in the snow are operational indicators that "someone went that way"; it takes only a whiff of a peculiar odor to "operationalize" a danger signal concerning a leaky gas main; the election totals are (somewhat shakily) interpretable as indicators of relative popularity of the candidates, and so on. In each case, the sample or indicator selected should be as nearly as possible an irrefutable surrogate for the concept it represents.

Theory *vs.* Reality: The Operational Compromise

As I tried to make clear in Chapter 1, our methodological tactics, including various modes of operationalization, provide us with rules and manipulations for transforming low-level observations into theoretical propositions of varying degrees of abstraction. Frequently, a set of theoretical propositions *suggests* a new theoretical relationship, which can be verified only through some kind of empirical investigation. The terms of the theoretical statements provide the concepts that must be operationalized. At this point the realities of the "world out there" strongly affect our selection of research operations; hence, specific research techniques represent a compromise between the ideals of theory and the practicalities of given research contexts.

In Cancian's research on economics and prestige in Zinacantan, his theoretical concerns with the matter of prestige probably would have been best satisfied if he could have gotten direct statements about the relative social worth of all adult persons in the community, together with similar rankings of the relative merit attached to each of the religious offices. But the Zinacantecos either would not, or could not, make such direct prestige ratings for Cancian, even though their behavior indicated that they held some sort of organized set of ideas of relative prestige that applied both to persons and to religious offices. This difficulty forced Cancian to look for more indirect roads to his theoretical goal. The chronicles of most field projects can be profitably conceptualized as the often frustrating, trial-and-error searching for adequate research operations that reflect theoretical concerns. Indeed, sometimes theoretical goals are changed because no means of adequate operationalization of the relevant concepts is possible.

Sometimes events and observations in a field-work situation suggest new theoretical propositions to the researcher in such a way that the means for systematic observation become apparent at the same time. Thus, the theoretically significant observation that "it looks like most of the vendors in this market are out-of-towners" contains within its logic the research tactic of counting the local vendors and "out-of-towners" (perhaps by asking them where they are from), to provide empirical support of the generalization.

Any theoretical "hunch" that arises during field work takes on meaning only because of a vast, complicated network of social meta-theory in terms of which the researcher sees and interprets his world. At the same time, it is useful to admit that the "hunching" of new propositions and concepts from the raw materials of field experience can produce important contributions to anthropological theory without in the least resembling the careful theorem-testing of classical deductivism. Even though such "field-grown" theoretical contributions depend for their structuring on a complex of concepts (often unrecognized) from previous anthropological history and experience, the immediate process at work can be labeled *induction*. And the transformational rules of observation—in the operationalization of variables—are not logically different from those employed in the deductive style of research.

While it is important to note that research operations only make sense in terms of particular theoretical constructs for which they provide supporting evidence, it is equally relevant to keep in mind that the tasks of operationalizing theoretical concepts are often crucial in sorting out the useful from the meaningless in theoretical discourse. Contentless tautologies and vague confusions of abstract discourse are often best exposed through examination of their operational implications. If a theoretical proposition eludes any sensible pattern of empirical testing, the chances are great that the proposition does not make sense, however elegantly phrased. Anthropology, like many other young sciences, includes a number of theoretical disputes for which there are no solutions because the arguments are methodologically meaningless.

Summary and Conclusions

In his research operations the anthropologist is probably as eclectic as a social scientist can get. Out of the complex, buzzing confusion of life in human societies the fieldworker picks out his "indicators" and traces of behavior complexes in a great many forms. Sometimes an informant's whole lifetime of worldly experiences is "operationalized" in the form of a few hours of mechanically recorded utterances on magnetic tape. A few days' worth of observations in the cornfields duly jotted down in field notebooks "stands for" the thousands of hours of the people's horticultural activities, which are then compressed into one chapter of the ethnographic monograph. For many kinds of activities a very small amount of direct observation suffices, because the activities are highly patterned and repetitious.

Thus, watching (like a human camera) and listening (like a tape recorder) constitute the core elements of practically all operationalized definitions in anthropology. But operationalizing requires specification of *what* was watched, or *who* was listened to, under what circumstances. Sometimes a special, standardized stimulus is presented to an informant in order to promote a stream of verbal material which will be interpreted in terms of personality characteristics. The standard stimulus in such cases may be a set of pictures such as the Thematic Apperception Test, or a Rorschach test, or perhaps some sentences that the informant is suppose to complete.

The products and effects of human behavior are a special, and very important set of materials, which can be observed systematically as surrogates for conceptual domains. Roads and paths mutely testify to volume of traffic; cartloads of produce stand for economic productivity; rows of lighted candles represent operationalized religion.

In Chapter 5 an inventory of the varieties of field research tools is presented. This is done so that their respective advantages and disadvantages can be weighed. Special problems of operationalization arise when cross-cultural comparative research is carried out by means of the systematic use of data from a number of different ethnographic sources. Operational definitions then become "transformational rules" whereby pieces of information from ethnographies are selected in a standard, intersubjectively replicable manner.

Before we move on to a discussion of various field research tools and techniques, one very general, all-encompassing methodological question should be examined. Much discussion has taken place in recent years concerning the relative validity and methodological usefulness of the "insider's (native's) view" versus the "outsider's" (the objective scientist's) categorizations as main organizing principles of cultural behavior. Chapter 4 is devoted to this special problem.

REFERENCES CITED

CANCIAN, FRANK
1965. *Economics and Prestige in a Maya Community.* Stanford: Stanford University Press.

FEIGL, HERBERT
1945. "Operationism and Scientific Method." *Psychological Review,* 52: 250–259.

FREED, STANLEY
1963. "An Objective Method for Determining the Collective Caste Hierarchy of an Indian Village." *American Anthropologist,* 65:879–891.

FREILICH, MORRIS
1970. *Marginal Natives.* New York: Harper & Row.

HIEBERT, PAUL
1967. "Structure and Integration in a Central Indian Village." Unpublished Ph.D. dissertation. University of Minnesota.

NAGEL, ERNEST
1961. *The Structure of Science.* New York: Harcourt, Brace & World.

SAHLINS, MARSHALL
1958. *Social Stratification in Polynesia.* Seattle: The American Ethnological Society.

Science
1967. Volume 162. American Association for the Advancement of Science.

WARNER, W. LLOYD, MARCHIA MEEKER, and KENNETH EELLS
1960. *Social Class in America.* New York: Harper & Row.

Man from Nuba Hills, Sudan

4. Units of Observation: *Emic and Etic Approaches*

In anthropology we want our concepts to be useful in the construction of more and more inclusive and empirically successful theoretical systems. The "success" of both concepts and broader theoretical structures is measured in terms of their efficacy in explaining human behavior. In recent years there has been a growing feeling among anthropologists that our science has been progressing too slowly toward a really successful system of explanations of human behavior. As a result, a considerable amount of critical attention has been focused on various aspects of anthropological theory and method.

One diagnosis that has been offered for the theoretical and methodological "crisis" in anthropology holds that our problems grow out of a particular kind of weakness in the strategy of conceptualization used in most ethnographic descriptions. According to this view, cultural behavior should always be studied and categorized in terms of the "inside view"—the "actors' definition"—of human events. That is, the units of conceptualization in anthropological theories should be "discovered" by analyzing the cognitive processes of the people studied, rather than "imposed" from cross-cultural (hence ethnocentric) classifications of behavior. This point of view is variously referred to as "the New Ethnography," "ethnoscience," or "ethnosemantics."

The contrast between the "New Ethnography" and other anthropological methodologies has often been expressed as the opposition between "emic" and "etic" approaches to classification. The terms appear to have been coined by Kenneth Pike. He states the idea as follows:

> In contrast to the Etic approach, an Emic one is in essence valid for only one language (or one culture) at a time. . . . It is an attempt to *discover* and to describe the pattern of that particular language or culture in reference to the way in which the various elements of that culture are related to each other in the functioning of the particular pattern, rather than an attempt to describe them in reference to a generalized classification derived in advance of the study of that culture. (Pike, 1954:8.)

> An etic analytical standpoint . . . might be called "external or "alien," since for etic purposes the analyst stands "far enough away" from or "outside" of a particular culture to see its separate events, primarily in relation to their similarities and their differences, as compared to events in other cultures, rather than in reference to the sequences of classes of events within that one particular culture. (*Ibid.*, 10.)

> Etic criteria have the appearance of absolutes, within the range of sensitivity of the measuring instrument (or the expertness of the analyst); emic criteria savor more of relativity, with the sameness of activity determined in reference to a particular system of activity. (*Ibid.*, 11.)

The Emic or "New Ethnography" Approach

The development of the "emic," or "New Ethnography," approach to anthropological methods owes its origins to certain important features of the Boasian historicalist paradigm. Much of Franz Boas' teaching of ethnological methods emphasized the importance of collecting data in the form of verbatim texts from native informants in order to preserve the original (i.e., "native") meaning of the information. The emicists' view of anthropological classification is clearly stated by Boas:

> In natural sciences we are accustomed to demand a classification of phenomena expressed in a concise and unambiguous terminology. The same

term should have the same meaning everywhere. We should like to see the same in anthropology. As long as we do not overstep the limits of one culture we are able to classify its features in a clear and definite terminology. We know what we mean by the terms family, state, government, etc. As soon as we overstep the limits of one culture we do not know in how far these may correspond to equivalent concepts. If we choose to apply our classification to alien cultures we may combine forms that do not belong together. The very rigidity of definition may lead to a misunderstanding of the essential problems involved. . . . If it is our serious purpose to understand the thoughts of a people the whole analysis of experience must be based on their concepts, not ours. (Boas, 1943:314.)

Edward Sapir expresses approximately the same point of view:

It is impossible to say what a person is doing unless we have tacitly accepted the essentially arbitrary modes of interpretation that social tradition is constantly suggesting to us from the very moment of our birth. Let anyone who doubts this try the experiment of making a painstaking report of the actions of a group of natives engaged in some form of activity, say religious, to which he has not the cultural key. If he is a skillful writer, he may succeed in giving a picturesque account of what he sees and hears, or thinks he sees and hears, but the chances of his being able to give a relation of what happens in terms that would be intelligible and acceptable to the natives themselves are practically nil. He will be guilty of all manner of distortion. His emphasis will be constantly askew. He will find interesting what the natives take for granted as a casual kind of behavior worthy of no particular comment, and he will utterly fail to observe the crucial turning points in the course of action that give formal significance to the whole in the minds of those who do possess the key to its understanding. . . . Forms and significances which seem obvious to an outsider will be denied outright by those who carry out the patterns; outlines and implications that are perfectly clear to these may be absent to the eye of the onlooker. (Sapir, 1927, as reprinted in Mandelbaum, 1949:546–547.)

Sapir's statement is similar to the position of some later emicists in that it involves an apparent denial of the idea of "definitional relativity" in adjudging the correctness or adequacy of concepts. Instead of assessing conceptual categories in terms of their relevance for theoretical problems, he adopts the assumption that the *native's categorization of behavior is the only correct one.*

Some of the most important recent programmatic statements concerning the New Ethnography have been made by Goodenough (1956), Frake (1962), Gladwin and Sturtevant (1962), and Sturtevant (1964). These statements have occasionally included rather extravagant claims about the scientific potential of the new paradigm. In an editor's introduction to a paper by Frake about "the ethnographic study of cognitive systems," Gladwin and Sturtevant state the following.

The significance of the methodology outlined [here] . . . goes beyond its contribution to descriptive ethnography. The strategies outlined here promise a revolution in cultural anthropology comparable to that which took place in recent decades in linguistics. Linguistic analysis has cast aside the mold of the classical grammars to describe each language in terms appropriate to its own structure. Ethnography is struggling to break the mold of the categorical outline of culture which most anthropologists now take with them to the field. These papers describe the first steps toward a new technique of description and analysis which will in the future be able to describe the totality of culture as it exists among its bearers—and most particularly in the functional form in which it is presented to each succeeding generation during socialization." (Gladwin and Sturtevant, 1962: 72–73.)

In the paper to which the above comments refer, Frake outlines the basic assumptions and methods of the New Ethnography. "The basic methodological concept advocated here—the determination of the set of contrasting responses appropriate to a given, culturally valid, eliciting context—should ultimately be applicable to the 'semantic' analysis of any culturally meaningful behavior" (Frake, 1962:76). As a first step the anthropologist must identify particular "segregates"—the meaningful behavioral items that are grouped together as sets of contrasting responses. He suggests that such forms will be found by observing verbal behavior, particularly in bounded sociolinguistic contexts. For illustration he tells us that observations at an American lunch counter are likely to result in an identification of segregates such as "ham 'n' cheese sandwich," "hamburger," "cheeseburger," and "hot dog." Identifying all the segregates that are substitutable for one another (the alternatives within a given type of "something to eat") results in the production of a "contrast set." The construction of logically arranged hierarchies of terms related to a given semantic domain (e.g., "something to eat") results in a "taxonomy." Frake's illustrative taxonomy from the lunch counter looks like this:

TABLE 2. **Taxonomy of Something to Eat**

Sandwich		Pie		Ice-cream bar
HAMBURGER	HAM SANDWICH	APPLE PIE	CHERRY PIE	ESKIMO PIE
A	B	C	D	E

ADAPTED FROM Frake, 1962:80.

After identifying this kind of taxonomy of "segregates" in a "contrast set," it is essential to find the relevant "attributes" which distinguish the items from one another. As Frake quite correctly points out, a "hamburger" can vary a great deal in a number of characteristics, yet still be identifiable as a "hamburger." Addition of a piece of cheese, however, quickly changes it into a "cheeseburger." Analysis of the attributes that distinguish segregates at particular levels of contrast permit the ethnographer to identify the dimensions of contrast that supposedly have semantic and cognitive significance. The systematic study of semantic domains is often called "componential analysis."

For Frake this method of analysis has as its goal the development of an "operationally explicit methodology for discerning how people construe their world of experience from the way they talk about it" (Frake, 1962:74). The method has been most frequently used in the analysis of kinship systems (Goodenough, 1956, 1965; Wallace and Atkins, 1960; Wallace, 1965; etc.), but it has also been utilized for describing color categories (Conklin, 1955), weddings (Metzger and Williams, 1963), religious behavior (Conklin, 1964), firewood (Metzger and Williams, 1966), ingredients for beermaking (Frake, 1964b), and a number of other semantic domains.

The method, as applied to a specific field problem in another culture, is well illustrated by Metzger and Williams' (1966) report on some procedures and results in the study of native categories: Tzeltal "firewood." The researchers found from systematic interviewing that the Tzeltal of Tenejapa (Mexico) conceptualize "the things of mother-earth" to be divisible into "people," "animals," and "trees-and-plants." One subcategory of "trees-and-plants," that of "trees/wood," was examined (Metzger and Williams, 1966:394) in terms of the contrast set of mutually exclusive uses consisting of:

1. house-(building) wood
2. axe handle
3. pruning-fork handle
4. hoe handle
5. dibble
6. (forked stick suspended from ceiling on which clothing, etc., is hung)
7. bench

. . . .

18. bridge
19. firewood
20. charcoal

The category firewood, it was found, can be internally differentiated by a set of criteria referring to "good" and "poor" firewood.

TABLE 3. Criteria of Firewood Evaluation

Lek ("good")	Ma Lekuk ("poor")
"hard wood" "be hard"	"soft wood" "be (middling) soft"
"burns strongly"	"burns quickly"
"burns strongly" (an alternate form)	"burns quickly"
"dries rapidly"	"dries slowly"
"its fire is hot"	"its fire is only little hot"

ADAPTED FROM Metzger and Williams, 1966.

The grounds for these differential evaluations of good vs. poor firewood were discovered through the systematic application of "frames" (questions) in the form of "Why is ――― good (as firewood)?" and "Why is ――― not good (as firewood)?"

Additional information about the domain *firewood* was structured in terms of "consequences of burning certain varieties of wood," "lengths" and "dimensions" in firewood, and so on. Metzger and Williams were able to show by means of this systematic questioning technique that the Tzeltal-speaking Indians, their Spanish-speaking *ladino* neighbors, and the Tzotzil-speaking Indians in the neighboring *municipio* of Chamula each have somewhat different systems for classifying and evaluating firewood, even though there are no differences in the kinds of wood/trees available to the three cultural groups. For example, the Spanish-speaking informants "are able to name or recognize fewer varieties, differentiate among fewer varieties, and in some instances make different allocations of class membership" (p. 402).

It is important to consider the methodological and theoretical issues involved in the emic method of research because at least some of the practitioners appear to claim that the New Ethnography is the only sound basis for progress in cultural anthropology. Sturtevant (1964:101) says, for example, that "ethnoscience shows promise as the New Ethnography required to advance the whole of cultural anthropology," adding that it "raises the standards of reliability, validity, and exhaustiveness of ethnography." A note on the pessimistic side is added when Sturtevant admits the following.

One result is that the ideal goal of a complete ethnography is farther removed from practical attainment. The full ethnoscientific description of a
single culture would require many thousands of pages published after
many years of intensive field work based on ethnographic methods more
complete and more advanced than are now available. (Sturtevant, 1964:
123.)

On the other side, in a paper entitled "Anemic and Emetic Analyses in Social Anthropology," Gerald Berreman (1966) has charged
that the proponents of ethnoscience have been immodest in their
claims, while their actual accomplishments are of a relatively trivial
nature. Robbins Burling, who has contributed several studies to the
materials on ethnoscience, has questioned some of the basic assumptions of the componential analysts in a paper entitled "Cognition
and Componential Analysis: God's Truth or Hocus-pocus" (1964),
in which he admits the usefulness of componential analysis as a
mode of organizing terminological systems, but denies that this kind
of study provides insight into the cognitive processes of peoples. He
sums up his position by stating:

It is always tempting to attribute something more important to one's work
than a tinkering with a rough set of operational devices. It certainly sounds
more exciting to say we are "discovering the cognitive system of the people" than to admit that we are just fiddling with a set of rules which allow
us to use terms the way others do. (Burling, 1964:27.)

Burling came to these rather harsh conclusions after noting the
great number of logically possible alternatives for grouping sets of
even very few items. He notes, for example, that there is "a total of
124 ways in which a set of four terms can be discretely but nonre-
dundantly apportioned into cells by the application of components.
Clearly with five or more items the possibilities would rapidly become astronomical" (Burling, 1964:23). He further points out that
the componential analysts have a whole series of other logical problems to cope with, including *homonomy* (splitting a single term
into two different meaning clusters), *nonbinary components,* and
redundancy.

The proponents of the methods (Hymes 1964:116; Frake, C.,
1964:119) have replied that most of the superfluous possible solutions are eliminated by the field worker, who does not just "fiddle
with sets of items," but carefully elicits the appropriate terms (and
related information) from informants in relevant sociolinguistic
contexts. To this Burling replied that he has not found in practice
that such clear and unambiguous sorting of terminological systems
is possible.

But is it too much to ask for demonstrations of the technique on whole systems other than kinship or pronouns? One need not go off to exotic parts of the world to do this, English would really be a better test case, since readers could more easily judge the results. How about a full analysis of American folk terminology for trees? I have the nagging fear that the reason full analyses have not been given is because the methods advocated are not equal to the goals. I would really like to be proved wrong, for I think componential analysis is lots of fun, but I will only be persuaded by substantive descriptions, not by methodological arguments. (Burling, 1964: 122.)

Considering our earlier analysis of the relationships between theory and method in anthropology (and science generally), we are struck with the question "But what theoretical problems are the componential analysts attempting to solve?" It would appear that the method has some pertinence to the general problem of describing "folk taxonomic systems." (Burling points out that this is an attainable and legitimate objective.)

However, as proponents of a new kind of taxonomic system for analysis of *all* cultural problems, the componential analysts (and other formal semantic analysts) have provided little in the way of a general theoretical framework, and they appear to believe that accurate description of semantic domains is a useful end in itself. (Most of the works of the componential analysts are programmatic papers on the new research methods, and provide only partial descriptions of the quite limited semantic domains with which they concern themselves.) Given that the field work was very carefully done, and the results are sound, one wonders what theoretical use other anthropologists will make, for example, of descriptions of Tzeltal firewood or ingredients for beer among the Subanum.

By the time the smoke had cleared away in the debates between Burling and Frake, Hymes, *et al.*, the ethnoscientists admitted that the "real meanings" of native cultural categories can be understood only by examining behavior, *including nonverbal behavior,* in a variety of contexts. What, we wonder, *are* the crucial differences between the emicists and eticists? All anthropologists, regardless of their theoretical aims, presumably test their categories of observation in a variety of ways (frequently unspecified), including in their observations the informants' use of local terminology, statements by informants about norms of behavior, and notes concerning relevant nonverbal behavior relative to particular categories of things or events under study.

Although the ethnoscientists have offered no comprehensive statement of theory in connection with which their methodological practices are invoked, we should nonetheless look at some of the pieces of theory, explicit and implicit, imbedded in their works. First and foremost, they are explicit in pointing out that the theoretical system from which their main assumptions are derived is that of linguistics. This theoretical model is one which generally assumes formal patterns or "mechanical models" of behavior, rather than probabilistic or statistical patterning. It is assumed that there *is one* *"right" description of, or logical organization of, a given semantic* *domain* (say, kinship or plants), and that all or most of the members of a given society "know" that particular system. The componential analysts do not generally explore the significance of variations from person to person in organization of cognitive domains, just as linguists usually do not concern themselves with the varieties of speech patterns in given communities.

The ethnoscientists, therefore, are seldom concerned with details of sampling and representativeness in the cultures they study. Their published descriptions are set forth as the single "best" unitary system derivable from the given culture.

The most comprehensive criticism to date of the New Ethnographic approach has been presented by Marvin Harris (1964, 1968). Concerning the general assumption of cognitive or semantic homogeneity of populations, Harris describes his own experience in eliciting puzzling variations of kin terms among the Bathonga.

What I encountered in some of my "ill-informed informants" was an even greater measure of confusion. Thus, while Junod attributed the substitution of the grandfather term (*kokwana*) for mother's brother (*malume*) as a dialect difference, I kept running across people who insisted that both *malume* and *kokwana* were appropriate! . . . It may be that these variations can be handled as subcultural or dialect differences taking place inside different heads. On the other hand, it is equally plausible that these variations take place inside the same head. Indeed, this is true for many Bathonga in the modern situation. If that is the case, then an "adequate" ethnography must express the ambiguity of the system, and it must do so statistically. (Harris, 1968:586.)

He makes a similar critique of Goodenough's (1965) (and others') analyses of "the American kinship system."

Goodenough's assumptions need to be tested against sample population responses under standardized conditions. . . . None of the attempts to define the basic cognitive features of American kinship terminology has thus far made concessions to the possibility that ambiguity is one of the salient characteristics of this domain. (*Ibid.*, p. 587.)

In the area of *nonverbal* behavior the assumptions of cultural homogeneity and unambiguity become strained even more than they were in the matter of "folk taxonomies." Harris has commented on this problem.

If permitted to develop unchecked, the tendency to write ethnographies in accord with the emic rules of behavior will result in an unintentional parody of the human condition. Applied to our own culture it would conjure up a way of life in which men tip their hats to ladies; youths defer to old people in public conveyances; unwed mothers are a rarity; citizens go to the aid of law enforcement officers . . . television repairmen fix television sets . . . [etc.] (Harris, 1968:590.)

Granted that this caricature is not altogether fair to the methods and assumptions of the ethnoscientists, it nonetheless clearly points up a central problem—that of intracultural variations, which requires answers to questions of representativeness of informants, statistical examination of data, and a host of related methodological issues.

In addition to the matter of homogeneity versus heterogeneity of cultural behavior patterns, the ethnoscientists appear to assume an excessively idealistic (implicit) theory of human behavior. Linguists and their admirers seem prone to place strong emphasis on the power of words and language forms as causal factors in human affairs. This tendency is evident in the frequent statements by the emicists that equate understanding of "native categories of thought" with predictability of cultural behavior. The importance of idea systems—for example, ideologies and religious-belief systems—cannot be denied, but any adequate description of human cultural behavior must surely involve careful consideration of nonlanguage factors, such as material conditions, social relationships, and technological equipment as part of the explanatory frame of reference.

The Eticists

MARVIN HARRIS: THE STREAM OF BEHAVIOR I

The problems that have been raised by the emicists are thrown into sharper relief if we examine the methodological and typological suggestions of the eticists. As the most outspoken critic of the emicists, Marvin Harris has proposed a "new ethnography" of his own. Harris believes that

the ultimate source of the emicists' difficulties lies in the attempt to impose upon nonverbal behavior the type of approach which has proved successful for verbal behavior, on the mistaken assumption that, since both verbal and nonverbal behavior are behavior, a single standpoint should be equally appropriate to both. (Harris, 1964:148.)

Harris argues that human communities invest a great amount of effort and training (mostly informally programmed) in insuring that members of society distinguish clearly among the units of verbal communication. The community consensus about verbal communication is essential and is possible because of the limited number of basic units (phonemes) of which the communication is constructed. As Harris puts it,

It is easy to decide between the right and the wrong way to pronounce 10,000 or so morphemes; it is another matter for a population to reach consensus on the right and wrong way to perform forty or fifty million episodes [of nonverbal behavior]. (Harris, 1964:150.)

Given the great number of different possible behavioral elements about which judgments must be made as to "similar or different," the problem

cannot be solved by asking the actors to vote on the issue. The community of observers themselves must decide this question. They alone can resolve it in the manner best serving the interest of theory-construction. To leave it up to the informants, is, in effect, to abandon social science to amateurs. On the other hand, if we want to know whether two vernacular messages are similar or different, there can be no higher authority than the actors themselves. (Harris, 1964:150.)

Harris' point of departure for studying human behavior is the classification of body motions, in terms of the effects these motions have on the environment. Hence his minimal unit of analysis is the "actone," which "is a behavioral bit consisting of body motion and environmental effect which rise above the threshold of the observer's auditory and visual senses" (*ibid.*, 37). In beginning his observations with these relatively microscopic units, Harris admits that

when the observer is confronted by a multi-actor situation, there will be many intervals during which he will be unable to note the actones of all the people within his field of vision. Recourse to a second or third observer and to motion picture cameras and tape recorders will solve part of this problem. (*Ibid.*, 45.)

Table 4 is a sample list of actone classes (actonemes) suggested by Harris.

In giving these examples, Harris tries to make clear that there are a great many words in ordinary language that are relatively specific in meaning (hence operationalizable) as contrasted with yet other classes of words which are useless for precise description (e.g., beautify, celebrate, betray).

Harris suggests that "episodes" can be built up from chains of actones. These consist of the combination of actone with information about actor-type, object-type, time, and place (the "stage coordinates" of analysis.) Such episodes can, by observation, be linked in "episode chains," in which certain episodes may be analyzed as "nodes" because they are the "logico-physical functional requisites" of the given chain. Such functionally requisite behaviors are identifiable in cases where "one may retrospectively assert, on the basis of simple logico-physical principles, that the later episodes could not have occurred unless the antecedent episodes had occurred" (*ibid.*, 78).

TABLE 4. **Actone Classes**

Actoneme	*Body part*	*Body motion*	*Environmental effect*
carry	hand	hand moves horizontally while fingers grasp	object moves horizontally
drink	mouth	mouth opens	liquid disappears inside mouth
drop	fingers	fingers open	object falls
pick up	hand	hand elevated while fingers grasp	object is raised
poke	hand	hand moves down rapidly, fingers grasping	object moves down rapidly

ADAPTED FROM Harris, 1964:47–49.

The next higher taxonomic levels in Harris' methodology are nodal chains, mono- and multi-actor "scenes" and then "serials." At this point, Harris is able to bring his detailed micro-observational terminology to bear on the identification of operationally valid groups, in terms of which he can discuss social structure, "social relations," and other larger questions. His analysis remains clear and cogent, but the terminology gets a bit complicated by the time he has defined "permaclones," "paragroups," "nomoclonic types," and "permaclonic super systems."

In his emphatic rejection of emic analysis of behavior, Harris, as we noted, is insistent that verbal behavior requires a style of treatment different from the analysis of nonverbal behavior. Most important, he feels that the actors' verbal descriptions should *not* be used as the main evidence for actual behavior, though he points out that actors' verbal descriptions are useful sources of information about where to look and what to expect in observations of complex scenes.

As for the more detailed noting of language behavior, Harris feels that verbal analysis of scenes makes possible the separation of these observational units into subtypes. For example, two closely similar scenes identified as academic "classes" can be distinguished as "class on Chaucer" and "class on social stratification" on the basis of verbal content.

The study of ethnosemantics (including what he calls "ethnoactonics") Harris feels is an important study in itself, notably as practiced by the componential analysts. Such study of the semantic systems of peoples should not, however, be thought of as providing anything like an adequate method for the description of nonverbal behavior.

ROGER G. BARKER AND ASSOCIATES:
THE STREAM OF BEHAVIOR II

Roger Barker and his associates (Louise Barker, Herbert Wright, and others) have sometimes been identified as emicists (e.g., by Harris, 1964:144 ff.), sometimes as eticists (e.g., by Adams, unpublished; and Sturtevant, 1964: 121–122). While Barker and associates are explicit in their rejection of "arbitrary" units of behavioral analysis, they do not propose the actors' own perceptions of units as essential observational criteria. In rejecting totally arbitrary units of observation, Barker observes:

Tesserae [arbitrary units of analysis] are the pieces of glass or marble used in mosaic work; they are created or selected by the mosaic maker to fulfill his artistic aims. Similarly, behavior tesserae are fragments of behavior that are created or selected by the investigator in accordance with his scientific aims. Maze-learning trials, five-minute segments of behavior, and answers to pollsters' questions are behavior tesserae. (Barker, 1963: 1–2.)

Instead of observing human behavior in terms of "tesserae," Barker feels that it is possible to identify natural behavioral units. "Behavior units are natural units in the sense that they occur without intervention by the investigator; they are self-generated parts of the stream of behavior" (Barker, 1963:2). Barker (who is a psychologist and relatively unaware of, or indifferent to, the recent debates in anthropology concerning emic *vs.* etic analysis) refers to his type of social science as psychological ecology. In this kind of analysis, "There are . . . two grounds for identifying and classifying behavior units. One ground is their structural-dynamic characteristics; the other is their material-content properties" (*ibid.*, 8).

To illustrate his method of analysis, Barker gives a portion of a record of behavior concerning "Brett Butley, 7 years 2 months of age on July 5, 1957 . . . member of the Upper Infants Class of the Yoredale (England) County School." Some of the behavioral segments observed are (simplified) as follows:

> Eating orange
> Watching cricket
> Noting hurt child
> Brett glanced at (girl)
> 10:40 Brett walked over to the boy who had been batting.
> He took the bat which was handed to him as though this was expected by both of them.
> He stood quietly with the end of the bat resting on the ground as he waited for the bowl.
> Orin bowled.
> Brett struck at the ball rather awkwardly though he failed to hit it.
> It was difficult for Brett to swing the bat.
> The ball was thrown back to Orin and he bowled again.
> This time Brett succeeded in hitting the ball.
> It went a short distance and was thrown back to Orin.
> Etc.

From this record (continued at some length) the observer identified the following behavioral units: eating orange, noting hurt child, watching cricket game, noting hurt child, playing cricket, waiting for boys to move away, etc. (*ibid.,* 10). Barker argues that "playing cricket" is the size of unit that is most useful for descriptive analysis, though the smaller units of observation are important for identifying the boundaries of the "natural units."

In addition to this plan of behavioral observation, Barker and associates are much concerned with the delineation of natural "behavioral settings"—the environmental contexts within which particular sequences of behavior regularly occur.

Because the list of settings which we have identified reads, for the most part, like a common sense directory of town's businesses, organization meetings, school classes, and so forth, it is sometimes overlooked that their identification involves highly technical operations and precise ratings of interdependence . . . the precise quantitative criterion which we have used to establish the limits of behavior settings . . . was selected so that the settings would fall within the usual range of laymen's discrimination. Nevertheless, the criteria for their identification are not lay criteria. (Barker and Barker, 1961:467.)

The research of Barker and Barker (and associates) is a most impressive attempt to develop methods for the systematic description of behavior. Their intentions, whether observing children at play, interaction between parents and children, or details of a movie, are generally aimed at developing methods for more and more precise delineations of the basic observational units in order to achieve quantifiable, statistical materials. It appears that their assumptions about the "naturalness" of behavioral units place Barker and associates' research style squarely between the emicists and the eticists —to the confusion of both. In their insistence on avoiding "unnatural units" or "imposed units of analysis," they "sound like" emicists. On the other hand, their criteria of the relevance and "validity" of behavioral segments are based on agreement among the observers, rather than on the statements (and verbal habits) of the actors.

As Harris has observed (Harris, 1964:144–148), the research assumptions of the Barkers appear to be based on a relatively great amount of intuitive delimiting of "molar units," which seems to work successfully in American (and English) cultural contexts, but would be likely to cause serious difficulties if applied to non-Western cultures. Although the Barkers list criteria for recognizing boundaries of "episodes," these criteria are difficult to interpret:

1. Action persists in the absence of instigating conditions.
2. Change in position toward a part of the environment is renewed after forced digression or delay.
3. Preparatory adjustments appropriate to imminent situational change, toward which the observed action contributes, accompany the action. (Barker and Wright, 1955:238–243.)

The list of "molar" segments from behavioral observations of Brett Butley "look like" reasonably identifiable patterns, as long as the action is not far from the life experiences of the trained Western observer. Emicists' fears about our inability to recognize "natural units" would probably be justified when we contemplate application of Barker and Wright's criteria to, say, a Melanesian pig feast or a Rajput wedding.

Both Harris and Barker propose strictly empirical, inductive research methods, although Harris (quite correctly) points out that units of observation *must* depend on some kind of theoretical structure. Both Harris and the Barkers place great reliance on the observation of nonverbal behavior, although verbal materials are admissible as evidence concerning the nature of behavioral events. One important difference between the two methodologies lies in the size of basic units and their operational definition. For Harris, the basic units—"actones"—are relatively small segments of behavior, and require careful operational definitions. Few assumptions are made about the "cognitive" relevance of the individual acts. The inductive building up from "actones" to "episodes" to "scenes" is a time-consuming process, and it is only when he gets into those larger units that Harris is operating at something like the "molar" level of description that the Barkers prefer. The Barkers, on the other hand, assume that their larger, "molar," units of analysis generally have cognitive and goal-directed significance, even though they do not rely on the actors' statements for delineating such goal-oriented responses.

Emic, Etic, and the Goals of Anthropology

The debates between emicists and eticists have been examined at some length in order to put into perspective what is probably the single most important theoretical disagreement in social anthropology—one which involves the foundations of all our methodological procedures. If either the emic or the etic "side" of the argument is overwhelmingly right in its assertions, the work of the other must be regarded as nearly totally worthless. The main directions of future anthropological strategy are clearly involved in the controversy.

Resolution of the emic-etic controversy requires a closer examination of the anthropological goals of the two paradigms. Colby (1966) has reviewed the literature on the emic side of the controversy, and he has made it clear that the goals of the ethnoscientists mainly concern "better ways to handle the semantics of the cultures they are describing." Thus, the focus of attention is on more clearly understanding "primitive thought patterns," as expressed in language systems. For some anthropologists "primitive thought patterns" are synonymous with culture, and the study of culture is what anthropology is all about. In the most extreme emic position, then, ethnoscience *equals* the New Ethnography *equals* study of culture *equals* cultural anthropology.

Etic anthropologists, on the other hand, do not equate "culture" and "thought patterns." Harris, for example, insists that he is studying culture, though his goals are clearly the description of behavior patterns, based largely on nonverbal data. In this view, verbal materials are of some use in understanding and classifying human behavior, but they are distinctly secondary.

Underlying these striking contrasts in research strategy are important differences in assumptions about causality. The emicists are frequently quite explicit in their support of an "idealist" explanation of human behavior. That is, causes of human actions are to be found mainly in the definitions, beliefs, values, and ideologies of the actors. Eticists, on the contrary, more frequently seek explanations of human action in the environmental situation—the constraints of the "real world" surrounding human actors. Given this more or less "materialistic" theoretical position, direct observations of human *action* become much more important than the collection of verbal statements *about* human action.

Different methodological strategies follow directly from these theoretical differences. The hallmark of ethnoscientific research is the long-term intensive interviewing of a few trained key informants; etic observation of cultural behavior, on the other hand, usually requires the definition of "action settings," within which the observer notes the behavioral regularities of the individuals who habitually appear in these settings.

Another crucial difference between the emic and etic approaches is concerned with their handling of the time dimension. For the most part the New Ethnographers organize data in a "timeless" logical structure. The methods of contrastive analysis imported from linguistic methodology are generally based on the premise that the people's patterns of thought, structured in terms of language usage, will "stand still" long enough for the componential analysis, or other logical manipulation, to be carried out.

Thus, because of the nature of their goals and strategies, the ethnoscientists direct their studies to descriptions of relatively stable cultural scenes. The literature of ethnoscience so far available contains very few descriptions in which acculturation, culture change, development, diffusion, or other processes of temporal change are treated. This is also partly a reflection of the fact that language as "crystallized knowledge" tends, in its more systematic aspects, to lag behind changes in behavior. This aspect of language has made possible the strategy of inferring past social behavior (preferential marriage patterns, corporate kin groups, etc.) from present kinship terminologies, a technique that was used by Morgan, Murdock, Lowie, and others.

Given the "timeless" nature of ethnoscientific methodology, those anthropologists whose main concerns are the study of acculturation, migration, urbanization, adaptation to national cultures, complex societies, or other aspects of changing cultural patterns are seldom able to make extensive use of the techniques of the New Ethnography in their work. Also, those studies that concentrate on intracultural differences and conflicts—such as research in factionalism, decision-making processes, "marginal subgroups," etc.—find the ethnoscientific paradigm unsuitable for coping with the heterogeneities and ambiguities of cultural behavior.

The Emic-Etic Compromise—"Imbedded Emicism"

In spite of the apparent difficulties inherent in the application of a strictly emic approach to most modern ethnographic problems, it should be noted that the overwhelming majority of anthropologists accept and make use of some fundamental tenets of the emic point of view. Practically all fieldworkers operate with the assumption that information about cultural behavior must be gathered as much as possible from "the actors' point of view." That is, the meanings and interpretations that "the natives" give to cultural happenings are of great importance for untangling their patterns of behavior.

Many anthropologists take the view that the problem of identifying the insider's point of view is solved by the fieldworker's use of the native language and by his learning to interact in the local setting in a manner that approaches local cultural acceptability. Through observation of day-to-day behavior, critical listening to the concerns and attitudes verbalized by informants, and studying the emphases of significant ritual enactments, the ethnographer systematically checks and rechecks his stock of working hypotheses concerning the insiders' definitions of experience. Some of these definitions and classifications of cultural materials are elicited from informants in systematic, patterned interviewing not greatly different from that utilized by the stricter ethnoscientists, but these specialized ventures are interspersed with other, less rigidly emic, research techniques.

Sydel Silverman has described a technique for studying prestige stratification in an Italian community that illustrates the "imbedded emic" approach. Although her field technique does not include extracting strict contrast sets, formal componential analysis, or other appurtenances that have become familiar in the reports of the ethnoscientists, Silverman states that "the strategy followed here builds on the efforts of the so-called "new ethnography" . . . to discover the principles by which the bearers of particular cultures organize their universe and respond to it in culturally appropriate ways" (Silverman, 1966:899). Her work makes it clear that the data gathered in the specialized study of community stratification can be profitably interrelated with other, more etically derived information, in testing hypotheses about cultural processes. Silverman's technique for eliciting informants' systems of prestige stratification is described more fully in Chapter 5.

As will be argued later in this book, anthropologists are frequently in a position where they must ask questions, and note information about research communities, in terms derived from cross-cultural ethnological practice and from their own special research hypotheses. In these cases the field worker does not wait to extract native categories of experience through the involved processes of the New Ethnography. He assumes that for purposes of testing theory and hypotheses of the anthropological researcher, *some* of the outsider's definitions of significant actions or cultural categories are useful. He does not, on the other hand, ignore completely the question of the local insiders' definitions and categorizations of behavior.

The test of "correctness" in each of these field research strategies is the same—its empirically determined productivity. The complete outsider's set of survey questions put to a sample of the local populace is often empty of meaning and devoid of predictability—the questions are out of touch with the definitions of reality operative in the local scene. But the local people are not invariable better than the ethnographer in categorizing their own social reality for the simple reasons that (1) they are not social scientists, and (2) their (arbitrary) categorizations were not constructed for the purpose of cross-cultural study of behavioral systems. When we keep in mind that no one taxonomy of cultural behavior (or any other semantic domain) can be inherently correct, and when we note that componential analyses and other ethnoscientific styles of study have often demonstrated that *several alternative interpretations or taxonomic styles are possible* (Goodenough, 1956; Burling, 1964; Wallace, 1965), we are in a position to adopt a free-wheeling pragmatism in our modes of categorizing cultural observations. Following Kaplan, the only useful test of our classifications is in the successes and failures of our hypothesis testing and theory building.

This is the strategy that will be adopted in our examination of research methods. Neither the "insider" nor the "outsider" in the cultural scene has the answers for appropriate categories and definitions of behavioral facts. The appropriate categories depend on their predictive consequences in research. But the field worker must be able to judge—and his critics must be able to interpret—the consequences of his conceptual strategies. Hence, he must operationalize his definitions of cultural terms in such a manner that at least hindsight can adjust for misjudgment. When the field worker needs to examine precise details of behavior in a number of action settings he will find the suggestions of Harris and the Barkers to be extremely useful. When theoretical tasks require careful analysis of the natives' categorization of behavior, and of the world around them, the techniques of the ethnosemanticists will be of great importance. Many research questions will require both techniques for their solution.

On the other hand, most important theoretical questions in anthropology involve cross-cultural comparison, and such comparisons almost by definition require etic categories and styles of data gathering. While emic studies, through componential or other semantic analysis, often provide significant guides to realistic "native" definitions of units of observation, these must be fitted to the researcher's cross-cultural (etic) concepts in order to test general propositions about human behavior. Goodness of fit with other theoretical results, and success in hypothesis testing, are often the main criteria for judging whether such cross-cultural behavioral observations are realistic in terms of local definitions and conditions of cultural action.

REFERENCES CITED

ADAMS, RICHARD N.
1962. "The Formal Analysis of Behavioral Segments: A Progress Report." Paper presented at the American Anthropological Association Meeting, Chicago.

BARKER, ROGER, ed.
1963. *The Stream of Behavior.* New York: Appleton-Century-Crofts.

BARKER, ROGER, and L. BARKER
1961. "Behavior Units for the Comparative Study of Culture." In *Studying Personality Cross-Culturallly,* ed. B. Kaplan. Evanston: Row, Peterson, 456–476.

BARKER, ROGER, and H. F. WRIGHT
1955. *Midwest and Its Children.* Evanston: Row, Peterson.

BERREMAN, GERALD
1966. "Anemic and Emetic Analysis in Social Anthropology." *American Anthropologist,* 68:346–354.

BOAS, FRANZ
1943. "Recent Anthropology." *Science,* 98:311–314; 334–337.

BURLING, ROBBINS
1964. "Cognition and Componential Analysis: God's Truth or Hocus-pocus?" *American Anthropologist,* 66:20–28; 120–122.

COLBY, BENJAMIN N.
1966. "Ethnographic Semantics: A Preliminary Survey." *Current Anthropology,* 7:3–32.

CONKLIN, H. C.

1955. Hanunoo Color Categories. *Southwestern Journal of Anthropology,* 11:339–344.

FRAKE, CHARLES

1961. "The Diagnosis of Disease Among the Subanum of Mindanao." *American Anthropologist,* 63:113–132.

1962. "The Ethnographic Study of Cognitive Systems." In *Anthropology and Human Behavior,* ed. T. Gladwin and W. G. Sturtevant. Washington: Anthropological Society of Washington, 72–85. Reproduced by permission of the Anthropological Society of Washington.

1964a. "A Structural Description of Subanum 'Religious Behavior.'" In *Explorations in Cultural Anthropology,* ed. W. Goodenough. New York: McGraw-Hill, 111–129.

1964b. "Notes on Queries in Anthropology." *American Anthropologist,* 66 (part 2):132–145.

1964c. "Further Discussion of Burling." *American Anthropologist,* 66: 119.

GLADWIN, T., and W. G. STURTEVANT

1962. Introduction to paper by Frake. *Anthropology and Human Behavior.* Washington: Anthropological Society of Washington, 72–73.

GOODENOUGH, WARD

1956. "Componential Analysis and the Study of Meaning." *Language,* 32:195–216.

1965. "Yankee Kinship Terminology: A Problem in Componential Analysis." *American Anthropologist,* 67 (part 2):259–287.

HARRIS, MARVIN

1964. *The Nature of Cultural Things.* New York: Random House. © 1964 by Random House, Inc. Reprinted by permission.

1968. *The Rise of Anthropological Theory.* New York: Crowell.

HYMES, DELL

1964. Discussion of Burling's paper ("Cognition and Componential Analysis: God's Truth or Hocus-pocus?"). *American Anthropologist,* 66: 116–119.

MANDELBAUM, DAVID G., ed.

1949. *Selected Writings of Edward Sapir in Language, Culture, and Personality.* Berkeley: University of California Press.

METZGER, DUANE, and G. WILLIAMS

1963. "A Formal Ethnographic Analysis of Tenejapa Ladino Weddings." *American Anthropologist,* 65:1076–1101.

1966. "Some Procedures and Results in the Study of Native Categories: Tzeltal 'Firewood.'" *American Anthropologist,* 68:389–407. Reproduced by permission of the American Anthropological Association.

PIKE, KENNETH

1954. *Language in Relation to a Unified Theory of the Structure of*

Human Behavior, Vol. 1. Glendale, Calif.: Summer Institute of Linguistics.

SAPIR, EDWARD (see MANDELBAUM)

SILVERMAN, SYDEL
1966. "An Ethnographic Approach to Social Stratification: Prestige in a Central Italian Community. *American Anthropologist,* 68:899–921.

STURTEVANT, WILLIAM G.
1964. "Studies in Ethnoscience." *American Anthropologist,* 66 (part 2): 99–131.

WALLACE, A. F. C.
1965. "The Problem of the Psychological Validity of Componential Analysis." *American Anthropologist,* 67 (part 2):229–248.

WALLACE, A. F. C., and JOHN W. ATKINS
1960. "The Meaning of Kinship Terms." *American Anthropologist,* 62: 58–80.

Gerald Berreman with Informants in North India

5. Tools of Research

For every scientific concept that appears in our theoretical statements there are likely to be a number of alternative procedures available for observing, or operationalizing the relevant phenomena. The concept *strength of electrical current* can be operationalized in measurements of heat change, intensity of light, electrical shock felt by a person, changes in speed of a motor, changes in magnetic fields, and so forth. The same idea applies in anthropology, and it is often useful to employ more than one measure or mode of observation in the study of particular cultural institutions. This is the principle of multi-instrument research. The anthropological fieldworker, thus, needs to have a number of different research tools in his "field kit." Unlike the situation in the laboratory sciences, research tools in anthropology involve relatively little in the way of "hardware" and gadgetry but do require great sensitivity and self-awareness on the part of the investigator. The fieldworker is his own principal research instrument, and the various methods of investigation are alternative techniques for objectifying and standardizing the fieldworker's perceptions.

The research tools to be discussed in this chapter are the most frequently encountered techniques of anthropological investigation. It is not a complete inventory, however, and every fieldworker should be constantly alert to the possibilities of developing new modes of observation to supplement the standard items. Usually, new field-work techniques are refinements or modifications of one or the other of these main techniques. A corollary of this statement is that in practically every instance of field research, the techniques employed—whether qeustionnaires, projective tests, specialized behavioral observations, or modes of informal interviewing—must be adapted by the fieldworker to the requirements of the local cultural scene. There are no ready-made instruments.

Participant Observation

Soon after I had established myself in Omarakana Trobriand Islands, I began to take part, in a way, in the village life, to look forward to the important or festive events, to take personal interest in the gossip and the developments of the village occurrences; to wake up every morning to a day, presenting itself to me more or less as it does to the natives. I would get out from under my mosquito net, to find around me the village life beginning to stir, or the people well advanced in their working day according to the hour or also the season, for they get up and begin their labors early or late, as work presses. As I went on my morning walk through the village. I could see intimate details of family life, of toilet, cooking, taking of meals; I could see the arrangements for the day's work, people starting on their errands, or groups of men and women busy at some manufacturing tasks. Quarrels, jokes, family scenes, events usually trivial, sometimes dramatic but always significant, form the atmosphere of my daily life, as well as of theirs. It must be remembered that the natives saw me constantly every day, they ceased to be interested or alarmed, or made self-conscious by my presence, and I ceased to be a disturbing element in the tribal life which I was to study, altering it by my very approach, as always happens with a newcomer to every savage community. In fact, as they knew that I would thrust my nose into everything, even where a well-mannered native would not dream of intruding, they finished by regarding me as part and parcel of their life, a necessary evil or nuisance, mitigated by donations of tobacco.

Later on in the day, whatever happened was in easy reach, and there was no possibility of its escaping my notice. Alarms about the sorcerer's approach in the evening, one or two big, really important quarrels and rifts within the community, cases of illness, attempted cures and deaths, magical rites which had to be performed, all these I had not to pursue, fearful of missing them, but they took place under my very eyes, at my own doorstep, so to speak. And it must be emphasized whenever anything dramatic or important occurs it is essential to investigate it at the very moment of happening, because the natives cannot but talk about it, are too excited to be reticent, and too interested to be mentally lazy in supplying details. Also, over and over again, I committed breaches of etiquette, which the natives, familiar enough with me, were not slow in pointing out. I had to learn how to behave, and to a certain extent, I acquired "the feeling" for native good and bad manners. With this, and with the capacity of enjoying their company and sharing some of their games and amusements, I began to feel that I was indeed in touch with the natives, and this is certainly the preliminary condition of being able to carry on successful field work. (Malinowski, 1961:7–8.)

Malinowski's famous statement illustrates the fact that participant observation is central to effective field work. Participation is, of course, a matter of degree; even the casual adventurer or traveler participates, if only momentarily, in the lives of the people he visits. The anthropological fieldworker, Malinowski stresses, should totally immerse himself in the lives of the peoples he studies; and that can only be done through long months of residence in the local scene. Whenever possible the fieldworker should master the language of the people he studies, even though much of the behavior available for observation is nonverbal. Residence in the research community ensures, as Malinowski suggests, that the fieldworker observes details of daily life and activity enacted by people who have become relatively indifferent to, and unabashed by, the presence of a "foreigner." The fieldworker sees elements of daily life repeated over and over again; they become commonplace to him.

Part of the fieldworker's ethnographic knowledge becomes imbedded in his own daily routines, for he acquires many of the habits and concerns of the local people. He "internalizes" significant aspects of behavior. Fieldworkers differ a good deal in the extent to which they take on local cultural characteristics; "going native" has its disadvantages as well as advantages for effective research. But it is difficult to overestimate the importance of the information that the anthropologist accumulates through direct participation in the local scene.

The relatively unsystematized scanning of information through participant observation is basic to all the other, more refined, research techniques. The preliminary data from participant observations provide the fieldworker with insights and clues necessary for developing questionnaires, psychological tests, or other more specialized research tools. Participant observation also provides the further checking and monitoring of field information that is necessary for evaluating data gathered by the specialized techniques. The chronicle of a field project usually consists of the interplay between participant observation and the other modes of data collection.

Every individual is a participant observer—if not of other cultures, then at least of his own. But the typical nonanthropological resident in a foreign community returns to his native haunts with a very unsystematic and incomplete picture of the scene he has observed. Field work requires much more than simply "being there" and passively watching what people are about. Often the fieldworker, in observing a particular pattern of behavior or an event, needs to find out a great deal more about that event than he is able to observe firsthand. His personal theoretical frame of reference suggests to him sets of questions to ask; relationships of this event to other types of data must be explored, and a host of other materials must be considered in order to make individual observations useful. In cases where the fieldworker feels that a significant block of information is available to him simply through his observation of a particular type of event, he may nonetheless need to devise ways of ensuring the representativeness and objectivity of his observations in a series of repetitions of the given event. By structuring observations and systematically exploring relationships among different events— through interviewing, watching, and perhaps administering "tests" —participant observation can be converted to scientific use.

Some individuals are keen observers, while others fail to notice or remember many of the details to which they are exposed. Some individuals are excellent witnesses and can provide detailed play-by-play descriptions of actions at which they were present. People differ with regard to which aspects of scenes and events most capture their interest and are thus subject to clear recall. For example, American women seem better than men at recalling details of clothing, colors, and features of decoration and adornment. Professional cooks notice food and cooking equipment that escape the eye of the novice, and farmers notice details of agricultural technique that city people miss. Every individual has areas of special interest and expertise that affect his habits of observation.

The anthropological fieldworker needs to become aware of his own strengths and weaknesses in observational style. He should practice observing and recording events in order to discover his observational biases and to develop more systematic techniques of recall. He should find out for himself how extensive his note taking must be in order to ensure accuracy of recall. He needs to learn to direct his attention to features he might ordinarily tend to neglect. Habits of participant observation are, of course, closely interrelated with theoretical orientation. An anthropologist trained in "structural-functional" theory will certainly see a feast or ceremonial action differently than would the anthropologist who is concerned with processes of historical diffusion.

Theoretical systems provide the concepts and other frames of reference for pigeonholing observations. The fieldworker needs to examine with great care the nature of the classifications and concepts he employs in field observation. A constant danger is the overly quick leap to abstraction. Primary reporting of concrete events and things in field work should proceed at as low a level of abstraction as possible. Thus, observational statements such as, "The two men were very hostile toward one another" or "The building was rather dilapidated" are overly general statements, which may seem perfectly adequate to the fieldworker at the time he writes them, but which may well be difficult to interpret in later months when the fieldworker sits down to sort out and analyze these notes.

LANGUAGE OF OBSERVATION IN FIELD WORK

The following paired comparisons of (hypothetical) field-note entries illustrate some differences between overgeneralized reporting and notes that preserve the sense "evidence" on which descriptive generalizations are based:

Vague notes	Concrete notes
1. A showed hostility toward B.	A scowled and spoke harshly to B, saying a number of negative things, including "Get the hell out of here, Mr. B." He then shook his fist in B's face and walked out of the room.
2. The boy was very uneasy in the presence of the strangers.	In the presence of these strangers, the boy appeared to be very uneasy. He shifted from one foot to the other, stammered while he spoke, and his voice was so low he could hardly be heard. He kept picking at a scab on his left arm. When the strangers began to walk toward the house he ran behind the house and disappeared.
3. The house was very dilapidated in appearance.	Compared to many houses in the community this house appeared quite dilapidated. The part of the roof that was covered with tarpaper had a number of large rips in it. The corrugated iron sheet on the part of the roof closest to the road was awry, with part of it hang-

Vague notes (cont.)   *Concrete notes (cont.)*

	ing down over the eaves. The log foundations of the house were partially rotted so that the house leaned markedly toward the west. Two windows were broken out, and there were several holes in the floor of the main room where rotted floor boards had been broken in and not replaced (etc., etc.).
4. The child was angry because the neighbor children would not let him play with them.	The child told me he was angry because the neighbor children would not let him play with them. He said he had gone toward the X (neighbor's) house with his bows and arrows, but K and L (neighbor's children) had chased him away shouting insults at him.

These examples direct our attention to some points that fieldworkers need to keep constantly in mind in the course of their research.

1. Our language in both ordinary usage and theoretical terms is full of concepts that can be used as "cover terms" for a very wide range of different specific actions and conditions. The observations to which cover terms such as *hostile, uneasy, indifferent, hospitable,* etc., refer may range from simple verbal statements or paralinguistic hints to violent overt action.
2. These general cover terms have very little meaning except as qualities assessed in relation to other events of the same type. Thus it is extremely easy for an individual fieldworker to be misled by his own cultural biases in judging whether a particular action is hostile, indifferent, etc.
3. When judgments in terms of these vague categories are inserted into field-work reports, the standard of comparison on which the judgment is based should also be inserted. Thus, if one judges that a particular house is *dilapidated,* it is important to note whether the judgment is in relation to other houses in the immediate neighborhood, or whether the fieldworker is using his own society as a reference point.
4. A commonplace that is often ignored by fieldworkers is the fact that a statement by an informant should not be accepted at face value as a statement "truth." Even if the informant's statement seems plausible it is best to record the observation simply as, "The informant said that . . ."
5. Thus in every case, the fieldworker recording his observations should describe *the observations themselves* rather than the low-level inferences he derives from the observations.

Key-Informant Interviewing

One of the mainstays of earlier anthropological work was the use of key informants as sources of information about their cultures. This methodology has been, of course, indispensable for recovering information about ways of living that have ceased to exist, or have been sharply modified, by the time the fieldworker arrives on the scene. Thus, most of the available descriptions of American Indian culture were reconstructed from informants' statements about a past way of life that was no longer in existence at the time of the anthropologist's field work. Participant observation was impossible, so the remaining source of available information was the recall of individuals who had been participants in the given culture.

From our experience with our fellow humans we know that individuals vary a great deal with regard to their knowledge and interpretations of their own social and cultural systems. People differ greatly in the extensiveness of their vocabularies; some of our peers appear to be walking books of etiquette, while others blunder about through ignorance of accepted practice. In the great variety of adaptive techniques and tools, some individuals are widely knowledgeable, while others seem dependent on their fellows for information concerning the most routine things. Most important of all, we notice that humans differ greatly in their inclinations as well as their capabilities for verbally expressing cultural information. Consequently, the anthropologist usually finds that only a small number of individuals in any community are "good key informants."

Some of the capabilities of key informants are systematically developed by the fieldworker, as he trains the informant to conceptualize cultural data in the frame of reference employed by the anthropologist. This is especially true in the case of linguistic and sociolinguistic field work, but the point applies to all anthropological interviewing. The key informant gradually learns the rules of behavior of his role vis-à-vis the interviewer-anthropologist, and, if the interaction lasts long enough, he may begin to employ the anthropologist's theoretical concepts in the analysis of his own culture. Thus, in some studies which have involved great dependence on key informants over long periods of time, the possibility cannot be ruled out that the interpretations of cognitive structuring, basic postulates, or functional relationships which appear to emerge naturally from the key informants were in fact shaped to a considerable extent by the anthropologist himself as he taught the key informant his role as expositor of a cultural system.

Frank and Ruth Young carried out an analysis of the effectiveness of key informants during their field work in Mexico (Young and Young, 1961). They found that key informants were most reliable and effective in giving information on subjects such as:

1. Physical geography and public buildings (E.g., "Is there a church here?")
2. Institutions and institutional roles ("Do you have a doctor here?")
3. Dates of important community events ("When did you get electricity in this town?")

On the other hand, they found that evaluative questions such as, "Has there been any change in religion in this community in the last ten years?" or "What percentage of the people here customarily eat eggs?" or "How friendly are people here?" show a much lower degree of agreement (hence, reliability) among informants. The interviews on which these findings are based were carried out with very little accompanying participant observation or other modes of research. Also, the interviews were carried out with relatively little prior contact with informants. The results of their study are instructive, however. Even though we would expect the key informants' performance to be somewhat different under conditions of long-term contact and good rapport, it is likely that "when the information concerns directly observable phenomena such as physical properties or stable institutions in the community, and in matters requiring little evaluation or inference," key informants show a relatively high degree of reliability. Another aspect of key-informant reliability reported by the Youngs deserves careful attention: "Reliability among informants is probabilistic," they report. "That is, there is seldom precise agreement on any question or for all communities. Reliability is typically a matter of a majority of informants in a majority of communities agreeing on an answer" (Young and Young, 1961:148).

Most studies of the effectiveness of key-informant interviewing have been in connection with large-scale survey research, rather than in situations in which intensive interviewing is used over long periods of time in relatively small communities. However, some of the main points that have emerged from these investigations should be kept in mind by the anthropological fieldworker. A point quite frequently made is that different interviewers can elicit different kinds of answers from the same informants. The social characteristics, the style of presentation of self, and other qualities of the interviewer have important effects on the persons he interviews. This is not the place to go into great detail about interviewing techniques, good and bad, but it must be remembered that the interaction between fieldworker and his informants is a complex social process. The data that are entered into the fieldworker's notebooks or interview schedules may differ a good deal, depending on how he managed the interview scene.

It is frequently claimed that the fieldworker can trust his key informants because of his long-term friendly relationship with them, but it must be kept in mind that the long-term, friendly relationship will inevitably create a style of interaction and a shared set of attitudes and tendencies that may significantly color the information given by the informant. A fieldworker who is especially interested in people's negative characteristics—their fears, hostilities, aggressions, and deviant behaviors—is likely to elicit descriptions of behavior from his informants that include a liberal sprinkling of such negative attributes. The fieldworker who dwells on the positive side of things may evoke information of a somewhat "pollyanna" quality as his friendship and interaction with key informants progresses.

Aside from interviewer-effect on the quality of key-informant responses, there are numbers of other problems in the interpretation and analysis of verbal data from selected individuals. Every individual human being has a particular image of himself and his position in the world of persons and things—an image he endeavors to maintain as a consistent presentation of self to fellow human beings. His verbal statements to anthropologists are affected by this tendency.

Key-informant interviewing is used to best advantage when it is closely integrated with participant observation. This is the point made by Malinowski when he emphasized that "whenever anything dramatic or important occurs it is essential to investigate it at the very moment of happening, because the natives cannot but talk about it, are too excited to be reticent, and too interested to be mentally lazy in supplying details." Whenever the fieldworker himself has observed an event and has command over a considerable portion of the relevant information, he is in a position to vastly improve his data by systematic checking with informants. Informants' recall of details are sharpest during an event and immediately after it. Their interest in talking about significant events is likely to be highest at the time of the event or just before (and after) it.

Also, through participant observation, the fieldworker notes which persons are most involved in the actions—they are the ones with the greatest amount of first-hand information. Furthermore, he learns about informants' particular "stakes" in social actions, so he can assess the likelihood that any given informant might distort information to maintain self-respect or for other reasons. If the field-worker has observed the battle he is less likely to be led astray by the distorted accounts of either the winners or the losers—he can interview both, or, better yet, he may be able to locate neutral spectators of the action. Participant observation is essential for checking and evaluating key-informant data.

A fieldworker's most important informants are frequently persons who occupy specialized positions in the local society. Often the anthropologist hopes to have special relationships with head men, skilled craftsmen, and other important persons. Thomas Rhys Williams (1967) relates:

In Sensuron we identified and selected a girl of 16 for our household assistant. Her grandmother was one of the leading female ritual specialists of the Tambunan area. The girl had been trained as a ritual specialist. In addition, she was closely related to six persons holding key positions in the community. She served as a key informant in Sensuron. Her special ritual knowledge and her ability to give meaningful and accurate details of widely shared aspects of her cultural were invaluable. (Williams, 1967:29.)

Such close social contact with a specialized key informant has disadvantages as well as advantages. Many anthropological reports include useful discussion of the selection and utilization of special persons as key informants in field work.

So much of anthropological field work is composed of participant observation and key-informant interviewing that a large portion of methodological writing in anthropology is devoted to these aspects of research procedures. Some of the autobiographical accounts of anthropologists are especially interesting and informative in this regard. Hortense Powdermaker has presented a lucid account of her own field-work experiences (Powdermaker, 1967); John Beattie's *Understanding an African Kingdom: Bunyoro* (1965) gives much insight into the elements of anthropological method; and Thomas Williams' description of field methods in the study of culture is a useful additional source of ideas about participant observation and interviewing (Williams, 1967).

Collection of Life Histories

As suggested, key-informant interviewing frequently becomes so important in anthropological field work that extensive personal documents are collected from a small number of persons with whom the anthropologist has especially good rapport. The anthropologist is attracted to collecting extensive materials from persons who are unusually eloquent and sensitive in their presentation of personal and cultural data. Thus, in most cases, life histories represent the exceptional rather than the representative or average persons in the community. In spite of this fact, the richness and personalized nature of life histories afford a vividness and integration of cultural information that are of great value for understanding particular life ways.

Some life histories of considerable anthropological importance have been collected by individuals who were not themselves anthropologists. One of the most famous of these is the narrative of John Tanner, written and edited by Dr. Edwin James in the 1820s (James, 1956). John Tanner was a skilled raconteur whose recall of the details of day-to-day activities was little short of phenomenal. He lived a life of such varied adventures that his narrative is frequently cited as data concerning the conditions of life among the Obijway (Chippewa) peoples in northern Minnesota in the early nineteenth century.

Life-history materials are often collected and presented by anthropological researchers in an attempt to relate the abstractions of ethnographic description to the lives of individuals. The aim of Paul Radin's biography of a Winnebago Indian was, in his own words, "not to obtain autobiographical details about some definite personage, but to have some representative middle-aged individual of moderate ability describe his life in relation to the social group in which he had grown up" (Radin, 1920:384).

L. L. Langness (1965) has examined the use of life histories in anthropological research. He discusses some of the main uses of this field technique, and also examines problems of rapport, translation, reliability, and sampling. To the objection that life-history data frequently cannot be checked against objective observations of real behavior, he replies that very frequently a chief anthropological concern is the patterning of peoples' beliefs and conceptualizations of past events, rather than the truth or falseness of these accounts. From that point of view, life-history materials may be more useful for examining the patterning of general values, foci of cultural interests, and perceptions of social and natural relationships than as "true histories." This point is well illustrated in the book *Cheyenne Memories* by John Stands-in-Timber and Margot Liberty (1967). John Stands-in-Timber presents a Cheyenne version of the Custer fight in great detail. His version of this famous battle is different from other accounts. While it is of importance for historians and others to use this information as they attempt to piece together the story of what probably happened on that day in June, 1876, Stands-in-Timber's narrative is probably of greater anthropological significance as evidence concerning the beliefs and views of modern Cheyenne Indians, who are experiencing difficulties in adapting to life as a reservation enclave within American society.

One of the most ambitious studies to date involving life-history materials is Cora DuBois's study, *The People of Alor* (DuBois, 1960). She collected eight personal biographies from the Alorese, supplementing them with collections of dreams, Rorschach tests, and other psychological materials. DuBois collected the life-history materials mainly for analyzing Alorese personality, but the narratives are rich in cultural information as well. The psychiatrist Abraham Kardiner analyzed the individual life narratives and derived personality sketches for each of the eight individuals. Generalizations about the personalities of these individuals were also obtained in a separate analysis of the Rorschach protocols. The considerable congruence in these personality descriptions provides some prima facie evidence for the validity of these methods of psychological study, though the results were not subjected to statistical analysis. DuBois' monograph includes description of her data-collection methods and is therefore valuable as a guide for other fieldworkers.

The People of Alor brings into focus a central issue in the use of life histories as data about cultures. The problem is the matter of representativeness. In most cases persons who willingly narrate their life histories for ethnographers appear to be atypical members of their communities. DuBois, in fact, makes it very clear that her eight informants were in no sense a representative sample of the local community. Thus, the data from the eight life histories can be generalized to the entire local population only if sweeping assumptions are made about the homogeneity of personality characteristics among these people. These same problems of representativeness are encountered in all studies involving life-history materials. One way of overcoming these problems is to use life histories as explanatory and illustrative materials in connection with other kinds of data that have been collected in a more representative manner.

Structured Interviews

Participant observation and key-informant interviews have generally formed the core of anthropological research, but, taken by themselves, these methods have exposed anthropology to some serious criticisms, some of which have already been mentioned earlier.

1. *Quantification.* Although Malinowski and other leading anthropologists insisted that the fieldworker should count events and measure things as much as possible, quantification has been notably lacking in most research reports.

2. *Representativeness.* In those cases where data have been collected from a number of different informants or from numerous personal observations the researcher has generally not specified the total population or "universe" from which these observations are a sample, and steps were not taken to ensure that the sample was representative of the population.
3. *Specificity of research procedures.* In many cases anthropologists give no information about the research methods underlying particular descriptive generalizations. References are generally made to participant observation and interviewing, but for specific pieces of field information the supporting data are usually not given. That being the case, the critical reader usually has no way of evaluating the reliability and validity of the information.

In recent times anthropologists have developed a number of refinements in field techniques which are designed to offset these criticisms. In practically all cases these techniques are outgrowths and modifications of the basic field-work tools of observation and interviewing. For example, preparation and use of an interview schedule is simply a formalization of basic interviewing techniques.

Much has been written, especially by sociologists, concerning the design, administration, and processing of interview schedules and other survey research instruments. Anthropologists are well advised to turn to those sources of advice and information when preparing to carry out structured interviewing. It will be sufficient, therefore, to take up only a few main points here. Goode and Hatt (1952), Madge (1965), Bernard S. Phillips (1966), and Festinger and Katz (1953) all carry excellent treatments of the steps and problems in questionnaire and interview schedule construction. Glock (1967) presents a collection of inventory papers, *Survey Research in the Social Sciences,* in which an article by Bennett and Thaiss summarizes main lines of anthropological use of these data-collection methods.

One standard and highly practical use of interview schedules is in the preparation of a basic census of a research population or community. In some cases such census taking is restricted to a simple enumeration of household composition, with very little additional data other than perhaps occupation, marital status, age, and place of origin. On the other hand, census procedures are often expanded in order to gather much more comprehensive data from the households in the research population.

Elizabeth Colson has described a rather extensive interview schedule used in connection with her enumeration of persons among the Plateau Tonga (Colson, 1954). The data she collected for each household included names, clan affiliation, ethnic affiliation and birthplace of parents; data on siblings, spouses, and children; name, alternative names, place of birth, approximate date of birth, ethnic affiliation and clan of household head; previous residences, labor history, details of puberty ceremony (for women only); marriage payments, religious affiliation, fields and crops, inherited succession, number of persons in household, and kinship category of ancestor to whom the household was dedicated. These data were, of course, checked by means of other types of field observations in the course of her research. Extensive, quantified data collection as part of census taking appears to have been particularly characteristic of the research of Audrey Richards and her colleagues at the Rhodes-Livingstone Institute in Africa (Mitchell, 1967).

John Beattie (1965) has described in some detail the kinds of data that he gathered by means of a standardized interview schedule among the Bunyoro. His survey form was designed to accommodate information "from all but the very largest polygynous families." Detailed information about every household member included age, sex, kinship ties, and affiliations both within and beyond the household, education, occupation, marital status, marital history, and so on. One section of the schedule provided for data on economically important property (land, animals, cash crops, etc.) of the household (Beattie, 1965:39–40).

Beattie reports that one of these interview schedules took about an hour to complete. He carried out most of the interviewing and recording himself, although he did have assistants working with him. Interviews were obtained with all the households in three upland villages, totaling about 115 cases.

A basic interview schedule of the type described by Beattie and Colson ensures adequate quantification of a large array of materials for which the fieldworker otherwise can usually assemble only informants' generalized statements and his own, far from random, observations in a complex scene of social action.

An important use of structured interview schedules in field work is in cross-checking key-informant data. The alert fieldworker will, of course, test all of his data with as many different kinds of validity checks as he can devise. Colson has presented some interesting examples of the utility of checking informants' statements against survey analysis data:

I originally assumed that the period of seclusion for girls at puberty had been progressively diminished by mission and school influence. When I compiled material on the length of seclusion, classifying the material according to the decade in which the woman had been born, I found that there had actually been a progressive increase in the length of time of seclusion in all areas, but that this trend had been reversed for the last group of women to reach puberty. I now suspect that the increased prosperity of the Tonga . . . enabled more families to indulge in the status-producing practice of lengthy seclusion. . . . (Colson, 1954:57.)

Colson also found that informants' statements about the age of women at marriage were at variance with the data from her interview-schedule materials. She notes that "today I find that when I make a statement about the Tonga I am inclined first to check it against the material drawn from the census to see whether or not I am coming anywhere near the facts of the case. Impressions can be thoroughly wrong; so can the statements of informants" (Colson, 1954:58).

Use of an extensive interview schedule requires fairly thorough knowledge of local cultural patterns and social groupings. When several different cultural groups are present in a region, it is important to obtain approximate population data so that stratified samples can be drawn. Patterns of land tenure, ownership of material goods, kinship relations, religious activities, and recreational practices cannot be effectively quantified in an interview schedule until fieldworkers have idenitfied the potentially significant questions by means of participant observation and key-informant interviewing. Beattie makes the same point when he notes that "obviously, statistical information is worse than useless if the material that is being quantified is incompletely understood in the first place or, worse still, misunderstood" (Beattie, 1965:36). Thus he began survey research operations a full year after his arrival in Bunyoro territory.

In a multicommunity study in rural northern Minnesota, our fieldworkers carried out informal interviewing and other preliminary work for several weeks, in order to identify significant questions for structured interviewing. We found, for example, that many of the households of the area had more than one source of income. Farmers usually had part-time employment in construction, pulp cutting, and various other occupations. It became clear that our interview schedule needed to provide for complex questioning concerning occupations. For our Indian subgroups, on the other hand, preliminary work pointed to importance of information about wild-rice harvesting, participation in summer powwows, and attendance at Indian council meetings. Initial data-gathering also established some of the terminology that was appropriate for interviewing in the region.

PRETESTING OF INTERVIEW INSTRUMENTS

When preliminary field work has made possible the construction of an interview schedule suited to local data and conditions, a pretest community should be chosen, preferably a community very similar to the main research site. Use of separate pretest communities prevents "contamination" of research communities; this is especially important in relation to procedures of random sampling.

In pretesting an interview schedule, fieldworkers try to ascertain people's responses to the style and content of questions, and are particularly sensitive to inappropriate wording of questions. In areas where local dialects of a national language are markedly different from the urban dialects, the choice of wording in a questionnaire will depend very much on local attitudes toward national speech patterns. In some cases attempts to use the local dialect in questioning may provoke hostility because the respondents feel that the interviewers are "talking down" to them.

TYPES OF QUESTIONS

In the interview schedules used by Colson and Beattie, most of the questions refer to specific states or events within the experience of the person interviewed; for the requested information there should be one "correct" answer. Also, the meanings of the questions are quite concrete. There will, of course, always be ambiguities in the data—uncertainties about assignment of an individual to full status in the household, faulty recall of year of birth, and so on. Where possible, though, fieldworkers should devise questions concerning concrete events, behaviors and possessions, instead of asking questions involving vague generalizations. As an example, consider the following:

Q. Do you often visit other communities?

As compared with:

Q. When did you last visit Community A? Community B? Community C? Are there any other communities you have visited re-recently? (Preliminary field work having established a tentative list of important communities with which these people have contact.)

Whereas the first question requires the respondent to interpret the word "often," which is highly ambiguous, the second question refers to specific actions requiring only that the respondent remember the specific occasions of his visits to other communities. Gathering data about visiting other communities in this form allows the fieldworker to make his own decisions about the meaning of "often" or "seldom."

Questions in interview schedules also differ in terms of whether they are relatively closed or open-ended. An open-ended question allows the respondent to give any type of answer he wishes, long or short. On the other hand the closed or "fixed-alternative" type of question requires the respondent to choose from a set of categories. For example, consider the following:

Q. If one of your children wished to marry a Protestant how would you feel about it?

or

Q. If one of your children wished to marry a Protestant would you
> Object somewhat
> Object strongly
> Not object
> (other answer)

In the first case the open-ended question makes it possible to obtain a wide variety of reactions from respondents. Also, the responses will be shaped by what the people consider to be important, rather than by the categories provided by interviewers. But open-ended questions usually require considerable work in the form of coding and content analysis before quantified analysis is possible. Also, the answers to open-ended questions may fall into several different domains of discourse so that comparability among different respondents is sacrificed. Sometimes open-ended questions give respondents the opportunity for evasion with vague and indefinite answers.

If an investigator is quite clear about the range of specific responses that will be of most usefulness, fixed-alternative questions may be the most appropriate, and they are certainly much easier to tabulate and analyze. Effective interview schedules often contain a mixture of both types of questions.

Questionnaires

Strictly speaking, questionnaires are distinguished from interview schedules in that the respondent himself fills out the answers to the questions on the form provided by the investigator. In complex societies questionnaires are often sent by mail to respondents, and return of the answers is voluntary. John Beattie reports that he sent questionnaires to some 300 head men and chiefs of the Bunyoro. The percentage of returned questionnaires was gratifyingly high (Beattie, 1965:38).

Questionnaires are not satisfactory as primary census-taking devices, because of the unevenness of returns. In any study involving complex statistical analysis, questionnaire responses are open to objection because of the probably nonrandom character of the sample. Where statistical analysis of materials is secondary to the gathering of general descriptive information, questionnaires can be quite useful, and once the schedules have been prepared, very little time is sacrificed in administration. If a researcher wishes to examine the general validity and representativeness of data gathered by means of a mailed questionnaire, interviewers can be sent out to the persons who did *not* return the original questionnaires, so that the characteristics of nonresponders can be ascertained. If the nonresponders appear to be randomly distributed throughout the population no serious problems arise in use of the questionnaire data. On the other hand, if the nonresponders are predominantly from a special segment of a population (e.g., lower socioeconomic groups) then corrections must be made to take that fact into account.

Anthropologists have developed many specialized questionnaires and interview schedules to explore particular domains of cultural and social behavior. Whiting and associates have developed a specialized interview for the study of child training and socialization (Minturn and Lambert, 1965); Landy used a carefully constructed schedule in interviewing mothers in a Puerto Rican village (Landy, 1965); Chance used the Cornell Medical Index to assess personality adjustment among north Alaskan Eskimos (Chance, 1965); Graves and associates have used a long interview schedule (approximately two hours) in exploring drinking and deviant behavior among Indians, Spanish Americans, and Anglos in a community in the Southwest (Graves, 1967; Jessor, Graves, Hanson, and Jessor, 1968); a variety of techniques have been used in the study of socioeconomic stratification, as mentioned in the preceding chapter (e.g., Warner *et al.,* 1960); and sociologists, of course, have developed specialized interviewing materials on practically every conceivable subject, since this is a main methodological strategy in that discipline.

Ratings and Rankings

The various possibilites of asking informants to group or rank people (or other entities) is a potentially important questioning device, since it results in an "inside" or emic view of social categories. Silverman used this technique to study stratification of prestige in an Italian community (Silverman, 1966). During her early months of fieldwork, Silverman found evidence (through observation and key-informant interviewing) that the people of the community exhibited deference to one another according to essentially occupational criteria, but that other, unknown, criteria affected the ranking in particular cases. She pursued the matter further with a selected list of key informants.

Each informant was presented with a number of cards naming various members of the community and was asked to try to sort them out as "higher" and "lower." No indication was given of the dimensions of hierarchy that I wanted, for my explicit aim was to permit the informant to establish the terms in which "higher" and "lower" are meaningful to him. . . .

Each informant indicated that there are various possible ways of distinguishing person as "higher" and "lower" (such as financial position and values attached to occupations). However in each case *Rispetto* was soon mentioned. This concept . . . seemed satisfying to the informants and they readily returned to it.

In addition to suggesting the relevant questions to be put to informants, the preliminary interviews yielded other information that affected the way in which the sorting task was set up. First, it became evident that *rispetto* regulates relations only outside the household; it is adjudged for the family group as a whole and (with a few exceptions) at the common level of all members. The unit taken in subsequent interviews, therefore, was the family (household) rather than the individual. It was also determined that in Colleverde assessments of the level of *rispetto* correspond to a discrete, small number of categories, rather than to a continuum of graded rank or a very large number of levels. Therefore, informants could be asked to sort families "into groups." Moreover, since these categories are correlated with objective attributes, it seems possible to identify these attributes by referring to a sufficiently large representative part of the population, after which the level of others who shared these attributes could be predicted.

The sorting task was carried out in two two hour interviews with each informant. The informant was given one hundred and seventy five cards, one for each family in the village and for a selected sample of the country-side families. He was asked to sort all the cards into groups, as many or as few as he wished, according to the level of *rispetto*. It should be noted that the special task I set did not force the informant to behave in ways that do not occur in natural events; rather, it was a stimulus for the informant to simulate his normal behavior, to make the same judgments as those required of members of the community in everyday situations. (Silverman, 1966:903–904.)

It is interesting that Silverman's informants did not produce identical groupings of families in terms of the concept *rispetto*. She reports that

there were discrepancies in the number of groups (Renaldo recognized six groups, Gianni four groups, and Alberto seven groups) and in the points at which groups were cut off one from another, although there was high agreement in the relative rank of most persons. (Silverman, 1966:905.)

Having established the hierarchy of *rispetto* by means of the sorting operation, Silverman turned to further informal interviewing and participant observation to provide further validation and behavioral description of this prestige system. She felt that her research strongly supported a social-ranking model with the following form:

Rank Rispetto Groups in an Italian Village

Landowners (those who live off their land income)
Professionals
White collar workers and merchants
* . . . .

Village artisans, "civilized"

** ————————————————————————————
Village artisans, "noncivilized"
Unskilled nonagricultural laborers, village residents
Unskilled nonagricultural laborers, country residents
* . . . .

Peasant proprietors and farm tenants
Agricultural wage laborers
Mezzadria peasants
Drifters

————————————————————————————————

* . . . indicates a minor line of differentiation
** . . . indicates major point of differentiation

A major point of procedure stressed by Silverman is that it is important to allow the informants to devise their own categories and criteria for categories—particularly in initial stages of this kind of sorting operation. Once major dimensions, such as *rispetto,* have been established, it is then possible to ask informants to use this dimension in their ranking operations. Simon has used the same procedure in studying social stratification in a Mexican rural community (Simon, 1968). She found that the major dimenison used by Mexican villagers was referred to as *categoría.* Several points should be noted in this kind of methodology:

1. The structured ranking task should be preceded by a considerable amount of work, so that the researcher can give a preliminary structuring to the situation from first-hand information.
2. Although the fieldworker may have hypotheses concerning the nature and dimensions to be ranked, it is extremely important to avoid forcing a particular structure on the informants.

3. Reasons and comments provided by the informants in the course of their ranking operations are an extremely valuable source of additional data. Simon used a tape recorder to record her informants' responses, and content analysis of the informants' comments add greatly to the understanding of the data.
4. Participant observation and informal interviewing should be used as a follow-up to this structured procedure, to obtain further validation of the ranked results, and to fit the rankings and ratings into the context of day-to-day behavior in the community.

It should not require great power of imagination for anthropological fieldworkers to devise other kinds of rating and ranking tasks for specialized purposes. In some cases it may be of importance to rate or rank political functionaries in their order of importance, supernatural personages in terms of their relative "sacredness," warriors in terms of bravery, and so on. Not all native classifications of persons or groups of other units need to be in the form of hierarchies, however. In response to the task, as structured by Silverman, the Italian peasants could as easily have arranged the persons in some other kind of array.

The Semantic Differential Technique

Charles Osgood and associates have developed a technique for investigating the *connotational* dimensions of people's cognitive worlds by means of a systematic interviewing procedure.

In the typical semantic differential task, a subject judges a series of concepts (e.g. *my mother, Chinese, modern art,* etc.) against a series of bipolar, seven-step scales defined by verbal opposites (e.g., *good-bad, hot-cold, fair-unfair,* etc.). The concept is given at the top of each sheet, and the subject judges it against each successive scale by putting his checkmark in the appropriate position, e.g., $+3$ *extremely good,* $+2$ *quite good,* $+1$ slightly good, 0 equally good and bad or neither, -1 *slightly bad,* -2 *quite bad,* and -3 *extremely bad.* (Osgood, 1964:172–173.)

Respondents' ratings on the various scales can be averaged in order to explore the range of "semantic space" assigned to a particular concept; these can then be compared with other concepts in the same semantic domain. It is also possible to analyze the patterns of response among various groups—e.g., cultures and subcultures—to find out about differences in the assignment of adjectival qualities such as "good" and "bad." Using factor-analytic techniques, the researchers found evidence that adjectival judgments in all societies tend to cluster into three main domains of connotational meaning.

They labeled these semantic dimensions *evaluation, potency,* and *activity.* This leads them to conclude that "human beings share a common framework for differentiating the affective meanings of signs."

The semantic differential technique appears to be a promising tool for making cross-cultural comparisons of people's cognitive definitions of their experiential worlds. Schensul (1969) has used a modification of this instrument for comparing rural peoples of Ankole (Uganda) and northern Minnesota in terms of their semantic definitions of the "rural-urban continuum." He had the respondents rate concepts such as "my village," "the market town," "the city," "the best life," and "myself" on a series of dimensions including "religious-irreligious," "clean-dirty," "much money–little money," "hospitable," and so on.

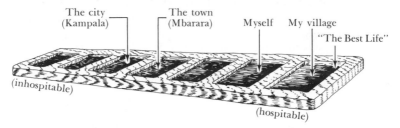

FIGURE 3. **Semantic Differential "Board" Used by S. Schensul in Uganda (With pattern of responses of typical villager.)**

To facilitate administration of the semantic differential, Schensul prepared a wooden board with seven indentations corresponding to the seven-point scale. (This "semantic board" was modeled after a board game that is very popular in East Africa.) Concepts were represented by small cards with symbols on them—e.g., "farmer" was represented by a banana tree for the respondents in Ankole. The respondent was given oral instructions about the appropriate terms for each end of the scale (e.g., inhospitable-hospitable) each time he was asked to consider a new dimension of meaning. Figure 3 illustrates the semantic differential board and a typical Banyankole response pattern for the "hospitable-inhospitable" dimension. Schensul was able to show that the rural people of northern Minnesota and Ankole had many similarities in the way significant geographical and social concepts are arranged in multidimensional semantic space.

Projective Techniques

There are a number of special psychological tests that were originally developed by clinical psychologists to obtain personality data, but which have been used by anthropologists in cross-cultural contexts. The best known of these is perhaps the Rorschach ink-blot test (Figure 4). Another popular projective personality test is the Thematic Apperception Test (TAT), first developed by Henry A. Murray for clinical use (Figure 5). A variety of other projective personality tests have been developed, most of them modifications or variants of these basic instruments.

FIGURE 4. **Example of Ink-blot Figure (Similar to Rorschach ink blots and other tests.)**

In most cases, projective personality tests are not, in essence, logically different from standard interviewing situations. The basic procedure involves asking informants (subjects) to respond verbally to *something* presented to him by the investigator.

The concept of "projection" involves the assumption that psychological characteristics of individuals dispose them to project certain personal needs, tendencies, inclinations, and themes into their verbal responses or descriptions of stimuli presented by the investigator. The original ideas behind both the Rorschach and Thematic Apperception Tests included the assumption that the stimuli presented to informants should be ambiguous (ink blots or vague pictures) so that the subject would have maximum freedom in exercise of imagination (and psychological tendencies) in responding to the situation.

FIGURE 5. **Thematic Apperception Test Picture**
REPRINTED BY PERMISSION OF THE PUBLISHERS, FROM Henry A. Murray, *Thematic Apperception Test*, Cambridge, Massachusetts: Harvard University Press, Copyright 1943 by the President and Fellows of Harvard College.

THE RORSCHACH INK-BLOT TEST

The Rorschach ink-blot test was developed by the Swiss psychiatrist Hermann Rorschach immediately after World War I. The test consists of 10 pictures in the form of symmetrical ink blots. Half of these involve color; the other half are composed of various shades of gray and black. The cards are presented to the respondent in a standardized order, and the subject is to report what the figures resemble or suggest. The time lag before the person responds is noted, and in the second phase of the testing procedure the respondent is asked to explain what features of the ink blots were important in determining his responses. Thus administration of the test is a complex procedure requiring a good deal of experience.

A number of different systems of scoring have been developed for the Rorschach test. The system devised by Klopfer (1956) has been the most frequently used. Scoring of the Rorschach responses generally involves considerations of "location," "determinant," and "content." "Location" refers to whether the subject responds in terms of the whole ink plot (W) or to some detail (D) within the blot. These in turn can be subdivided into categories of "small" (Dd) and "rare" (Dr). "Determinants" refer to whether the subject's association is primarily in terms of form or shape (F); color (C); movement (M) (an element within the ink blot is perceived as moving); or whether the response is determined by shading in the pictures (kk). Mixtures or blends of determinants can be expressed in terms of combinations, such as CF, in which color and form are both important, with color predominating as an influence; or the opposite situation, in which form plays the predominant role (FC).

Content of responses is scored in terms of human (H), nature (N), animal (A), abstract responses (Abs), and so on. Also responses are scored in terms of whether they are common or popular (P) or, on the other hand, original (O). Popular responses are those which have been found to occur very frequently among many different populations of subjects.

The scoring categories such as "whole responses," "small detail," "animal movement," "human detail," and so on are but a first step to interpreting the Rorschach protocol. That is, these response categories are translated into personality characteristics following a set of "transformation rules" that have been developed from clinical experience among American and European populations. A high incidence of animal responses (A) is translated to mean "shallow, ineffective intellect." Subjects that produce a large number of popular responses (P) are labeled "conventional" and "conforming." A high frequency of color responses (C) is translated as direct and uninhibited emotionality, although an unusually large number of pure color responses would be expected only from psychotic persons. Responses labeled FC, in which color is involved but subordinate to form, are translated as "socially acceptable emotionality." Complete absence of color response is interpreted as "impoverishment of emotional life." The ratio C–M (the ratio of color responses to movement) is used as a measure of the degree to which an individual is an introvert (paraphrased from Lindzey, 1961).

This description is not by any means a complete detailing of the scoring procedure. Rorschach-test advocates suggest that the scoring categories be examined in their interrelationships, and the test is usually employed in a semiclinical fashion. The quantified indexes provide a background against which the trained Rorschach clinician makes global assessments about personality characteristics in terms of a wide range of experience with Rorschach protocols. It is common, therefore, for anthropologists using the Rorschach test to have the protocols scored by clinical psychologists with extensive experience in scoring of these materials.

George and Louise Spindler's study of personality characteristics related to acculturation among the Menominee provides a good example of the use of Rorschach projective tests in testing a hypothesis (Spindler, 1955; Spindler and Spindler, 1958). On the basis of religious affiliation and other social characteristics, the investigators divided the Wisconsin Menominee into five groups as follows:

1. Native-oriented group (Medicine Lodge-Dream-Dance group)— least acculturated.
2. Peyote Cult group—transitional in acculturation.
3. Transitional group—characterized by little participation in any religious activity.
4. Lower-Status Acculturated group—associated with the Catholic Church.
5. Elite Acculturated group—associated with the Catholic religion.

These groups were shown to differ one from another in terms of income, group affiliations, use of Menominee language, and other characteristics. Twelve white subjects living on the reservation were included as a control group.

The Spindlers divided the scores on each of the Rorschach items into the "highs" and "lows," and compared each of the social groups to every other group in terms of their scores on the 21 Rorschach indexes. They found that the two extremes of the acculturation continuum (the Native-oriented compared to the Elite Acculturated) showed significant differences in eight of the 21 Rorschach variables. They also found that the Peyote group was the most different from all the others in psychological characteristics.

The Spindlers then constructed group "psychograms" for each of the groups. They found:

The typical native-oriented Menominee personality is highly intratensive, sensitive to the environment but able to maintain equilibrium despite its variations, lacking generally in overt emotional responsiveness and exhibiting a high degree of rational control over it when it does appear, motivated more by biologically oriented survival drives than by self-projective imaginatively creative ones, intellectually uncomplicated but adequate in terms of its setting, lacking in rigidity or constriction, without evidence of the usual forms of anxiety, tension or internal conflict and, in general, psychologically adequate to the demands placed upon it within its own socio-cultural setting. (Spindler, 1955:206.)

The Elite Acculturated group was also found to have a relatively adjusted personality profile, while the intermediate or Transitional groups appeared to have more disturbed personalities. This use of the Rorschach technique is a fairly successful and sophisticated example for a number of reasons.

1. The selection of the sample of subjects, while not employing a random procedure, appeared to ensure adequate representativeness from each of the socioeconomic groups.
2. All of the Rorschach responses were collected by one individual (the investigator himself).
3. All of the subjects were from the same general cultural milieu (Menominee reservation), thus insuring their comparability.
4. The procedures, including statistical analysis, were clearly described.
5. The statistical differences that were found to exist among the different Menominee groups were calculated in terms of the coded Rorschach variables themselves; hence they do not depend on the personality *inferences* which are involved when personality profiles are constructed from Rorschach data.
6. The total of 68 male subjects (a 20 percent sample of adult male Menominee above the age of 21) is large enough to justify the comparisons undertaken.

In a later study the Spindlers obtained Rorschach responses from 61 female subjects selected so as to correspond with the social characteristics of the male population in terms of the acculturation continuum. The male and female subjects were compared in personality characteristics, with the finding that the females appeared to have more satisfactory personality adjustments than did the males.

Bert Kaplan (1955) used the Rorschach test to examine differences and similarities among Zuñi, Navaho, Mormon, and Spanish-American subjects. He examined a total of 170 responses. By means of chi-square statistical tests, Kaplan found that there were significant differences among these four groups, particularly on five of the Rorschach scoring categories. He also examined these data by means of an analysis of variance, and found that there was *much greater within-group variance than between-groups variance*. This finding throws considerable doubt on the usefulness of the personality descriptions that have been used to demonstrate alleged differences among cultures. As Kaplan notes,

A very high degree of overlap among the groups is present, and this, coupled with the small size of the differences that do appear, indicates the variability of individuals in any one culture is greater than the variability between cultures. (Kaplan, 1955:18.)

Rorschach ink-blot tests have been scored by DeVos in a manner somewhat different from the scoring techniques described above. Instead of using the standard scoring variables, such as FC, C/M, P, etc. DeVos scored the verbal responses of the subject in terms of variables such as "rigidity," "maladjustment," "anxiety," "hostility," "body preoccupation," and so forth. He used his scoring system to examine Rorschach protocols collected by Horace Miner from Oasis and Urban Arab groups in Algeria. There were a number of statistically significant differences between the two groups. The higher scores on "rigidity," "unpleasant content," and "hostility" among the Urban group suggested the possibility that they were experiencing psychological strain because of acculturation to city life.

The use of Rorschach tests by anthropologists has declined a great deal from the peak period in the 1940s and 1950s. The reasons for this decline are complex, but the following factors appear to be important:

1. There has been heated debate among clinical psychologists within American culture concerning the validity of Rorschach-test interpretation.
2. The scoring procedures are very complex, as described above, and usually require that the anthropologists get assistance from clinical specialists. This is costly in terms of both time and money, and it is becoming more and more difficult to obtain expert Rorschach scoring for materials collected in the field.
3. Serious objections have been raised concerning the cross-cultural comparability of Rorshcach interpretations. It has been suggested, for example, that numbers of animal responses or numbers of movement responses may be related to environmental factors, rather than simply reflecting psychological tendencies. Similarly, interpretation of color responses has been criticized on the ground that various cultures place differing interpretations and weights of social and supernatural meaning on different colors.
4. The personality generalizations derived from Rorschach analysis are by nature fairly broad and vague qualities, divorced from specific behavioral observations. In recent times anthropologists have become concerned with more concrete elements of personality, including styles of interpersonal behavior, acquisitiveness and achievement orientation, self-esteem, and other characteristics which are not easily derivable from Rorschach responses.
5. To a certain extent the decline in Rorschach tests is associated with a general disenchantment with culture and personality studies, particularly those aimed at describing "modal" personalities, "national character," and other characterizations of group personality.

The Thematic Apperception Test was originally developed by Henry A. Murray and associates in the 1930s (Morgan and Murray, 1935). Murray's TAT (as it is commonly called) consists of 20 pictures with a variety of content, including a small boy looking at a violin; a farm scene with a man plowing, watched by a woman and a girl; a man and a woman in a semiembrace, in which the woman appears to be restraining the man; an elderly man and a younger man apparently in conversation; a woman and child; a woman and young man (frequently interpreted as mother and son); a pastoral scene with a boat moored under a tree, no persons visible; and a number of other pictures, most of which suggest some sort of social interaction.

These pictures are presented to the subject one at a time with the request that he invent a narrative to account for what he sees in the picture. He is asked what led up to the scene in the picture, "how the people feel about it," and what will happen afterward. The story told by the subject is recorded as nearly word for word as possible. It is desirable that the investigator not interfere with or prompt the subject.

There is no single standardized scoring procedure for TAT responses. Analysis of responses has been carried out in two main styles. Clinically oriented researchers, both psychologists and anthropologists, have examined the themes and styles of action in TAT stories in order to make inferences about qualities such as aggressiveness, dependence, sex conflict, and other general personality traits. For example, Henry states:

The TAT gave data on the following points: intellectual capacities, creativity and use of imagination, social behavior, sexual adjustment, emotional relationship to parents and other people in general, emotionality (in the sense of being generally submissive, passive, or cautious, or aggressive in dealings with other people), presence of anxiety or insecurity, relation to the Indian-White culture conflicts, general estimate of personality adjustment, and finally an overall picture of the relationship between the intellectual and emotional aspects of the individual and of these to his overt behavior. While not all TAT analyses gave data on each of these points, these were the ones that appeared most frequently. (Henry, 1947:24.)

In this clinical mode of TAT analysis researchers sometimes mention counting of particular thematic elements and even of ratios among these elements, but the procedures of content analysis are not made specific, and no statistical analysis of supposedly quantified elements is given.

William Henry's (1947) comparison of Hopi and Navaho children's TAT responses was the first significant cross-cultural use of the instrument, and his monograph provides a clear and thoughtful account of the procedures and results. TAT responses had been collected in five Indian tribes (Hopi, Navaho, Papago, Sioux, and Zuñi) in the course of the Indian Education Research Project, conducted jointly by the United States Bureau of Indian Affairs and the Committee on Human Developments of the University of Chicago. The children ranged in age from 6 to 18 and were selected in such a manner as to provide a reasonable representativeness of sampling from the different levels of acculturation in these groups. Henry collected 104 responses from Navaho children and 102 from the Hopi.

As is commonly done in cross-cultural use of TATs, special pictures were drawn so that the facial features and the cultural elements in the pictures would be congruent with Indian life in the Southwest.

The following are some examples of Hopi children's responses to these TAT pictures:

1. The man is talking. He is their father. He tells them he wants help. They will help him in the field.
2. Some mother is taking care of the baby. The little boy and girl playing with the turtle. They found it.
3. This man wants to sell his horse to him. He will take it. He is a white man.
4. The little boy is crying because his father scold him.
5. This man is talking to these two men. These are listening to him. They are his friend. They are talking about animals, sheeps. He wants them to herd his sheep. They will do it.
6. These two children are playing with the turtle. This turtle is going toward that boy. This lady is watching them. She is nursing the baby. These two are playing and talking to each other.
7. Somebody hurt him and he is crying. He is crying on the rock. When he got through crying, he went home. (Who hurt him?) A little boy hurt him. He (the other boy) does not like this little boy. He (the other boy) is a bad boy and too mean.

In seeking validation for psychological constructs derived from the TAT responses, Henry and his colleagues compared TAT interpretations with data from Rorschach tests, life histories, free drawing, and other materials. They found that there was a fairly high degree of agreement in psychological content from these different data sources, but he notes that "it is clear that the validating techniques were subjective in nature and some were of unknown validity themselves" (*ibid.*, 81).

Summing up this validation procedure, Henry stated that

of all the statements made by the Rorschach on any given area of the outline, on which the TAT also commented, 98.8% agreed with those made
by the TAT; of those made by the Life History, 97.2% agreed; of those
made by the Battery, 98%, and by the free drawing, 94.1%. (*Ibid.*, 81–82.)

One problem in this impressive validation attempt is that the procedures and rules for determining agreement or lack of agreement in
interpretation were not clearly specified.

In the resulting comparison of Hopi and Navaho (children's)
personalities, Henry noted that whereas Hopi children completed
their stories in a definite fashion, Navaho responses were frequently
incomplete—the outcome of the story was not stated. For example,

1. (Hopi) He is mad. His mother must have scold him because he refused
   to do it. He is going to do it.
2. (Navaho) I don't know what this boy is saying, maybe he is crying.
   When they get a scolding, they cry.

Compared to the Navaho, Henry found that Hopi TAT stories
contained numerous incidents involving aggression or intended aggression, followed by suppression and punishment:

He hurt his sister. His mother whip him.
He was bad. He not do what told. His mother spank. He will be good.

In fact, the most repeated theme is that of the punishment of
aggression or autonomy and the following reversion to correct,
obedient, and nonaggressive behavior (*ibid.*, 87).

Although there are some gaps in Henry's description of his methods of data analysis, his monograph provides much greater detail
about the responses and methods of interpretation than has been
common in later studies employing the TAT. Any anthropologist
intending to explore methods and techniques in TAT analysis can
profit from a detailed examination of Henry's monograph.

A much more systematically quantitative and statistical analysis
of TAT responses has been developed by a number of social psychologists, including John W. Atkinson, David C. McClelland, and
others. Their use of TATs has also involved specially designed pictures; most of these studies have been experimental in nature, involving American subjects (frequently college students). In *Motives in Fantasy, Action, and Society,* Atkinson and his associates
have assembled an impressive body of materials concerning TAT
research, including a variety of hypothesis-testing situations, essays
concerning fundamental assumptions of projective techniques, and
carefully worked-out scoring techniques for analysis of "achievement," "affiliation," and "power" motivations. An example will illustrate their research methods.

A Projective Measure of Need for Affiliation
(THOMAS E. SHIPLEY, JR., and JOSEPH VEROFF)

The psychologists used fraternity groups at the University of Pennsylvania for this study. For one fraternity group a sociometric test was introduced in which each subject was asked to describe the other members of his fraternity in terms of a number of adjectives such as "aggressive," "antisocial," "argumentative," "conceited," "cooperative," "entertaining," "friendly," "sincere." The researchers theorized that this sociometric procedure would arouse the subjects' concerns and motivations about affiliation.

"Need for affiliation" involves the general idea of concern about

establishing, maintaining, or restoring an affective relationship with another person. This relationship is most adequately described by the word friendship. . . . Affiliative concern is also readily inferred from some statement of how one person feels about another or their relationship. Some statement of liking, or the desire to be liked or accepted or forgiven reveals the nature of the relationship.

The affiliative concern of one of the characters may be apparent in his reaction to a separation or some disruption of an interpersonal relationship. Feeling bad (negative affect) following a separation or disruption implies concern with maintaining or restoring a broken relationship. For example sorrow in parting, shame or grief over some action that has led to a separation, or similar instances imply the desire to restore the affiliative relationship of the past. (Heyns, Veroff, and Atkinson, 1958:205–207, their italics.)

After the investigators had administered the sociometric task to the fraternity group, they introduced the TAT instrument, consisting of five pictures (including four from the standard TAT set and "a fifth picture showing a group of young men seated around a table with another young man in the background"). The subjects were asked to write stories about each of the pictures.

The control group (another fraternity group) was given a preliminary task concerning food preference, which presumably would not arouse motivations or "need for affiliation." They completed the same TAT after the food-preference test. Shipley and Veroff scored these TAT responses in terms of the following subcategories: "affiliation imagery," "unrelated imagery," "need" (affiliation), "instrumental activity" (concerning affiliation), "goal anticipation," "obstacle," "affective goal state," and "general theme" (concerning affiliation). Mean scores for the two groups in each of these scoring categories were calculated, and mean differences were statistically compared by means of the t test. They found that on six of the eight scoring categories there were differences between the two groups at the .05 level of statistical significance. The researchers concluded that the experimental device (sociometric task) had aroused motivations and anxieties concerning affiliation, and that their content-analysis methods were effective in detecting these differences in motivational states.

The methods of content analysis used by Shipley and Veroff (and a number of other contributors to the volume edited by John W. Atkinson) involve a minimum of clinical or other inferences about personality since the thematic items that are counted in the analysis refer to relatively common-sense categories of behavior. These content-analysis methods of the social psychologist provide a model for TAT use that could be adapted to many anthropological research problems. An example of this kind of use of TATs in a study of Chippewa Indians of Minnesota is instructive.

Comparisons of James Lake Indians and White Respondents in Psychological Characteristics
(WHITAKER, 1967)

In this research project the TAT was administered to randomly selected samples of 30 White and 30 Indian respondents in the community of James Lake in northern Minnesota. Since the Indians and Whites in the sample live in the same community and experience the same general natural environment, comparisons between the two groups are facilitated.

Much has been written about the alleged introverted character of the Chippewa Indians; examination of the general personality dimension "introversion-extraversion" was therefore a central concern of this research. Eysenck has described "extraverted" and "introverted" personality tendencies as follows:

> The typical extravert is sociable, likes parties, has many friends, needs to have people to talk to . . . He craves excitement, takes chances, often sticks his neck out, acts on the spur of the moment, and is generally an impulsive individual.

> The typical introvert, on the other hand, is a quiet, retiring sort of person, introspective . . . he is reserved and distant, except with intimate friends. He tends to plan ahead . . . He keeps his feelings under close control, seldom behaves in an aggressive manner and does not lose his temper easily. (Eysenck, 1965:59–60.)

This description of extraversion-introversion, and descriptive remarks from Barnouw, Hallowell, and others concerning the introversive character of Chippewa personalities afforded the basis for establishing a systematic content analysis. The responses of the subjects to each of eight TAT cards were examined for presence of extraversive and introversive thematic content. Thus, if an individual gave extraverted content in every card he would have a total "extraversion score" of eight. The following kinds of content were considered to be indicators of extraversion:

1. In the narrative group behavior is participated in with enjoyment, including mention of friendship, parties, etc.
2. The subject's narrative involves studying for or occupying a job which implies or involves service to others, or frequent involvement with others.
3. The subject's response tells of interaction, or attempts to interact, with others.
4. The subject mentions loneliness or feelings of "being left out." (Includes going out and looking for somebody.)
5. The person in subject's story is asking for help.
6. The narrative includes expression of grief for another person.
7. Persons in the story express concern, interest, and attention to others.

An individual's "introversion score" was derived in essentially the same manner. An introversion-extraversion ratio was then calculated for each of the Indian and White respondents. It was found that Chippewa subjects were not significantly more introverted than White persons in the community of James Lake. Whitaker notes:

what is most striking in these results is that differences in introversion-extraversion are much more marked when we turn from inter-ethnic comparisons to an examination of contrasts between males and females. When the Indians and Whites are grouped together, males are more introverted than females. Also it is important to note that among female respondents, Indians are more introverted than Whites. (Whitaker, 1967.)

The finding that the Indian males are not significantly more introverted than White men living in the same community reminds us of the Spindlers' White control group in the Menominee study, mentioned above. They, too, found that the White men living in the *same environment* were not substantially different in personality from the transitional and acculturated Menominee group. (They were, however, psychologically different from the "native-oriented" and Peyote groups.)

All studies that involve detailed rating and ranking for purposes of cross-cultural or intracultural comparisons run the risk of "contamination" through subconscious distortions in favor of the hypotheses being tested (or overreaction *against* the hypotheses being tested). For this reason, content analysis of TATs and other projective tests should be carried out by persons who are unaware of the hypotheses being tested. Sometimes the same kind of protection

from "rater contamination" can be achieved by disguising the identities of the individual protocols.

THE SENTENCE-COMPLETION TEST

While the Rorschach and TAT projective tests (and a number of
other instruments modifed from these prototypes) involve presentation of some kind of visual or pictorial stimulus to subjects, a variety of analogous procedures have been explored using *verbal* stimuli. The most common verbal projective instrument is the *sentence-completion test,* in which standardized sets of incomplete sentences or stems of sentences are presented and the subjects are asked
to complete the statements in any way they like. Thus, the procedure resembles the word-association test—in fact, it can be considered a variant type of word-association task. (A variant of this *ver-
bal-completion* projective technique is the *story-completion test*
[Murray, 1938].)

Thai Peasant Personality
(PHILLIPS, 1965)

Herbert Phillips used the sentence-completion test technique for
gathering personality data among the people of Bang Chan in rural
Thailand. His monograph describes his research methods in full detail. His first concern in preparation of the sentence-completion instrument was to identify the various problem areas to be covered by
the technique.

On the basis of the available literature on Thai personality, it was apparent that three areas—aggression, dependency, and attitudes toward
authority—loomed particularly large in the psychic lives of most Thai, and
that items descriptive of these areas should be included in my version of
the SCT. Too, during my early months in the field, there were several
facets of the villagers' behavior that were mystifying—for example, the
mechanisms they use in orienting themselves to other people—and it was
decided to include items that would tap such areas. Most of these items
were derived from the events and conversation of the work-a-day world:
the villagers' repeated use of the phrase of *maj daj* (I cannot do it); I am
not able; I do not know how; their ambivalent attitude toward *nagkleengs*
(the aggressive, daring, sometimes bullying individuals who speak their
feelings from their hearts). It should be noted that although these items
were derived from Bang Chan culture, a concerted effort was made to
phrase them for the SCT schedule in more universal, non-culturally specific
terms. In addition there were several specific items which were standard
fare on most versions of the SCT, but which seem to represent universal
psychological issues or problem areas, that is, "he is most afraid of . . ."
(anxiety); "he often daydreams of . . ." (psychological isolation).

When the final version of the instrument was ready for informants, there were thirteen general categories, although not all were of equal significance in the lives of villagers, and were not equally productive of meaningful data. These thirteen categories were:

aggression; causes and reactions	attitudes toward authority
achievement-failure	dependency
reactions to crises	self image
dominant drives and aspirations	anxiety; causes and ways of handling
kinship relations	
psychological isolation	orienting toward others
notions of good and evil	love, sex, and marriage

Phillips describes in detail the work involved in translating the sentence fragments into the Thai language and arranging these in acceptable order for presentation to the subjects. After pretesting the instrument, he administered the SCT to a stratified sample of 111 individuals—approximately 11 percent of the population over 21 years of age).

In analyzing the sentence-completion responses Phillips counted the frequencies of main types of predicted responses. For example, for the sentence "When he was asked if he wanted to become boss, he . . ." the tabulation listed responses as follows: reject offer (69 percent); unsure (9 percent); accept offer (21 percent). Again, "The best way to treat a subordinate is . . .": agreeable words (35 percent); feed well (19 percent); not overwork (15 percent). (Phillips, 1955: 1952–1953). To the sentence stem "He was most afraid of . . ." the Bang Chan people replied in terms of: threats to physical well-being (61 percent); actions of others (20 percent); and malevolent spirits (10 percent) (*ibid.*, 177).

Unfortunately, in spite of the considerable variation of responses in Bang Chan, Phillips did not make comparisons among subgroups or categories within the community. He was more concerned with describing the generalized *group* personality of Thai villagers. With no internal comparisons, and no external control group for cross-cultural comparison, the interpretation of the Thai sentence-completion responses remains somewhat vague and incomplete.

Personalities of Cane Cutters and Fishermen in a West Indies Community
(ARONOFF, 1967)

Joel Aronoff used the sentence-completion technique in a sophisticated study of personality characteristics related to occupational choices in the little community of Dieppe Bay in the West Indies. The investigator and his wife carried out a number of months of field work in the research region, during which they developed hypotheses about the importance of personality variables in explaining why some individuals remain cane cutters while other individuals choose fishing as an occupation (a much more desirable and monetarily rewarding occupation, according to Aronoff). Relying on his first-hand acquaintance with individual cane cutters and fishermen, Aronoff constructed a sentence completion test to test his hypotheses. He also devised a series of projective questions, another variant form of *verbal* projective technique. An interesting problem in his field work developed when Aronoff found that the people of Dieppe Bay did not conceptualize verbal patterns in terms of "sentences." Following are some examples of his sentence-completion items:

1. Money is . . .
2. Food . . .
3. I am proud of . . .
4. A friend . . .
5. A father . . .
6. I get vexed when . . .
15. I am sad because I . . .
21. I am good at . . .
28. The people around here . . .

Some of his projective questions included:

1. If you were given two thousand dollars, what would you do with it?
2. What kind of friend would you choose?
3. What should be done with people who ride bicycles carelessly?
5. What is the worse thing that could happen to you?
6. What is the nicest thing that could happen to you?
11. What is the best thing about women?
12. What should be done with people from another island who do rudeness?

Aronoff employed a content analysis technique based on the scoring systems of McClelland and Atkinson and associates. His statistical analysis of these materials is examined in Chapter 7.

The psychological characteristics which Aronoff examined in his sentence completion protocols were derived from the personality theory of Abraham Maslow and associates. In this body of theory, concepts such as *self-esteem, self-image, concern with physiological problems* (e.g., hunger and food), *concern about safety, capacity for love and belongingness,* and *self-actualization* are seen as important variables in terms of which "more successful" personalities can be distinguished from the "less successful."

Some of the aspects of Aronoff's study which deserve special attention include the following.

1. The fact that his hypothesis testing involves comparisons between groups living in the same community makes the comparisons more credible than those involving distinctly different cultures.
2. Construction of the sentence completion instrument was carried out *after* extensive field work in the research community.
3. Methods of content analysis were specified in detail.
4. The reliability of scoring techniques was tested by comparing Aronoff's own ratings with those of an independent rater.
5. Results of comparison were subjected to statistical analysis.
6. The data from the psychological tests were related to behavioral data concerning activities of fishermen and cane cutters—for which extensive observations and interview data were available.
7. Some alternative hypotheses concerning the research findings were examined statistically and rejected.

OTHER PROJECTIVE TECHNIQUES

Many other projective techniques have been used from time to time in anthropological research. Some of these have been directly borrowed from the research kit of clinical psychologists, while others have been developed by anthropologists themselves in their particular field-work contexts. Doll-play techniques were used by Henry and Henry (1953) to examine psychological characteristics of Pilagá Indian children. The Goodenough test, the Machover test, and other drawing tests have been used by numbers of anthropologists for the collection of psychological materials. Probably there are scores of collections of children's drawings in the files of anthropological field workers that have never been published or even mentioned in research reports; but a number of selections of drawings have been submitted to detailed psychological analysis by anthropologists and their collaborators. Children's drawings were an important adjunct to DuBois' study of the Alorese; free drawings were part of the psychological data collected in the research project on Indian education (mentioned above in connection with Henry's TAT analysis of Hopi and Navaho children); and many other anthropologists have used drawings as projective tests. Recently Wayne Dennis (1966), after statistically examining Goodenough draw-a-man scores for 40 different cultural groups, proposed that the independent variable most directly related to the diversity of scores is the amount of experience with representational art. Such variation in exposure to representational art may be due to differences in development of native art, to the degree of exposure to Western art, or to both. He suggested that if we control for the levels of development of indigenous art, Goodenough draw-a-man projective scores can be used to infer different degrees of acculturation to Western civilization.

Auditory-perceptive techniques (involving music and other sounds) have sometimes been employed by clinicians and experimental psychologists, but have not been employed very much in anthropological research, although data about music preference has occasionally figured in anthropological hypothesis testing. This is but one example of the many relatively unexplored areas of human behavior that may offer significant possibilities for research.

ADMINISTERING PROJECTIVE TESTS

Projective tests and other psychological instruments were, for the most part, developed in the context of psychological laboratories and clinical situations. Under those circumstances the methods of administration could be fairly carefully standardized in order to ensure comparability of the stimulus situation. Administration of projective tests in field work, on the other hand, involves presenting and administering materials in an unpredicatable variety of contexts. Frequently projective tests are presented to respondents in their homes, in circumstances where it is extremely difficult to prevent other members of the family, particularly the children, from interfering. Tests have been administered by field·workers in the field where farmers were working, in the kitchen as a housewife prepared a meal, in the shade of a tree in the village square, with children playing about, and in many other situations.

In some cases fieldworkers can find temporary quarters in which to conduct their interviews, but usually they must meet each respondent on his own home ground. Interviewing respondents in their homes or fields has some advantages, however. It can be argued that the respondent is more natural and relaxed in familiar surroundings, and that he may therefore be more expressive and cooperative in the task set by the psychological instruments. This probably varies from one society to another.

Although he may be faced with the problem of variations in the test settings, the fieldworker should try to standardize his procedures as much as possible. The following items provide a partial framework for this standardization:

1. The opening explanation of the test should be presented in the same manner to each respondent. Instructions should be (as nearly as possible) the same, word for word, to each subject. E.g., "I would like you to tell a story about what you see in this picture. It can be any kind of story that you wish to tell, and you can let your imagination roam as freely as you like. Tell what is happening in the picture, what led up to this scene, and then what will happen afterward."

2. Questions asked during administration of the instrument should be standardized so that every individual is asked the same set of "probes."

3. The pictures (or other stimuli) should be administered in the same order to every individual in the sample (or else in randomized order).

4. If the fieldworker makes comments to individuals concerning their stories, such as, "That's fine, let's go on to the next one," the same comments should be used for each person tested.

5. The researcher should become aware of mannerisms and other paralinguistic communications through which he may be influencing respondents to answer in a particular manner. Recent studies in social psychology have demonstrated that test administrators can exert significant influence on persons being tested in extremely subtle and subliminal ways (Rosenthal, 1966).

6. The fieldworker should suggest to his respondents that they not discuss the nature of the test with other persons in their community until he has finished gathering these materials, since he wants to get each person's *own* individual response, unaffected by suggestions or influences of kinsmen, friends, or other persons.

7. In some cases the researcher may wish to point out some feature in a picture which he wishes to serve as a standardized stimulus to his respondent. For example, in research with TATs in northern Minnesota, respondents were instructed that one of the persons in a particular picture was an Indian and the other a White man. This instruction was intended to ensure high salience of the interethnic component in the picture. Special information or instructions should be presented in a uniform manner to all respondents. The information should be presented in a neutral tone, unless the test administrator has very special purposes in mind in arousing emotional reactions.

8. In some cases TAT responses (or other projected materials) are collected by a number of different fieldworkers in the course of a project. In such cases, comparisons between groups may be contaminated by the fact that different persons (with possibly different stimulus characteristics) carried out the research in the different groups to be compared. More effective research design to guard against "investigator effect" would divide up the administration of tests in such a way that *all* workers collected tests in *all* of the groups to be compared. That is, if comparisons are to be made between village A and village B, and four fieldworkers are available to collect the psychological responses, it would be best if the four fieldworkers all worked in village A and then moved to village B. Even more effective controls on investigator bias would be ensured if assignment of particular researchers to particular respondents were randomized by means of coin tosses or tables of random numbers.

In field work in northern Minnesota, our TAT materials were collected by a number of different persons in four research communities. In one of these communities, "Ashville," TAT responses showed a higher rate of depressive responses than in the other communities. Before making any other interpretation of the finding, we had to rule out the possibility that one or two of our fieldworkers may have been responsible for eliciting this high rate. We therefore examined the Ashville responses to see which interviewers produced high depressive imagery and which interviewers had interviewed low in depressive imagery. Table 5 presents the results.

TABLE 5.   **Depressive Imagery Among Ashville and Draketon Respondents**

Interviewer	High	Low
Hochberg, A.	12	11
DeKrey, D.	4	5
Schensul, S	3	2
Others	1	1

From these results it appeared that no particular interviewer was responsible for the tendencies toward high depressive imagery among the people of Ashville. This strengthened our belief that the results represented characteristics of the sample population rather than "interviewer effect" (Upper Mississippi Research Project, 1968).

Other Psychological Research Instruments

In recent times a number of other psychological tests and measurements have been used in cross-cultural and anthropological research. Most of these are not usually regarded as projective techniques, though the distinction is often difficult to maintain.

PERCEPTION OF ILLUSIONS

Segall, Campbell, and Herskovits (1966) have devised a test involving several simple optical illusions for examining differences in perception related to differences in types of environment.

The investigators found support for the hypothesis that people who live in "carpentered environments" (with rectangular buildings, right-angle street intersections, and other angular features) tend to be more deceived by optical illusions, such as the Müller-Lyer illusion (Figure 6), than people who live in environments less dominated by man-made angularities (Segall, Campbell, and Herskovits, 1966).

FIGURE 6. **The Müller–Lyer Illusion**

ACUITY OF PERCEPTION

Winter (1964) has tested Kalahari Bushmen, African laborers, and a White population to determine their accuracy in perceiving relative sizes of discs at various distances. The Bushmen proved to be superior to the other groups in this perception task. Robbins and collaborators have examined perceptions of time lapse as well as perceptions of perspective in a standardized picture test among Ganda peoples. These techniques were used to test hypotheses about perceptual correlates of acculturation and urbanization (Robbins and Kilbride, 1968; Kilbride *et al.,* 1968). The psychologist Doob has used a picture test among African peoples in his research on "eidetic imagery." This perceptual pheonomenon involves the experiencing of visual images "persisting after stimulations relatively accurate in detail, colored positively, and capable of being scanned." Like most other studies of differences in styles of perception, the matter of eidetic imagery is of theoretical importance in relation to problems of acculturation (Doob, 1964, 1965).

JUDGMENTS OF ESTHETIC QUALITIES

Irvin Child and colleagues (social psychologists and anthropologists) have used pictures of art objects to elicit opinions concerning esthetic excellence from "art experts" in New Haven (Child and Siroto, 1965), mask makers in Africa, Fiji carvers (Ford *et al.,* 1966), and Japanese potters (Iwao and Child, 1966). The techniques involved in this kind of research are similar to the ranking and rating of social position and prestige tasks described on page 106. That is, selected informants are asked to sort out, group, rank, or otherwise differentiate a series of items (art pictures in this case). Average ratings or rankings of the individual items are calculated statistically, and degrees of consensus among the expert raters are compared. In these cross-cultural studies Child and associates have found evidence of panhuman similarities in esthetic judgment.

They emphasize that these agreements in esthetic judgment are found among *"experts"*; artistic judgments of ordinary lay persons in different societies do not seem to demonstrate these similarities.

PSYCHOMOTOR SKILLS

Robert J. Maxwell has used pursuit-rotor tests and manual-sorting operations (such as block sorting) to examine the psychomotor characteristics of Samoans. Differences in performance and in persistence in these psychomotor tasks are thought to be related to extraversion-introversion, as well as to other personality qualities.

GAMES PEOPLE PLAY

John M. Roberts and associates have suggested that people's recreational games are significant expressions of cultural and psychological processes. Thus, they report that simpler societies, such as hunting-and-gathering peoples, do not generally have games of strategy but find their off-hour enjoyments in games involving physical skill and chance. Games of strategy, apparently, are found in more complex societies and seem to reflect psychological conflicts over mastery of complex social relationships (Roberts, Arth, and Bush, 1959; Roberts and Sutton-Smith, 1962).

Content analysis of games in terms of chance, physical skill, and strategy (or combinations of these), or any other distinctive features provides yet another projection domain for developing quantifiable reflections of the psychological, cultural, and social attributes of peoples. For example, girls' games in a Mexican village have been found to dramatize conflict with sexually predatory males, while boys' game-playing reflects their ambivalent reactions to authority figures. Part of the research technique in a study by Maccoby, Modiano, and Lander (1964) included the experimental introduction of new games to the Mexican villagers. Since games are usually considered to be harmless pastimes, introducing a new game provides significant information about community behavior without disrupting normal social life. (It may even help to increase the fieldworker's rapport!)

A GAME AS A LABORATORY DEVICE

Murray and Jacqueline Straus (Straus, 1968; Straus and Straus, 1968) have developed an experimental game for the cross-cultural laboratory study of family interaction and problem-solving behavior. The game is played on a nine-by-twelve court, with wooden "targets" at one end toward which the subjects push colored balls, somewhat after the manner of shuffleboard. The problem-solving feature of the game is that the players (a man, his wife, and child) must infer the rules of the game from the informational feedback of red (error) and green (correct play) lights. The laboratory set-up is shown in Figure 7.

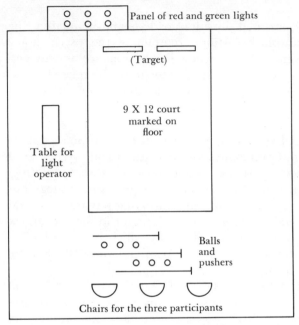

FIGURE 7. **Laboratory Game for Study of Family Interaction Patterns**
ADAPTED FROM Straus and Straus, 1968.

The rules the family must learn in order to solve the puzzle are quite simple:

1. The *color* of the pusher, the ball, and the subject's armband must all match.
2. The ball must hit the wooden target.
3. The ball must not roll out of the court after hitting the target.

The game is reported to be quite enjoyable by most participants, even though there is marked variation in the participants' success in solving the problem. This research technique was used with subjects in San Juan, Puerto Rico; Bombay, India; and Minneapolis, Minnesota in a study of middle class *vs.* working class differences in family problem-solving styles. It is important to note that the logic of the research design was based in *intra*societal comparison, with cross-cultural replication. In all three areas the middle-class families demonstrated greater game-solving success than the working-class families. Communication patterns as well as individual creativity (in suggesting and trying out various tactics and solutions) were related to these socioeconomic differences.

One of the most important methodological features of this laboratory game is that a number of different measures of behavior can be effectively observed. All interaction (conversation, gestures, etc.) of the participants can be recorded; also, the scores of the player groups provide a quantified measure of success in problem-solving. Total number of shots attempted provides a measure of "activity-level"; and various other elements, including "creativity," can be given quite precise operational meanings.

There is no reason why anthropologists cannot develop experimental games (or other situations) which would permit controlled testing of certain kinds of theoretical propositions. Such games need not be elaborate, and they could be quite entertaining for the respondents. The apparatus in the Straus research requires an electrical system; hence it is not easy to carry it out in remote areas, but innovative anthropologists could develop simpler analogs for controlled observation of interaction styles in small groups, reactions to authority, intersex behavioral patterns, modes of verbal and nonverbal communication, and so on. Such games could be modeled after locally prevalent pastimes, games, or work arrangements.

Unobtrusive Measures

Research techniques employing questionnaires, interviews, and psychological tests all involve confronting particular individuals with situations that are, to a considerable extent, outside their daily rounds of living. Thus, the researcher interposes some kind of stimulus—whether a set of questions or a performance task—assumed to be in some way an *analog* of ordinary behavior. The researcher assumes that habitual behavioral tendencies of subjects will be reflected in reactions to the situations structured by the anthropologist. Even informal conversations between anthropologists and research subjects are "obtrusive" in that the anthropologist is to some extent an "outsider" in the research community. On the other hand, anthropological fieldwork involves observation that is "unobtrusive" whenever the anthropologist watches ongoing behavior—feasts and festivals, daily work, meetings and discussions, recreation, and other habitual activities. These latter types of observations are among the research methods reviewed by Webb, Campbell, Schwartz, and Sechrest in *Unobtrusive Measures: Non-reactive Research in the Social Sciences* (1966). The authors of this excellent little book point out that all *obtrusive measures* are somewhat suspect because they involve "artificial" stimuli presented to subjects; the research subjects' awareness of these stimuli may cause them to change, modify, falsify, or otherwise distort their habitual behavioral tendencies. Therefore, obtrusive research observations should, whenever possible, be checked against data involving unobtrusive methods.

PHYSICAL TRACES: EROSION AND ACCRETION

In their field work, anthropologists have a long history of Sherlock Holmes–like acuity in deriving data from physical traces. A well-worn path is excellent, though incomplete, evidence concerning volume of traffic between two communities; different states of disrepair of buildings provide possible indexes of relative affluence; extensiveness of refuse heaps give testimony to durations of occupation—a type of evidence that has been raised to full professional status by archaeologists. On a more mundane note, numbers of liquor bottles in garbage cans (and other places) have been used as evidence concerning differential alcohol consumption (Webb, Campbell, Schwartz, and Sechrest, 1966:41).

These are examples of fairly obvious unobtrusive measures. The fieldworker with imagination will find many other possibilities for inferring social information from the physical marks of wear and tear (and pollution) men habitually impose upon their physical environments. Air photos, too, have been used by archaeologists, geographers, and occasionally by social anthropologists to examine the physical traces of human cultural behavior.

ARCHIVES AND OTHER WRITTEN RECORDS

In most parts of the world nowadays governments and their appointed agents maintain a variety of records concerning population sizes, births and deaths, crimes, marriages, and other social statistics. These kinds of data are of relatively recent origin in many parts of the world, and anthropologists carry out field research among many peoples for whom no such records exist. Nonetheless, fieldworkers should make every attempt to obtain official archival data whenever possible, even though these materials frequently are incomplete or distorted for particular communities. Fieldworkers will in most cases need to check official census statistics by means of other kinds of observation in their research communities.

In many areas of the world, churches and other private organizations have been more important than governmental agencies in the maintenance of records concerning vital statistics. Subject to their own particular kinds of distortions, church records may be very important sources of data on genealogies, ritual relationships (such as godparenthood), as well as on religious activities and practices.

Another significant archival data source is the local cemetery, whose monuments often give information about kinship groups, birth and death dates, and relative social importance as reflected in the size and elaborateness of tombstones and excellence of upkeep.

One of the most extensive uses of the archival material of cemeteries is that of Warner (1959) in his monograph *The Living and the Dead*. Warner consulted official cemetery documents to establish a history of the dead, and through interviewing, observation, and trace analysis added further data to his description of graveyards. The archaeologist Deetz has made an extensive investigation of cemeteries in New England in studying problems related to archaeological theory (Deetz and Dethlefsen, 1967).

In many of the societies studied by anthropologists, written materials are imported from the outside world in the form of newspapers, magazines, books, religious tracts, hymnals, and so on. If the local population contains only a few people who are literate, their habits with regard to written materials are of course not representative of the thinking of the entire community. But (when corrections are made for the degree of literacy in a local community) the inventories of reading materials found in people's homes, plus their attitudes about particular kinds of such materials, can constitute important information for the ethnographer. Also, the written output of the schoolchildren in the local school is sometimes an important source of information, again subject to the distortion introduced by the schoolteacher and *his* particular interests. Often the ethnographer can ask the teacher to have the schoolchildren write thematic materials especially for the ethnographer. Such an exercise, of course, is no longer a completely "unobtrusive measure," but many fieldworkers have found schoolchildren's themes to be important supplemental data. Beattie sponsored an essay contest among the Nyoro in which he offered prizes for the best essays on the general topic "customs of the country." This competition was open not only to the schoolchildren but to all literate Nyoro (Beattie, 1965:31–33).

In many societies "archival materials" are found in a mixed form —some of the data are stored in the memories of older members of the community, but portions are available in written records.

Frank Cancian (1965) based an important part of his study *Economics and Prestige in a Maya Community* on the archival information concerning *"cargo* careers" in the community of Zinacantan. To test propositions about the functioning of the system, Cancian needed to have information about all the *cargos* held by the people in his sample. He describes his collection of the "total career sample" as follows:

> The total career sample includes all recorded cases of men who have passed more than one *cargo*. Only name, hamlet of residence, and *cargos* passed are included. These cases were taken from several sources. All of the cases from the Hteklum and Apas censuses and the Paste economic sample are included. In addition there are several cases that Juan was able to remember in the course of doing the Paste census. All the cases recorded in interviews on diverse subjects and in casual conversations are also included. A major source of information about *cargo* careers was the responses of informants to open ended questions like: "Name all the people you know who have passed an Alferez *cargo*." Manuel produced the overwhelming proportion of the answers elicited by this method. This method of questioning produced more information on people who had passed prestigious *cargos* than on people who had passed lesser *cargos*. This is a defect in the sampling, but I have no reasons to believe that this defect significantly affects the results of the analysis of the total sample. (Cancian, 1965:203–204.)

Cancian also had available to him one significant written archival source concerning the *cargos*. Sometime during the 1940s, the people of Zinacantan began keeping waiting lists of people who had requested particular *cargos* for the future. "The lists are kept in hard-cover notebooks, and a page or more is devoted to each year in the future to the last year for which there is a *cargo* requested" (Cancian, 1965:176). This data archive was of crucial importance to Cancian in his analysis of the functioning of the *cargo* system.

FOLK TALES AND MYTHS

The folk tales and myths of nonliterate societies constitute an "archive" of thematic materials that have been a rich mine of information for various kinds of analysis. Sometimes these archives are used to infer psychological characteristics of the people; they are often invoked for the analysis of religious beliefs; and they also serve as evidence concerning transmission of information (diffusion) from culture to culture. Songs, proverbs, riddles, jokes, and other standardized verbal lore are a significant adjunct to them. Benjamin Colby has used a complex statistical method in analyzing the contents of folktales and other text materials in several societies. He proceeded as follows:

> By using a revised set of word-groups . . . and by dividing a collection of Eskimo folktales . . . and Japanese folktales . . . into sections, an unexpected number of statistically significant patterns emerged. Each tale was divided into nine equal parts. These were then grouped into nine sections.

All the first parts of the folk tales were put into section one, the second parts into section two, and so on up to section nine. The word group frequencies of these sections were then graphed and tested for statistical significance. Out of 195 independent word-groups counted for the Eskimo material, forty five or 23% were statistically significant at the .01 level using a chi-square test for "flatness." For the Japanese material, 23% were also statistically significant at this level. (Colby, 1966a:382.)

Table 6 details the patterning of the words *fight* and *death* in a sample of Eskimo folk tales. From these tabulations it would appear that the theme of fighting reaches a climax shortly after the mid-point of Eskimo tales, and tapers off at the end. Death, on the other hand, shows a steady increase from the beginning to the end of these tales, so if only one death occurs in an Eskimo folk tale, one would be fairly safe in predicting that it comes near the end of the tale. By comparing Eskimo and Japanese folk tales, Colby has demonstrated that the patterning in these archival materials varies significantly in ways that are congruent with other aspects of these cultures. Thus,

the pattern of the concept of death in the Eskimo tales . . . reflects the continual preoccupation with life and death of people in a difficult environment. It illustrates the Eskimos' inevitable concern with such basic matters as food, hunting, maintaining physical strength, and staying alive. The Japanese, on the other hand, are more concerned with subtle social situations and strategies than with human survival. (Colby, 1966b:796.)

TABLE 6.   **Patterns of Occurrence of "Fight"**
             and "Death" in Eskimo Folk Tales

1	1--(2)
2---(3)	2
3-(1)	3---(3)
4-(1)	4----(4)
5------(6)	5
6--------(8)	6------(6)
7-------(7)	7--------(8)
8-----(5)	8---------(9)
9-(1)	9----------(10)
Fight	Death

DIRECT OBSERVATION—AGAIN

Under the heading *participant observation* I discussed at some length the importance of direct observation by the ethnographic fieldworker. It is important, however, to examine more closely the possibilities for "objectifying" these data. Field ethnographers would do well to study the increasingly sophisticated observational techniques of students of animal behavior. In recent times a large number of new studies of apes and monkeys, herds of deer, wolf packs, field mice, and many other animal groupings have demonstrated very carefully defined procedures for observing (and counting) behavioral elements. A most significant aspect of observations among animal groups is the matter of physical location. A great amount of information concerning the social organization of baboon troops, for example has been inferred from observations of physical spacing (DeVore, 1965). Edward T. Hall (1966) has explored what he calls "the hidden dimension" (of spacing and position) among human groups, and it appears from his discussion that observers of human behavior have thus far been relatively unsystematic and impressionistic in observing "social spacing" in human interaction.

The importance of physical position in human social organization is dramatically illustrated by recent events and discussions concerning integration, segregation, and related interracial problems in the United States. Seating patterns on buses (Jim Crow laws), restrictions concerning domicile (segregated housing practices), and a number of other highly controversial social practices in the United States demonstrate how physical spacing relates directly to social facts. Campbell, Kruskal, and Wallace (cited in Webb, *et al.*, 1966) studied the seating of blacks and whites in classrooms as indexes of racial attitudes. Classes in four schools were studied, in which there were significant variations in degrees of mixed seating; investigators took this as a presumptive index of the degree to which acquaintance, friendship, and social preferences were influenced by race.

A recent controversial book, *The Territorial Imperative* by Ardrey (1966), serves to point out some of the gaps in our existing data about human territoriality. Ethnographers' reports often include maps showing locations of households, land holdings, and boundaries of the community. However, it is surprising how often this significant information is omitted from ethnographic reports. Usually the ethnographies have failed to include information about significant transactions occurring at the boundaries of local territories.

Practically every fieldworker has made significant use of data on physical locations in households and seating arrangements and other positioning in ritual events as important social data concerning community behavior. In ritual events—weddings, funerals, festivals, sacred ceremonies, etc.—the positioning of persons in the scene of social action practically always reflects important social information. Important persons are frequently at the head of the table; seating at feasts often reflects extended kinship relations; and social inferiors are often identifiable because of their locations at the margins, or back in the shadows, away from the center of social action.

THE STREAM OF BEHAVIOR AND MEASUREMENT OF SOCIAL INTERACTION

Closely related to observations of physical location and spacing are the fieldworker's systematic recording of social behavior of individuals and the social contacts among different kinds of individuals. Here again, recently developed techniques in the naturalistic study of animal behavior might prove useful to anthropological fieldworkers. Two of the most important problems facing the fieldworker in his recording of behavioral observations are:

1. Ensuring representativeness when his observations can encompass only a small fraction of all the booming, buzzing confusion of events in a human community.
2. Defining useful behavioral units or "inherent" segments for identification and observation. Earlier, in my discussion of etic research strategies, I examined the methods suggested by Marvin Harris and by the Barkers for coping with the problem of obtaining systematic behavioral observations. Painstakingly complete behavioral observations of the type employed by the Barkers and by Harris are feasible only for highly selected aspects of social life in human communities. The fieldworker must be guided by his own theoretical concerns, plus his scientific hunches and intuitions, in selecting certain behavior settings for intensive study, leaving other social scenes for less systematic modes of observation.

The study of interaction, in terms of frequencies of dialogue and nonverbal interaction, energy levels, response patterns, dominance in interaction, etc., has been highly systematized and mechanized by Elliot Chapple with his "interaction chronograph" (Chapple, 1949). His device for measuring interaction has been developed particularly for studying factory social systems and other communities within American society, but the general idea embodied in this research technique can provide the fieldworker (equipped only with notepad, pencil, and watch) with ideas for observations of great value in the field context. In drawing on the "interaction chronograph" model of research—for example, in studying a meeting—the fieldworker might concentrate on some of the following questions:

1. What are the physical locations of the different persons (and groups) in the meeting?

2. Who initiates major segments of the action?
3. Who speaks? For how long?
4. Which speakers respond to what other speakers?
5. What kinds of reactions are observable in the nonspeakers?
6. What kinds of spaces (pauses) segment the interaction?
7. Do different kinds of persons specialize in different aspects or topics in the meeting (e.g., finances, procedural rules, entertainment, lines of authority)?

In the Six Cultures Study (New England, East Africa, Mexico, Philippines, Okinawa, and India) developed by John M. Whiting, William Lambert, and associates, it was decided that children's behavior would be observed in carefully timed segments, with a specially developed code system for recording different aspects of interaction (Lambert, n.d.). At prescribed and measured time intervals, the children were observed at play and other activities, with note taken of such actions as:

1. Child plays alone.
2. Child's reaction to interference by others.
3. Child initiates aggression to others.
4. Child interacts with mother.
5. Child responds positively to approach of another.

The detailed, standardized, observational procedure permitted quantification of aspects of behavior such as "number of aggressive acts," "independence," "competitiveness," and so on. These systematic observations were imbedded in the context of more generalized qualitative observations of social behavior. Thus, general interviewing, key-informant observations, and other ethnographic research methods were employed to generate descriptions of these six different cultural settings. It is important to stress here that highly systematized modes of observation, such as those suggested by Elliot Chapple and the Barkers, can result in very misleading and incomplete data if they are not supported by large amounts of qualitative information collected by standard anthropological field techniques.

Technical Equipment in Field Work

Compared with many other sciences, methods of observation in anthropological work generally require very little in the way of specialized measuring and observing devices. The anthropologist himself is the main instrument of observation, and most of the "tools" of research discussed in this incomplete inventory are simply methods for sharpening his perceptions and standardizing his recording of observations. Interaction chronographs are not generally taken out into the kinds of communities that anthropologists most frequently study. Recent developments in recording devices and photographic equipment have provided some important supplemental items to the anthropological fieldworker's kit, however.

TAPE RECORDERS

Mechanical recording devices were already being used by anthropologists in field work in the late nineteenth century (Rowe, 1953), particularly for recording folk tales and other oral literature. But the old Gramophones and other recording devices were too cumbersome for most field-work purposes. When magnetic tape recorders came into use after World War II, it became feasible for ethnographers to record relatively large amounts of conversation and other aural materials in the field.

During the 1960s tape recorders have become extremely compact, portable, reliable, and therefore invaluable as field-work equipment. Life-history materials and other longer narratives from key informants are frequently tape-recorded in order to ensure accuracy and completeness. It is advisable that whenever possible respondents' replies to TATs and other psychological instruments be recorded fully on tape. The ethnographer with his pencil and notepad is physically incapable of recording verbatim the statements of respondents if these are given in a natural manner. Improved microphone equipment makes it possible for the fieldworker to record all of the verbal transactions in meetings, conferences, and other important events.

Since the tape recorder as note taker is so far superior to the paper-and-pencil ethnographer in most instances, fieldworkers are sometimes tempted to try to "get everything on tape." This strategy is ill advised, however. Transcribing materials from tapes into typewritten notes is an extremely tedious and time-consuming task at best; one suspects that there are great numbers of untranscribed tapes in the files of those ethnographers who have been most avid in the use of this equipment. Also, there are many contexts in which presence of a tape recorder—even a small one—is resented by the people in the research community; or at least it introduces a foreign element into social action, and may seriously interfere with the naturalness of the people's behavior. Fieldworkers should therefore use tape recorders with discretion, and should seek to minimize the intrusive effects of mechanical recordings. It is of great importance that the fieldworker be so familiar with his tape-recording equipment that he can operate it with a minimum of distractions and uneasiness. The flustered fieldworker fiddling with his tape-recording equipment has little chance of maintaining the naturalness of conversational flow.

CAMERAS AND PHOTOGRAPHY

It is rare indeed that an ethnographer goes into the field without photographic equipment. Also rare in anthropological fieldwork is the conscious and carefully planned use of photography as a research tool. Most fieldworkers are content to snap pictures for use in slide-illustrated lectures; also desired are those engaging "human-interest" shots for one's expected major book. These are worthwhile uses of photography in field work, but they are far from exhausting the potential usefulness of photographic equipment. Bateson and Mead (1942) made a relatively extensive study of the Balinese by means of photography as a central observational technique. Mead also collaborated with MacGregor (1951) in a photographic study of Balinese childhood based on photographs by Gregory Bateson. In recent years John Collier, Jr., has been an outstanding advocate of the use of photography in anthropological research. His new book, *Visual Anthropology: Photography as a Research Method* (1967), is a must for all anthropological fieldworkers. Collier describes some of the routine uses of photography in providing general orientation to research sites, in surveying and mapping, and in documenting complex events such as festivals and celebrations. He also points out important possibilities for using photographs in interviewing. Respondents' reactions to photographs can be an important projective technique, though anthropologists have not yet experimented much with this method of research. Collier describes his own research project, in which a sample of 22 Indian households in the San Francisco Bay area were studied photographically.

After contact and sufficient rapport had been established by one of the project interviewers, each of the families . . . was photographed on a single visit with consent and by appointment. The fieldworker was present as well as myself, the photographer. In all cases living rooms and kitchens were thoroughly photographed. In all but four houses one or more bedrooms were also covered. The focus was chiefly upon the contents of the household and its arrangements, with wide angle shots to show placement of the various items and furniture and the relationship between rooms, and with close-up shots to show areas of particular interest such as mantels and bureaus and the tops of television sets where small but presumably valued objects were collected. (Collier, 1967:82.)

The analysis of the data

consisted of an inventory of the objects in each of the houses, a comparison of the inventories, with each other, and a comparison of the inventories with what was known about the families from the interview and question-naire data. Finally there was an attempt to bring these together with the general concerns of the project. This was done by indicating how the houses reflected the attitudes toward "Indianness" and the attitudes toward the dominant culture, and by attempting to identify the value systems by which the various families operated in the urban settings. (*Ibid.*, 83–84.)

Although Collier did not employ any complex statistical analysis, the definitions of observational elements are relatively clear and objective. Collier's monograph includes important technical infor-mation concerning photographic equipment.

CINEMATOGRAPHY IN ANTHROPOLOGICAL RESEARCH

In *Visual Anthropology* Collier also gives attention to the use of ci-nematography in anthropological research. He points out that, in addition to their pioneering work in use of still photography, Mar-garet Mead and Gregory Bateson have also carried out research using films. Otherwise, he notes, movie filming has played only a minor part in anthropological research. Movie films as research tools should not be confused with the making of ethnographic mov-ies such as Flaherty's *Nanook of the North* (1925) or more recent classics like *The Hunters* by John Marshall and Robert Gardiner (1956). These ethnographic movies are much more pertinent as ed-ucational and informational devices than as research techniques.

Collier notes that

film is *the* tool for analysis of process where technological innovation or subtle abstraction on technological change is needed. In anthropology film is not only the complete way of recording choreography but also the most direct way of analyzing dance or ceremony, where so many elements are in motion together. In this situation human memory in notebook recordings becomes wholly inadequate and highly impressionistic. (*Ibid.*, 128.)

He continues:

. . . *only* the moving picture film can record the realism of time and mo-tion, or the psychological reality of varieties of interpersonal relations. As an example, it is hard to evaluate the character of love between children and parents from still photographs, whereas film can record the family tempo, the nature of touching, how long, how often, and the way an older expresses fondness for a younger brother. (*Ibid.*, 128.)

Gregory Bateson has developed an observational training film for psychiatrists consisting of two sequences of behavior—giving the baby his bath and feeding the baby—in three families. Collier him-self has produced an experimental film called *A Family's Day* which was made with a total budget of only $400.

Sorenson and Gajdusek (1966) have made extensive use of cinema for recording behavior—especially children's behavior—and socialization scenes among a number of New Guinea peoples. These researchers are particularly interested in detailed study of development of motor patterns in children, especially children raised in distinctly non-Western social environments. They note that the opportunities for studying relatively "untouched" peoples is rapidly drawing to a close, and the research film is one important way to preserve these "nonrecurring ethno-environmental data."

We may look at fondling, close bodily contact, nursing, feeding, carrying postures, swaddling, rocking, sleeping, grooming, sucking, genital handling, pacifying, attention to crying, encouragement of walking or talking, enforcement of modesty, language and gesture, singing, associated movement of speech, styles of sitting and gait, mannerisms associated with emotional tension, modes of skilled motor performance, and many other aspects of behavior in a culture and study the range of style manifested by the culture or even by single individuals in it. This we can often do as well from extensive photographic records as while in the field and, in some cases, even better than in the field . . . similarly, we can capture the components of motion in rapid complex movements as in gestures or gesticulation; climbing trees, vines or ladders; tumbling or falling; jumping and running; and quarreling or fighting and find standardized styles or unusual components differentiating the actions as performed by children of one culture from that of another. . . . At present we are only learning to look—slowly discovering what to see. To do this successfully we find that the ability repeatedly to review photographic data on child behavior with convenience, and to look at it in the various frame per second partitioning provided by cinema—returning to the same sequences time and again, continually comparing and contrasting—is of utmost importance, and is an advantage often totally unavailable in the study of the fleeting unrecapturable events and moments often witnessed while in the field. (Sorenson and Gajdusek, 1966: 156–157.)

A number of research films are available from Gajdusek and Sorenson at the National Institutes of Health. This fact illustrates an important point about research films, namely, that they provide a form of data easily loaned by one researcher to another so that independent studies can be made of the same materials. Production of useful research films is clearly an expensive process, and requires expertise on the part of the movie maker. On the other hand, the films do not require much editing and finishing, for ideally, research films are assembled with as little editing as possible in order to preserve the original raw data intact and in correct chronological sequence.

Recent growth of interest in aspects of nonverbal communication, as discussed by Edward T. Hall in a number of papers on "proxemics," as well as in his recent book on human uses of space (*The*

Hidden Dimension, 1966), and by a number of other anthropologists, suggests the likelihood that there will be increased use of visual materials (both still photography and movies) in the systematic cross-cultural study of human behavior. Harvey Sarles (in a personal communication) has suggested that television provides a more versatile medium for such studies than does movie film. Highly portable and flexible television equipment is now available, and the processing and manipulation of television footage may indeed prove to have some advantages over film. In any case, there are many kinds of human behaviors and social interactions that are so technically complex and rapid that adequate study of these actions in full detail can be accomplished only by means of well-prepared visual records. Not all anthropologists need to become movie makers (or television producers), but it seems clear that photography as a research tool has much potential usefulness that has not yet been exploited by anthropologists.

Multi-instrument Research

Each of the research tools and techniques mentioned in this chapter has serious limitations. Interviews, questionnaires, tests, and many other instruments involve confronting individuals with somewhat artificial stimuli, and the "awareness of being studied" may produce important distortions in people's responses. On the other hand, various "unobtrusive" observations often have a contrived and inadequate character. Therefore, examining cultural behavior with a *variety of different approaches* greatly enhances the credibility of research results.

Webb, Campbell, Schwartz, and Sechrest (1966) have discussed this point in terms of the concept of *outcroppings,* based on an analogy from geology. The physical pheonomena pertaining to the different ages and stages of formation of the earth's crust are for the most part buried deeply in the ground. However, the warping and folding of the earth's crust and erosion by glaciers, winds, and streams have left exposed for observation numerous *outcroppings,* which are traces or samples from which inferences about the "parent population" of geological pheonomena can be made. These outcroppings vary in their structural relationships to other features of the earth's crust, and various tools of observation are combined in examining the different outcroppings. Similarly,

it can be noted that a theory predicting a change in civic opinion, due to an event and occurring between two time periods, might be such that this opinion shift could be predicted for many partially overlapping populations. One might predict changes on public opinion polls within that universe, changes in sampled conversation on commuter trains for a much smaller segment, changes in letters mailed to editors and the still more limited letters published by editors, changes in purchase rates of books on relevant subjects by that minute universe, and so on. In such an instance, the occurrence of the predicted shift on any one of these meters is confirmatory and its absence discouraging. If the effect is found on only one measure, it probably reflects more on the method than on the theory . . . a more complicated theory might well predict differential shifts for different meters, and again the evidence of each is relevant to the validity of the theory. The joint confirmation between pollings of high income populations and commuter train conversations is much more validating than either taken alone, just because of the difference between the methods in irrelevant components . . . any given theory has innumerable implications and makes innumerable predictions which are unaccessible to available measures at any given time. The testing of the theory can only be done at the available outcroppings, those points where theoretical predictions and available instrumentation meet. Any one such outcropping is equivocal, and all types available should be checked. The more remote or independent such checks, the more confirmatory their agreement. (Webb, Campbell, Schwartz, and Sechrest, 1966:28.)

The field anthropologist has practically always used the multi-instrument and "multioutcropping" approach, as he checked the statements of one informant against another, checked them both against his own experiences in the field community, and then dug into the archives for supporting evidence. Adding specialized tools such as projective tests, rating and ranking tasks, and census-gathering should not lead the researcher to abandon his strategy of "the qualitative-quantitative mix" in research operations. Some outcroppings can be quantified and then analyzed numerically; other outcroppings related to the same basic sociocultural phenomena may be essentially "noncountable," but their richness and concreteness lend special credibility that is lacking in the more structured observations. The multi-instrument approach to the study of "outcroppings" in human behavioral systems implies not only the testing of hypotheses in a number of different ways, but also a continued shifting back and forth between qualitative and quantitative observations.

REFERENCES CITED

ARDREY, ROBERT
1966.   *The Territorial Imperative*. New York: Atheneum.

ARONOFF, JOEL
1967. *Psychological Needs and Cultural Systems: A Case Study.* New York: Van Nostrand. © 1967 by Litton Educational Publishing, Inc. By permission of Van Nostrand Reinhold Company.

ATKINSON, JOHN W.
1958. *Motives in Fantasy, Action, and Society.* New York: Van Nostrand.

BARKER, ROGER G., ed.
1963. *The Stream of Behavior.* New York: Appleton-Century-Crofts.

BATESON, GREGORY, and MARGARET MEAD
1942. *Balinese Character: A Photographic Analysis.* New York: New York Academy of Sciences Special Publication.

BEATTIE, JOHN
1965. *Understanding an African Kingdom: Bunyoro.* New York: Holt, Rinehart and Winston. © 1965 by Holt, Rinehart and Winston, Inc. Reprinted by permission of the publisher.

BILLIG, OTTO, JOHN GILLIN, and WILLIAM DAVIDSON
1947–1948. "Aspects of Personality and Culture in a Guatemalan Community: Ethnological and Rorschach Approaches." *Journal of Personality,* 16:153–187, 328–368.

CANCIAN, FRANK
1965. *Economics and Prestige in a Maya Community: The Religious Cargo System in Zinacantan.* Stanford: Stanford University Press.

CHANCE, NORMAN A.
1965. "Acculturation, Self Identification, and Personality Adjustment." *American Anthropologist* 67(2):372–393.

CHAPPLE, ELLIOT D.
1949. "The Interaction Chronograph: Its Evolution and Present Application." *Personnel,* 25:295–307.

CHILD, IRVIN L., and L. SIROTO
1965. "Bakwele and American Esthetic Evaluation Compared." *Ethnology,* 4:349–360.

COLBY, BENJAMIN
1966a. "Cultural Patterns in Narrative." *Science,* 161:793–798.
1966b. "The Analysis of Culture, Content and the Patterning of Narrative Concern in Text." *American Anthropologist,* 68:374–388. Reproduced by permission of the American Anthropological Association.

COLLIER, JOHN, JR.
1967. *Visual Anthropology: Photography as a Research Method.* New York: Holt, Rinehart and Winston.

COLSON, ELIZABETH
1954. "The Intensive Study of Small Sample Communities." In *Method and Perspective in Anthropology,* ed. R. F. Spencer. Minneapolis: University of Minnesota Press, 43–60.

DEETZ, JAMES, and EDWIN S. DETHLEFSEN
1967. "Death's Head, Cherub, Urn and Willow." *Natural History,* 76
(3):28–37.

DENNIS, WAYNE
1966. "Goodenough Scores, Art Experience and Modernization." *Journal of Social Psychology,* 68:211–228.

DEVORE, I., ed.
1965. *Primate Behavior: Field Studies of Monkeys and Apes.* New York: Holt, Rinehart and Winston.

DOOB, LEONARD W.
1964. "Eidetic Images Among the Ibo." *Ethnology,* 3:357–363.
1965. "Exploring Eidetic Imagery Among the Kamba of Central Kenya." *Journal of Social Psychology,* 67:3–22.

DUBOIS, CORA
1960. (First published 1944.) *The People of Alor* (2 vols.). New York: Harper Torchbook.

EYSENCK, H. J.
1965. *Fact and Fiction in Psychology.* Harmonsworth. Middlesex: Penguin Books.

FESTINGER, LEON and DANIEL KATZ
1953. *Research Methods in the Behavioral Sciences.* New York: Holt, Rinehart and Winston.

FORD, CLELLAN S., T. PROTHRO, and I. CHILD
1966. "Some Transcultural Comparisons of Esthetic Judgment." *Journal of Social Psychology,* 68:19–26.

FREED, STANLEY A.
1963. "An Objective Method for Determining the Collective Caste Hierarchy of an Indian Village." *American Anthropologist,* 65 (4):879–891.

GLOCK, CHARLES Y., ed.
1967. *Survey Research in the Social Sciences.* New York: Russell Sage Foundation.

GODWIN, THOMAS, and S. B. SARASON
1953. *Truk: Man in Paradise.* New York: Wenner-Gren Foundation.

GOODE, WILLIAM J., and PAUL K. HATT
1952. *Methods in Social Research.* New York: McGraw-Hill.

GRAVES, THEODORE D.
1967. "Acculturation, Access, and Alcohol in a Tri-ethnic Community." *American Anthropologist,* 69 (3–4):306–321.

HALL, EDWARD T.
1966. *The Hidden Dimension.* Garden City, New York: Doubleday.

HALLOWELL, A. IRVING
1955. *Culture and Experience.* Philadelphia: University of Pennsylvania Press.

HENRY, JULES, and ZUNIA HENRY
1953. "Doll Play of Pilagá Indian Children." In C. Kluckhohn, H. A. Murray, and D. M. Schneider, eds. *Personality in Nature, Society and Culture*. New York: Knopf.

HENRY, WILLIAM E.
1947. *The Thematic Apperception Technique in the Study of Culture-Personality Relations*. Genetic Psychological Monographs, 35.

HEYNS, ROGER W., JOSEPH VEROFF, and JOHN W. ATKINSON
1958. "A Scoring Manual for the Affiliation Motive." In *Motives in Fantasy, Action, and Society*, ed. J. W. Atkinson. New York: Van Nostrand, 205–218.

HIEBERT, PAUL
1967. "Structure and Integration in a Central Indian Village." Unpublished Ph.D. dissertation, University of Minnesota.

HONIGMANN, J. J.
1949. *Culture and Ethos of Koska Society*. New Haven: Yale University Publications in Anthropology, 40.

IWAO, S., and I. CHILD
1966. "Comparisons of Aesthetic Judgments by American Experts and by Japanese Potters." *Journal of Social Psychology*, 68:27–33.

JAMES, EDWIN
1956. (First published 1830.) *Thirty Years of Indian Captivity of John Tanner*. Minneapolis: Ross and Haines.

JESSOR, RICHARD, THEODORE GRAVES, ROBERT HANSON, and S. L. JESSOR
1968. *Society, Personality and Deviant Behavior*. New York: Holt, Rinehart and Winston.

KAPLAN, BERT
1955. *A Study of Rorschach Responses in Four Cultures*. Cambridge: Peabody Museum of Harvard University Papers, 42(2).

KILBRIDE, PHILIP L., MICHAEL C. ROBBINS, and ROBERT B. FREEMAN, JR.
1968. "Pictorial Depth Perception and Education Among Baganda School Children." *Perceptual and Motor Skills*, 26, 1116–1118.

KLOPFER, BRUNO
1956. *Developments in the Rorschach Technique*. Vol. 2, *Fields of Application*. New York: Harcourt, Brace & World.

LAMBERT, WILLIAM W.
n.d. Personal communication (concerning the Six Cultures Project).

LANDY, DAVID
1965. (First published 1959.) *Tropical Childhood: Cultural Transmission and Learning in a Puerto Rican Village*. New York: Harper Torchbooks.

LANGNESS, L. L.
1965. *The Life History in Anthropological Science*. (Series of studies in anthropological method.) New York: Holt, Rinehart and Winston.

LINDZEY, GARDNER
1961. *Projective Techniques and Cross-Cultural Research.* New York: Appleton-Century-Crofts.

MACCOBY, M., N. MODIANO, and P. LANDER
1964. "Games and Social Character in a Mexican Village." *Psychiatry,* 27:150–162.

MADGE, JOHN
1965. (Originally published 1953.) *The Tools of Social Science.* Garden City, New York: Doubleday Anchor.

MALINOWSKI, BRONISLAW
1961. (First published 1922.) *Argonauts of the Western Pacific.* New York: E. P. Dutton. Reprinted by permission of E. P. Dutton & Co., Inc.

MAXWELL, ROBERT J.
n.d. Personal communication.

MEAD, MARGARET, and FRANCIS COOKE MACGREGOR
1951. *Growth and Culture: A Photographic Study of Balinese Childhood.* (Based upon photographs by Gregory Bateson.) New York: Putnam.

MINER, HORACE, and GEORGE DEVOS
1960. *Oasis and Casbah.* Ann Arbor: University of Michigan Press.

MINTURN, LEIGH, and W. W. LAMBERT
1965. *Mothers in Six Cultures.* New York: Wiley.

MITCHELL, J. CLYDE
1967. "On Quantification in Social Anthropology." In *The Craft of Social Anthropology,* ed. A. L. Epstein. London: Tavistock, 17–47.

MORGAN, CHRISTIANA D., and HENRY A. MURRAY
1935. "A Method for Investigating Fantasies: The Thematic Apperception Test." *Archives of Neurology and Psychiatry,* 34:289–306.

MURRAY, H. A., *et al.*
1938. *Explorations in Personality.* New York: Oxford University Press.

OSGOOD, CHARLES
1964. "Semantic Differential Technique in the Comparative Study of Cultures." In *Transcultural Studies in Cognition,* ed. A. K. Romney and R. G. D'Andrade. *American Anthropologist,* special number.

PELTO, PERTTI J.
1967. "Psychological Anthropology." In *Biennial Review of Anthropology,* 1967, ed. B.J. Siegel and Alan R. Beals. Stanford: Stanford University Press, 140–208.

PHILLIPS, BERNARD S.
1966. *Social Research: Strategy and Tactics.* New York: Macmillan.

PHILLIPS, HERBERT P.
1965. *Thai Peasant Personality: The Patterning of Inter-Personal Behavior in the Village of BangChan.* Berkeley and Los Angeles: University of California Press.

POWDERMAKER, HORTENSE
1966. *Stranger and Friend.* New York: W. W. Norton.

RADIN, PAUL
1920. *The Autobiography of a Winnebago Indian.* Berkeley: University of California Publications in Anthropology, Archaeology, and Ethnology, 16:381–473.

ROBBINS, MICHAEL C.
1968. "Perceptual Environments and Pattern Preferences." *Perceptual and Motor Skills,* 26:545–546.

ROBBINS, MICHAEL C., and PHILIP L. KILBRIDE
1968. "Time Estimation and Acculturation Among the Baganda." *Perceptual and Motor Skills,* 26:1010.

ROBERTS, JOHN M., M. J. ARTH, and R. R. BUSH
1959. "Games in Culture." *American Anthropologist,* 61:597–605.

ROBERTS, JOHN M., and BRIAN SUTTON-SMITH
1962. "Child Training and Game Involvement. *Ethnology* 1(2):167–185.

ROSENTHAL, ROBERT
1966. *Experimenter Effects in Behavioral Research.* New York: Appleton-Century-Crofts.

ROWE, J. HOWLAND
1953. "Technical Aids in Anthropology: A Historical Survey." *Anthropology Today,* ed. A. L. Kroeber. Chicago: University of Chicago Press, 895–940.

SARLES, HARVEY
n.d. Personal communication.

SCHENSUL, STEPHEN
1969. "Marginal Rural Peoples: Behavior and Cognitive Models Among Northern Minnesotans and Western Ugandans." Ph.D. dissertation, University of Minnesota.

SEGALL, MARSHALL H., DONALD T. CAMPBELL, and MELVILLE J. HERSKOVITS
1966. *The Influence of Culture on Visual Perceptions.* Indianapolis: Bobbs-Merrill.

SHIPLEY, THOMAS E., JR., and JOSEPH VEROFF
1958. "A Projective Measure of Need for Affiliation." In *Motives and Fantasy, Action, and Society,* ed. J. W. Atkinson. New York: Van Nostrand, 83–94.

SILVERMAN, SYDEL F.
1966. "An Ethnographic Approach to Social Stratification: Prestige in a Central Italian Community." *American Anthropologist,* 68(4):899–921. Reproduced by permission of the American Anthropological Association.

SIMON, BARBARA
1968. "Social Stratification in a Modern Mexican Community." In *Social and Cultural Aspects of Modernization in Mexico,* ed. Frank C. Miller and Pertti J. Pelto. Minneapolis. (Mimeographed.)

SORENSON, E. RICHARD, and D. CARLETON GAJDUSEK
1966. *The Study of Child Behavior and Development in Primitive Cultures.* Supplement to *Pediatrics,* 37:(No. 1, Part II).

SPINDLER, GEORGE
1955. *Socio-Cultural and Psychological Processes in Menominee Acculturation.* Berkeley and Los Angeles: University of California Publications in Cultural Sociology 5.

SPINDLER, GEORGE, and LOUISE SPINDLER
1965a. "The Instrumental Activities Inventory: A Technique for the Study of the Psychology of Acculturation." *Southwestern Journal of Anthropology,* 21:1–23.
1965b. "Researching the Perception of Cultural Alternatives: The Instrumental Activities Inventory." In *Context and Meaning in Cultural Anthropology,* ed. M. E. Spiro. New York: Free Press, 312–337.

SPINDLER, LOUISE, and GEORGE SPINDLER
1958. "Male and Female Adaptations in Culture Change." *American Anthropologist,* 60:217–233.

STANDS-IN-TIMBER, JOHN, and MARGOT LIBERTY
1967. *Cheyenne Memories.* New Haven and London: Yale University Press.

STRAUS, MURRAY
1968. "Communication, Creativity, and Problem-Solving Ability of Middle- and Working-Class Families in Three Societies." *American Journal of Sociology,* 73(4):417–430.

STRAUS, MURRAY, and JACQUELINE STRAUS
1968. "Family Roles and Sex Differences in Creativity of Children in Bombay and Minneapolis." *Journal of Marriage and the Family,* 30: 46–53.

Upper Mississippi Research Project Final Report (prepared by Paredes, Pelto, and others).
1968. Upper Mississippi Research Project. Bemidji, Minnesota. (Mimeographed.)

WARNER, W. LLOYD
1959. *The Living and the Dead.* New Haven: Yale University Press.

WARNER, W. LLOYD, MARCIA MEEKER, and KENNETH EELS
1960. (First published 1949.) *Social Class in America: A Manual of Procedure for the Measurement of Social Status.* New York: Harper Torchbooks.

WEBB, EUGENE J., DONALD T. CAMPBELL, RICHARD D. SCHWARTZ, and LEE SECHREST
1966. *Unobtrusive Measures: Non-reactive Research in the Social Sciences.* Chicago: Rand McNally.

WHITAKER, GRETEL
1967. "Personality and Social Integration in a Chippewa Community."

Paper read at the sixty-sixth annual meeting of the American Anthropological Association, Washington, D.C.

WILLIAMS, HERBERT H., and JUDITH R. WILLIAMS
1965. "The Definition of the Rorschach Test Situation: A Cross-cultural Illustration." In *Context and Meaning in Cultural Anthropology*, ed. Melford E. Spiro. New York: Free Press, 338–356.

WILLIAMS, THOMAS RHYS
1967. *Field Methods in the Study of Culture.* (Series of studies in anthropological method.) New York: Holt, Rinehart and Winston.

WINTER, W.
1964. "Recent Findings from the Application of Psychological Tests to Bushman." *Psychogram,* 6:42–55.

YOUNG, FRANK W., and RUTH C. YOUNG
1961. "Key Informant Reliability in Rural Mexican Villages." *Human Organization,* 20(3):141–148.

John Lozier Collecting Names of Voluntary Workers on a Village
Road Project in Mexico

6. Counting and Sampling

In earlier chapters, particularly in the discussion of operationalism,
we examined the arguments in favor of "counting things" in field
work and other anthropological research. Anthropological research
reports always include statements that *imply* counting, even when it
was not consciously and systematically carried out. Thus, the typical
monograph includes statements such as, "Most of the people participate in the festival"; "Very few of the people can avoid paying their
taxes to the chief"; "They often work as much as 10 to 12 hours a
day"; "Very little in the way of news or other contact reaches the
village from the outside world"; and so on.

The ubiquity of such quantitative statements in anthropological
literature stems, I believe, from basic processes of human psychological functioning. In fact, not only humans, but other animals, are
constantly "counting things" in the process of adapting to their en-

vironments. Basic processes of learning, as described by experimental psychologists, most often imply some kind of counting or measurement that permits an animal (human or otherwise) to distinguish between one condition and another as a relevant stimulus for appropriate action. In the simplest experimental situation with animals, the subject (e.g., a rat or monkey) can quickly learn that pressing a bar rewards him with food, even when the reward does not occur every time the bar is pressed. The animal is able to make some approximation or estimate of the correlation between his pressing of the bar and the appearance of food. If the "correlation coefficient" between bar pressing and food pellets falls below certain limits, however, the animal may "decide" that there is no relationship between his bar pressing and the food. Extinction of the response results.

Similarly, a hunter may, through long years of experience, accumulate a store of information concerning the habits of animals based on frequencies of particular behaviors, without, however, consciously totaling up the instances in favor of his inferential knowledge as compared with the instances in which his inferred correlation or observation does not hold true. Another way of stating the case is that human knowledge in general is based on observations of probabilities of occurrence of particular events and situations in relationship to other events, things, and situations. When we say that an infant has learned an attachment for his nurturant mother, we are saying in effect that the infant has developed an inference of the probability that contact with his mother will be associated with some kind of nurturance; i.e., food, fondling, or other good things.

A similar position has been proposed by Charles Erasmus in his book *Man Takes Control*. Erasmus states:

Cognition as a causal factor in cultural behavior takes the form of probability predictions-frequency interpretations derived from inductive inference. Experience or observation is the raw material from which frequency interpretations are inductively derived. Tossing a coin, for example, provides experience or observation from which it can be inductively inferred that the frequency of occurrence of each face is the same. It can be predicted, then, that in repeated throws the coin will land heads up 50% of the time. Human knowledge, on which cognition builds, is made up of predictions, which are simply tentative probability statements—never final truths.

Frequency interpretation is not an exclusively human phenomenon. Experiments have shown that birds have a number sense which enables them to select boxes with the same number of spots (never more than seven) as those presented on a cue card. Even in simple trial-and-error learning among animals, certain positive associations are built up when successful choices frequently lead to a reward. The experimental animal is clearly anticipatory in its actions; and as successful responses grow more strongly motivated, one might even consider the animal's behavior "predictive." (Erasmus, 1961:22–23.)

Frequency interpretation may be arbitrarily divided into correlation (simple or sophisticated) and the derived causal assumption that serve as a basis for action. The latter are essentially predictions, which, like probable knowledge, are never final and never foresee all the consequences of action. (*Ibid.*, 32.)

In his discussion about frequency inferences, Erasmus describes humans as adapting to their various environments by accumulating repeated observations of events in their phenomenal world. Compared to other animals, man is peculiarly and richly endowed in the extensiveness of his ability, through language and other symbolic systems, to pass on to his fellow humans the accumulation of probability inferences that form the essence of human cultural knowledge and belief. Thus we do not expect every child in our society to learn completely on his own about the probabilities of being hit by automobiles in the street, burned by hot stoves, or made ill by eating contaminated materials. These and thousands of other pieces of cultural-probability knowledge are taught to individuals in verbal form without the necessity of direct personal experience. The knowledge pools of various cultures, even in the simplest of societies, have grown to tremendous proportions, representing stored probability inferences that would appear to be far beyond the learning capability of a single individual in a single lifetime.

When the anthropologist goes into the field to do research, his processes of learning are substantially the same as those just described. At first tentatively, and later with greater assurance, he makes probability inferences about various forms of behavior in the community he is observing. He links these probability inferences together into what we call "culture patterns." The logic of probability inference is not different when the anthropologist shifts his attention from the culture patterns of one society to the search for cross-cultural regularities.

Examples of Counting in Ethnographic Reports

Ethnographic reporting in recent decades has shown a great variation in sensitivity to the matter of counting and other numerical analysis. It is instructive, for example, to compare the two books on Tepoztlán by Robert Redfield (1930) and Oscar Lewis (1963). Redfield's monograph contains very few instances of numerical description. Lewis, on the other hand, gives table after table of information on the population of Tepoztlán and surrounding villages (p. 29); sex and age distribution (p. 30); birth and mortality rates (p. 31); language and literacy (p. 33); family size (p. 59); hours spent by women of a family at various activities (p. 72); frequency distribution of age at marriage (p. 74); inter- and intrabarrio and -village marriages (p. 77); occupations in 1926 and 1944 (p. 102), and so on throughout the monograph. It is clear that anyone returning to Tepoztlán today would be able to make extremely useful quantified assessments of culture change if he collected statistical data similar to Lewis' materials.

In his study of culture change in Tzintzuntzan, George Foster has presented many "qualitative" statements about social changes; at the same time he presents a number of quantitative statements. Particularly interesting is the list of innovators he has accumulated in his years of field work in Tzintzuntzan. He is able to state, for example, that

the second thing that is noteworthy is the relative infrequence with which potters appear on this list. Only 15 or 28% are potters, compared to 55% (of family heads) in the community at large who are potters. Potters, by this measure, are only half as likely to innovate as non-potters. This indication of general conservatism is again strikingly borne out by census data. (Foster, 1967:295–296.)

In examining changes in material style of life among people in Tzintzuntzan, Foster presents an inventory of material contents of households, including raised hearth, raised bed, water tap, latrine, and electricity—each of these with the percentage of homes having the particular item. He is able to show quantitative changes between 1945 and 1960 in these items of household equipment.

In contrast with the cases just cited, Charles Leslie's monograph *Now We Are Civilized* (a study of the world view of the Zapotec Indians of Mitla, Oaxaca) reports very little quantification of social data. The monograph does, however, contain a number of statements that imply quantification. For example, "Townspeople *generally agreed* that *mal de ojo* was the most common malady of children and parents *usually* attributed the deaths of their offspring to this cause" (Leslie, 1960:46). Also, "The opinion was also *commonly* expressed that other towns spawn witches and these occasionally appeared in Mitla at night. *Few* townspeople seemed to fear these magical beasts, however" (p. 37, italics supplied).

I think it is fair to say that the reader is left wondering about the actual frequencies of the statements and beliefs Leslie described. Twenty years before Leslie's field work, Elsie Clews Parsons studied the same community and described some of the same beliefs and practices. Since neither author provided quantified information, it is difficult to estimate the extent of social change that occurred in Mitla between 1933 and 1953.

In his monograph *Coast Lapp Society* (1965), Robert Paine provides a number of tables concerning incomes of families in the community, size of households, numbers of unmarried persons in different age groups, and many other items. It appears that Paine counted many elements of behavior and situations because he was concerned with examining differences among local households and individuals in terms of decision-making and adaptation to social change. If he had made the assumption that the people are homogeneous in their modes of adaptation, he would probably not have felt it necessary to give as much numerical information.

British social anthropology, too, exhibits a wide range of variation in the use of quantification in ethnographic materials. The earlier structural-functional studies of Radcliffe-Brown, Evans-Pritchard, and others were usually concerned more with abstract patterns of social groupings than with numerical analyses of observable behavior. In a recent review of quantification in social anthropology, Mitchell (1967) has suggested that the main stimulus for numerical analysis in ethnographic reporting probably came from Malinowski, although his own works show little evidence of the quantification he advocated. Several of Malinowski's students have made extensive use of quantitative data, especially Firth in his field work in Tikopia (1959) and Richards in her description of Bemba economic organization and marital patterns (Richards, 1939 and 1940).

Mitchell feels that counting elements of social behavior is particularly notable in the work of the Rhodes-Livingston Institute. He says:

Godfrey Wilson, the first Director of the Institute, set the tone thereafter to be followed by making extensive use of quantitative data in his study of Broken Hill in 1939–40 (1941–1942). Subsequently, Gluckman and the agriculturalists who worked among the Plateau Tonga of Mazabuka, quantified their analysis of land-holding and usage (Allan *et al.*, 1948). The practice of gathering full data in quantifiable form was established particularly in a field-training trip to the Lamba near Ndola (Mitchell) and (Barnes, 1950), where quantitative information was collected on population characteristics, kinship and clan composition of villages, marriage and divorce, labor migration and family income and expenditure. (Mitchell, 1967:19.)

In his own work, Mitchell has made extensive use of quantification, particularly in a survey of Copper Belt mining towns in Rhodesia. He gathered statistical information on occupations, religion, tribe, marital status, education, wages, and length of residence in the mining towns. A 10 percent random sample of houses in the four towns was used to represent the population. Intensive anthropological studies were then conducted on a selected subsample of the households from the larger survey (Mitchell, 1954). This study also illustrates the usual anthropological pattern of combining qualitative investigation with numerical analysis.

John Beattie in *Understanding an African Kingdom: Bunyoro* (1965) has described the rather extensive quantitative techniques that he employed in research on the Bunyoro kingdom of Uganda. He sent questionnaires to chiefs and headmen at all levels of administration. He also gathered quantified data from 369 private estates in the Bunyoro territory, in addition to which he administered a complicated interview schedule to 100 percent samples of households in his three research communities (Beattie, 1965:39).

There appear to be three principle research situations that have encouraged numerical analysis by anthropologists:

1. *Large and heterogeneous populations.* Anthropologists have turned in increasing numbers to the study of relatively complex societies, many of which are experiencing rapid social change, including urbanization, industrialization, and nationalization. The growing interest in anthropological studies of American metropolitan populations illustrates this trend. These large research populations have forced anthropologists to develop new field techniques to supplement the face-to-face methods appropriate to the study of small communities.
2. *Comparative studies of social change.* The increasing focus on social change, in place of the earlier concentration on supposedly stable social systems, leads anthropologists to seek quantifiable measures of social developments such as migration rates, acculturation, changes in family stability, and so on.
3. *Hypothesis-testing in research.* A number of field studies in recent times have been directed to the testing of specific hypotheses, often by means of specialized research instruments developed in other areas of the social sciences. In field work involving Thematic Apperception Tests, specialized interview schedules, Q-Sort techniques, and other such instruments, anthropologists have become increasingly sensitized to the need for numerical analysis.

While there are clear trends toward increased use of quantification in ethnographic reporting, as well as in other kinds of anthropological research, not all researchers accept the usefulness of these techniques. John W. Bennett and Gustav Thaiss have suggested that a main reason for anthropological resistance to quantified research procedures has been a commitment to what they call "holistic depiction." This style of field work is generally exploratory and highly flexible. The investigator adjusts his activities to the pace of community life rather than to the requirements of his research instruments. Techniques of participation, open-ended interviewing, and keeping up with the daily activities of the people are adjusted to a personalized form of investigation in which laboratory procedures and door-to-door surveying appear to be foreign intrusions. Bennett and Thaiss feel that these techniques of field work "should not be viewed as 'traditional' or 'imprecise,' as some social scientists have done, but rather as simply another approach to the gaining of knowledge of social behavior" (Bennett and Thaiss, 1967:273).

Problems of Representativeness: Sampling

As soon as the anthropologist decides to quantify some of his observations of social behavior, he is faced with the problem of defining his universe of observation and devising ways of ensuring that his observations fairly represent that universe. Counting is relatively useless, or even misleading, if there are no provisions against biased selection of the observations (units of study) that are to be quantified.

In some cases the researcher may find it convenient and important to include all the people of his research community in a numerical analysis. For example, in small communities it is a common anthropological practice to make a complete census of households, and in this situation information on family size and composition, as well as size of land holdings or other economic assets, can be based on a 100 percent sample.

Often, however, the anthropologist is confronted with research populations or communities whose size makes the prospect of 100 percent sampling too costly and time consuming. In a town of 4000 or 5000 people it is neither necessary nor practical to interview everyone in order to make legitimate generalizations. In dealing with relatively large populations, anthropologists have sometimes "sampled" the range of variation by means of a small number of selected "typical" cases. For example, Manning Nash, in his monograph *Machine Age Maya* (Nash, 1958), contrasted workers and farmers of Cantel by presenting extensive information about one worker household and one farmer household. His generalizations about family interaction, spending patterns, religious activities, and other characteristics were, of course, based on observation of, and interviews with, a number of families within the community (a population of about 1700).

In selecting informants and in presenting "typical" cases, the anthropologist often uses unstated, intuitive criteria as a guide to the "sampling." An improvement on this intuitive approach to sampling is evident in David Landy's study of child training in a Puerto Rican village (1965). Landy completed a full census of the community of El Camino (113 families), obtaining many categories of demographic, sociological, and psychological data. He felt that the survey procedure was very useful for developing relationships with all the resident households. From these census data he then selected 18 lower-class families for intensive study. His selection criteria included geographical representativeness, consideration of family size and composition, father's occupation, and other aspects which he felt to be important for their effects on socialization practices. Landy's procedure may be considered a special kind of *quota sample*.

A rather unusual variation in sampling techniques is presented by Gladwin and Sarason in *Truk: Man in Paradise* (1953). In this case, the researchers sought to obtain a wide range of contrast in personality types. Gladwin, the anthropologist, obtained ratings from the Trukese concerning the most liked and the most disliked persons in the population. From these preliminary categories,

six of the most "liked" and six of the most "disliked" of each sex were set apart, and three were selected by chance out of each such group for intensive study; there were thus six persons of each sex in our sample who were putatively "unusual." Of those remaining in the middle range, five of each sex were again selected by chance for inclusion in the sample, making a total of eleven men and eleven women. (Gladwin and Sarason, 1953:211.)

This Trukese example can be considered a three-part *stratified sample,* with stratification criteria derived from a sort of popularity rating.

The examples we have just reviewed illustrate various ways in which anthropologists have sought representativeness in their field-research materials. Of these, only the procedure followed by Gladwin produced a sample that approximates randomness. Strict random sampling requires that every individual (or other unit of observation) in the population has an equal probability of being selected. Randomness in sampling is required of any quantified data which are to be analyzed by means of inferential statistics.

DEFINING THE UNIVERSE

No matter what sampling procedures are used, the first problem that must be solved is the delimiting of a population (of people, events, or other units) from which the sample is to be drawn. Often this is a difficult task. The favorite population unit of anthropologists has tended to be "the community" but that is often hard to define. Among many East African peoples, for example, homesteads and neighborhood clusters are spread across the land in such fashion that it is difficult to say where one community ends and another begins. On the other hand, in some societies (e.g., Eskimo local groups and urban neighborhoods) membership is often quite variable depending on economic opportunities, seasonal residence changes, and so on.

In northern Minnesota we found that people identified with different communities depending on whether reference was made to postal address, trade areas, school districts, township lines, or other political/geographical subdivisions. We finally concluded on the basis of informants' statements and other data that "school district" provided the most useful and unambiguous way of defining our research populations.

Quite often single communities are highly inadequate as representations of the variability within their regions. Ties of kinship and marriage, occupational specializations, and many other social facts cut across community boundaries and suggest that certain kinds of numerical data should be gathered from a multicommunity universe.

Sometimes effective universes for sampling can be defined in terms of natural ecological features, such as "along the river," "in the valley," or "in the coastal zone." Such definitions of sampling populations depend, of course, on whether they fit with the specific purposes of the research.

In city populations it is often very difficult to delimit the boundaries of sub-groups such as ethnic enclaves. For example, if one is studying Indian populations in an urban setting it may be necessary to restrict research to certain census tracts known to contain a large number of Indians. Sometimes it is practical to limit observations to "all the people who are listed in the files of the ——— (Name) settlement house," although such a "universe" is clearly biased toward the more socially visible or active members of the ethnic group. All the possible solutions to defining research populations in urban settings involve arbitrary boundaries (hence biases), which should be kept in mind when generalizations are offered about these populations.

There are many other kinds of sampling universes besides human populations and communities. The universe of "all marriages" (for a given population) is a particularly difficult aggregate to isolate; yet estimates of divorce rates, endogamy, preferred marriage partners, and many other analyses depend on effective delimiting of this domain. Barnes (1967) has discussed this problem in detail, pointing out that one effective definition of the "population" of all marriages is obtained if one includes all the marriages ever experienced by the living members of the (designated) community. In societies with adequate written records it may be possible to select a research universe consisting of "all marriages recorded in (particular church or civil register)." Naturally the usefulness of such a universe depends on preliminary ethnographic research, to find out if all or most marriages in the area are in fact recorded in the register.

Similarly, other written registers, censuses, police records, or archives may or may not be useful as research universes, depending on their correspondence (or lack of it) to the real events they purport to list.

Whether populations for sampling are to be based on written records, or on natural, observable aggregates in the research area, field work in the form of participant observation and interviewing is usually necessary in order to select the best possible ways of defining such universes.

TYPES OF SAMPLING

The statistical operations used for making inferences about populations (of persons, events, or other units) require that samples must be drawn randomly from known populations. This is because statistical procedures are based on complex calculations concerning the patterns of equiprobable events. Textbooks in statistics and probability often begin their explanations with an examination of the probabilities of various patterns, such as those associated with flipping coins or throwing dice, assuming that the dice are not loaded and that the coins flipped are "fair."

The term *random sampling* thus has a very specific meaning, even though the word *random* is sometimes wrongly equated with haphazardness. Even today there are many research operations by anthropologists and others in which samples have been gathered by some sort of casual process to which the investigator then attaches the label *random*. If, for example, the investigator enters a room in which there are about a hundred persons and haphazardly interviews 10 of these persons, he may be tempted to claim that he has taken a 10 percent random sample. But, is it really true that each of the persons in the room had an equal chance of being selected for interview? Perhaps a number of persons were sitting in the corners of the room, and the interviewer did not go to these corners, so those persons did not have any chance of being selected. Or perhaps the interviewer has an unconscious bias against persons with red hair; consequently he did not interview any red-haired persons. We can easily imagine a number of other reasons why the casual interviewer unintentionally selects a biased sample. In anthropological field work, researchers may in fact encounter situations in which strict procedures for ensuring randomness cannot be achieved. The "haphazard sample" may be the best that can be obtained, given the situation at hand. The researcher should be aware, however, that such a sample does *not* correspond to the strict definition of random sample and should be treated with appropriate caution.

Often the best way to obtain a true random sample is by means of a table of random numbers. In this procedure, a given research population is delineated, and each individual in that population is assigned a number. The researcher then selects a table of random numbers (these are provided in most standard textbooks on statistics), and begins reading these numbers in consecutive order, starting at any point left or right, top or bottom, in the number table. Each time he encounters a number corresponding to one of the numbers in his population, the person with that number is selected for the sample. The investigator continues scanning the table of random numbers until he has selected the requisite-size sample. It should be clear that this method of choosing a sample requires that the researcher be able to designate each individual (or other unit) in his population uniquely. For a research community, this requires a total census of the local population.

Frequently, the researcher has defined for himself a population that he cannot enumerate individually in advance, but which he feels he can identify as individual units during the process of the survey. This is frequently the situation in fairly large populations, in which 100 percent census enumeration is impractical (thus eliminating the possibility of using a table of random numbers). In the Copper Belt towns studied by Hortense Powdermaker, for example, a random sample was obtained by designating every nth (household) unit for interviewing. In such cases, the sampled individuals may be designated as every third, every fifth, every tenth, every twentieth (or other nth), depending on the ratio to total population desired in the sample.

A similar method of sampling by designating every nth unit is usually necessary if one is sampling events. For example, a sample of business transactions in a market might require that the observer sample every fifth or every tenth transaction (depending on the frequency of such transactions), since he would ordinarily have no way of assigning random numbers to such events in advance. An alternative sampling technique in market transactions might be to sample at regular time intervals—e.g., every 10 minutes or every half-hour.

Frequently a research population contains important subgroups such as castes, social classes, or ethnic groups. In such cases, the investigator may want to ensure that each subgroup is adequately represented in his sample. The Tri-Ethnic Research Project, carried out by Richard Jessor, Theodore Graves, and their associates, is an excellent example of this kind of situation. They studied alcohol use, antisocial behavior, and other patterns related to acculturation in a small southwestern town whose population is about one-half Anglo-American, one-third Spanish-American, and one-sixth Indian. Since comparisons among the three ethnic groups was a main aspect of the research design, random samples were drawn separately from the three subgroups. The population was also stratified by sex.

Names were drawn from an alphabetized complete census list of the adult members of the communities; the sampling ratio was 1 in 6 for the Anglos and Spanish, and because of their smaller proportion in the community, 1 in 3 for the Indians. Cooperation was excellent: 96% of the designated respondents who were still living in or near the community were interviewed. The final sample size was 221, comprised of 93 Anglos, 60 Spanish, and 68 Indians. (Graves, 1967.306–321 and Jessor *et al.*, 1968.)

Subdivision, or stratification, of a research population is often necessary, even if the specific intentions of research do not focus on differences among these subpopulations. In many studies, for example, it is important to stratify samples between males and females. Frequently it is a good idea to stratify a sample in terms of age categories to ensure adequate representation of all generations. In each case the research operation involves the division of the target population into subgroups, after which random sampling is carried out separately in the subpopulations. Stratification by sex, age groups, and other social criteria ensures that these variables can be controlled in later analysis.

For some research purposes, once the designation of strata or subpopulations has been accomplished, samples are drawn from these subpopulations in accordance with their percentages in the overall population. Thus if one-ninth of the population is Indian, one-ninth of the respondents should be selected from among Indians. In many cases, however, this is not necessary or feasible. In the Tri-Ethnic example given above, a major intent of the sampling procedure was to provide enough respondents in each of the three ethnic groups so that comparisons could be made among them. This required that a larger portion of Indians be selected than would be called for strictly on the basis of their percentage in the population.

When a researcher samples disproportionately from subpopulations, he departs from strict randomness for the population taken as a whole. Consequently, he must be cautious in generalizing about that total population.

CLUSTER PROBABILITY SAMPLES

Cluster sampling, or *area-probability sampling,* is a technique used to simplify problems of enumerating the total population to be surveyed, by first breaking up the population into equivalent geographical units such as counties, neighborhoods, blocks, and so on. This method of sampling is intended to preserve the criteria of randomness without the necessity for enumerating every individual in the population in advance. In a Mexican peasant *municipio,* for example, it is often possible to divide the population into a series of named subcommunities and to select a certain proportion of these subunits randomly for inclusion in the survey. Within each unit selected there can be a further subdivision into blocks or subareas of some sort, again selected randomly. Once these smallest territorial units have been selected, individual households or persons can be enumerated and random samples of respondents obtained. Such a procedure eliminates the necessity for a complete enumeration of all dwellings, persons, families, or other primary units within the entire community. It should be noted, however, that this method of sampling can lead to omission of some significant, however small, segment of the population. Thus, in our hypothetical Mexican community, random selection of small subcommunities might result in elimination of all the wealthy people (or some other small but important subgroup) who happen to be concentrated in a single *barrio.* This point illustrates the need for a preliminary ethnographic survey of geographically defined subunits before any cluster sampling is attempted.

As in the case of our other sampling patterns described above, it should be clear that cluster or area-probability sampling can be carried out for other kinds of units besides people or households. That is, it is possible to conceive of clustering events in time sequences, by types of transactions in a commercial scene, by categories of vendors in a large complicated market, and so on.

NONPROBABILITY SAMPLES

As already mentioned, the statistical operations usually used with quantified social data are based on the assumption that sampling has been random from a designated universe or population. The realities of field research, however, frequently present us with situations in which deviations must be made from the ideals of randomness. While haphazard selection of informants, test families, or other units of observation is too naïve for most research purposes, the fieldworker must often make compromises in order to produce data without undue expenditures of time, effort, and money. Where such compromises are necessary, they should be made with full knowledge of the logical weaknesses they entail, and should be acknowledged in research reports. Some types of nonprobability sampling in anthropological research will be further examined in the chapter on cross-cultural research methods.

QUOTA SAMPLING

Even fairly sophisticated survey research in the United States is often based on sampling procedures that are not strictly random. For example, most public-opinion polls are based not on strict probability samples but rather on so-called *quota sampling*.

In quota sampling the first step is to ascertain some of the important characteristics of the general research population—age, occupations, ethnic groups, income levels, number of years of education, and so on. The sample from the population is then selected to match the general population in all these characteristics. Interviewers collecting individual responses are given considerable latitude in their selection of respondents as long as they keep their designated quotas in mind. After a large portion of the sample has been collected, the researchers can tell by inspection whether the proper proportion of each age category (and other elements of the quota) has been obtained. If the sample is short of respondents in a particular category, interviewers are sent out to get more respondents who fulfill those particular requirements. For example, it may be found that not enough blue-collar workers have been included in the sample. Interviewers then return to the field to correct this shortcoming.

Quota sampling is used in public-opinion polls and other kinds of surveys because it is cheaper and easier than fully random sampling. The researcher who uses this technique should keep in mind that, however carefully a quota sample has been constructed to correspond with the total population (in terms of age distribution, occupations, and numbers of other characteristics), this does not ensure that it is representative in other significant social characteristics. Such samples are approximations which may be quite useful for certain rough-and-ready purposes. When the anthropologist (or other social scientist) makes compromises in his sampling procedure, he does so most frequently to save time and money. Short cuts are sometimes justified, particularly in exploratory studies, in which the anthropologist is testing new research methods and instruments. Also, in some "applied" situations speedy feedback of information to the "client" may be more important than exactness of sampling.

In some cases the anthropologist may feel that the contrast between two research populations are so clear that slight deviations of procedure will not damage the usefulness of the research. For example, in studying mixed Indian-White communities, anthropologists have frequently observed that there are marked differences between the two groups in their patronage of particular stores, bars, and other business establishments. It would be useful to provide some sort of quantified documentation of these observations. If the fieldworker makes several preliminary counts of Indians and Whites at, for example, the two different laundromats in the community, and finds his hunches strongly supported, he may be justified in assuming that the energies and time required for more adequate sampling procedures would not add much additional credibility to his generalizations. However, sampling procedures in connection with questionnaires, psychological tests, and other specialized research instruments should always be as thoroughgoing as time and resources permit, since the data from such instruments are usually employed for a number of different descriptive and correlational analyses.

PROBLEMS OF SAMPLE SIZE

It has been pointed out that effective random sampling makes possible some reasonable estimates of the characteristics of very large populations using information gathered from relatively small numbers of persons. For example, a statistically adequate random sample from a population of one million needs to include only about two-tenths of one percent (ca. 2000) of the people (Phillips, 1966:265). Enlarging the sample size beyond that point accomplishes very little compared to the cost involved. On the other hand, with small populations of, say, 300 to 500 persons, samples need to comprise a considerably larger percentage of the population. Goode and Hatt have presented a formula according to which the researcher can estimate the size of population necessary for a particular level of accuracy. This formula is $N_s = (\sigma Z/T)^2$, where $N_s = $ the required sample size, σ preliminary estimate of the standard deviation of the universe, $Z = $ number of standard error units equal to a desired probability, and $T = $ permissible tolerance of variation in the sample mean. They present the following demonstration of this formula.

The purpose here is to estimate reliably the average annual income of families in the \$10-to-\$15-a-month income stratum in a hypothetical population. The permissible range of variation of result (T) is given as \$100; the standard deviation of the universe (σ) is estimated at \$500, and the standard error equivalent to the desired probability, taken as 99 to 1, has a value of 2.57. These figures then yield an equation of

$$N_s = 500(2.57/100)^2 = 165.$$

By that computation, a random sample of 165 cases would be sufficient to produce the desired level of accuracy (Goode and Hatt, 1952:228–229).

Examining this equation (and recollecting our experiences in flipping coins or throwing dice), tells us that the larger the sample, the greater the accuracy of predicting from this sample to the universe it represents. From this argument it would follow that our samples should always be as large as possible, which gives small comfort to the lonely fieldworker who has plenty of other problems on his hands besides trying to get very large samples of all his research populations.

There is another element to be considered in this problem of sampling, however. Paul Meehl (1967) has pointed out that the larger our samples, the greater the probability that we will pick up small differences between any populations being compared. If we hypothesize that there are differences in IQ between rural and urban populations, we are likely to get *some* result, provided we collect samples of several thousand individuals in the two populations. Large samples can, therefore, provide us with materials in which differences do become apparent as predicted, even though the differences between the sample populations may be very small in magnitude (and theoretical relevance).

Meehl's argument can be used to support research that is designed in terms of relatively small populations. In small samples, relationships among variables must be relatively large in order to reach statistically significant levels. Thus, any differences that are identified in relatively small samples are likely to be large enough to be *socially significant* as well as statistically significant. While this argument should not be overextended to justify small samples of respondents in every piece of research, it gives some comfort to anthropologists who frequently deal with small populations.

The fact that the anthropologist frequently studies rather small samples of individuals in small populations should lead him to be all the more careful about the selection of his sample. While it may seem that a sample of 50 men from a total population of 85 adult males is such a large percentage of the available population that there should be no problems about representativeness, it is important to note that neither a large total number nor a large percentage of respondents ensures that a sample is unbiased. Sometimes larger samples are more biased than small samples. This was, of course, glaringly evident in the famous case of the *Literary Digest* election polls of 1936. The very method of collecting the sample involved bias toward the more affluent in the society (those with telephones); thus the larger the sample the greater the resulting bias. Similarly, an anthropologist in a small community may collect a large number of respondents for some particular purpose, but if he is not systematically guarding against his unconscious biases, he may be collecting a sample that is distorted in favor of those persons who like him, those who are more available at certain times of the day or week; those in a particular kin network; or those with other unnoticed tendencies that make his sample the more distorted the larger it grows.

Small sample sizes (40 to 50 respondents) are not uniformly and universally ideal for the many different purposes for which anthropologists may wish to employ them, but it is useful to point out that small sample sizes are not in themselves automatic barriers to the use of statistical procedures. We occasionally hear researchers claim that their sample was so small that statistical analysis would have been inappropriate. Since samples as small as 10 or 15 (persons, items, observations) permit statistical analysis under given conditions, the small size in itself is not sufficient grounds for neglecting statistical analysis. The more likely problem in such cases is that the sample was not collected with statistical procedures in mind, and hence it could not meet the assumptions of representativeness.

Patterning and Sampling

Our common-sense experience in field work and elsewhere tells us that certain kinds of cultural data are so publicly available, homogeneous in patterning, or otherwise uniform that random samples of informants or other kinds of observations are quite unnecessary for establishing their veracity. In most cases, it is perfectly clear that a community has or does not have a school building, that men "hunt with bows and arrows," or that it is against the law to "burn down public buildings without permission." Also, we do not require a large sample of linguistic informants to produce a working description of standard grammatical forms in English (or any other language). (On the other hand, reliance on single, highly sophisticated key informants reduces the credibility even of linguistic data.)

No guidelines have been worked out by anthropologists for selecting adequate "panels" of key informants. However, as attention is focused more and more on the great amount of *intracultural* variation in beliefs, attitudes, and practices among most human groups, it becomes obvious that some kind of sampling procedure is necessary if the ethnographer is to be sure that his sources of information fairly represent intracommunity variations in cultural and social opinions and patterns. Schwab has commented on this problem of selecting informants in connection with his research in a West African urban community:

The selection of reliable and representative informants became crucial as well as difficult. It was not only a question of whether an individual or group was typical or atypical, but also one of selecting informants who were representative of the diverse social components of the community. (Schwab, 1960:408-421.)

Robbins and associates have suggested that factor analytic techniques be used to isolate main dimensions of variation within local populations (based on survey or census data) in order that key informants be selected in terms of their representativeness along these main lines of intrapopulation diversity. On the other hand, if a fieldworker feels that the kinds of data he is collecting are most clearly related to a single dimension of variation, say acculturation or socioeconomic status, it may be sufficient to devise an index or scale for this one sociocultural dimension, and to select informants to be representative, for example, of the high, middle, and low points of this scale.

In addition to the problem of representativeness of key informants, the fieldworker is often confronted with the question of how many informants are enough to inform him about different kinds of cultural patterns. Sometimes the careful selection of four or five persons who are representative of significant intracommunity variations produces such high levels of interinformant reliability that it is unnecessary to add more individuals to the panel.

It may be that there is a marginal zone of data collection, which requires at the outset careful quantitative procedures that include several (independent) informants, but within which the presence of highly patterned responses from a small number of persons can be taken as strong evidence that no further sampling is needed. The general rule might be: "When addition of informants has little effect on the general structure of a complex pattern of data, then the present sample is satisfactory." Unfortunately, no statistical procedures have been worked out for assessing this situation in data collection. This is only one of a whole series of problems in data analysis for which anthropologists and their numerically inclined friends will need to work out some new guidelines and some new procedures.

Summary and Conclusions

One of the important elements in the operationalizing of research is in counting things in order to provide numerical statements of frequencies of different behaviors, ownership of goods and prerogatives, indexes of change from one time period to another, and so on. Counting procedures provide clear specifications of the kinds of probability inferences that anthropologists have always worked with in the field (and elsewhere). Also, formalizing one's counting procedures forces the researcher to develop clear definitions of what it is that he claims to be observing. For example, when the anthropologist is asked to be more specific about what he means when he says, "Most of the people visited the city at least once during the year," he may have to redefine the population, saying, "That is, most of the adult males. . . ."

Misplaced quantification is often worse than none at all. Quantification without clear conceptualization of the relevant population, careful selection of a representative sample from the population, and other operational precautions leads to error and mystification. Also, it is clear that many of these methodological precautions require extensive supporting field work—participant observation, interviewing, and other qualitative back-up research, to give reality and meaning to the numbers and percentages.

REFERENCES CITED

BARNES, J. A.
1967. "The Frequency of Divorce." In *The Craft of Social Anthropology,* ed. A. L. Epstein. London: Tavistock, 47–100.

BEATTIE, JOHN
1965. *Understanding an African Kingdom: Bunyoro.* New York: Holt, Rinehart and Winston. © 1965 by Holt, Rinehart and Winston, Inc. Reprinted by permission of the publisher.

BENNETT, JOHN W., and GUSTAV THAISS
1967. "Sociocultural Anthropology and Survey Research." In *Survey Research in the Social Sciences,* ed. Charles Y. Glock. New York: Russell Sage Foundation: 269–314.

ERASMUS, CHARLES
1961. *Man Takes Control.* Minneapolis: University of Minnesota Press.

FIRTH, RAYMOND
    1959.   *Social Change in Tikopia*. London: Allen and Unwin.
FOSTER, GEORGE
    1967.   *Tzintzuntzan*. Boston: Little, Brown.
GLADWIN, THOMAS, and SEYMOUR SARASON
    1953.   *Truk: Man in Paradise*. Viking Fund Publications in Anthropology, 20.
GOODE, WILLIAM J., and PAUL K. HATT
    1952.   *Methods in Social Research*. New York: McGraw-Hill.
GRAVES, THEODORE
    1967.   "Acculturation, Access, and Alcohol in a Tri-ethnic Community." *American Anthropologist*, 69:306–321.
JESSOR, RICHARD, THEODORE GRAVES, ROBERT C. HANSON, and S. L. JESSOR
    1968.   *Society, Personality, and Deviant Behavior*. New York: Holt, Rinehart and Winston.
LANDY, DAVID
    1965.   *Tropical Childhood*. New York: Harper Torchbooks.
LESLIE, CHARLES
    1960.   *Now We Are Civilized*. Detroit: Wayne State University Press.
LEWIS, OSCAR
    1963.   (First published 1951.) *Life in a Mexican Village: Tepoztlán Restudied*. Urbana: University of Illinois Press.
MEEHL, PAUL
    1967.   "Theory-Testing in Psychology and Physics: A Methodological Paradox." *Philosophy of Science*, 34(2):103–115.
MITCHELL, J. CLYDE
    1954.   *African Urbanization in Ndola and Luanshya*. Rhodes-Livingstone Communication, 6.
    1967.   On Quantification in Social Anthropology. In *The Craft of Social Anthropology*, ed. A. L. Epstein. London: Tavistock, 17–46.
NASH, MANNING
    1958.   *Machine Age Maya*. American Anthropological Association Memoir, 87.
PAINE, ROBERT
    1965.   *Coast Lapp Society II*. Tromsö: Tromsö Museums Skrifter IV, 2.
PHILLIPS, BERNARD S.
    1966.   *Social Research*. New York: Macmillan.
REDFIELD, ROBERT
    1930.   *Tepoztlan, a Mexican Village*. Chicago: University of Chicago Press.
RICHARDS, A. I.
    1939.   *Land, Labor and Diet in Northern Rhodesia*. London: O.U.P. for the International African Institute.
    1940.   *Bemba Marriage and Present Economic Conditions*. Rhodes-Livingstone Paper, 4.

ROBBINS, MICHAEL C., ANTHONY V. WILLIAMS, PHILIP L. KILBRIDE, and RICHARD POLLNAC
in press. "Factor Analytic Techniques for Case Selection: An Example from Buganda." *Human Organization.*

SCHWAB, WILLIAM B.
1960. "An Experiment in Methodology in a West African Urban Community." In *Human Organization Research,* eds. Richard N. Adams and Jack J. Preiss. Homewood, Illinois: Dorsey, 408–421.

SILVERMAN, SYDEL F.
1966. "An Ethnographic Approach to Social Stratification: Prestige in a Central Italian Community." *American Anthropologist,* 68(4):899–921.

SIMON, BARBARA
1968. "Social Stratification in a Modern Mexican Community." In *Social and Cultural Aspects of Modernization in Mexico,* eds. Frank C. Miller and Pertti J. Pelto. Minneapolis, pp. 25–33. (Mimeographed.)

Tappers of the Maguey Cactus Pour *Agua Miel* (Sap) into Vat
for Brewing Native Alcoholic Drink in Mexico

7. Measurement, Scales, and Statistics

Anthropological observations and probability inferences vary from
the completely unsystematic "quasi-counting" of some of the old-
style ethnographic work to the computerized multivariable data
processing of some recent analyses. It is important for us to realize,
however, that in most cases the underlying *logic-in-use* of the different studies is much the same, even though they look very different
in their presentations. As an example, let us briefly examine the
logic of Benjamin Colby's computerized analysis of folk tales, mentioned in Chapter 5. At first glance his analysis seems complex and
strange because (1) the entire process was carried out by computer
and (2) the patterns of data as illustrated in Table 6 are different
from usual renditions of folk-tale analysis. But we need only look
for a moment at these materials to see the simplicity of the entire
research plan. It can be conceptualized as follows.

1. (idea) Perhaps folk tales of different peoples can be distinguished in terms of variations in thematic patterning.
2. One way to analyze thematic patterns in folk tales is to look at different uses (different frequencies, etc.) of particular words and clusters of words. (Hundreds of folk-tale analyses have depended on some variation of this essentially simple process.)
3. Counting the frequencies of a great number of different words in a collection of folk tales is an incredibly time-consuming process; a computer (if properly programmed) can do the same task much more quickly and accurately.
4. Setting up the folk-tale materials for the computer requires a more precise format and set of instructions than those generally used by researchers who produce such counting of thematic materials "by hand."
5. Some of the formal trappings of Colby's presentation are derived from the computerization format. However, it would be possible for him to report simply the thematic counts such as presented in Table 6 and make systematic comparisons between Eskimo and Japanese folk tales, *without reference to his use of the computer, and without reference to his statistical tests*—the essential logic of the study involves a simple comparison of thematic (word) frequencies in patterned arrays.

Even the most complicated statistical research operations are often quite simple in their logic. Understanding the underlying structure of these procedures is an essential first step to deciphering statistical analyses in the anthropological literature, as well as to developing some elementary numerical operations in one's own work. In the following sections, I will review examples of common statistical usages in anthropological literature. Further information about the mathematical formulas and other features of these procedures can be found in standard textbooks.

Some excellent books in statistics have been written in such straightforward and informative style that anyone with a little background in simple mathematics can follow (and make use of) at least the more elementary computations. *Non-parametric Statistics for the Behavioral Sciences* by Sidney Siegel (1956) is one such book. Each procedure is illustrated in terms of a simple well-defined problem case. A more recent text, entitled *Elementary Applied Statistics: For Students in Behavioral Science,* by Linton C. Freeman (1965) is also very helpful as a guide to simple statistical procedures. The book is especially useful in that it includes descriptions of the *coefficient of predictability* (lambda), the *coefficient of ordinal association* (gamma), and several parametric procedures, none of which are included in Siegel's text. I am not suggesting that these sources constitute sufficient background in statistics for the well-trained graduate student; but they do provide a do-it-yourself beginning in the use of quantitative tools.

Murdock, Social Structure, and the Chi-Square Test

Murdock's *Social Structure* (1949) contains an awesome array of numerical data that strikes fear into the hearts of some anthropology students. The propositions that Murdock set out to examine statistically consisted of a large series of probability inferences deduced from a very general theoretical model. His theoretical system focused attention on the relationship between features of kinship terminological systems and the systems of social behavior within which the kinship terms are used. In terms of our methodological paradigm in Chapter 1, this aspect of Murdock's study can be depicted as follows:

General Theory: Principles of learning theory and habit formation (psychology), functional factors (social structural and cultural), and historical events all contribute to the patterning of kinship terminological systems, and the relationships of these to the social structural systems of human groups.

The Basic Postulate: "The relatives of any two kin-types tend to be called by the same kinship terms, rather than by different terms in inverse proportion to the number and relative efficacy of (a) the inherent distinctions between them and (b) the *social differentials* affecting them, and in direct proportion to the number and relative efficacy of the *social equalizers* affecting them." (Murdock, p. 138, italics added.)

A Basic Assumption: Systems of social structure may be regarded (among other things) as systems of "social differentials" and "social equalizers," with reference to the basic postulate to be tested.

Specific Hypothesis: "In the presence of exogamous matrilineal or patrilineal lineages, sibs, phratries, or moieties, terms for lineal relatives tend to be extended, within the same sex and generation, to collateral kinsmen who would be affiliated with them under either unilinear rule of descent." (Murdock, p. 162.)

Explanation: Thus the unilinear descent groupings (or the principles of social structure underlying them) are believed to operate as "social differentials" (with regard to people in different kin groups) and "social equalizers" (with regard to people within the same kin groups).

Methods of Observation: Presence or absence of unilinear kin groups, and presence or absence of the relevant features of kinship terminology were adjudged from available ethnographic descriptions for a worldwide sample of 250 societies.

Test of the hypothesis: Supporting evidence for the hypothesis should consist of clusters of observations in the pattern shown in Figure 8.

Exogamous Unilinear Kin Groups

	Present	Absent
Terms for "equalized" kin types are the *same* (e.g., Mother, Mother's sister)	a X (hits)	b (misses)
Terms for "equalized" kin types are *different*	c (misses)	d X (hits)

FIGURE 8. **Relationships Between Kin Groups and Kin Terms**
HYPOTHESIZED BY G. P. Murdock.

Thus, Murdock suggests that where unilinear kin groups are present the kinsmen presumed to be grouped ("equalized") should be lumped under the same kin terms; in societies lacking unilinear descent groups, the corresponding kin pairs should not be lumped.

Since other differentiating and equalizing factors besides unilinear kin groups are presumed to be operating, the observed relationships are not expected to approach a perfect correlation. Rather, the test of the hypothesis requires only that the data show a *nonrandom skewing* in favor of the "hits" (cells *a* and *d* in Figure 8). Thus, Murdock, in using this research model, scanned the available information from a whole series of "events" (societies), and looked for a clustering as predicted by his theoretical hypothesis. Generalizations made by other anthropologists about relationships between social systems and kinship terminology have often involved the same kind of scanning, but without either specification of the list of cases scanned or statistical analysis of the resulting data.

From the examination of his population of 250 societies, Murdock found the data as given in Table 7.

TABLE 7.   **Relationships Among Exogamous Unilinear Kin Groups and Features of Kin Terminology**

	Exogamous Unilinear Kin Groups Present		Exogamous Unilinear Kin Groups Absent		Statistical Indices	
PAIRS OF RELATIVES	SAME TERM	DIFFERENT TERMS	SAME TERM	DIFFERENT TERMS	Q	X²
Mother–Mo Sis	106	53	31	51	+.51	1000
Sister–Fa Bro Da	125	29	64	22	+.19	2
Sister–Mo Sis Da	114	31	62	23	+.15	2
Daughter–Bro Da	107	37	34	43	+.57	1000
Daughter–Wi Si Da	38	25	15	15	+.21	2

FROM Murdock, p. 163.

Murdock's table of data looks a bit different from our Figure 8, because he included a number of tests of his hypothesis in a single block of numbers. *Each kin pair* in the table constitutes a separate set of observations. Therefore, we can take the first group (mother–mother's sister) and recast the information in the same form as given in Figure 8.

When we reorganize Murdock's first group of observations in the form of a two-by-two contingency table, we have results as shown in Table 8.

We note that there is, in fact, a tendency for the societies to be clustered in the "hits" (cells *a* and *d*), as compared with the "misses" (cells *c* and *b*). By inspection we can see that the clustering *does* seem to support Murdock's hypothesis; however, it is important to ask whether such a skewing of the numerical distribution could have occurred quite easily because of *chance sampling factors*.

Murdock's analysis of his numerical data included both the computation of a measure of association (Yule's Q) and a statistical "test of significance," or a "test of independence," referred to as the chi-square test.

This statistical calculation is especially useful for the type of data involved in Murdock's hypotheses.

The basic idea of the chi-square calculation involves a computation of the differences between the observed frequencies in each of the four cells in Table 8, compared with the frequencies that would be expected in each of the four cells *if the distribution of cases occurred simply by chance*.

TABLE 8.   **Exogamous Kin Groups and Extension of Kin Terms**

Pair of Relatives	*Exogamous Unilinear Kin Groups*		
MO–MO'S SIS	PRESENT		ABSENT
Same term used	*a*	106|*b*	31
Different terms used	*c*	53 |*d*	51
			$N = 241$ societies

DERIVED FROM Murdock, Table 35, p. 163.

Using a standard formula (available in Siegel, Freeman, and most other statistics texts), Murdock found that a pattern of skewing as extreme as that found in Table 8 would occur *by chance* less than once in a thousand times. This information, which is usually expressed as $p < .001$, suggests to the investigator that there are at least 999 chances in 1000 that *some kind* of nonrandom relationship exists between the two variables. (This is the meaning of the figure 1000 given at the right-hand margin of Murdock's table of data, Table 7). Applying the same computation to his *second row* of observations, the chi-square probability estimate tells us that these results could occur *by chance* 50 percent of the time. Clearly it is not wise in this case to discard the alternative hypothesis that this pattern of data occurred because of the vagaries of sampling rather than because of some sort of causal link between the variables.

According to strict statistical practice the researcher should establish his level of acceptable statistical significance (p-value) before making his computations. That is, he should decide in advance how much risk he is willing to run of accepting apparently significant results that are caused merely by chance. It is common in anthropology, as in some of the other social sciences, to regard a significance level of $p < .05$ as sufficient to reject null hypotheses. If there is less than one chance in twenty that the observed pattern of frequencies could have occurred by chance alone, the investigator feels justified in assuming that the observed variables are related. In the case of Murdock's data, the chi-square analysis lends support to the general theoretical proposition in the first and fourth rows of observations only. The other three computations are "statistically nonsignificant."

Although the chi-square test is most frequently used in situations in which the data can be arranged in a two-by-two contingency table, it should be noted that the calculation can be made with data arranged in any number of columns and rows. For example, if one wished to examine differences in the patterns of kinship terms among matrilineal, patrilineal, bilateral, and duolateral societies the data could be arranged in the form of a four-by-two table, as in Table 9.

TABLE 9. **Relationship of "Type X" Kinship Terms to Types of Descent Systems**

Kin terms	Societies			
	PATRILINEAL	MATRILINEAL	DUOLATERAL	BILATERAL
"Type X"	40	10	2	0
Non-X	45	30	10	50
		(Imaginary data)		

SOME CAUTIONS IN THE USE OF
THE CHI-SQUARE TEST

It should be noted that all inferential statistical tests such as the chi-square test are based on an assumption that the data to which computations are applied are a random sample from a definable universe. One of the criticisms that has been made of Murdock's statistical analysis is that his samples were not, in fact, random samples from a universe of human societies. His data were drawn as a special kind of quota sample based on such criteria as the availability of kinship information on particular societies, representation of societies from all of the major culture areas of the world, and avoidance of overrepresentation of any particular culture area. The justification for using a statistical test on this imperfect sample (and in many other similar situations) is that frequently it is impossible to achieve the ideal in sampling, yet it is useful to do the best that one can with available resources. If Murdock's hypothesis testing had depended on only a few chi-square calculations, the deficiencies in the sample would create serious doubts about the usefulness of his work. The fact is, however, that *Social Structure* is based on over a hundred chi-square computations. Since these computations tended overwhelmingly to support his major hypotheses (or theorems), the massed pattern of data is a partial compensation for the weaknesses in sampling. Just as "one swallow does not make a summer," one or a few statistical tests may not prove much, but a large number of computations in support of a *network* of hypotheses has considerable credibility.

In applying the chi-square test, the calculations are not reliable if the expected frequencies in some of the cells are too small. In the two-by-two contingency table the expected frequencies of each of the cells must be at least five. When the number of rows or columns is larger than two the chi-square test may be used if no more than 20 percent of the cells have an expected frequency of less than five. (Also, no cell can have an expected frequency of less than one in this case.) Frequently researchers encounter situations where a number of cells in a large contingency table may have small expected frequencies, and it is necessary to group or combine cells in order to prepare the data for a chi-square calculation. In cases where the expected frequencies of cells fall below the requirements for chi-square computations, the researcher may turn to the Fisher Exact Probability Test, which is particularly useful when dealing with small numbers of cases.

The chi-square test, as mentioned, is a particularly widely used statistical computation because it can be applied to data which are assigned simple, categorical values. That is, the chi-square test requires the theoretical minimum of measurement sophistication. On the other hand, many kinds of anthropological observations involve more complex and sophisticated measurement principles. Field data very often include observations about people and events that permit rank ordering in terms of dimensions, such as social stratification, wealth, household size, "modernization," and so on. The different kinds of measurements make possible different kinds of statistical procedures. Textbooks in statistics are usually organized in terms of the statistical procedures applicable to particular types of scales of measurement.

Types of Measurements: Nominal, Ordinal, Interval, and Ratio Scales

NOMINAL SCALES

In the research problem just examined we notice that Murdock made his observations concerning kinship terminology and social structure in terms of discrete categories. That is, societies were rated as either having, or not having, unilinear kinship groups. Similarly, the kinship terminological systems were assigned to two categories with no intermediate cases. These observations constitute measurements in terms of what statisticians refer to as *nominal* categories. Each such category is unique and cannot be permutated by degrees into another category. There are no gradations.

In the social sciences there are many kinds of observations that are usually best considered as nominal scales, including sex, political affiliations, and religion. In anthropological literature one encounters nominal classifications such as Indians and Mestizos, herders and agriculturalists, farmers and workers, matrilineal, patrilineal, and bilateral societies, monolinguals and bilinguals, and many other typological categories. But types of measurement are not absolutes. It is frequently possible to develop more refined techniques of observation that go beyond the simple categorizations of nominal scales. Returning to Murdock's categories, it is not hard to imagine the possibility of ranking societies in terms of their *degree* of unilinearity. Ethnographers have frequently observed that some societies are "more patrilineal than others," and matrilineal societies appear to range from those with strongly corporate unilinear groups (e.g., the Trukese and the Hopi) to societies such as the Kaska and Yukaghir with their relatively weakly developed matrilineal features. Thus, with more refined techniques Murdock's nominal categorization of social structure might be converted into a rank ordering of societies (on the dimension of unilinearity). Such a set of rank-order observations is referred to as an *ordinal* scale.

ORDINAL SCALES

Like nominal scales, ordinal scales provide for the classification of observations into mutually exclusive categories. There is an important additional feature in ordinal scales, however: The classes or categories of an ordinal scale form an ordered series.

In the discussion of research tools in Chapter 5 the observations related to social stratification are particularly good examples of ordinal scales. In Warner's description of class structure in American communities, the "Upper Upper Class" is treated as a discrete category; at the same time, it is considered to be the "highest" class in an ordered series. The highest class is thought of as having "more of something" (e.g., prestige, material goods) than any of the classes farther down the scale.

It is important to note in connection with ordinal scales that the measurements do not specify *how much* difference exists between any two categories. We do not know for example, whether the distance from "Lower Middle Class" to "Upper Middle" is the same as the distance from "Upper Middle" to "Lower Upper Class." If we were to use numbers as labels for these social classes we might designate them classes 1, 2, 3, 4, 5, 6 to preserve their rank ordering. However, we could just as well label them 1, 4, 7, 11, 17, and 25— for we make no assumptions about the magnitudes of the differences among the series.

Any series of observations in an ordinal scale can be simplified into a nominal scale. Warner's six classes can be treated statistically as discrete nominal categories if their ordering is ignored.

There are a great many kinds of observations in the social sciences that are best treated as ordinal scales. Redfield's folk-urban continuum is based on the assumption that societies can be ranked in terms of degrees of "urbanness" or "folkness." Acculturation is commonly seen as a matter of degree, as, for example, in the Spindlers' research on the Menominee, mentioned on page 114. The series from "Native Oriented" to "Elite Acculturated" can be treated as an ordinal series measuring degree of acculturation.

Many personality characteristics are also best expressed in terms of rank ordering. When we say that an individual is "achievement oriented" we generally mean that he has more of that personality element than many other people.

Many psychological tests and personality inventories are expressed in terms of scores with numbers that appear to be precise. That is, IQ test scores are frequently treated as if the distances between the scores are absolutely equivalent. If this were true, we could be assured that the distance from an IQ of 100 to one of 110 is in some mathematical sense the same as the distance between IQs of 140 and 150. However, at this stage of development in the social sciences it would appear that such test scores are so loose and indeterminate that no such claim of equivalence should be made. In fact, it could be argued that all data regarding human behavior (in the social sciences) are sufficiently inexact that measurements and scores should be regarded as ordinal scales only.

THE INTERVAL SCALE

The essential difference between an ordinal scale and an interval scale is that the distance between any two numbers on the interval scale is of known magnitude. The fact that the distances between any two points on the scale can be precisely defined means that many kinds of mathematical processes can be used in the data analysis. Thus the interval scale is a more powerful tool of measurement than the ordinal scale.

Our measurement of temperature (in terms of Centigrade and Fahrenheit scales) presents a good example of interval scales. Temperature scales can, of course, be treated as ordinal scales. That is, we are sure always that 60° is warmer than 50° and that 50° is warmer than 30°. In addition to this ordinal information, however, the measuring capabilities of high-grade thermometers assure us that we can treat the difference between 100° and 99° as equivalent to the difference between 30° and 31°. These properties of interval scales make it possible for us to use arithmetic manipulations to convert Centigrade temperature information to Fahrenheit and vice versa.

THE RATIO SCALE

The ratio scale has all the qualities of an interval scale, plus one additional feature. That is, it has a true zero point as its origin. Measurement of weight or mass is possible in terms of a ratio scale since the condition of weightlessness (no longer only an imagined theoretical possibility since the advent of space flights) is acceptable as the zero point of the measurements. Thus, the numbers associated with a ratio scale are "true" numbers and only the unit of measure is arbitrary.

The ratios between any pairs of numbers are preserved when the numbers are multiplied by a positive constant, and all kinds of mathematical transformations can be applied to ratio scales without fear of distortion.

The "level of measurement," or type of scale, involved in a particular set of observations depends on two factors—the things measured and the techniques employed by the researcher. As already pointed out, nominal observations often can be converted into ordinal measurements by improved research techniques. As ordinal measures are refined they increasingly approximate interval scales. On the other hand, some measurements that have the appearance of interval scales may be so imprecise that they are best regarded as ordinal scales. Thus the types of scales should not be regarded as absolute nominal categories, but rather as central tendencies in observational procedures. In fact, measurements in the sciences are best regarded as a continuum, ranging from "rough-and-ready" nominal observations at one end of the spectrum to highly refined interval and ratio measurements at the other extreme. Even though it is desirable to refine measurement techniques wherever possible, statistical techniques have been developed to maximize the usefulness of observations in each of the general categories outlined here.

It follows from our examination of different types of measurements (scales) that a researcher must be quite clear about what kinds of data he has in hand before he can select appropriate statistical procedures. Often the anthropological fieldworker has data in the form of a ranking (ordinal scale) for two different cultural groups (nominal categories). He should therefore use a statistical procedure which is optimally designed for an ordinal-nominal combination of variables. Examples of some of the more usually encountered statistical tests will help to illustrate these points.

Tests of Independence and Measures of Association

If we return for a moment to the example of Murdock's statistical procedures, we note that the numerical analysis was aimed at two main goals. First, with the chi-square calculation Murdock tested the hypothesis that two different "populations" (those with unilinear kin groups and those without) are different in terms of a given dependent variable (kin-term patterns). The result of the chi-square test, as we have seen, allowed him to state with a high degree of probability that the two populations are indeed different (in their kin terminological features). This type of statistical test, which is a most familar hypothesis-testing device in social sciences research, is called a *test of independence*. A test of independence tells us about the probability that two populations, defined in terms of some variable X, are different from each other with respect to another variable Y. If they are different, then the variables X and Y (e.g., types of societies and systems of kinship terminology) *are related to each other in some way*.

Measures of association, on the other hand, are designed to provide a statement about the *amount of relationship* between two variables, X and Y. In Table 7 Murdock used a measure of association called Q and gives these measures for the five separate relationships examined. It should be noted that, with large samples, relatively small amounts of association (or correlation) between two variables can sometimes be statistically significant (high probability that variables X and Y are not independent); on the other hand, with small samples, an association that *looks* impressive may be statistically nonsignificant. This point will be discussed in more detail.

In addition to the widely used chi-square test, there are several other tests of independence that are frequently encountered in recent anthropological work. Also, for each of the measures of association commonly used by behavioral scientists there is a (usually simple) method of computing the probability that a given level of association is a chance result of sampling. Thus, although the two kinds of statistical tests should be clearly differentiated conceptually, they are usually used together.

THE FISCHER EXACT PROBABILITY TEST
(NOMINAL VARIABLES)

This statistical tool is particularly useful in cases of very small samples, for which chi-square computation is inapplicable. Like the chi-square test, the Fisher Exact test is a calculation for discrete data in either nominal or ordinal form. (Actually interval or ratio-scale data can also be used in these statistical calculations, since the more powerful kinds of measurements can always be treated as if they are "weaker" in form—i.e., as nominal or ordinal data.)

Aronoff's comparisons of fishermen and cane cutters in the West Indies include several Fisher Exact Probability computations, among them those in Table 10.

TABLE 10.   **Response to Projective Question: "What happens when the man over you doesn't treat you right?"**

	Active Response	Passive Response
Fishermen	10	4
Cane cutters	4	11
		$p < .025$
		Fisher Exact Test

ADAPTED FROM Aronoff, 1967:137.

In this case it would have been technically possible for Aronoff to use the chi-square computation, but the small sample makes the Fisher test more applicable. In a case of this sort the Fisher test is a more "powerful" tool than the chi-square test, since the latter provides only an approximation, rather than a calculation of exact probabilities. The computation of the Fisher Exact Probability is a tedious procedure, but Siegel's text provides short-cut tables for finding the probability values of small samples (up to 30 cases) without any computations. With larger samples it is best to turn to calculators or electronic computers.

THE MANN-WHITNEY U TEST
(ONE ORDINAL AND ONE NOMINAL VARIABLE)

In the examples thus far the data have been arranged in the form of contingency tables, in which all of the information was treated in the form of nominal categories. When one of the variables is in the form of ranked or ordinal data, the use of chi-square or Fisher Exact tests results in throwing away the information about rank differences. The Mann-Whitney U test is a more appropriate test where ordinal measurements are available. This is a powerful test that can be used to determine whether two groups have been drawn from the same population. Like the Fisher Exact test, the Mann-Whitney U test is applicable to very small samples.

Another of Aronoff's statistical analyses from the West Indies can serve as an illustration of this analytic technique.

As described in Chapter 5, Aronoff used the sentence-completion technique to compare fishermen and cane cutters. He suggested that the fishermen of the community are higher in self-esteem than the cane cutters. The relevant data are given in Table 11.

TABLE 11. **Frequency Distribution of the Cane Cutters' and Fishermen's Responses on the Esteem Level**

```
    C
    C     C
    C     F
    C C C F F
    C F C F F
C   C C F F F F C       C        F  F      F     F
0   1 2 3 4 5 6 7 8 9 10 11  12 13 14 15    18    20
```

(Number of esteem responses)

$p < .001$
(Mann-Whitney U test)

FROM Aronoff, 1967:76.
F: fishermen
C: cane cutters

If we consider these data to represent a ranking in terms of the number of "esteem responses," we note that the man with 20 responses is rank one, 18 responses is rank two, and so on. The top four ranks are all fishermen. At the bottom end of the ranking there is a group of nine cane cutters who have fewer esteem responses than any of the fishermen. The Mann-Whitney U test is an excellent technique for assessing the probability of "no difference" in the rank ordering of the two groups. As indicated in the statement $p<.001$, it is highly unlikely that this pattern of observations occurred by mere chance.

MEASURES OF ASSOCIATION

The measure of association known as Yule's Q was one of the earliest statistical computations of covariation and is called Q in honor of Quételet, the nineteenth-century statistician. Q is a very easy statistic to compute, but Driver (1961:321) and others have pointed out that the arithmetic derivation of Q is arbitrary, hence the "meaning" of this measure of association is difficult to interpret. Also, the value of Q will be 1.00 (spuriously indicating a perfect covariance) if one of the cells in a two-by-two matrix happens to be zero.

PHI CORRELATION COEFFICIENT
(NOMINAL VARIABLES)

The computation of a phi correlation is slightly more complicated than that for Q but this statistical operation has some distinct advantages. The value of phi as a statement of covariation does not automatically go to 1.00 if one of the cells in the matrix happens to be zero. Also, unlike the Q computation, phi can be directly related to the computation for chi square. That is (in two-by-two tables), $X^2 = \phi^2 N$.

If we apply this formula to the chi-square value in the first of Murdock's kin terminology hypotheses, we find that $\phi^2 = .276$. We notice immediately that phi is smaller than the .51 Q value that Murdock presented in his data tables. This is generally true of phi as compared to Q, except in certain extreme cases. Driver (1961) has presented a useful discussion about chi square, phi, and related statistical computations.

Since the value of phi approaches 1.00 as any two variables are more and more closely related, we can see that the relationship between Murdock's kin group type and kin terminology are not particularly close, even though, as previously noted, the relationships are statistically significant. We may make the assumption that, although there may be some kind of causal relationship between the two variables, many other (unknown) factors must be affecting the occurrence of the two variables.

When the data are such that only nominal measures have been obtained and when the data can be organized in the form of a two-by-two contingency table, the phi coefficient of correlation would appear to be an appropriate computation. In cases where the extent of the relationship between the two variables in such a table is not immediately obvious, the researcher makes more information available if he presents the phi computation as well as the test of significance. This is all the more useful when a whole series of computations is presented; we may wish to compare the magnitudes of relationships in the series, regardless of the computed levels of significance. Examination of phi coefficients may enable us to make some judgment concerning the theoretical and practical significance (as opposed to the statistical significance) of particular sets of relationships.

GUTTMAN'S COEFFICIENT OF PREDICTABILITY:
LAMBDA (NOMINAL VARIABLES)

The coefficient of predictability (lambda) is a more recently developed statistical technique that has considerable logical appeal. We can look upon measures of association as aids in guessing or estimating the value of variable X from our knowledge of Y (e.g., the likelihood of correctly guessing the kinship terminological system of a given culture if we know their type of descent system). Increased values of phi or Q (or some other measures of association) all imply improved possibilities of prediction. Lambda, unlike our other correlational computations, is a direct arithmetic statement of the *improvement of prediction* of a variable X provided by knowledge of Y.

Poggie (1968) examined the relationship between occupational categories and aspirations for sons' education among people in the vicinity of a new industrial city in Mexico. Table 12 presents his data on the two variables.

TABLE 12. **Relationships Between Occupation and Aspirations for Son's Education**

Desired Education for Sons	Workers	Young Farmers	Old Farmers
Primary	15	71	42
Secondary	13	9	8
Professional	59	21	7
Other	8	10	6

ADAPTED FROM Poggie, 1968:166.

Lambda: Workers *vs.* Young Farmers   .37
        Workers *vs.* Old Farmers   .38

The computation of lambda (which is relatively simple) shows that 37 percent of the errors in "guessing" the level of education desired for a son can be eliminated by knowing whether the respondent is a worker or a young farmer. Slightly higher predictive success is obtained in the comparison of workers and older farmers. In this kind of calculation, the variable to be guessed is considered the dependent variable. A combined coefficient of predictability can be calculated, involving the estimates in both directions of dependence. Freeman (1965) provides a clear description of the logic and computations of lambda.

THE KENDALL RANK CORRELATION COEFFICIENT:
TAU (ORDINAL DATA)

Sometimes a researcher is fortunate enough to have ranked, or ordinal, measurements of the two variables whose relationship he is examining. Such ranked data can always be broken down, or collapsed, into two-by-two tables for computing simple measures of association. However, that means throwing away some of the information. When two variables to be examined are both in the form of ordinal data, Kendall's tau is a very useful statistical computation.

An example will make clear the simplicity and usefulness of the Kendall tau coefficient of correlation. In some recent research, I have been interested in differences between "tight" and "loose" societies (Pelto, 1968). I developed a Guttman scalogram of societies ranked in terms of 12 elements of social structure which I felt registered relative "tightness" of the social system. In examining possible causal factors associated with relative tightness of societies, I examined the relationship between tight societies and density of population. Table 13 shows the rank order of societies in relative tightness, and the estimated densities of the populations.

The Kendall tau computation is an estimation of how well the rank ordering of a second variable (in this case, population density) compares with the rank ordering of the other variable (relative tightness of society). If the rank order of population densities were in exactly the same order as the rank ordering of social systems we would say that there is a perfect correlation. However, examination of Table 13 points out that the correlation in this case is far from perfect.

Using the Kendall tau formula in Siegel (1956) we learned that tau is .276. Since even relatively small values of tau are statistically significant, it would appear that there is some kind of direct or indirect causal link between population density and the relative tightness of the social system. The actual probability of a given tau value can be computed by converting it to a z score. This procedure is described by Siegel (1956:213–223). In our example, the z score turns out to be 5.5, which has an associated level of significance so extreme that many tables of z do not go that high. Therefore, we feel justified in rejecting the null hypothesis in favor of the alternative statement that there is a significant relationship between population density and tightness of societies.

TABLE 13.   **Relationship Between Population Density and Relative Tightness of Society**

Society (in descending order of tightness)	Estimated Pop. per Sq Mi	Rank Order of Population Densities
Hutterites (North America)	50.0	12
Hano (Arizona)	1.3	18
Lugbara (Uganda)	150.0	5
Pahari (Northern India)	100.0	8
Kibbutz (Israel)	110.0	7
Hidatsa (Northern Plains)	70.0	9
Samburu (East Africa)	2.7	16
Taira (Okinawa)	1440.0	1
Ting Hsien (China)	850.0	2
Mixtecans (Mexico)	120.0	6
Serbians (Eastern Europe)	160.0	4
Orchard Town (New England)	52.0	11
Napaskiak (Eskimo)	0.5	19.5
Aritama (Colombia)	66.0	10
Tarong (Philippines)	2.0	17
Gusii (East Africa)	450.0	3
Basseri (Iran)	8.0	15
Kapauku (New Guinea)	9.0	13.5
Skolt Lapps (Finland)	9.0	13.5
Cubeo (Brazil)	0.5	19.5
Kung (South Africa)	0.1	21

Siegel also described a procedure which Kendall developed for a *partial* rank correlation coefficient. This statistical computation is useful for comparing ranked data on three variables. In such a case, we may wish to determine the relationship between variables X and Y when variable Z is held constant, or partialed out. Also of interest is Kendall's coefficient of concordance: w. This coefficient is computed to determine the agreement among a whole series of variables. The calculation is particularly appropriate if a researcher has a set of data that have been ranked or rated by a number of different judges. For example, Freed obtained rankings of the cast hierarchy in an Indian village from a sample of 26 raters (Freed, 1963:879–891). Although Freed did not use Kendall's w for his computation of agreement among his raters, these are the kinds of data for which that statistical operation is particularly useful.

THE SPEARMAN RANK CORRELATION COEFFICIENT: RHO (ORDINAL DATA)

The Spearman rank correlation coefficient was the first of the correlation coefficients to be developed for ranked data, and is perhaps the best known today. This statistic is often referred to simply as rho. Whereas Kendall's tau computations involve the concept of "the natural order of rankings in the second variable," Spearman's rho is based on the computation of the "aggregated differences between the two rankings."

An interesting use of the Spearman rho correlation of rank is presented by Stanley Freed in "An Objective Method for Determining the Collective Caste Hierarchy of an Indian Village" (Freed, 1963:879–891). Freed examines the hypothesis that individuals in Indian villages will consider their own caste to be of higher rank than do the rest of the people in the village. He first obtained a set of average rankings of the castes in the village and then compared these village averages with the rankings of the people in particular castes. That is, he compared the Brahman self-ranking with the village average, the self-ranking of the Jats with the average of the village as a whole, and so on. The results of these comparisons are given in Table 14.

TABLE 14. **Correlations Between Self-rating and Community Consensus in an Indian Caste Structure**

Castes	Correlation coefficient of "rating of own caste" and rankings by other members of the village
Brahman	.97
Baniya	.96
Jat	.98
Bairagi	.94
Mali	.97
Jhinvar	.95
Gola Kumhar	.86
Nai	.85
Chamar	.95
Churha	.98

ADAPTED FROM Freed, 1963.

Freed concluded that most members of caste groups in this Indian village assign ranks to themselves in approximately the same way as do other members of the village; however, the two castes whose members' correlations with the rest of the village fall below .90 show a tendency to rank themselves higher than do other members of the community.

GOODMAN AND KRUSKAL'S COEFFICIENT OF ORDINAL ASSOCIATION (GAMMA)

Linton Freeman considers gamma to be "the most generally useful ordinal measure of association" (Freeman, 1965:79). Its attractiveness lies in the fact that, like lambda, gamma is a measure of the improvement in guessing about *X*, given information about *Y*. Hence it is a coefficient of predictability. Since gamma is a relatively new statistical device, few anthropological researchers have used it thus far.

Parametric and Nonparametric Statistics

Until recently it has been common for statisticians to insist that only nonparametric statistics should be used in the analysis of nominal and ordinal data, particularly in cases where a normal distribution of values or frequencies cannot be assumed. In fact, all of the statistics for which I have given examples above *are* nonparametric procedures. As stated by Siegel,

A nonparametric statistical test is a test whose model does not specify the conditions about the parameters of the population from which the sample is drawn. Certain assumptions are associated with most nonparametric statistical tests, i.e., that the observations are independent and that the variable under study has an underlying continuity, but these assumptions are fewer and much weaker than those associated with parametric tests. Moreover, non-parametric tests do not require measurements so strong as that required for the parametric tests; most nonparametric tests apply to data in an ordinal scale, and some apply also to data in a nominal scale. (Siegel, 1956:31.)

Parametric tests, on the other hand, are generally acknowledged to be more powerful statistical operations if the assumptions underlying their use can be met. The *t* and *F* tests are among the commonly used forms of inferential parametric statistics. In recent years there has been increasing evidence that use of parametric statistical procedures does not lead to invalid results even though some of the assumptions and conditions of such tests have been violated. Occasionally it is useful for researchers to check statistical results using both parametric and nonparametric procedures. Many of the more complex statistical procedures that are increasingly being used by anthropologists involve parametric analysis. Researchers should not shy away from these research tools simply because of fear that all the statistical assumptions cannot be rigorously met. On the other hand, use of these statistics challenges the anthropologist to improve his basic measurement procedures.

I have presented basic nonparametric statistics because these procedures provide certain advantages for anthropologists, particularly at the precomputer stage of data analysis. These advantages include the following:

1. For very small samples there is sometimes no alternative to using nonparametric statistics, unless the population distribution can be described exactly.
2. Since nonparametric statistics make no assumptions about the equivalence of distances between scores in a series of ranks, we do not need to worry about the exactness of our measurements, as long as we are sure that, e.g., X is greater than Y and Y is greater than Z. In some cases nonparametric statistics are employed on materials that can be categorized only as plus or minus (more or less; better or worse).
3. Nonparametric methods can be used on data that are simply classified in terms of a nominal scale. Parametric tests usually cannot be applied to information of that type.
4. It is especially interesting to note that nonparametric statistics are typically much simpler than their parametric counterparts; hence, they are easier to learn and often may be carried out without recourse to calculators or other "hardware." Frequently provisional statistical analyses should be carried out *during* field work. The ease of computations of nonparametric statistics is a distinct advantage under field conditions.
5. Some of the nonparametric procedures involve logical manipulations that are quite clear, and intuitively pleasing—as, for example, the Mann-Whitney U test described above.

It is only fair to list here some of the disadvantages of nonparametric tests.

1. Nonparametric tests are wasteful of the data. Since nonparametric statistical operations treat of rank orders and/or nominal categories, the additional measurement power inherent in interval ratio scales is simply discarded in nonparametric analysis. Such wastefulness means that the power-efficiency of nonparametric tests is lower than that of equivalent parametric tests.
2. Nonparametric methods have not been developed for the testing of interactions in the analysis of variance model, unless certain special assumptions are made. In general, problems of multi-

variable analyses have not been fully worked out in terms of nonparametric statistics.

More Complicated Statistical Operations

The anthropological literature includes many studies that have more complicated statistical operations than any we have so far examined. There is, of course, no limit to the complexity of statistical operations that may prove useful in the study of human behavior. Naturally complexity (whether of statistics or anything else) is not valuable in and of itself. As a matter of fact a cardinal rule of science is frequently given as: "Other things being equal, the simplest explanation (or operation, or statistical computation) is the preferred one."

MULTIPLE REGRESSION ANALYSIS

In most of the statistical techniques employed by anthropologists, only two or in some cases three variables can be examined simultaneously. Thus, from a complex, multifaceted world of interrelated events and things, the investigator must pick out just two or three theoretically important concepts for analysis, trying to "hold everything else constant." This is a difficult and frequently unrewarding assignment, since in natural events the effects of many extraneous, uncontrolled variables are always affecting the outcome of observations.

Sometimes the anthropologist would rather devise some way to examine a whole series of variables, X_1, X_2, X_3, X_4, X_5, and so on, to see what *combination* of these variables best predicts the values of a particular dependent variable, Y. Multiple regression analysis offers one means of accomplishing this complicated assessment of interrelated data.

Schensul (1969) used multiple regression analysis in a study of cognitive responses to modernization in Uganda (see Chapter 5). He used a structured interview schedule to collect a mass of information about his Banyankole informants, including size of household, income, number of coffee trees owned, number of cows, measures of "modern information," a scale of material style of life, and so forth. Also, as described earlier, he obtained informants' responses to a modified semantic differential task.

Schensul's statistical adviser suggested that he experiment with a multiple linear regression analysis in order to identify predictors of the semantic differential responses. From the computerized analysis, it appeared that among the sample of Banyankole people the 10 most important predictors of responses in the overall semantic differential task were as follows:

1. Number of brothers and sisters who have left the area
2. Income (cash)
3. Percent of income received from wages
4. Number of moves the household has made
5. Number of coffee trees (major cash crop)
6. Age
7. Number of cows (important factor of wealth)
8. Traditional goods (Guttman scale)
9. Religiosity (Guttman scale)
10. Articulation (Guttman scale)

As an example of the information produced by the multiple regression analysis we can look at the relationships between the independent variables and responses concerning "Inhospitable-Hospitable" as applied to the informants' ratings of themselves. In Table 15 we see that the independent variable with the strongest predictive power (highest correlation with the dependent variable) is income, with a correlation of .32. The next predictor variable is number of cows, which adds .07 of predictive power to that provided by the first variable. The third variable, siblings who have migrated,

TABLE 15. **Multiple Regression Analysis to Predict Informant's Ratings of Self on Dimension of Hospitable-Inhospitable**

Variable	Multiple R (cumulative)	Increase in R (rounded)	Direction of Relationship
Income	.32	—	high income = inhospitable
No. of cows	.40	.08	more cows = hospitable
Siblings migrated	.44	.04	more siblings migrated = inhospitable
Age	.46	.02	high age = hospitable
Possession of traditional goods	.49	.03	more traditional goods = inhospitable
Number of coffee trees	.51	.02	more trees = hospitable
Knowledge of national system	.54	.03	high knowledge = hospitable
No. of people in household	.55	.01	more in household = hospitable
Religiosity	.56	.01	more religiosity = hospitable
Changes in residence	.56	.007	more moves = hospitable

FROM Schensul, 1969, Appendix.

adds only .05 more predictive power, and so on down to the tenth variable, number of changes of residence, which makes very little further contribution to the linear regression equation. The multiple R of .56 indicates that the combined force of the 10 most significant independent variables leaves a considerable portion of the variance unaccounted for.

This statistical analysis allowed Schensul to make the following inferences:

1. Banyankole perceptions of their social world (defined in the semantic differential task) vary intraculturally in relation to economic position (income, number of cows, coffee trees, etc.), and a number of other factors.
2. Although economic factors were important in the list of predictor variables, such noneconomic factors as "religiosity" and "knowledge" were also significant.
3. The independent variables that were importantly related to particular conceptual definitions (decisions in the semantic differential) differed in ways that "make sense" in terms of the contemporary ethnographic picture of the Banyankole. For example, hospitality behavior involves significantly increased expenses for wealthier people. Hence the higher-income people are ambivalent about hospitality.

Although this example of multiple regression analysis represents a tentative exploration in a relatively new and unknown realm, it would appear that, because it permits examination of the simultaneous effects of a large cluster of variables, it has much intuitive appeal for the holistically inclined anthropologist.

FACTOR ANALYSIS

One of the more commonly encountered complex statistical techniques is that of factor analysis. Basically, factor analysis is a technique whereby a large number of categories of data and their intercorrelations can be reduced to a small number of basic "factors," to simplify further analysis of the data.

Sawyer and Levine (1966) used factor analysis in an examination of Murdock's World Ethnographic Sample, which consists of a table of 30 basic economic, ecological, social, and political characteristics for a sample of 565 societies. They first computed product-moment correlations between each pair of variables. The intercorrelations between all pairs of variables formed a matrix of data from which the factor-analysis procedure (computerized) was used to select clusters of interrelated variables. (A number of different factor analysis procedures are possible, and they produce somewhat different results.) Each succeeding cluster of variables (these clusters are called *factors*) selected in this process is statistically independent of other such clusters.

Sawyer and Levine found that 10 factors, or clusters of variables, accounted for 74 percent of the variance in Murdock's World Ethnographic Sample. Tables 16 and 17 show their results. Some of the inferences one can draw from inspection of these data are surprising.

1. The "patrilineality complex" (factor 6) is surprisingly independent of matriliny (factor 7), cross-cousin marriage (factor 8), animal husbandry (factor 2), and even father-uncle differentiation (factor 10). One might well have expected, instead, a high negative relationship between patrilineality and matrilineality.
2. A high positive correlation between patrilineality and animal husbandry has often been claimed, and partially demonstrated; and a number of theoretical statements suggesting correlations between patrilineality and several other variables fail to find support in Sawyer and Levine's data.
3. It is also quite surprising that family composition (factor 5) generally is unrelated to either subsistence systems (factors 1, 2, 3) or to kinship systems (factors 6 and 7).
4. One can argue from these data that, at least for Murdock's particular sample of societies, the subsistence factors are the most powerful in predicting variation in other cultural traits, although the patrilineality factor is also important.
5. Conversely, cross-cousin marriage (factor 8) and father-uncle differentiation (factor 10) seem relatively insignificant as predictors of cultural variation according to this set of data. Devotees of theories concerning marriage alliances could do well to ponder the implication of these findings.

Naturally one should take Sawyer and Levine's factor analysis results with a large grain of salt, for there are a great many criticisms that can be made concerning the basic quality of the World Ethnographic Sample data. The results suggest directions for further exploration, rather than finished theoretical propositions. Nonetheless, the careful researcher can examine these data with profit—telling himself that "something is going on" that requires much further study with other techniques of analysis. The impression that "something is going on" in these data is strengthened by Sawyer and Levine's demonstration that broadly similar results are obtained if one considers the intercorrelations and clusters of variables separately for the six major cultural regions of the world.

Driver and Schuessler (1967) have also factor analyzed Murdock's World Ethnographic Sample. Their methods differed somewhat from those of Sawyer and Levine in that they derived phi coefficients of correlation rather than product-moment correlations for their matrix of 30 cultural variables. The factors that they extracted bear a considerable resemblance to those produced by Sawyer and Levine. The authors include some methodological notes in their presentation of these materials.

TABLE 16.   **Thirty Cultural Variables on 10 Factors**

	1A Agriculture		
I	1B Male involvement in agriculture		6A Patrilineality
			6B Patrilineal Exogamy
	1C Cereal agriculture	VI	6C Patrilocality
	1D Permanence and clustering		6D Bilateral descent of kindreds
			6E Community exogamy
	2A Animal husbandry		6F Bride price
II	2B Male involvement in animal husbandry		
	2C Domestication of animals		7A Matrilineality
		VII	7B Matrilineal Exogamy
	3A Fishing, etc.	VIII	8A Cross-cousin marriage
III	3B Male involvement in fishing, etc.		8B Cousin-sibling differentiation
	4A Hunting and gathering		9A Social stratification
IV	4B Male involvement in hunting & gathering		9B Political integration
		IX	9C Slavery
			9D Hereditary political succession
	5A Nuclear family household		
	5B Extended family structure		
V	5C Household size	X	10A Father-uncle differentiation
	5D Polygyny		

ADAPTED FROM Sawyer and Levine, 1966:715.

Child, Bacon, and Barry (1965) have presented another very interesting use of factor analysis in their cross-cultural study of drinking behavior. These authors extracted data about alcohol use from a sample of 139 societies. From these data they were able to make ratings on 19 different variables. The matrix of correlation coefficients among the 19 variables was then factor analyzed by means of the "principal factors method." Using a varimax rotation, they extracted 4 factors. Of the total variance (80 percent for the 4 factors) 37 percent is accounted for by the first factor, 24 percent by the second factor, 12 percent by the third factor, and 7 percent by the fourth factor. Table 18 presents the 19 variables and their loadings on the 4 factors (Child, Bacon, Barry, 1965:10). The authors then use the factor scores of their societies to examine a series of hy-

TABLE 17. Loadings of 30 Cultural Variables on 10 Factors

Variable	1	2	3	4	5	6	7	8	9	10	Commu- nality
1A	.88	.16	−.03	.00	−.05	.05	.06	.00	.01	−.20	.85
1B	.72	.08	−.14	−.10	.01	−.13	−.09	.04	.09	.03	.60
1C	.63	.30	−.30	.20	.04	−.01	−.01	−.01	.19	.16	.68
1D	.78	−.02	.25	−.09	−.11	.05	.03	.02	.09	−.08	.71
2A	.12	.84	−.23	−.16	.02	.15	−.06	.09	.16	.06	.87
2B	.07	.86	−.18	−.07	.02	.09	−.09	.03	.14	−.07	.83
2C	.27	.84	−.09	−.16	.05	.14	.00	.02	.09	−.05	.85
3A	−.12	−.31	.85	−.03	−.03	−.09	.05	.01	.00	.06	.85
3B	.03	−.13	.90	.05	.00	−.10	−.01	.06	−.01	.10	.86
4A	−.50	−.37	−.01	.64	−.02	−.02	.04	−.06	−.14	.05	.83
4B	.04	−.13	.02	.88	.04	.07	.02	−.02	.00	.01	.80
5A	11	−.16	.01	−.16	.81	−.19	−.08	−.06	−.04	.11	.78
5B	.20	−.11	.01	−.12	−.70	.03	−.01	−.06	.17	.00	.59
5C	.05	−.39	.05	−.14	−.61	−.17	−.06	.08	−.21	.30	.71
5D	−.34	.20	.08	.33	−.37	.24	−.01	.01	.17	−.43	.68
6A	.11	.19	−.11	−.02	−.02	.86	−.20	.17	.05	−.05	.87
6B	.04	.01	.01	.10	−.05	.82	.15	−.32	−.10	.01	.82
6C	−.07	.10	−.09	−.08	−.02	.70	−.40	.03	.15	.03	.69
6D	−.15	−.13	.11	.04	.04	−.68	−.35	−.34	−.08	.08	.78
6E	−.30	.11	.02	.07	−.09	.59	.15	−.10	.02	−.06	.50
6F	−.06	.50	−.10	.14	−.04	.35	−.15	.08	.25	−.14	.51
7A	−.01	−.07	.01	−.01	.00	−.10	.89	.18	.02	−.14	.86
7B	−.03	−.15	.04	.03	−.04	.11	.88	−.28	.07	−.11	.91
8A	.07	.05	.11	−.07	−.04	−.08	−.10	.89	.05	−.03	.84
8B	−.08	.14	−.10	.08	.04	.39	.37	.52	−.08	.18	.64
9A	.23	.29	.05	−.24	−.06	−.04	−.03	.01	.71	.18	.74
9B	.28	.39	−.04	−.19	.04	−.06	−.06	.03	.59	.19	.65
9C	.06	.19	.02	.19	−.08	.08	−.06	.01	.68	−.13	.57
9D	−.11	−.28	−.14	−.03	−.11	.21	.12	.04	.52	−.41	.62
10A	−.21	−.09	.03	.05	−.05	.02	−.20	.02	.06	.80	.74
Percent of total variance	10.6	11.7	6.3	5.5	5.7	10.9	7.4	4.9	6.4	4.6	74.0

ADAPTED FROM Sawyer and Levine, 1966:715.

potheses concerning relationships of drinking behavior to socialization practices, social organization, and other variables. The authors find that "the hypothesis that high levels of use of alcohol are in part motivated by a need to relieve frustrated or conflicted dependency needs seems to be supported by most of these relationships and contradicted by none of them" (Child, Bacon, Barry, 1965:46).

TABLE 18.   Factor Analysis of Variables in the Use of Alcohol (Loadings of 19 Variables on 4 Factors)

	1st Factor: Integrated Drinking	2d Factor: Inebriety	3d Factor: Hostility	4th Factor: Quantity
1. Frequency of Drinking as Religious Ritual	.94	—.04	.00	.05
2. Frequency of Ceremonial Drinking	.90	.10	—.15	.20
3. Extent of Ritualization	.88	—.02	—.03	—.27
4. Quantity of Ceremonial Drinking	.86	.37	—.12	.06
5. Quantity of Drinking as Religious Ritual	.85	.08	.07	.05
6. Approval of Drinking	.76	.17	—.06	.45
7. Extent of Drinking	.57	.08	—.09	.45
8. Quantity Consumed on One Occasion	.12	.85	.17	.16
9. Duration of Drinking Episode	.24	.79	.04	—.10
10. Frequency of Drunkenness	.13	.77	.37	.43
11. Approval of Drunkenness	.53	.65	.03	.35
12. Boisterousness	—.13	.61	.55	.13
13. Typical Intensity of Hostility	—.13	.08	.93	—.05
14. Extent of Change in Hostility	—.03	.13	.89	—.08
15. Occurrence of Extreme Hostility	.04	.17	.87	.10
16. General Consumption	.45	.29	.03	.77
17. Frequency of Drinking	.23	—.18	—.17	.74
18. Procurement Effort	—.15	.35	.10	.67
19. Extent of Problem	—.17	.57	.23	.67

FROM Child, Bacon, and Barry, 1965:10.

It appears that factor analysis is growing in popularity generally in the social sciences, and may become more prevalent in anthropological work. Several of the researchers who have used factor analysis point out that the method should be considered only as a technique for clustering data, not as a mode of theory testing. There is reason to be cautious about the use of factor analysis in those situations in which the investigator has few guidelines for deciding the appropriateness of a specific type of factor analysis and no external criteria for judging the acceptability or usefulness of the factors produced. J. Scott Armstrong (1967) has presented a discussion of the usefulness of factor analysis (subtitled "Tom Swift and His Electric Factor Analysis Machine") in which he factor analyzed the dimensions of 63 metal boxes. He used the "principal-component method" of factor analysis with an orthogonal rotation. The 11 variables were found to group into 3 principal factors, accounting for 90.7 percent of the information contained in the original 11 variables. Armstrong then changed his rules of factor analysis slightly and produced a solution with 4 factors. He felt that neither of these factor-analytic solutions was, in fact, theoretically justified. He said:

. . . those people who have read the literature in metallurgy, geometry and economics will recognize that, in the initial study, all of the information is contained in five of the original eleven variables—namely length, width, height, density and cost per pound. The remaining six variables are merely built up from the five "underlying factors" by additions and multiplications. Since a rather simple model will give a perfect explanation, it is difficult to get excited about a factor analytic model which "explains" 90.7% of the total information (Armstrong, 1967:19.)

The objections that may be raised about the use of factor analysis appear to be concerned mainly with the arbitrariness of the results. Depending on what arbitrary plan of factor analysis is employed, different results may be produced. If there are no theoretical or empirical criteria against which to judge these differential results, the researcher may be left to wonder what the factors mean and how many factors are "enough" to structure his data. Factor analysis clusters together those items that are highly intercorrelated, regardless of their meaning. In fact, it may be said that the clustering by factor analysis is essentially theoryless. Thus, whenever the researcher has reasons for clustering certain variables because he is operating in terms of a particular theory, it may be well to let theoretical considerations rather than mechanical computation determine the specific factors.

These statements should not be read to mean that factor analysis has no place in the social sciences. Useful discussions of factor analysis have been presented by psychologists, anthropologists, and others, and it seems likely that the technique will continue to be one of the statistical tools used by social scientists. In this as in all other decisions about research methods, the researcher is well advised to consult with statisticians and other specialists and to make clear to himself just exactly what his own research intentions are. Once his research strategies are generally laid out, competent statisticians and other advisers can help in the decisions to use, or not to use, factor analysis as part of the procedures.

Tests of Independence
Do Not Prove Causation

The notion is widespread (especially among laymen) that it is possible to "prove" theoretical propositions by means of statistical operations. This is definitely not the case, and we need to be very clear about the logic involved in the use of statistical tests of independence. When our computations lead us to reject the null hypothesis in a particular instance, we are able to say (in terms of given degrees of probability) that the variables we have been examining are linked in some way; the distributions of the independent and dependent variables are not random with respect to one another. If by this operation we have demonstrated the probability that a variable X is in some way linked to a variable Y we do not know whether X causes Y, or whether Y is an antecedent to X. And we must also assume the possibility that the variables are related to each other through the action of other, unknown factors. Our particular theoretical explanation of the observed relationships must compete with all possible alternative explanations.

In general, it is now widely agreed that statistical tests of independence have been overdone in the literature of the social sciences. Frequently the data to which such tests have been applied cannot meet the requirements of random sampling. Since these tests tell nothing about the magnitude of the observed relationships, it is usually more informative to provide some form of correlation coefficient or other measure of association.

The literature of the social sciences is full of cases in which the concept of "significance level" is misused. Frequently it is apparent that the individual researcher has not established any particular level of significance for accepting or rejecting the null hypothesis, but rather has made his statistical computations and decided about his level of significance afterward. Thus we find instances in which the researcher has found that his chi-square or Fisher Exact test computation results in a p value of .065. He then declares that the relationship is "almost significant." In discussing this "almost significant" finding he may make such statements as "The data show a strong tendency in support of the hypothesis."

Strict application of the logic of these statistical tests leaves no room for this kind of post hoc interpretation of data. If the researcher was operating with a .05 level of significance, then his finding of a p value of .065 requires that he accept the null hypothesis. If he had intended to consider a p value of .065 as representing "strong tendencies toward support of his hypotheses" then he should have established a significance level of .10 before proceeding to statistical analysis.

We should note that there is no absolute rule about what level of significance should be used. Some social scientists appear to consider anything that does not reach the .01 level of probability to be unworthy of further consideration. (There is a widespread understanding that certain journals of psychology are extremely hesitant to accept any research results that do not operate with a .01 significance level.) Above I have mentioned that the .05 level of significance is quite commonly applied in anthropological work.

The central point to understand is that levels of significance are a simple technical device for assisting the researcher in making decisions to accept or reject particular hypotheses. It would seem likely that the researcher is most interested in making the correct decisions from his statistical analysis. If he insists that his results must be at the .01 level of statistical significance, he can be relatively confident that he is making no mistakes involving rejection of the null hypothesis when it should not be rejected. On the other hand, when such stringent requirements are invoked, the researcher greatly increases his chances of *accepting* the null hypothesis, when it in fact is "not true." Statisticians refer to these two different mistakes as Type I and Type II errors. Rejecting the null hypothesis when the null hypothesis is correct is a Type I error. Failure to reject the null hypothesis when one should do so is a Type II error. From the discussion above we can easily see that the probabilities of these two types of error vary inversely. Thus the overly strict researcher does not maximize correct decision making. Rather, he is maximizing a particular kind of decision for which he is paying a cost—in the form of a higher probability of making a Type II error.

Different statistical tests have different efficacies in promoting correct decision making. The efficiency of a statistical test in furthering correct decisions is referred to as the *power* of the test. Comparisons of the relative powers of different tests are often given in statistics texts. Statistical computations are also available to determine the respective probabilities of Type I and Type II errors, given a particular statistic.

Statistical significance does not mean the same thing as theoretical or practical significance. As already noted, with a very large sample of subjects one can always find *some* statistically significant differences between populations. Yet the true differences between the populations may be relatively trivial. Triviality, of course, is itself a relative matter, depending on the nature of the subject. If the question is the relative numbers of Republican and Democrat voters in a given population, a true difference of 1 percent in either direction can be highly significant practically (that is, politically), even though the amount of difference is not particularly large. On the other hand, if we are interested in examining, say, the differences in "intelligence" between population A and population B, a difference of 1 or 2 percent between the two populations may be significant statistically, yet the information is not particularly useful theoretically or practically, for it would not enable one to predict very much about the performances or activities of the two populations.

Statistical computations cannot, therefore, tell us all we wish to know about our data. The calculations assist us in making certain decisions and statements about these data, but beyond the point of accepting or rejecting null hypotheses and making some other descriptive statements, including the degree of association, we should step back from statistics and exercise "common sense." Independently of statistics, we must make our decisions about the magnitude of contribution, or the usefulness as information, of particular research findings. Usefulness must be assessed in terms of how well the particular data help to fill gaps in the network of propositions in social sciences theory, and at the same time individual research findings can be evaluated in terms of the possibilities of making correct, practical predictions of human behavior related to social problems.

The Meehl Paradox: Some Problems
in Hypothesis Testing

In psychology, sociology, and other sectors of the social sciences it has become increasingly usual to find research structured in the following general form:

1. Statement of a problem involving two or more variables and their interrelationships.
2. Presentation of research hypotheses.
3. Statement of methods of research.
4. Statistical tests of significance concerning the hypotheses.
5. Acceptance (on the basis of statistical tests) of the hypotheses.
6. Explanation concerning one or two relationships that "didn't turn out" in the predicted manner.
7. Statement concerning the theoretical advances achieved.

It is important to note in connection with this research paradigm that the main efforts of the researcher are directed toward finding some sort of statistically significant differences between his two populations, or his two sets of observations. This general model of theory testing has been subjected to a damaging critique by Paul E. Meehl (1967).

Meehl points out first that there is a basic contrast in the way measurements are used in physics (and the other "hard sciences") and in the social sciences. Measurements in physics are intended to present *point values* of variables, while the research designs of the social sciences are concerned not with point values but with predicting *probable differences*.

For example, temperature as a dependent variable in a physics experiment is usually predicted exactly from a mathematical equation; in a social science situation a comparable dependent variable is most likely to be predicted in a general form, such as: "It will be greater," "It will vary inversely with (another variable)," or simply, "It will be correlated with." The exact *value* of the variable is not predicted. Meehl points out that, given this fundamental difference in measurement strategy, increased precision in physics (and related sciences) logically should lead to more and more rigorous testing of theoretical propositions, while increased precision of measurement in the social sciences *logically leads to the increasing probability of finding some differences, hence a weaker corroboration of the hypotheses tested*. Meehl shows that, "in most psychological research, improved power of a statistical design leads to a prior probability approaching one half of finding a significant difference in the theoretically predicted direction" (Meehl, 1967:103). This same argument would of course apply to similar hypothesis testing in other social sciences, including anthropology.

One of the ways in which researchers in the social sciences regularly "improve" their research designs is to increase the size of the sample. Increasing the size of the sample, as already pointed out in earlier discussions, can lead to a situation where there will be a high likelihood of finding statistically significant differences between populations. To demonstrate this proposition empirically, Meehl and his associates used a sample of over 55,000 Minnesota high-school seniors and tested the interrelationships among such variables as sex, birth order, religious preference, number of siblings, vocational choice, club membership, college choice, mother's education, interest in dancing, interest in woodworking, liking for school, and so on. They found statistically significant relationships in 91 percent of the pair-wise associations tested. The logic of limited possibilities assures us that, since differences in populations (generally) can have only two directions, the researcher's hypothesis is bound to be right *one half of the time* in randomly appearing *but statistically significant differences* in the populations.

Meehl points out that two populations will "quasi always" differ, since there is an infinite number of external factors, problems of reliability, and other elements that will differentially affect the two populations. Improvement of psychological measuring devices (or other social sciences operations) is likely to *increase* the probability of such differences becoming statistically significant.

Meehl also points out that researchers typically find that some of their predicted associations do not turn out the way they had expected, and in such cases the investigator usually presents a post hoc explanation of the results, pointing to contaminating variables that had not been considered in an earlier analysis of the research design. Such post hoc analysis of statistical results cannot be regarded as successful tests of a hypothesis; they have no status in theory building other than as suggestions for future research.

If social scientists take Meehl's argument seriously (as they should) the entire structure of theory building by means of statistically manipulated hypothesis tests is called into question. Particularly questionable are any results of hypothesis tests based on extremely large samples of cases (however paradoxical this statement may appear at first glance). Also open to suspicion are all propositions about relationships which have been tested *only once*. However, there are some roads that may lead past the apparent impasse.

Clearly, any theoretical investigation which involves the testing of whole networks of hypotheses, on several different samples of data, with each general theorem examined in terms of a series of subhypotheses, is a much stronger research design than is the one in which only one hypothesis is tested with one statistical operation. For example, the cross-cultural testing of a series of social-structural theorems by Murdock (1949) presents a fairly strong statistical case, because he tested his general ideas with a battery of over a hundred statistical operations. Similarly, Aronoff's theoretical structure concerning psychological differences between fishermen and cane cutters in the British West Indies is supported by a network of 30 or 40 statistical tests of hypotheses.

Anthropological research usually includes a feature of methodology that is often lacking in psychological and sociological research. The anthropologist, however much significance he attaches to statistical tests of parts of his data, generally prefers to have a large amount of contextual information, including personal observations, anecdotal evidence, descriptions of logical interrelationships, demonstration of linguistic behavior, and other nonquantified support and explanation built up in support of the proposition he is testing. Thus the "credibility" of the statistical material is enhanced.

Some of the main ways in which social scientists can minimize the effects of Meehl's metholological paradox are as follows.

1. Any given general theorem should be tested in the form of a large network of hypotheses. Support for the general theorem should involve confirmation in the overwhelming proportion of the individual statistical tests.
2. Propositions should be tested on a number of different populations.
3. The proposition should be subjected to test by a series of different research instruments.
4. The proposition should be subjected to a re-examination by other investigators using the first investigator's carefully specified operations.
5. Random samples should be carefully selected, and should not be particularly large.
6. If statistically significant results are found in an examination of relatively large sample populations, these differences should not be accorded much theoretical importance unless the demonstrated associations are fairly large in absolute magnitude.

Specialized Competence in Statistics

From even a casual review of recent anthropological literature, it seems clear that an increasing number of anthropologists have developed competence in the use of inferential statistical procedures. This trend will continue in the future. But statistics represents only one of a number of different new areas of competence that anthropologists may feel a need to acquire. Boundaries between disciplines become blurred, and some anthropologists have invested considerable effort in learning the tools and theoretical procedures of sociologists, for example. Others, interested in economic patterns among primitive and peasant peoples, have felt the need to learn new research techniques from the economists. Ecologically oriented studies frequently appear naïve if the anthropologist researcher has not familiarized himself with the expertise of geographers, agricultural economists, biologists, and so on.

The fact is that anthropologists have been committed for a long time to the study of "whole cultures," and this can only lead the researcher to a desperate struggle to master the main lines of competence of some adjacent social sciences, in addition to other related bodies of knowledge. Mastery of statistics, then, presents but a further indignity to the already thinly spread efforts of the anthropologist. It is even more discouraging when the anthropologist has made a considerable attempt to learn the rudiments of statistics and finds that his new research tools only increase his vulnerability to criticism from people with (supposedly) more statistical sophistication.

In many cases anthropologists (and other social scientists) would be well advised to seek the counsel and friendship of competent statisticians. It often requires some searching to find statisticians who are interested in the problems of the social sciences, and who are willing to be somewhat flexible in the face of the harsh realities of anthropological field work—in which samples are, strictly speaking, never absolutely random, and many supposedly crucial assumptions of statistical procedure must be violated. Our experience has been that, for every statistician who throws up his hands in horror at the looseness of statistical usage in anthropology, another can be found who finds no difficulty in making a few methodological compromises because of the realities of anthropological data. The anthropologist who needs statistical help should, therefore, keep searching until he finds a flexible statistician—one who has some knowledge of the problems of the social sciences.

Any anthropologist undertaking a project that involves quantification, population sampling, and statistical testing of hypotheses should seek the advice of a professional statistician. Larger projects should, if possible, employ statisticians as part of their multidisciplinary staffs. But the anthropologist should be aware of differences among statisticians, for not all statisticians will fit in satisfactorily with a social scientist research team.

All this does not excuse the anthropologist from learning the rudiments of statistics for himself. There are three main reasons why every anthropologist needs to develop a certain minimal competence in statistical analysis.

1. In many areas of research the anthropologist will encounter situations in which at least elementary statistics are needed. A certain minimum level of statistical orientation is necessary so that the anthropologist can recognize these situations and either apply statistical procedures himself or seek competent advice.
2. On those occasions when the anthropologist clearly needs statistical advice of a more sophisticated nature, he must be able to communicate with the statistician—to describe his research intentions in ways that "make sense" to the statistician, and to understand the advice that is offered.
3. Finally, the anthropologist nowadays must be able to read and understand a wide variety of literature that involves statistical operations. While the producers of statistically analyzed research usually make attempts to present their data in such form that it is easily understood by nonstatistical readers, an increasing number of complicated debates and discussions concerning interpretation of statistical material are appearing. It is no longer possible for the general anthropologist to ignore the statistical problems

current in the literature; and it is not easy to make an honest assessment of those materials without at least an elementary background in statistics.

REFERENCES CITED

ARMSTRONG, J. SCOTT
1967. "Derivation of Theory by Means of Factor Analysis *or* Tom Swift and His Electric Factor Analysis Machine." *American Statistician,* 21:17–21.

ARMSTRONG, J. SCOTT, and PEER SOELBERG
1968. "On the Interpretation of Factor Analysis." *Psychological Bulletin,* 70(5):361–364.

ARONOFF, JOEL
1967. *Psychological Needs and Cultural Systems: A Case Study.* New York: Van Nostrand. © 1967 by Litton Educational Publishing, Inc. By permission of Van Nostrand Reinhold Company.

CHILD, IRVIN, MARGARET K. BACON, and HERBERT BARRY, III
1965. *A Cross Cultural Study of Drinking.* Quarterly Journal of Studies on Alcohol Supplement No. 3, p. 10. Copyright by Journal of Studies on Alcohol, Inc., New Brunswick, N. J. Reprinted by permission.

COHEN, JACOB
1968. "Multiple Regression as a General Data-Analytic System." *Psychological Bulletin* 70(6):426–443.

DRIVER, HAROLD E.
1961. "Introduction to Statistics for Comparative Research." In *Readings in Cross-Cultural Methodology,* ed. Frank W. Moore. New Haven: Human Relations Area Files.

DRIVER, HAROLD E., and KARL F. SCHUESSLER
1967. "Correlational Analysis of Murdock's 1957 Ethnographic Sample." *American Anthropologist,* 69:332–352.

FREED, STANLEY
1963. "An Objective Method for Determining the Collective Caste Hierarchy of an Indian Village." *American Anthropologist,* 65:879–891. Reproduced by permission of the American Anthropological Association.

FREEMAN, LINTON C.
1965. *Elementary Applied Statistics: For Students in Behavioral Science.* New York: Wiley.

MEEHL, PAUL
1967. "Theory-testing in Psychology and Physics: A Methodological Paradox." *Philosophy of Science,* 34(2):103–115.

MURDOCK, GEORGE P.
1949. *Social Structure.* New York: Macmillan. © 1949 by The Macmillan Co. Reprinted with permission.

PELTO, PERTTI J.
1968. "The Differences between 'Tight' and 'Loose' Societies." *Transaction,* 5 (5)37–40.

POGGIE, JOHN J., JR.
1968. "The Impact of Industrialization on a Mexican Intervillage Network." Unpublished Ph.D. thesis. University of Minnesota.

RUMMEL, R. J.
1968. "Understanding Factor Analysis." *Journal of Conflict Resolution,* XI (4)444–479.

SAWYER, JACK, and ROBERT A. LEVINE
1966. "Cultural Dimensions: A Factor Analysis of the World Ethnographic Sample." *American Anthropologist,* 68:708–731. Reproduced by permission of the American Anthropological Association.

SCHENSUL, STEPHEN
1969. "Marginal Rural Peoples: Behavior and Cognitive Models Among Northern Minnesotans and Western Ugandans." Unpublished Ph.D. thesis. University of Minnesota.

SIEGEL, SIDNEY
1956. *Non-parametric Statistics for the Behavioral Sciences.* New York: McGraw-Hill.

Reindeer Roundup in Lapland

8. Art and Science in Field Work

Strategies in the Art of Field Work

Anthropologists have awakened to the great need for a thorough examination of the processes of data collection in the field. Research in human communities is inevitably complex and personalized, but many parts of it can become more systematic than they have been in the past. Open discussion of ethnographers' experiences and methods is removing some of the mystique of field work and is helping to identify those aspects which can be made more explicitly operational and quantified. Some of the important new literature on field work includes edited collections of papers such as Freilich's *Marginal Natives* (1969), Epstein's *The Craft of Social Anthropology* (1967), and *Anthropologists in the Field* (Jongmans and Gutkind, 1967). Powdermaker's autobiographic recollections in

Stranger and Friend (1966), Bowen's *Return to Laughter* (1954), Beattie's *Understanding an African Kingdom* (1965), and Berreman's *Behind Many Masks* (1962) are good examples of the growing collection of illuminating personal documents about field work.

Anthropological research has most often been carried out through intensive study in one or a few relatively small communities. Thus, the anthropologist who engages in field work in a society (e.g., Navaho, Zulu, Tiv, Mexican peasants) does not generally take that entire society as his unit of analysis. Instead, he chooses some community within that society as a primary base of operations. Intensive study is carried out in the chosen community, and observations about other villages, localities, or groups in the general population usually assume a secondary role.

If there are important differences among the communities of a particular society (e.g., the coastal *vs.* upland peoples), the anthropologist may limit his generalizations to one group or the other. Often, however, community studies are presented as "typical" of a given culture or subculture, without regard for the possible subcultural variations among the towns, villages, or other local units of the society.

Community study has persisted as a principal mode of anthropological field work because of some very important advantages. It generally provides a clear definition of the research area; boundaries can be drawn, and the population to be studied can (usually) be clearly delimited. Second, transportation requirements are minimized if much of the researcher's time is to be spent in a single village, hamlet, or town. Many of his informants or research subjects will be within walking distance.

Anthropologists have made important assumptions about the naturalness of communities as social units. It is generally felt that villages or towns are semiautonomous and "complete" social systems, in which most of the significant variables or factors affecting individual behavior are to be found within the local system. Influences from the "outside world" must certainly be noted and described, but these are frequently thought to be less important than the local cultural patterns and, particularly, the primary, face-to-face social relationships that occur within the bounds of the community.

One important reason for anthropological concentration on community studies is often overlooked. Since field-work projects, whatever their structure, usually involve months and sometimes years of residence in cultural milieus that are much removed from the anthropologist's home base, it is likely that the fieldworker has strong psychological needs to develop a network of local social ties, at least to organize the procurement of the basic necessities of life. Housing must be obtained; clothes must be laundered; food must be purchased, traded for, or produced by the fieldworker himself; and dozens of other everyday details of living require attention. These requirements of living imbed the fieldworker in his community of residence. However much he tries to gather data to an equal extent from a number of different areas, he always turns out to have far more information about, and involvement with, his primary base of operations. (Generally anthropologists have found it unsatisfactory to commute to their research sites, though exceptions can be noted.)

In addition to fulfilling standard physical needs, the community comes to satisfy more diffuse psychological needs as well. Usually the anthropologist establishes special friendly relationships with one or two best informants. He may confide in them about his problems of adjustment, he often spends off hours in idle conversation or other recreation with these friends, and he may need to rely on them for special help, even including loans of money and supplies. The lone anthropologist is, of course, especially in need of companionship, but married couples are not immune to these psychological needs. However amiable the relationships between spouses in the field, both man and wife will often feel the need for solid friendships outside the tight confines of the research team. These psychological needs do not require that field work be structured in the form of community study, but maximum congruence between the fieldworker's personal needs and his research goals is often best attained in the community-study research structure.

CHOOSING A SITE

John Beattie has described in some detail how he chose a research community among the populous, geographically dispersed Bunyoro:

First, the community I settled in had to be, so far as I could judge, a reasonably representative one; as typical as possible of rural Bunyoro. Of course I could not at that time know with certainty exactly what *was* typical, but at least I could exclude from consideration areas that were obviously not so; those which were close to and therefore affected by either of Bunyoro's two towns, for example, or which neighbored one of the country's few nonnative estate. . . .

Secondly, my chosen area had to be reasonably remote not only from Hoima, but also from the local county or subcounty chief's headquarters. These were generally on or near main roads, and to have lived too close to one, with its office and court and, sometimes, its English-speaking clerks, would have made direct contact with the rural community itself more difficult. . . .

. . . thirdly (and not perhaps wholly consistently with the foregoing), my base had to be accessible, if not too easily so, by motor vehicle, so that

I could move my equipment there, obtain supplies and mail, and maintain some contact with the outside world without undue difficulty and expense.

And lastly, and most importantly of all, I wanted to find an area where not only did the local subcounty chief and his headmen seem to be reasonably cooperative and to have some understanding of what I was aiming to do, but also where the people themselves . . . seemed willing to put up with an intrusive European and even to help him in his task. (Beattie, 1965:13–14.)

Beattie's statement about his criteria for selecting a research site illustrates some common tendencies in anthropological practice. The typical village (or hamlet or district) is sought among those that are relatively removed from towns and villages, for in some sense they are thought to be more "pure." On the other hand, the community selected for research must be socially tolerable. Other things being equal (and even if they are not), the anthropologist will tend to study those communities in which the people seem cooperative and friendly.

Anthropologists have not always stressed the search for a typical community. Some research sites appear to have been selected because they were *atypical*. The most isolated and traditional community is often chosen; sometimes the most impressively beautiful town is selected; in other cases the anthropologist chooses a community because he happened to establish social contact with some of its members before he actually arrived on the local scene. In a significant number of cases anthropologists have selected particular research communities because the same community had been studied earlier by an anthropologist, thus providing a baseline for comparisons (Gallagher, 1961; Phillips, 1966; Oscar Lewis, 1963; Charles Leslie, 1960; and many others).

ASPECTS OF "IMPRESSION MANAGEMENT"

Usually the fieldworker's first concern after selecting a research community is to find a suitable headquarters—a combination household-and-research-center. Locating such a base of operations often depends on obtaining "official" permission to carry out research in the community. The researcher's quarters should be relatively central to "where the action is," but ideally it should be neutral with regard to significant social cleavages in the community. That is, the fieldworker nearly always assumes that his choice of living quarters will be a significant item of information in terms of which the local people judge his social role and affiliations. To accept housing in, for example, the governmental office building, the rectory, or the police station requires careful consideration of the local people's attitudes toward these authorities.

In some relatively tight communities, with well-developed bound-ary-maintenance mechanisms, the fieldworker may find that he must accept the dictates of local authorities with regard to the selection of his residence, if he has been successful in obtaining permission for the research activity. For example, those anthropologists who have studied "total institutions," such as prisons and mental hospitals often have to accept the quarters allocated to them by the administrators.

The fieldworker frequently has a choice between living with a family in the community or setting up a separate household. His decision in the matter involves a number of factors—willingness of local families to accept a stranger, extent of personal equipment, information about the social characteristics of potential "landlords," type of research intended (study of family interaction and socialization practices may be greatly facilitated by living with a local family), and relative centrality of the available alternatives. Thomas Rhys Williams maximized centrality in his choice of living arrangements among the Dusun:

In Sensuron we rented the village headman's house for about five dollars a month. The house was already a focal point of daily village routines and centrally located. The headman moved next door into another house. (Williams, 1967:14.)

In many communities there are no "vacancies," and new houses must be built for newcomers. Powdermaker has described some features of her house in Lesu:

Both men had supervised the finishing of my house (begun before my arrival for visiting government patrols), the building of the privy, the making of a primitive shower, adding a room to the cook-house for a servant's bedroom, and all the other details of settling in. Compared to the one-room village huts whose floor was the ground, my house seemed luxurious. It was raised from the ground and had two windowless rooms with a wide veranda between them and a narrow one around the sides of the house. One room was for sleeping and the other for keeping supplies. I worked, received company, and ate on the wide section of the veranda. The thatched roof was an advantage in the tropics. (Powdermaker, 1966: 51–52.)

Berreman (1962, 1963) was able to find rather less than comfortable quarters for his research in a Pahari village in north India. He comments, "My village house consisted of three small connecting rooms, one of which was occupied continuously by two to four water buffalo, and all of which were inferior to those inhabited by most villagers."

Joel Halpern, in his study of a Serbian village, lived at the home of the secretary of the local village council. In this case the decision about residence was made by the local officials.

Upon our arrival in Orasac, a conference as to where we would be lodged was immediately held among the leading officials: the Director of the school, the President and Secretary of the Village Council, and the President of the Village Cooperative. The house of the Secretary of the Village Council was unanimously agreed upon, and there we remained for our year's stay.

His house had the disadvantage of being located some distance from the center of the village. This was more than compensated for by the fact there were six members—three generations—in the household: his parents, his wife, and his young son and daughter, all of whom were very friendly and later proved themselves to be eager and dependable informants. (Halpern, 1958:xii.)

There are, of course, many field-research situations in which housing as such is not a problem, since the people—particularly in nomadic herding and hunting-and-gathering groups—rely on relatively simple and portable dwellings. In such cases the anthropologist can erect his tent in whatever location the local group suggests; he is rather more concerned with establishing social ties than in finding a place of residence. In extreme cases the would-be researcher may have major difficulties even in finding the group he has chosen to study. Allan Holmberg described his initial (and successful) contact with the nomadic Siriono as follows:

We followed the rude trails which had been made by the Indians about 3 months earlier, and after passing many abandoned huts, each one newer than the last, we finally arrived at midday on the eleventh day of March just outside of a village. On the advice of our Indian companions, Silva and I removed most of our clothes, so as not to be too conspicuous in the otherwise naked party—I at least had quite a tan—and leaving behind our guns and all supplies except a couple of baskets of roast peccary meat, which we were saving as a peace gesture, we sandwiched ourselves in between our Indian guides and made a hasty entrance into the communal hut. The occupants, who were enjoying a midday siesta, were so taken by surprise that we were able to start talking with them in their own language before they could grasp their weapons and flee. Moreover, as their interest almost immediately settled on the baskets of peccary meat, we felt secure within a few moments' time and sent back for the rest of our supplies. (Holmberg, 1969:xxi.)

In obtaining permission for research, selecting living quarters, announcing oneself to the populace, contacting prospective informants, and making other opening moves of field work, the fieldworker is highly conscious of the importance of what Berreman and others have referred to as *impression management*. Success in the art of field work depends, to a considerable extent, on establishing a very special social role that legitimatizes a kind of information-getting behavior which was not previously part of social expectations within the community. Thus, it is not true that the anthropologist tries to become "just like" the people he studies. He may identify with them vis-à-vis certain kinds of outsiders, eat the same foods and subject himself to the same diseases and hardships, learn some of their special skills and crafts and learn to dance and sing "like a native," but his role as gatherer of information, persistent asker of questions, and stranger from another culture are always part of his local social identity. The local people do not forget that he will ultimately leave them, carrying his notebooks, films, and other information-storage apparatus back to that other world from whence he came.

Normal human communities do not include within them social roles which permit individuals to ask relatively personal questions from all families, factions, and social types. In the first place, much of the information gathering is unnecessary for persons *within* the system, for they already know the answers. Also, even in the most benign human groups there are sharp limits to the amount and kind of social information that is allowed to pass from one family or group to another.

The situation in a Ladino community of Chiapas, Mexico, described by John C. Hotchkiss (1967) illustrates a fairly extreme expression of these common human tendencies. The walls of their houses, the shawls that women pull tightly around their faces (and over their market baskets), and the conversational habits of both men and women sharply restrict the flow of social knowledge within the community. For the Teopiscanecos, as Hotchkiss notes,

Information about oneself that becomes a topic of general gossip has escaped one's control. It might be used in ways that are damaging to one's reputation. A Teopiscaneco is concerned about his reputation because he knows that in his face-to-face encounters with others, the image of self that he presents must be congruent with his reputation, which nearly everyone in town has knowledge of or holds opinions about. (Hotchkiss, 1967: 713.)

Because of the severe restrictions on the flow of information, children of the community are trained to gather gossip as they go about their errands of shopping, vending, carrying water, and delivering messages. "When a child returns from an errand, he is extensively interrogated by an adult of his household to find out what the child has learned" (*ibid.,* 715).

Not all human communities restrict the flow of social information as much as do these Ladinos of Chiapas, but the work of an ethnographer requires that he be permitted to elicit much more of such gossip than can ever be customary anywhere. Since members of every human society seek to suppress knowledge of their personal failures, family secrets, economic and social strategies, and many other topics, the anthropologist must, in seeking access to such information, establish for himself a radically new kind of role in the community—that of neutral observer. In some respects he must be like the children of the Teopiscanecos: he must be defined as outside the adult social-prestige system. On the other hand, children are known to carry tales back to their parents; the anthropologist must make it known that he does not betray confidences.

Some people have written as if the ethnographer gains access to local private information to the degree that he becomes identified as a local—an *insider*. This is, of course, very important—up to a point. Beyond that point the fieldworker is privy to significant social information because he is an *outsider*—someone who is different from every other member of the community. He is different because his core prestige ultimately rests on membership in another, socially distant society; he is neutral in the local competitive scene; he can be trusted; he does not generally judge people's conduct in moral terms; and he offers social rewards in exchange for information. Occasionally he pays in cash or goods. Often he can be relied on for medicines and transportation. But, perhaps most important of all, he provides the possibility for social intraction in which the rules are suspended to a certain extent. Friendship and social affiliation can be obtained from him with relatively little social risk, because he is not competing for prestige in the same social arena. In some respects his role is not unlike that of the psychotherapist, as described by William Schofield (1964) in his *Psychotherapy: the Purchase of Friendship*. The difference is that the ethnographer receives information rather than money in the exchange.

Hazards and Punishments of Field Work

Maintaining an effective researcher role appears to be relatively easy in some types of societies, particularly those lacking well-defined boundary-maintenance mechanisms or serious intracommunity social cleavages (Pelto, 1969). Even in unusually benign instances the field researcher must be very sensitive in his presentation of self and management of social interactions. In most cases, though, the fieldworker encounters social complexities and problems at every turn, and successful role maintenance demands great presence of mind, flexibility, and luck. (Serendipity in scientific research always looms large, as Beveridge and others have demonstrated [see Chapter 2]; field work is no exception.)

Even the fieldworker's good luck often has ambiguous consequences. In the opening moves of field work he may be overjoyed when certain individuals begin to overwhelm him with information and attention. But every firm social relationship with a particular individual or group carries with it the possibility of closed doors and social rebuffs from competing segments of the community. This "social-competition effect" may be particularly operative in early phases of field work, when the anthropologist is highly vulnerable psychologically and before he has had a chance to teach his audience the dimensions of his special participant-observer role.

Berreman's (1962) play-by-play description of social management and field work in a Himalayan village is a striking illustration of how complex the fieldworker's problems can become, frequently without his awareness.

Having selected his research site with considerable care, Berreman entered the village accompanied by his high-caste interpreter-assistant and bearing a letter of introduction from a merchant who had had contacts with the village. Unknown to Berreman (1962:6), the merchant had engaged in sharp practices in his dealings with the villagers, so that, "As might have been expected, our benefactor was not beloved in the village and it was more in spite of his intercession than on account of it that we ultimately managed to do a year's research in the village." (Furthermore, the note was addressed to a high-caste man who was one of the most suspicious people in the village.)

After weeks and months of initial difficulties and frustrations the social identification of Berreman's assistant enabled the research team to develop relatively good rapport with some of the high-caste families of the community, so they were able to gain entrée to some "backstage" aspects of community life. On the other hand, social contacts among low-caste groups were correspondingly distant and frustrating. Thus, Berreman found:

> Our informants were primarily high-caste villagers intent on impressing us with their near conformity to the standards of behavior and belief of high-caste plainsmen. Low-caste people were respectful and reticent before us, primarily, as it turned out, because one of us was a Brahmin and we were closely identified with the high-caste villagers. (*Ibid.*, 9.)

Here enters serendipity disguised as catastrophe. Berreman's highly capable and loyal assistant became ill and had to leave the field. Morale dipped to a new low as the researcher cast about for a substitute to fill this delicate role. His new assistant was a Muslim, who was immediately defined by the community as low in general status, though his age engendered a measure of respect. As field work progressed under these new social conditions (which inevitably had strong effects on Berreman's role in the eyes of the village), a new and different side of the community began to emerge. The researcher soon developed rapport with low-caste groups, who proved to be much more open and informative than the Brahmins and Rajputs. Gradually a coherent picture of the intricacies of local social organization began to emerge. Had he entered the village initially with this assistant, however, the whole research effort might have failed, Berreman felt. "I might well have been unable to establish rapport . . . if my initial contact had been in the company of a Muslim interpreter" (*ibid.*, 21).

Sources of Tension in Field Work

While the problems of gaining acceptance in the local community (and a host of other frustrations and dangers) may have been exceptionally difficult in Berreman's Himalayan village, it is likely that most field ethnographers work under severe psychological tension much of the time. Köbben (1967) noted about his field work among Bush Negroes of Surinam that

since an ethnographer studies people and not insects, his field work also causes emotions in himself. Personally, I lived under great psychological stress and felt little of the proverbial peacefulness of "country life." Few books touch on this subject, but I know that the same is true of quite a number of other field workers. Perhaps it is even a *sine qua non* for field work. (Köbben, 1967:46.)

Another important source of these psychological tensions is the moral conflict that arises whenever the human values of the fieldworker conflict with events in the community (and with his scientific attitudes). The anthropologist, who is generally assumed to be a more than usually sensitive human observer, is, in the course of field work, frequently introduced to human misery that he could prevent if he used his social power and economic resources to interfere in local affairs. In some cultures he may encounter food practices that systematically deprive children of an adequately balanced diet (Gerlach, 1964), yet, as an outsider and guest of the community, he cannot interfere. On occasion he may have information that would permit subservient or disadvantaged people to protect themselves from the actions of the dominant élite of a community, but any interference by the fieldworker would mean that he would have to violate the confidences of his informants, and this would seriously jeopardize his work.

A scientific purist might insist that the anthropologist in no way interfere with the course of local cultural behavior. However, most fieldworkers have felt no qualm (scientific or otherwise) in providing medicines, drugs, and other special aid to people who would normally have no access to these facilities. Fieldworkers have also been generous with transportation (the research jeep, Land Rover, or station wagon often becomes the village bus), as well as other resources that would not have been available had the fieldworker not entered the village.

The dilemma of the fieldworker, then, is not *whether* to interfere in the local cultural scene, but *how much* to interfere. Beattie has commented on the moral dilemmas of field work as follows:

Anthropologists have sometimes written as though all that need be considered is the effect of field work on the fieldworker himself; much less attention has been given to its effects on the people studied (Barnes 1963 is a notable exception). But, consciously or unconsciously, the anthropologist is affecting the people he is working with all the time. Obviously no responsible anthropologist will betray to the authorities the fact, say, that a neighbor has been distilling illicit liquor, or has successfully evaded a tax obligation. But it is very much a matter of degree. When I learned, for example, that a respected neighbor, employed in the local hospital, was stealing syringes and giving injections with an unsterilized needle to local people for a fee, I felt justified in suggesting to the medical authorities that increased vigilance might be desirable (and in attempting to persuade the amateur physician of the importance of asepsis). But I did not feel justified in reporting the matter to the police. The anthropologist who learns a good deal about his neighbors in confidence must respect that confidence, except for overwhelming reasons, though it is of course conceivable that there might be occasions when he should not. No hard and fast rules can be laid down; these are matters of conscience rather than of science. (Beattie, 1965:55.)

Some anthropologists have found themselves in serious difficulties because of complex political machinations touching on, and affected by, their research activities (e.g., Diamond, 1964); it is therefore generally taken for granted that the fieldworker should avoid getting into politics. Lisa Peattie (1968) has, on the other hand, described her intentional involvement in political action in the course of work in the Venezuelan "new city" of Ciudad Guayana. Valentine (1968) goes even further. He argues that the fieldworker *should* become a political activist on behalf of the people he is studying, if they are (as is frequently the case) relative have-nots in the developing world.

This view of participation also makes it possible for the ethnographer, within the limits of his own value system, to act from the ethical position that he has major obligations to the people he is studying. . . . It is in these ways that some ethnographers have become advocates or spokesmen for groups among whom they have worked, on occasion acting as vigorous partisans. (Valentine, 1968:188–189.)

His position stems in part from the fact that it is presented in the context of research on the urban poor—particularly the poor of the black ghettos. Frequently the anthropologist who engages in this kind of research is already committed to partisanship before he enters the field. But these political (and ethical) issues are becoming more and more directly relevant in every field-work setting. Making choices about these issues adds to the psychological pressures on the fieldworker.

Thus, to the complexities of assuming and managing the ambiguous role of resident researcher are added a series of problems in self-management—of maintaining emotional balance and effectiveness under severe pressures. (I have not discussed here the serious problems of physical health often faced by ethnographers. Berreman describes the importance of this factor, and Allan Holmberg's [1969] accounts of struggles with disease, fatigue, and plagues of insects are a vivid illustration of the physical side of the field-work experience.) Unless the anthropologist can maintain his balance in these social and psychological aspects of research, his good intentions about operationalizing variables, sampling procedures, and other elements of methodological rigor are useless.

Rosalie Wax has written a vivid account of the anxieties she experienced during research in a Japanese Relocation Center. In the early stages of field work—that period nearly every researcher experiences in which nothing is going well, when informants are hostile and evasive, and when the entire effort seems meaningless and farcical—she "succumbed to an urge to eat enormously and in three months gained thirty pounds" (Wax, 1960b:175).

Although solid data on this subject are scarce, widespread anecdotal evidence suggests that most fieldworkers experience periods of anxiety, depression, and helplessness, often accompanied by a strong tendency to withdraw from all data-gathering activity. One fieldworker tells privately of a considerable span of field time during which he spent most of his days perusing *The Reader's Digest* and eating peanut-butter sandwiches. It is perhaps not surprising that we find numbers of instances in which fieldworkers mention eating as an anxiety-relieving mechanism. Jean Briggs reports from her field work among the Eskimo: "My tent had become a refuge, into which I withdrew every evening . . . to repair ravages to my spirits with the help of bannock and peanut butter. So reviving were those hours of self-indulgence that I dreaded their loss" (Briggs, 1968: 333). The psychiatrist Ronald Wintrob has examined the various ways in which anthropologists react to the stresses of field work (Wintrob, 1969).

A number of fieldworkers have noted that brief vacations away from the research community can be excellent tension relievers—for both informants and researchers. After all, at least in small communities the ubiquitous presence of "the man with the notebook and a thousand questions" can be very taxing for the local inhabitants. They must surely wish that for once they could enact a small bit of local custom without having to explain it all to the anthropologist. A few days away—or even longer—in the city, at the beach, hiking in the mountains, or visiting a nearby game reservation—can give the fieldworker time to dissipate his anxieties and hostilities, get some needed physical rest, and perhaps restock some supplies. At the same time, the research community itself gets a rest. Often the return of the fieldworker after even a brief vacation is an occasion for a warm welcome, a reaffirmation of friendships. He may be treated like a returning relative, and a few slightly reluctant informants may have been opened up a bit in their willingness to give information.

The social-psychological hazards of field work, which make every successful research project an elaborate combination of scientific techniques and social artistry, may account for some of the mystique that has grown up around the subject. At this stage of our discipline we know distressingly little about the personalities of anthropologists and the effects on personality of the field-work "rite of passage," although Dennison Nash, in his essay "The Ethnologist as Stranger," has reviewed psychological data (Rorschach tests, etc.) on 25 anthropologists that indicate that "these anthropologists would be able to tolerate the ambiguity, inconsistency and predictable flux of the stranger's experience without resort to the perceptual distortions that more authoritarian types would find necessary" (Nash, 1963:161).

Any extensive discussion of the art of fieldwork should include (among other things) sections on selection of informants, on gifts and payments, on when to take notes, or tactics with photographic equipment, on interactions with outsiders, on the giving of parties, on when to break taboos, and on many other subjects related to the central issue of "impression management." In the course of successful fieldwork the anthropologist builds up and maintains a complicated role of "inside-outsider," "privileged stranger," or some variant on this theme, but the specific content and dynamics of this presentation of self varies a great deal from one community to another, and from one anthropologist to another. Because human communities differ a great deal in their cultural context, and because the personalities of anthropologists exhibit great variation, fixed rules and procedures for the artistic social-management side of fieldwork cannot be prescribed.

SEX AND FIELD WORK

The fieldworker's sexual relationships with his research community can be quite complex and difficult, but very little information has been published concerning sexual behavior in the research setting. Since the typical field ethnographer is a lone male, the local people are usually concerned about his intentions regarding their women. At John Beattie's "housewarming party" (during his first days in a Bunyoro community), an important man of the settlement admonished him "not to make friends with the local women" (Beattie, 1965:16). Robert Maxwell (1969) has commented on sexual involvement in the course of his field work in Samoa.

Female anthropologists, on the other hand, generally have the difficult task of making clear to local males that they are sexually unavailable. In fact, among those many peoples of the world who are unaccustomed to seeing women of marriageable age going about with no evidence of husband and family, the female anthropologist has some difficult explanations to make to both sexes in the research community. Powdermaker told her Lesu friends that she had been married and was divorced, adding that her exhusband "had not worked well, one of the reasons for native divorce" (Powdermaker, 1966:63). Apparently this explanation was accepted. Establishing a successful role definition with regard to sex requires subtlety in nonverbal communication, as well as verbal statements. Young female anthropologists who have persistent trouble in warding off the sexual advances of local males are often causing difficulties by inadvertent behavior patterns that are sexually provocative by local standards.

On the other hand, there has been a good deal of exaggeration concerning the difficulties of field work for female anthropologists in societies where males are considered highly predatory. In Mexico, for example, a great many young women have carried out effective field research without experiencing serious difficulties.

The matter of sexual relationships with the research community becomes important in another way in later phases of field work. Sexual relations are an important aspect of amicable ties within communities, and it is not uncommon for the anthropologist to be offered access to females as a gesture of friendship. Such a situation presents the fieldworker with a complex dilemma: sexual involvement with local women can lead to serious difficulties; on the other hand, to refuse can be interpreted as an unfriendly act. Adding to the problem are the insistent psychophysiological pressures of un-relieved sexual needs.

More than a simple expression of in-group solidarity was at stake in an incident described by Colin Turnbull (1962), in which he found himself suddenly presented with a beautiful sleeping partner from one of the Bantu villages of the northeast Congo region. Apparently one of the subchiefs, in seeking to cement relationships with the elusive Pygmies, hit upon the idea of creating an alliance by giving his daughter to the anthropologist. "No doubt the chief had in mind the considerable bride-wealth he could demand should, by any chance, his daughter bear a mulatto child. Still, it was good of him to send his prettiest daughter" (Turnbull, 1962:143). Turnbull reports that he extricated himself from this delicate situation by a complex agreement with Amina (the chief's daughter). "She was to stay with me and cook my food—and mend leaks in the roof every night. This way she would preserve her reputation and I mine, and there would be no complications. And so it was" (Turnbull, 1962:144). This arrangement lasted for some while, until the Pygmies moved camp, at which time Amina took the opportunity to return to her village.

In some areas of Mexico researchers have, in the context of fiestas or other convivial events, been offered sexual access to local women (Kilbride, n.d.). Since sexual prowess is a large element in the male-prestige system of Mexican communities, it may be difficult for the anthropologist to give a convincing reason for declining such a gesture of hospitality, particularly when the "host" is an important official of the town. As in the example above, the fieldworker must decide which course of action is the least harmful one in terms of self-image as well as field-work rapport. It is probably not realistic to make any categorical pronouncements about correct courses of action in these (and many other) complex social situations.

CLOTHING, PERSONAL HABITS, AND
IMPRESSION MANAGEMENT

Very little is known about the effects of anthropologists' clothing styles on their research. When we consider that in every human society styles of clothing are important signals of social status and role, it follows that the fieldworker can *always* influence local attitudes toward him by adopting particular habits of costume. At first thought we would be tempted to conclude that the anthropologist should dress "like everyone else in the village." But there are many reasons why this is not always the solution to be adopted.

1. In some cases fieldworkers have been admonished by their in-formants that they should *not* dress like the ordinary villagers,

since that would be a form of condescension. "If you dress up in a suit to go to see government officials, why do you not dress that way when you visit other people?" Naturally the attitudes of people vary greatly with regard to such interpretations.

2. Where the local populace has a distinctive local costume, early adoption of that mode of dress by the fieldworker may be regarded as presumptuous, since it implies an insider status which he has not as yet attained. On the other hand, at a later stage of field residence, it may be expected, or even required, that the anthropologist adopt local garb, as he gets to be defined as a member of the local community.

3. The mode of acquisition of local items of costume can be quite important. During field work in Lapland, I had the opportunity to sit in on a card game in which the stakes consisted of a multi-colored Lappish tunic. During the excitement of the game, expressions of opinion among the surrounding kibitzers made it clear to me that *if I won the tunic* my possession and use of it would be regarded as legitimate, since many tunics among the local men were obtained in a similar manner, at card games. After my highly opportune victory in the card game, several persons suggested means by which I could acquire other articles of Lapp costume.

4. Many peoples in the world of anthropological experience seem to be willing to accept the suggestion that the fieldworker comes from a cultural background where people have different customs, which legitimate his somewhat unusual tastes and habits. Laura Nader apparently had a bit of difficulty in convincing her Zapotec friends in Talea and Juquila that she was legitimately different from them, but when she did, she gained some important advantages.

The women constantly badgered me to grow my hair, to change my clothes. By experimenting I finally discovered that the best reply was to tell them that were they to visit my home country dressed as they were with such long pigtails they would be ridiculed. Much laughter would result from such conversations. I capitalized on their indecision as to how to categorize me and gained the greatest freedom of movement among both men and women. (Nader, 1964:vi.)

5. Many male anthropologists return from the field with luxuriant beards. In many cases the decision to grow a beard arises in part from the difficulties and discomforts of regular shaving (e.g., procurement of hot water may involve complex procedures), but beard growing has certain psychological accompaniments as well. Some times the extended field-work situation is the first time an individual ever really had a chance to try growing a beard. On the other hand, Michael Robbins and Philip Kilbride report that they were discouraged from growing beards by their Baganda informants. Having a beard was associated with certain disliked

people from another region. In some areas wearing of beards is associated with missionaries, which invokes status imagery that anthropologists usually try to avoid. Again, male fieldworkers in Mexico frequently grow mustaches after a time—possibly as a response to one signaling element in the general *machismo* complex of male prestige.

6. One of the most important clothing "regulations" for anthropologists is to avoid elements of dress that symbolize locally disliked types of persons, such as administrators, missionaries, rich merchants, and the like. If the "people from the government" wear shiny leather boots, the anthropologist finds other types of foot gear; if the police wear heavy leather belts, it is perhaps best to find some other type of trouser support; and so on. The same principles apply with female fieldworkers, though they usually have a broader variety of symbols to work with. Sometimes the simple practice of wearing fairly visible lipstick is enough to disassociate oneself from undesirable roles, such as that of missionary lady.

It is important to keep in mind relationships between habits of dress and the signaling of sexual attitudes. Sometimes wearing lipstick is, in itself, considered provocative; slacks and shorts are not appropriate attire in many areas of the world (though they are perfectly acceptable in others); and miniskirts may be quite advantageous in some aspects of research in urban societies.

7. While the status-signal aspect of clothing and personal adornment is extremely important, practical considerations should not be lost sight of. The fieldworker must protect himself from cold, heat, and other physical hazards; at the same time he must be able to carry certain minimal equipment—at least notebook and pencil—at all times; and fussing with the complexities of clothing must not interfere with his field work. Since the anthropologist does *not* generally become defined as a complete insider, some defiance of dress style, whether dictated by practical needs or other motives, is usually feasible.

8. Research in complex urban environments presents a whole new set of problems about clothing strategies. Frequently the anthropologist does well to adopt the rule: Dress inconspicuously. In some situations (e.g., door-to-door interview work) it is important to signal a certain measure of prestige and status by wearing coat and tie. At other times, in working with low-status groups in an informal setting, much more casual costume is called for. The fieldworker who attends parties among urban hippies should probably not wear a suit and tie.

All of the comments here are intended only as general suggestions about dress habits in field work; few anthropologists report on these things, so each new fieldworker must explore these problems for himself.

At this point some observers of the anthropological scene would suggest that the nature of ethnographic work, because of the kinds of problems reviewed above, makes "scientific" field studies impossible. But examination of the stuff of anthropological work demonstrates to us that fieldworkers have, despite these hazards and problems, been able to carry out a truly amazing variety of specialized and relatively standardized data gathering. In their complicated insider-outsider roles, anthropologists have collected meticulous census and genealogical data; they have gathered information about private family activities and possessions; their notebooks have been filled with details of juridical cases and other special events that would astound the most intellectual and knowledgeable of local leaders; and they have obtained psychological tests, blood samples, urine specimens, accounts of dreams, life histories, and myriad other data which, had these been gathered by any *insider* in the community, would have resulted in his being lynched, or at least removed from social respectability.

Since descriptions of ethnographic field work provide extensive documentation of *both* the artistic and the scientific sides of research, we should now turn our attention to the empirical aspect of field data gathering. In spite of the large role of intuition in fieldwork, we have no reason to shrink from the possibility that a considerable portion of our field materials can be operationalized and quantified.

Elements of Community Study

Several important works in the anthropological literature set out details of *what* the fieldworker should study in the community, though these sources often give few details of how the tasks should be carried out. *Notes and Queries* (1951) has long been an important field guide for anthropologists, and Murdock's *Outline of Cultural Materials* (1950) is also a standard item to include in one's field research kit. There are also a number of more specialized guides to field operations, such as the *Field Guide for the Study of Socialization* by Whiting and associates (1968). If we examine the kinds of data that are present in most good ethnographic studies, it appears that certain field-work operations can be regarded as fundamental to general community description, however specialized the theoretical orientation of the anthropologist.

CENSUS TAKING AND MAPPING

The fieldworker should try to make a full enumeration of all family units and their membership near the beginning of field work. This is often an ideal first task for one's local field assistants; the accuracy of their work can be checked systematically by spot inspection. In many research contexts today, some sort of enumeration of household units is available from the records of the municipal authorities, the school system, church records, the post office, or other authorities. These records may also provide additional information, such as occupations and birthplaces of householders. Where written records are available, the fieldworker will need to spend a considerable number of hours and days in transferring these basic census data to his own records—preferably onto large file cards to which he can add much more information as field work progresses.

Besides enumerating social units within his research area, the fieldworker should map out the spatial relationships of significant social groups, man-made physical features, and other elements of the sociophysical landscape. (It is a source of constant surprise that many ethnographic reports do not contain maps of the physical setting within which social behavior takes place.) Such maps should locate major action settings (e.g., ball field, religious places, market places), major social divisions of the community, agricultural areas, directions and distances of neighboring communities, and major natural features such as rivers, mountains, and swamps.

Mapping and preliminary census taking often do not require a great deal of rapport with informants or language facility, so these activities can be carried out before the fieldworker is fully assimilated into the community. Problems can easily arise, of course, and the fieldworker must be aware of the possibility that his actions will be misinterpreted by the local people. A most common fear, increasingly encountered in modern times, is that census taking is part of a governmental attempt to increase tax collection in the community. A related concern is that mapping may be preliminary to some new land confiscation. The fieldworker therefore needs to develop effective explanations for this behavior. If he is able to establish this data collection as legitimate and harmless, he will usually find that these activities are very effective in introducing him to the majority of local inhabitants. In fact, introducing himself to everyone in the community can be one of the rationales for carrying out a preliminary census operation. Powdermaker's comments about her census taking in Lesu are useful in this connection (1966:60–62).

A constant feature in field work is the rechecking of data collected in earlier phases of the study. Thus, a census collected at the beginning of field work should be frequently spot checked, corrected, and updated. Colson (1954) has pointed out that among the Tonga she observed a great deal of intercommunity mobility, but was unable to document this impression with quantified material. Other fieldworkers have from time to time commented on the local mobility (intra- and intercommunity) of particular peoples. Such movements, if carefully studied, may be extremely important for understanding the dynamics of household and familial structure, but the data can be obtained only if the fieldworker periodically rechecks his basic census materials (or some selected sample thereof).

Köbben (1967) has described the joys and sorrows of collecting extensive census data among the Djuka of Surinam. It required a great sacrifice of time, during a year of field work, to collect these quantified data on a mere 176 persons (all adults in the village of Langa Uku).

People at first objected: "Where are you going to take those figures? Perhaps you'll take them to other villages! They'll be jealous when they find out how many children we have here." It was only after I had been there some months and after I had made the necessary libations (like everywhere else the living here help their ancestors drink) that I was permitted to take my census. (Köbben, 1967:49.)

There were all kinds of problems—refusals to talk about dead children, lack of exactness in people's numerical concepts, male mobility as an obstacle to assigning residence in particular households, and so on. In the end, Köbben felt rather unsure of the validity of some of his data, but his extensive fieldwork made it possible to assess the usefulness of different portions of the materials. Adoption patterns and genealogical relationships among the people in the community were illuminated by his numerical data, as were comparisons concerning religious experience.

In my village 20% of the adult population were mediums of some deity, on the Tapanahony river 37%. Even before my co-fieldworkers and I had collected these data it was already our impression that the Tapanahony people experienced their religion more intensely than the people of my region, but this was no more than an impression. We took the percentage of mediums as an operational definition of "intensity of religious experience." The difference indicated above we regard as a confirmation of our hypothesis. (*Ibid.*, 52.)

Many writers have commented that serious misinterpretations of survey and census data can result if the interview procedures are not carried out in close articulation with intensive ethnographic field study. Leach has presented one such example in "an anthropologist's reflections on a social survey" (1967), dealing with a survey of 58 villages in Ceylon (Sarkar and Tambiah, 1957). He points out that the sampling unit in the survey was the household, defined as "persons who cook their rice from the same pot." In his ethnographic work, however, he found that every young married couple has a separate cooking pot even when they live in an extended family household (a very common pattern). Thus, in the case of a man with three married sons, four separate households are recorded in the social survey. Therefore,

my anthropological appreciation of the total situation has led me to suspect that a proportion of the 335 landless households were landless simply because the householders were young, recently married adults who were heirs to still living parents. (Leach, 1967:80.)

He introduces similar technical problems concerning the identification of sharecroppers and owners and the calculation of the degree of bias toward males in inheritance patterns.

Some of the problems Leach describes could be corrected, it would seem, through a careful analysis of the survey protocols in the light of detailed ethnographic information. For example, spot checks in a few of the research communities might make possible a correction factor in terms of which the problem of multiple separate rice-cooking pots in extended households could be adjusted. But some of the survey data were inaccurate because the questions —the mode of operationalizing key variables—were not shaped realistically.

Clearly the quantified data of survey research or other standardized interviewing requires close support from participant observation and general informal interviewing. But the converse is equally true. The lesson in all this, as Köbben makes clear, is that field research entails a great amount of tedious, time-consuming work— both qualitative and numerical.

GENEALOGICAL INQUIRY

In addition to a complete enumeration of a population in terms of household of residence and major kinship affiliation, the field-worker usually needs much more detailed data concerning the consanguineal and affinal linkages that knit the community into a complex fabric of kinship. This body of information may be of crucial importance for making sense of great numbers of social events and transactions, so the researcher is often well advised to begin this work as soon as possible.

In a classic paper published in 1910, W. H. R. Rivers set out the procedures for collecting individual informants' "pedigrees" with such clarity and order that his description can still be regarded as a primary field-work guide. Referring to his sample genealogy from Guadalcanal, Rivers tells us:

I began the inquiry by asking my informant, Kurka or Arthur, the name of his father and mother, making it clear that I wanted the names of his real parents and not of any other people whom he would call such by virtue of the classificatory system of relationship. After ascertaining that Kulini had had only one wife and Kusua only one husband, I obtained the names of their children in order of age and inquired into the marriages and offspring of each. . . . I obtained the names of (his mother's) parents, ascertaining as before that each had only been once married, and then asked the names of their children and obtained the marriages and descendants of each. . . . In collecting the pedigrees the descendants in both the male and female lines are obtained, but in writing them out in order to use them for the purposes to be considered in this paper, it is well to record on one sheet only the descendants in one line with cross-references to other sheets for the descendants in the other line. (Rivers, 1910:1–2.)

It is important to note that in this initial phase of the method the only relationship terms normally required are those of father, mother, child, husband, and wife. Rivers notes:

A most important feature of the method is to record as far as possible the social condition of each person included in the pedigrees. In order that the pedigrees may be used in the ways I propose to describe it is necessary to be satisfied that they are trustworthy. In collecting the pedigrees of a whole community, there will be much overlapping; people who belong to the paternal stock of one informant will come in the maternal stock of another, and in the wife's ancestry of a third, and there will thus be ample opportunity of testing the agreement of the accounts of different informants. In nearly ever community in which I have worked I have found that there are people with especial genealogical knowledge, and it is well to make use of these as much as possible. In my experience it is very dangerous to trust to the young men, who nearly everywhere are no longer taking the trouble to learn the pedigrees from their elders. (Ibid., 3.)

Turning to the use of the genealogical data for eliciting kinship terminological systems, Rivers says that

my procedure is to ask my informant the terms which he would apply to the different members of his pedigree, and reciprocally the terms which they would apply to him. . . . I am in the habit of supplementing the genealogical method by asking for a list of all the people to whom a given man applies a term of relationship. (Ibid., 3–5.)

The highly complex network of relationships obtained in this fashion can be used as a frame of reference against which to elicit information about property rights, succession to special offices, residence rules, prescribed and prohibited marital or sex partners, and many other topics. In earlier decades ethnographers sometimes used genealogical data simply to establish the presence of supposedly unitary cultural "traits," such as lineality of descent, matrilocal or patrilocal residence, and marriage rules, but recent treatments of kinship structure concern themselves rather more with highly complex behavioral systems.

Commenting on Rivers' statement on genealogical inquiry, J. A. Barnes says that

> his method can scarcely be improved, except for one alteration. I suggest that it is often useful, before beginning on a sequence of inquiries structured by the ethnographer, to record first whatever information about his kinfolk the informant thinks important, in the form in which he presents it . . . it provides the best indication of how the informant perceives his kinfolk and what version of their names, status, numbers, and relationships he wishes to present to the ethnographer. (Barnes, 1967:106.)

Barnes' paper on the genealogical method is an important addition to Rivers' work.

Ethnographers going into the field have sometimes been advised that the collecting of genealogies is an excellent opening gambit, since these data are usually considered to be very interesting and nonthreatening. Perhaps there is some general change taking place in the world with regard to the meaning of kinship; at any rate, there are increasing reports of peoples who feel quite threatened by inquiries about genealogies. Gerlach reports, for example, that the Digo of East Africa are extremely wary of giving genealogical information, because these data are central to numerous disputes over property rights in a situation where matrilineal, patrilineal, and bilateral principles of reckoning are all invoked and debated in the course of litigation (Gerlach, personal communication). Also, it appears that in a world full of new kinds of social striving, the rubrics of pedigree have taken on added significance in connection with racial, aristocratic, or other standards of presumed social excellence. One of my Lappish informants proudly informed me that *his* biological father was an Englishman who occasionally visited Lapland on fishing excursions.

INVENTORY OF OCCUPATIONS AND MATERIAL GOODS

Without espousing any kind of economic determinism in one's social and cultural theory, it is reasonable to assume that the subsistence basis of any community is primary for any descriptive or theoretical study. The fieldworker will usually find it quite easy to learn a good deal about the agricultural practices and other income-producing behavior of the people, though in most cases systems of distribution and exchange of goods and services constitute a much more complicated area of study. Communities in which everyone has the same basic economic pursuit are becoming increasingly rare, and inventorying the basic occupational subdivisions of a community is an important step in the early phases of field work. These data can, of course, be included in a general census-taking operation.

In every human community there are differences among persons and families in their access to, or control of, the local good things in life. In all societies, too, some of these scarce resources are material goods, whether they are primarily food, clothing, housing, or other things. Although many ethnographic descriptions of earlier times have stressed the egalitarianism and homogeneity of local groups, such facile characterizations have in recent years been subjected to much criticism. (Social historians some day will be concerned to explain why anthropologists during much of the twentieth century showed rather little interest in local social stratification, except in such obvious situations as the caste system of India.)

An important point of concentration, then, in the study of local culture patterns is the differences between the materially more successful and those less wealthy (by local standards). The assumption should not be made that all aspects of social differences follow the lines of material differences, but the variations in what can be called material style of life are often easiest to discern in early phases of field inquiry.

Differences in house style will usually be noticeable to the fieldworker on his first day in his research community. In some cases the differences may simply reflect differences in optional use of local materials; or they may reflect subcultural differences that have no connotations of stratification. In most instances, though, some of the variations in construction and materials of roofs, windows, walls, etc., will indicate differential economic success among the members of the community.

House furnishings and other equipment generally follow this same pattern. Some households have kerosene lamps; others do not. Factory-made beds, tables, or other furniture may be in evidence in some households. In many parts of the world the presence of radios (or even television sets) distinguishes the economically more successful households. Often these marks of relative wealth are simultaneously evidence of the intrusions of generalized Western technology, so the fieldworker needs to begin early to sort out (where possible) the conceptually separate dimensions of affluence and acculturation.

Differences in occupation naturally result in significant differences in material possessions. Town-dwelling artisans may be without plows, draft animals, and other items that are standard for agriculturalists in the same community. Perhaps only the local smiths have a large array of iron tools, even though they are otherwise not among the wealthy of the community.

Inventories of material things are useful in examining many social distinctions and relationships. Also, examination of material things is, in many communities, a relatively nonthreatening procedure. People enjoy showing off their possessions, even to outsiders, and in any case establishing the presence or absence of these kinds of materials is usually easier than with nonmaterial cultural elements.

Any community, of course, contains hundreds of thousands of material things. The fieldworker needs to select a list of representative items that appear to be significant both as functionally useful equipment and as social differentiators.

LAND TENURE

Perhaps the most ubiquitous mark of social position is differential access to useful land. Land is, of course, physical and identifiable, so the patterns of ownership should be readily researchable, but such is not usually the case. Agriculturalists are often quite secretive about landholdings, and the rules of land tenure are usually so complex that the anthropologist must work for weeks, or even months, before the system (or systems) of landholding are clear to him. In some societies, local records or other sources offer quick and easy data on individual landholdings. Again, there are societies in which people make no secret of the size and productivity of their plots.

Careful description of the rules of landholding (and transactions in land) as well as the differential holdings of the social units (individuals, families, or other social units) is crucial for understanding the basic social processes in most food-growing communities. Where land is of great importance the researcher should expect to start early on this aspect of fieldwork and continue on it throughout most of his stay in the research site.

ANIMAL HUSBANDRY

Among some peoples—in East Africa, Southwest and Central Asia, and elsewhere—ownership of valuable animals is of much greater concern and significance than are matters of landholding. Here again the fact that animals are physical and observable makes the beginnings of fieldwork seem relatively simple, and pastoralists generally are more than willing to talk about their animals at great length. But the complex social relationships and obligations involving the animals can be at least as intricate as matters of land tenure. To add to this, keeping large numbers of animals requires land, so that economic processes in pastoralist communities may involve very complicated interrelationships among people, land, and animals. Robert Pehrson has described some of these kinds of relationships in a Lappish reindeer-herding community (Pehrson, 1957); the work of Vayda and others (Leeds and Vayda, 1965; Rappaport, 1967) illustrates the interrelations of populations, pigs, and territory in New Guinea.

Where herds of animals are of paramount importance in local affairs, the fieldworker can begin with rough estimates of herd sizes (often available nowadays from official tax sources, though very inaccurate). At the same time, a most important task is to learn the taxonomic system for identifying and describing the animals. Usually this involves at least the dimensions of sex, age, and major physical (usually color) characteristics. Most pastoralists are eager to impart this kind of information to anthropologists, and even young boys of the village are often excellent informants, since the lore of animal management is central to the male role they are most interested in.

EVENT ANALYSIS

So far our discussion of field work has concentrated on the physical things in the research setting—the people, habitations, material goods, geographical features, land, and animals. Although there are exceptions to this idea, the opening moves of field work can often begin most fruitfully in this sphere of concrete, observable things. Social relationships will often be manifest in these physical things, and discussions of social relationships in the abstract, without reference to physical spacing, ownership of resources, and differential control of scarce goods, is an empty, unrealistic exercise.

Much essential information about those physical objects and relationships is imbedded in nonmaterial social action. To study more directly these social actions and relationships, the anthropologist must shift his attention to the analysis of significant private and public events that take place in his research community. Such events come in all sizes, and eventually the fieldworker seeks to study as many as he can, but it is useful to turn first to examination of major public events, for these often mirror (however distortedly) important social relationships. Moreover, they have frequently been a focus of anthropological concern, and usually the major events (fiestas, religious ceremonials, annual fairs, market days, etc.) are publicly open to the fieldworker even before he has established strong social ties in the local community.

As an example of a major public action I will describe some aspects of a Lappish reindeer roundup. Like many public events, it has significant practical purposes, yet it is considered to be a festive celebration as well. Simply the fact that considerable numbers of people from many different communities assemble in one place (with an air of excitement and suspense) gives a clue to the relevance of the scene. My analysis of reindeer roundups is not intended as a full theoretical treatment, for only certain main highlights will be examined here as a guide to field-work procedure. The location for the following observations is the Muddusjärvi Association roundup site in northeastern Finnish Lapland.

In Finnish Lapland, reindeer roundups or "separations" occur several times a year in each of the 58 reindeer districts. The separations are usually carried out at permanent locations that are equipped with a complex of inner and outer corrals for capturing and holding fairly large numbers of animals. Some of these corrals are located in distant backlands, but others are situated near main roads, making them more accessible to meatbuyers, peddlers, and (nowadays) tourists.

The principal activity in these roundups is the capture of individual reindeer by lassoing. The herds that are brought to the roundup sites are usually very mixed in ownership, so that individual owners must recognize and sort out their own animals one by one from the milling throng of reindeer and people. Captured individual animals may then be sold, given over as debt payments, marked and turned loose, or taken home for winter herding (Pelto, 1962). Recognition and proof of ownership of reindeer throughout Lapland is achieved through a complex system of notches, slits, holes, and other marks in the ears of the animals.

Observing the reindeer roundup for the first time, the fieldworker can set out a number of key questions that should be answered if he is to understand the over-all events; for example:

1. Who are the different kinds of people involved in this action?
2. How are these people grouped in alliances, oppositions, partnerships?
3. What are the sequences of action in which these people express these relationships?
4. Are the social relationships among these people visible in terms of geographical spacing in the roundup corral and adjacent areas?
5. Are there symbols of status—e.g., clothing, emblems, equipment —that differentiate among some of these groups?
6. Which groups have the most "power" or decision-making capacity in this action?
7. Are there police, judges, referees, or other agents of social control?

Earlier it was suggested that mapping and census taking are important beginnings for community study; the same applies to the study of an event. I found, in my first exposure to a reindeer roundup, that mapping the physical structure of the corral and nearby dwelling units provided a nearly complete outline of the structure of the social interaction taking place (Pelto, 1962: 124–140). Figure 9 shows the geography of the corral and the cubicles immediately adjacent to the arena into which reindeer are brought for separation, or sorting. The first observation to be made about these cubicles is that the Skolt Lapp positions tend to be bunched together on one side of the corral, although this segregation of Skolt Lapps from other groups is not complete. Second, the cubicles of any one reindeer association tend to be together, and the relative positions of the associations are visible in the organization of the cubicles. That is, the Muddusjärvi Association owns the corral, and the other associations present (Utsjoki, Paatsjoki, Paistunturi), are neighboring associations whose animals often stray into the herds of the Muddusjärvi people.

The placement of the Paatsjoki "visitors" indicates that they are socially closer to their fellow Skolt Lapps of the Muddusjärvi Association than to other groups in the area. The positions of the cubicles in this case correspond to both social and territorial placement of

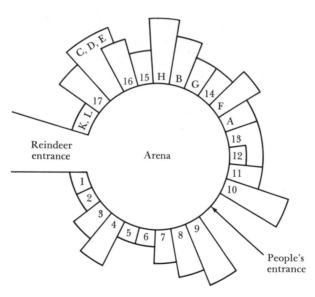

1	Paistunturi Association	
5,6,7	Utsjoki Association	
14	Muddusjärvi Association	
K,L	Paatsjoki Association (including Skolt Lapps)	
9	Meat buyers	

1–17 Cubicles of non-Skolts (Finns, Inari Lapps, etc.)

A–L Cubicles of Skolt Lapps and their associates

FIGURE 9. **Reindeer Roundup Site in Northeastern Lapland**

these people. (Of course, the verification of the social observations comes from intensive field work in other contexts.)

Also evident in the geography of the corral scene is the fact that the cubicles of the reindeer herders tend to sort out into those of Skolt Lapps, Inari Lapps, Tundra Lapps, and Finns. These cultural groupings are not coterminous with the reindeer districts, however, and the separation into the four cultural groups is not complete.

But what are the relationships within the groups which "own" each cubicle? This is a relatively easy piece of information to obtain, and it is of great importance. Generally speaking, a cubicle is "owned" by men who herd their reindeer together throughout the winter. They are the basic "winter herding groups." But there are exceptions. Some of the cubicles are "owned" by confederations of two or three winter herding groups.

During the action of sorting reindeer in the corral, it is possible to observe that each individual reindeer herder generally brings reindeer to only one cubicle, the one with which he is associated. Here, together with some of his neighbor and kinsmen (usually 4 to 10 owners), he collects his own herd for transfer back to home pasturage. But there are some exceptions. When one of these exceptions occurred I found it important to ask (that person, or some other handy informant) why this person brought a reindeer to someone else's cubicle. The answer is usually clear: he was helping someone. In some cases, though, he was paying a debt.

There were two cubicles, however, to which many people brought animals as they caught them. Before long it was possible to observe that one of these was a reindeer meat buyer. The meat buyer and his assistants kept careful tally of their purchases, and later, at the coffeehouses, the cash settlement of these transactions could be observed. The other cubicle that received some reindeer from a number of different persons turned out to be owned by the Muddusjärvi Association itself. Animals brought to that cubicle were mainly unmarked or unidentifiable animals that were auctioned off, proceeds going to the association.

The other important physical features in the Muddusjärvi reindeer separation site are a number of cabins, ranging from tiny two-man huts to the four large centrally located "coffeehouses." Inquiry into the ownership and use of the cabins showed that living accommodations at the roundup site tend toward congruence with arrangements in the corral itself, but many exceptions appear. Table 19 presents the winter herding group affiliations of a number of persons who domiciled in the cabins with which the Skolt Lapps were most closely associated. The list is incomplete, and the patterns changed somewhat from one occasion to the next, but certain important generalizations emerge from this mapping. A principal observation that begins to come clear from the mapping and census of cabins and their occupants is that social relationships, as expressed through sleeping and eating patterns, are very flexible and individualized.

Mapping the reindeer roundup site and making a census of the categories of persons at the roundup produced a great amount of information about important social relationships. Many of these observations were made, however, in the course of watching the principal *actions* in this complex event. From the outset it was clear that most, but far from all, significant action occurred in and near the corral itself. After the second day it was clear that the general sequence of events would be the same, day after day, until the end of the roundup.

Each morning at dawn the association herders brought a herd of reindeer into position for driving into the corral. Volunteers were then called out to man the "wings" of the "trap," as the animals were lured into the enclosure. When this capturing operation was completed, the animals were allowed to remain undisturbed in the outer enclosure for an hour or so, during which time the men walked quietly through the herds, identifying animals and noting which calves followed particular cows. (During the milling around in the inner corral calves become separated from their mothers and cannot be identified as to ownership unless they have been "recognized" during this earlier inspection period.)

The preliminary inspection completed, part of the herd is driven into the inner enclosure, and roping begins. As the number of uncaught reindeer diminishes, more and more herders drift off to the coffeehouses to rest, drink coffee, eat, and talk, until another portion of the herd is brought into the inner corral. When all the identifiable animals in the inner corral have been caught, the remaining, unidentified reindeer are driven into the association cubicle for auctioning. The (usually brief) auction is the final phase before a fresh herd is brought into the inner corral and the entire sequence is repeated. When all the animals in the outer enclosure have been processed, the day's work is over and the men retire to the coffeehouses and cabins to eat, drink, play cards, or otherwise pass the time.

The sequence of events that make up a separation is an ideal target for the anthropologist at an early stage of field work because patterns of action are repeated many times in approximately the same format, so the fieldworker can usually depend on the next day's repetition to fill in details that were missed earlier. There are few crucial moments, and no serious losses of data occur if the fieldworker

takes a break for coffee or gets into a long conversation with one of
the participants.

TABLE 19.   **Some Residence Patterns at the Muddusjärvi Reindeer Roundup
(Demonstrating Mixing of Skolt Lapp Sleeping Arrangements)**

Camp Owners	"Guests"	Herding Group Affiliation
1. Jankkilan Jussi (a Finn) (coffee house)	Most of the Skolt Lapps from Sevetti village	Group H
2. Karpis Pekka (a Finn) (coffee house)	Most of the Skolt Lapps and others from Paatsjoki District	I, K, L
3. Oskari and Erkki Fofanoff	Oskari's son Vasko A. Feodoroff P. Semenoja Two Sarre boys	A E K Λ
4. Olli Gauriloff Ev. Semenoff	Jakkima Feodoroff and son Aapo Aikio Saveli Fofanoff	G F E G G
5. Piera Porsanger Jaakko Gauriloff	J. Högman Eero Aikio Veikko Paltto Illep and Elias Fofanoff	G G H G Paatsjoki C
6. Nikolai Killanen Aleksi Fofanoff	Nikolai's four sons Evvan Kiprianoff Matti Sverloff	F B F H H
7. Evvan, Erkki, Mikko, and Aleksi Sverloff	Jussi Gauriloff	D D
8. Seurujärvi (a Finn) (coffee house)	Paavo, Vasko, and Kiurel Fofanoff Vasko R. Fofanoff	B C
9. Valle Niiles (Inari Lapp) (coffee house)	Jeffim Feodoroff Timo Gauriloff	F G

FROM Pelto, 1962.

The roundup corral is not the only scene of important social action, however. At the coffeehouses there is music and other entertainment, a huckster of clothing and miscellany holds forth for several hours a day outside one of the larger cabins, and occasionally one or another of the groups may hold a meeting to discuss some issue that has arisen.

When the roundup was completed, and I was back with my field notes at the village, it was possible to put together the "big picture" of the event. As I filled out my description, I found that the questions raised by the first field work in a roundup pointed in two directions. First, it was important to see the gaps in the data about the roundup itself—these gaps would have to be filled in when I had a chance to observe another roundup. Second, I needed to find out if social relationships in other big events, and in day-to-day social transactions, corresponded with the inferences that I had made from this first Muddusjärvi reindeer roundup.

I have gone into some detail about preliminary field analysis of the reindeer roundup because it is a clear case of an important, repeated social action that offers the fieldworker an opportunity to observe a very considerable amount of social information as it is dramatized in spatial and interactional terms. The repetition of this kind of large-scale social event provides an important part of the anthropologist's data concerning social processes. The following generalizations can be made concerning analysis of these social events:

1. As indicated above, all social events occur in some kind of physical setting, and the use of the physical setting, especially the spacing and movements among the participants, provides the first important clues to social relationships and processes. The fieldworker's first task, therefore, should be to identify the kinds of persons present in an event, and to map out their spacing in relation to the physical stage on which they act out this particular drama.
2. Key informants are very important as an information source but are best used in connection with the concrete events observed by the fieldworker. The important kinds of questions to ask are often in the following forms: What is that (building, enclosure, object) used for? Who is that man who is carrying the platter of food? Why is he going first to those people in the corner? Why is the man in the center dressed differently from the others?

    During a pause in the event it is possible to ask questions about previous events of the same type, such as the following inquiries. Is the action that we just witnessed very much the same as, or very different from, the previous enactment of this same event? How is it different? Which parts seem to you to be exactly the same? (Key informants often show much better recall of a past event when they are immersed in the memory-jogging setting pertinent to that event.)

3. Any social events that are repeated a number of times during the field period should be treated as a series of intracultural comparisons. That is, variations in the size and structure of a social event may be related to important social patterns. The size of weddings and fiestas may be indicators of relative wealth and/or social centrality; the sequence of actions in a ceremonial may be different depending on the ritual excellence and status of the central actors; law cases may result in different kinds of resolutions, depending on differentials in social status and political power. It follows, then, that any social events that occur a number of times should be observed systematically in ways that can permit numerical analysis.

4. Certain standard elements of any action can, and should, be quantified. The number of persons in particular categories should be counted. Counts of persons should be made at several different times during the course of the event, if possible. Counting makes it possible to give substance to such statements as: "This fiesta is bigger than the one last year," or "There are fewer costumed dancers now than there were in the winter ceremonial." In general, the fieldworker should make an attempt to predict the kinds of quantified statements he will need in describing the event. He can imagine himself writing portions of the analysis, and note the points at which he uses such expressions as "many," "few," "more than," "shorter than," "constantly increasing." These are clues to significant points to be counted. In addition to counting types or categories of persons, some usual items to be quantified include:

   a. Amounts of significant material things, such as platters of food, jugs of beverage, roast pigs, candles, musical instruments, cars and other vehicles, placards, bolts of cloth, gifts (of all types).

   b. Repetitions of important acts, such as prayers, ceremonial drinks or bites of foods, speeches, dances, bows, gestures.

   c. Distances—from one group to another, of races run, of processions, etc.

   d. Amounts of elapsed time of important activities, time of beginning events, time at termination of events.

   e. Cash amounts of transactions, usual cost of particular items, total expenditures for special events, etc.

5. It should be clear that quantification of aspects of an event is not the primary objective. Many other aspects of events are more important than counting persons or items or costs, but quantifica-

tion should be seen as an *essential* secondary feature in the analysis of events.

MICROEVENTS

In practically all significant social events there are features which are repeated a number of times or are sequences which involve a large number of different combinations of persons in identifiable *microevents*. Some examples of such repeated actions or combinations include "helping" in the reindeer roundup, transactions in the market, ceremonial drink exchanges, choosing dance partners, speaking in a meeting, presentations of gifts, racing or taking part in other contests; renditions by performers, and acts of harassing initiates.

For each type of microevent the fieldworker may want to amass certain standard information. Of what kin group were the persons? How much did the initiate cry out or show fear? What was the price of the item? What were the social identities of the persons who cooperated? How much did the buyer and seller haggle over price? And so on. Decisions about *which aspects,* of microevents require systematic recording depend on the fieldworker's theoretical orientation and the social nature of the persons involved in the events.

These items, and many more that the reader will be able to think of, represent observational problems for the fieldworker because he will need to generalize about the patterning of these actions, but in most cases he will not be able to observe all of that class of transactions. Usually the fieldworker resorts to stating the "typical" example of the transaction, but a much more satisfactory procedure is to observe a *sample,* especially a random sample, of such actions.

Most of the above cases can be handled in an approximation of a random sample if the fieldworker makes his plans carefully. In observing a busy market, for example, the fieldworker can use his preliminary map of the scene to select a number of segments or subtypes for sampling. He may then select particular vendors by such rough-and-ready means as "every third one in the row," or "three each (at random) from each of the five rows of fruit-vegetable stands." Where the number of actions is very great (e.g., roping of reindeer in the roundup), timed samples, such as "every instance of roping in this section during the first ten minutes of every hour," or "all instances of roping in the section during alternating one-hour periods (10–11, 12–1, 2–3, etc.)" may be effective. The inventive fieldworker will be able to devise many other ways of field sampling, especially if he uses his mapping and census data as aids.

RARE EVENTS

Significant social events differ a great deal in their periodicity. The fieldworker usually has several opportunities to observe the weekly market, monthly dances, semiformal family parties, and certain kinds of sports events. On the other hand, he may have only a single opportunity to witness a wedding, a funeral, or an initiation ceremony. Accordingly, the researcher should as far as possible prepare a list of the major events likely to occur in his research area. For the events that he may have only one or two opportunities to observe, he should, through questioning, form a tentative framework, or plan of action, in terms of which he will organize those precious moments of field observation. It may be wise to arrange a short period of rest before the event, for many important occasions turn out to be endurance contests for the fieldworker, especially if interminable drinking, eating, and celebrating makes up an important part of the action.

As part of his preparation the fieldworker can write up an outline of main pieces of data to be obtained. Each expected event requires its own specialized "notes and queries," as a generalized framework of expected information. Appendix D is an example of such a "guide to event analysis," developed as a format for study of community celebrations in northern Minnesota.

THE CASE METHOD

The term *case method* has usually been applied to the study of some delimited class of social events of which the fieldworker can observe a large number of instances. The study of law cases is the most common example. The method could also be profitably applied to the study of curing, witchcraft, aspects of religion, economic transactions, and many other facets of culture.

The fieldworker who adopts the case method must be careful to identify all the times and places in which the given social event regularly occurs. Curing, for example, may take place at the home of the sick person, at the "doctor's office," or at another specially designated area, such as a shrine or religious center. The researcher must devise means to gather cases from each of the relevant settings. Usually the fieldworker cannot observe all instances of the given social event, so he should develop some means of sampling systematically from the total population of "cases."

A. L. Epstein recently reviewed the methodological problems and issues in "The Case Method in the Field of Law" (Epstein, 1967a). As he points out, the case method has been long and usefully employed in anthropological studies of law, for careful analysis of a body of legal cases has distinct advantages over the research method that relies on the interviewing of juridically important persons about their "legal rules." He suggests that legal processes may operate very effectively even though the jurists in the system are not willing or able to formulate clear abstract principles or rules on which their legal decisions are supposed to be based.

Through the detailed examination of a series of cases the researcher seeks to define the regularities in recognized rules of conduct (e.g., rights and duties of particular social persons) as they are applied by judicial bodies, as well as the formal procedures and reasoning used for arriving at legal decisions. Epstein discusses a case from one of the Urban Courts of the Copper Belt to illustrate the concept of "the reasonable man" as a measuring rod by means of which members of the court judged a divorce case.

In handling the case, the Urban Court took into consideration the total nature of the marital relationship, which involved behavioral expectations between the spouses, but also includes codes of conduct regarding consanguineal and affinal kinsmen.

After establishing that the marriage had been properly contracted, the court inquired about previous misunderstandings between the couple. The wife said that there had been trouble in the past, and once before her father had wanted to see the marriage dissolved. She then embarked upon a lengthy account of how her husband had not come to offer his sympathy when her father was ill; he did not greet his father-in-law with the customary salutation when the latter returned home from work; on another occasion he had refused to go into the bush to seek medicine for a sick child; and so on. Let us see how the court took up these points.

COURT: Is it true that you refused to fetch medicines for a sick child?
HUSBAND: No, I did not refuse to fetch it.
COURT: But did you go and get it?
HUSBAND: No.
COURT: Do you think the relatives of your wife would have been pleased about that?
HUSBAND: No, they were not very pleased.
COURT: Yes, you see. That is where you were very foolish. And don't you know that whenever your father-in-law comes back from work in the evening you should clap before him in accordance with our Bemba custom?

Another member of the court who was of the Kaonde tribe intervened:

MEMBER: According to the customs of the Kaonde, if I were to come to you and seek to marry your daughter, what would you say?
HUSBAND: I would be pleased.
MEMBER: Would you not say this son-in-law of ours will help us in all our difficulties?

HUSBAND: Yes, I would.

MEMBER: Well, that is exactly the point here. You should know that you made a mistake by refusing to go where your father-in-law directed you. Listen now, if your chief came and married my daughter I would be entitled to make him climb trees. (This was a reference to the Bemba custom of performing service for one's in-laws by cutting trees and making gardens for them.) There is a proverb in Bemba that a chief does not marry the daughter of a fellow chief unless he is anxious to cut trees. Now what have you to say about your wife? (Epstein, 1967a:220–221.)

This instance of the court's reasoning about the expected marital conduct of a reasonable man is doubly revealing because it involves cross-cultural regularities in the sense that the court made reference to both Bemba and Kaonde behavioral codes in reaching a verdict. As Epstein points out, the Urban Court had no intention of enforcing a specific rule—that the husband must climb trees for his wife's people—but they were concerned with the general matter of whether the husband had shown reasonable care and respect for the wife and her kinsmen.

A study of the principles and procedures of particular judicial bodies requires the scrutinizing of a number of cases in order to sort out the relatively invariant from the more variable and idiosyncratic patterns of decision making. In this kind of research the anthropologist must know a great deal about the cultural patterns of the society studied, and he may spend as much time observing behaviors of everyday life as he spends in collecting and analyzing cases. He does not need to study "everything" in the culture in detail, but he does need to consider the *possibility* that any particular aspect of culture may be relevant for understanding his selected topic.

Concerning observation in the court scene itself, Epstein states that

. . . we must note where the hearing takes place, whether in a court-house or yard or in an open space; what persons are involved and the capacities in which they are present or serve; when and under what circumstances the body is convened; what powers it has and how far these are limited by jurisdiction, by the right of appeal, or otherwise. But the central problem here is the nature of the adjudicatory process itself: the aims which the process is designed to serve, and the means by which they are achieved. (*Ibid.*, 219.)

He goes on to say:

All this requires much more than a summary of the facts and arguments of a case. It demands careful and detailed recording of all that passes at at the hearing, including where possible the murmured *obiter dicta* of the judges, as well as the reactions of the audience. This is at the best of times a laborious and time-consuming task, and even when the field worker has a fair degree of fluency in the vernacular the use of idiom and meta-phor and elliptic references to persons, events, or topography make it all too easy to miss vital points in the cut and thrust of argument. (*Ibid.*, 222.)

Whether the research topic is law or economic exchanges or some other specialized cultural feature, the scene which the anthropologist must try to record and understand is often a veritable three-ring circus, with many different events and conversations taking place simultaneously. How is the fieldworker to do this job effectively? Epstein's own solution to the problem is to train an assistant to record the proceedings as carefully as possible, and

at the same time I myself took notes of the hearing, recording passages or phrases verbatim in the vernacular. The two records were then checked against each other, discussed and clarified, and combined in a final typed record of the case. (*Ibid.*, 223.)

DELINEATION OF GROUPS AND NETWORKS

Because of the powerful impact of the British school of social anthropology (supported by some influences emanating from sociology) much ethnographic fieldwork has been devoted to the exploration of social groups, their corporate natures, and their interrelationships. Although some emphases have changed, this aspect of field analysis is still very important. The significant social groupings vary from one community or culture to another, but many recurrent types, such as unilineal kin groups, bilaterally reckoned groups like the Lappish herding bands described by Pehrson (1957), voluntary associations of the sort described by Kenneth Little (1965) for West Africa, as well as territorial groupings of varying degrees of complexity have all received deservedly intensive study concerning their significance in the organization of social action.

In communities that are relatively "nondocumentary," socially significant groups are often most easily identified, and their roles most easily blocked out, through intensive analysis of major events, as illustrated above in the case of the reindeer roundup. In large annual celebrations major social groups make their presence known through joint participation, symbolic enactments, and many other communications. Newman has described how he identified significant kin groups among the Gururumba of the New Guinea highlands by watching and recording their ritual enactments (Newman, 1965).

Legal cases in local dispute settlements also can be a rich source of data about the nature and properties of social groups. The following are some of the main points about social groups that aid fieldworkers in their identification:

1. Social groups usually have a name.
2. Often they have distinctive clothing or insignia.
3. They may have special rites for admission to membership.
4. They carry out activities, including ritual performances, as a visible collectivity.
5. They defend property and other rights, *vis-à-vis* other groups and individuals.
6. They may have special words and slogans that help to make them (and their ideologies) distinct from other social bodies.
7. They have special rules of behavior which help to make them distinct from other groups (e.g., special ways of eating, special norms of honesty in commercial transactions).
8. They have modes of communicating, as a group, with other significant social bodies (e.g., some kinship groups exchange women in marriage as part of their general structuring of alliances).
9. They often have internal differentiation or "structure" in terms of which communication and decision making are carried out (e.g., there may be a "leader" and possibly other "officers," as well as internal segments).

No communities are without some kind of important social groups, even though their presence and operations may in certain cases be difficult to delineate. Sometimes, however, fieldworkers have been so imbued with the idea that social action is shaped by social groups that they have sought group corporacy where there was none, at the same time failing to observe other patterns of social interaction in which groupness and corporacy were not paramount features (see, e.g., Pelto, 1969).

In many complex scenes and events observed by the ethnographer, the patterning of action involves interconnecting links of reciprocities (or other contacts) among chains of individuals who do not sort out into bounded groups. These situations may be effectively studied in terms of the "personal networks" that individuals utilize in trying to realize personal goals. Aspects of behavior in complex societies may be particularly amenable to this kind of descriptive analysis.

Adrian Mayer (1966) has studied an election in Madhya Pradesh (India) by means of a network analysis. He found it useful to trace out the chains of individual relationships of a political candidate in order to understand the basis of his political power. The actual field procedure involves observing and interviewing numbers of individuals, in each instance exploring for further links and connec-

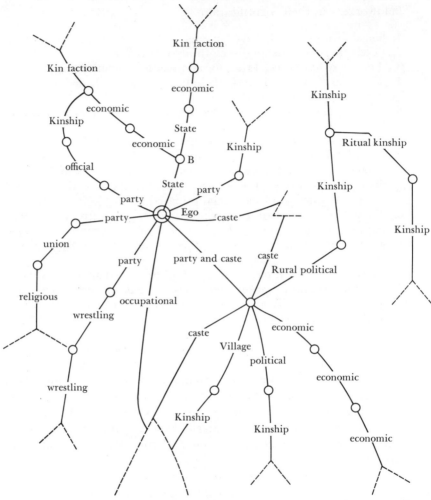

FIGURE 10. **The Congress Candidate's Linkages in the Election Campaign**
ADAPTED FROM Mayer, 1966:107.

tions through which some element of social action (in this case vot-
ing) is mobilized on behalf of a particular protagonist. Social
groups may, of course, play an important part in defining some
paths of personal networks, but socially corporate aggregates are far
from defining the total structure of the election. (See Figure 10.)
Mayer tells us:

It is clear that a candidate cannot be elected on the support of a single
caste, or of a single occupational interest. Hence, pressure has to be
brought on various sections of the electorate. This may be in terms of

policy, or it may be through linkages stretching from each candidate directly or through intermediaries to the voter. The pattern of the Congress candidate's linkages, as they were described to me and as I observed them, is given in the diagram. (Mayer, 1966:106.)

In his discussion of the election Mayer pointed out

these are not the only contacts made by the candidate with the public; nor do they show all the reasons why people supported him. Some, for instance, may have done so because of his party's official policy; others may have voted for him because of the auspiciousness of his party's electoral symbol—the best example in the election of purely ideological support, which in other cases might underlie other reasons (e.g., support of a caste-mate is partly ideological and partly self-interested. (Mayer, 1966:107–08.)

The research strategy of exploring networks, of the sort just described, was set out in some detail by Barnes (1954) in his study "Class and Committee in a Norwegian Island Parish." This approach also proved useful for Elizabeth Bott (1957) in her study of urban kinship relations, and Whitten (1965) has shown the importance of personal networks in the social organization of Negroes in a coastal Ecuadorian town.

Description and Hypothesis Testing

Regardless of his area of topical interest or specific theoretical framework, the fieldworker is, in effect, continually forming hypotheses and testing them. Frequently the hypotheses he shapes are simply descriptive, such as, "most of the people in the village own land" or "the rate of divorce and separation seems high in this community." The evidence used to "test" such hypotheses is often of a qualitative, anecdotal nature in most monographs, but fieldworkers can devise means by which such statements are given the additional credibility of quantified analysis.

Robert Paine's two volumes on *Coast Lapp Society* (1957, 1965) are good examples of simple quantification inbedded in the context of extensive community study. Generalizations about numbers of bachelors, out-migration of females, family incomes, age at marriage, and a great many other social facts are supported with numerical data. Paine moves back and forth between his tabulated data and the more interesting, flesh-and-blood descriptions of individual events and social processes. With data of this type the use of complex inferential statistics is often unnecessary (Paine uses none), since the aim of the ethnographer at that point is description, rather than theory building.

Anthropologists enter the field with research plans that range

from highly specific hypothesis testing designs to general commit-
ments to "study the ecological adaptation of these people." The
more specific the research plan, the more likely it is that the researcher finds the realities of the field situation incompatible with
his stated research aims. Generally the first weeks and months of
field work produce detailed information about local conditions
which force significant modifications in the research plan. Research
procedures that worked well in some other society may turn out to
be ineffectual because the local people either refuse to cooperate or
do not understand what the researcher expects of them. Also, the
significant social divisions within the community may be quite different from those that advance information had suggested.

In any case, from his first days in the field the researcher is concerned with adjusting his research plans to the realities of the study
site, and he is looking for the "significant questions" in the aspect
of culture or social structure that constitutes his main research
focus. It is often an excellent idea to make lists of significant questions pertaining to several different aspects of culture and social
structure. These questions can be phrased in quite general terms
at first, but later they must be refined and operationalized. The following section illustrates this "deductive-inductive" process of field
problem solving as it developed in the course of research in a marginal rural area.

A major assumption underlying our research plan in northern
Minnesota (Schensul, Paredes, and Pelto, 1968) was that the region
is "economically depressed." The national "war on poverty" had
been declared during the early phases of the project, and we soon
realized that an important research task revolved around the question, "What is poverty?" This very general question could be broken up into a series of smaller, but still quite vague, queries.

1. What do the people of the area *lack* compared to supposed ideal
   standards and compared to people of other areas?
2. What do the people of the area *have* that other populations
   lack?
3. How much effort must they expend to maintain this balance of
   advantages and disadvantages?
4. What information and attitudes do the people have concerning
   the "affluent society"?
5. How do the people conceptualize "the good life," "our town,"
   "the city," and so on?

To answer the first question we needed information about incomes, household furnishings, and other material goods, as well as
data about patterns of behavior such as recreation and visiting.
Therefore, an interview schedule was administered to random sam-

ples of persons in five communities of the area. Formal and informal questioning about life in the area gave us at least the idealized information about the advantages the people felt they had over city people and other populations. Through interviews and participant-observation we learned about the working hours, jobholding, and other aspects of the people's "effort levels."

Special research methods seemed to be necessary in order to examine the ways in which people conceptualized aspects of their life style in relation to supposedly more affluent sectors of our society. If possible we wanted to make quantified, systematic comparisons between the northern Minnesotans and some other population. Also, it was important to compare different groups *within* our northern Minnesota communities. The research instrument which seemed best suited to this task was a modified version of Osgood's "Semantic Differential" technique, which was described in Chapter 5 in connection with Schensul's comparison of northern Minnesotans and East Africans (Schensul, 1969).

The people's responses to this instrument provided quantified confirmation of our impression that northern Minnesotans regarded their rural communities as close to *the good life* except in matters of economic opportunity. *The city* was seen as offering more possibilities of earning satisfactory incomes. It was interesting to note that the people did not see the city as markedly less religious than their own communities.

When we had put together some preliminary answers to the questions raised above, we noted the ways in which the socioeconomic conditions in northern Minnesota were different from situations of poverty in urban slums and in the rural poverty pockets of Appalachia and the Deep South. From these data we put together our description of "the twilight zone of poverty." In this situation people have adequate food supplies and housing, as well as most other basic necessities, but they see themselves as "deprived" to the extent that they make unfavorable comparisons between their lives and the "affluent society" which they observe on television and read about in magazines and newspapers.

One paradigm of problem-solving during field work can be summarized as follows:

1. Delineate an important question to be examined, based on information particular to the research site. Often the significant question is derived from some particular body of social sciences theory.
2. Through observation and interviewing, locate the persons and the settings which will provide the most information related to the research question.

3. From the inventory of research techniques that have been used by anthropologists and other social scientists select the procedures that appear most likely to produce the desired information.
4. Modify the chosen research instrument to accord with local conditions.
5. Select a representative sample from the (theoretical) population of all possible observations. The sample may be cases, persons, time periods, or other units.
6. Collect the data.
7. Examine the data to see if the questions raised have in fact been answered. If they have not, some other method of data collection will be necessary.
8. The data obtained by these research operations will frequently leave many facets of the question unanswered. Through participant observation and informal interviewing, additional information can be accumulated that will throw further light on the problem and will also strengthen the credibility of the information derived from the more formalized research operations. (As a general rule, *every* research finding should be supported by more than one kind of data.)
9. The several different pieces of data that have been obtained must be logically interrelated, and they must also fit in with other aspects of the local culture. This process of conceptualization should also relate the specific local data to some body of general theory.

Every field project can be seen as a series of key questions and answers imbedded in the ongoing routines of standard data collection. Much of the fieldworker's time is taken up with the routines of collecting census materials, maps, and a large range of other general descriptive material, but the isolating and answering of key questions should never be lost sight of in this sea of routine.

Multicommunity Research Projects

During the past two decades there appears to have been a significant increase in the numbers of longer-term multicommunity research projects in anthropology. These studies often preserve the design feature of intensive community description, but a number of additional objectives concerning intracultural variation and controlled comparisons are achieved by adding extra communities to the analysis. Also, multicommunity research makes it possible for a number of fieldworkers to work together without disrupting local populations through "oversaturation" of research activity.

Redfield's comparisons among folk cultures of the Yucatán (1941) is an example of an earlier multicommunity study. By selecting a series of communities at different points of sociogeographic distance from the urban center of Mérida, Redfield sought to demonstrate regularities of cultural change that accompany the expanding impact of cities on their hinterlands.

The Sterling County Project in Maritime Canada (Alexander Leighton and associates), which was inaugurated in the 1950s, involves systematic comparisons of a number of communities that represent a range of variation in degree of organization-disorganization. Thus, a community variable (degree of disorganization) is examined for its effects on the dependent variable of individual psychiatric disorder. The nature of this project makes it strongly interdisciplinary. Anthropologists, sociologists, psychiatrists, and others have been involved in various phases of the work. A large number of fieldworkers have participated in the project over the past two decades; oversaturation of communities has been avoided, however, because of the number of different communities involved, the spreading of research over more than ten years, and the division of labor made possible through team research (Leighton, 1959; Hughes *et al.,* 1960; Leighton, D., *et al.,* 1963).

CHOICE OF RESEARCH SITES
IN MULTICOMMUNITY RESEARCH

When a multicommunity project is inaugurated, it is important to select the communities in terms of very clear criteria. In some instances it may be useful to draw a random sample of communities from a region, but this is seldom done. More usually, communities are selected in terms of some main dimensions of variation that are relevant to the dominant hypotheses of the research project. Thus, in the instance of Redfield's study of folk communities in the Yucatán, the selection of research sites was guided by his interest in the "folk-urban continuum." The range of variation from "most contact with outside world" to "most isolated" appears to have been involved in the selection of research communities in a number of projects.

Some measure of control over extraneous variables may be made possible by careful selection of communities. Thus, size of community and "distance from urban contact" may vary together, yet some communities can be selected in which size is held constant while the major independent variable changes systematically. Another research design could involve the selection of one community from each subgroup in the area, where major differences (and similarities) among them are to be described. Then a central concern might well be to select the "most typical" community from each of the subgroups of the region. Such a selection necessitates some systematic pilot research, such as a preliminary interview of officials (or other key informants) in each community. A preliminary survey of a region may help to spot possible "natural experiment" situations.

We should, of course, note that project research in which a number of different communities and/or cultures are studied by different members of a research team is not a new phenomenon in anthropology, but goes back at least to the Torres Strait and Jesup expeditions late in the last century and the beginning of this century (cf. Lowie, 1937).

MULTICOMMUNITY PROJECTS
AND SURVEY RESEARCH

A basic requirement in multicommunity research is that comparability among the several sites be established through use of survey research. For example, in the Saskatchewan project of John W. Bennett and associates,

> a single basic survey instrument—a detailed open-ended interview schedule—was administered to a large sample of persons and families from each of the several ethnic, religious, and occupational groups in the region. . . . A basic regional foundation was thus laid for the interpretation of the very different slices of data obtained by many other methods from the separate cultural groups. (Bennett and Thaiss, 1967:300).

It needs to be repeated that in projects of this sort the use of a basic survey instrument with a wide sample of respondents is *not* considered a substitute for the standard anthropological methods of participant observation and detailed interviewing. The use of a standardized interview process is *a necessary addition* to other methods of data collection.

In Chapter 5 we examined some of the main elements in the preparation and use of surveys and questionnaires. As suggested in that chapter, the anthropologist, when planning this kind of data collection, is well advised to look into the rich literature of those sociologists and others who have specialized in survey research.

Frequently, though, the anthropologist's use of survey techniques will be carried out in situations and with intentions that are somewhat different from the usual research modes of the sociologists. Most often the anthropologist carries out his research in a culture quite different from his own, and this requires meticulous care in translating questions into the local language, to mention just one obvious problem.

In the Sahagun Project in Mexico, it was found useful to engage the services of the Mexican Institute of Social Studies to help carry out the survey portion of field research (Poggie, 1968; Poggie and

Miller, 1969). This arrangement permitted the collection of over a thousand interviews in a relatively short period of time, with fairly effective standardization of training for the field interviewers. Such contracting for a basic survey should be carried out only when the anthropologists in the field have close contact with the organization carrying out the interviewing. Frequent conferences should be held with the field team, and the anthropologist must devote much time to looking for weaknesses in the interviewing procedures. Also, organizations hired to carry out survey research ideally should be experienced in the type of social milieu in which interviewing is required. Interviewers who are highly trained for urban surveys may not be suited for rural agricultural communities. (Contracting with local research organizations has also been successful in parts of Africa and elsewhere.)

As mentioned, survey research methods often uncover significant areas for investigation which require more intensive informal interviewing and observation. In some cases it may even be useful to plan on a follow-up interview schedule, after intensive field work has ironed out the main issues involved in certain complex areas of questioning. In matters of land tenure, for example, finding out the relevant questions may require months of field work. Once such field work has made clear how "the system" operates, a specialized interview schedule can be extremely useful in obtaining the quantified data relevant to aspects of landholding.

When an interview survey has been carried out in a research region, each fieldworker (regardless of his special area of interest) has available to him the standardized basic information about the particular community he has chosen to study. Knowledge of the range of variation in his community (in material style of life, kinship behavior, landholdings, etc.) gives him a standard against which to measure his contacts with informants. He may find that for one reason or another he tends mainly to encounter persons in the top of the local material wealth and prestige hierarchy. (This is often the case, though the problem is not always recognized by fieldworkers.) Data from the survey tell him *what kinds of persons* he has thus far failed to reach through his informal contacts in the community.

Assistants

It is more and more usual nowadays for the anthropologist to take with him to the field a crew of assistants (usually graduate students) who can aid in the administration of survey instruments as an early phase of their training in the field. Unfortunately, students from the home university may not be fluent enough in the local language to carry out this task effectively. Often the fieldworker finds it convenient to hire local persons to assist in administering interview schedules. Sometimes assistants may be recruited from regional universities or they may be local bilinguals, such as teachers or social workers. In some areas the best local assistants may be students in secondary schools (e.g., Schensul, 1969; Beattie, 1965; Powdermaker, 1966).

Writers have occasionally expressed doubts about the dependability of native research assistants. As in most other aspects of field work, the situation varies greatly from one cultural setting to another. A brief excerpt from A. J. Köbben's field notes is useful as an anodyne:

19th Jan. Today went to Pikin Santi to count the huts. The *kutu* took a long time and the gods proved to be very thirsty indeed. As we were going back Fanaili (my informant) said: "It is really a waste of time . . . couldn't we count the huts clandestinely from now on?"

15th April. To Agitiondro for the great mortuary feast. Took advantage of the occasion to count the huts, which wasn't easy since they are planted pell-mell with no sort of order while moreover we were continually interrupted by other visitors to the feast who greeted us. To have some means of checking our results Fanaili and I each counted separately. He came to a total of 219 huts, I had 215. I resignedly wrote down the average, 217 in my notebook, but Fanaili was not so easily satisfied: "No, we must do it well if we do it at all, let's start again." (Köbben, 1967:54.)

The use of local persons as researchers has been of great importance to the work of anthropological field research. Boas, for example, many times emphasized the magnitude of the contribution that his informant and field assistant, George Hunt, made to his research on the Kwakiutl. Boas trained Hunt in phonological transcription, and set him to collecting texts on every conceivable aspect of Kwakiutl culture. White (1963) and Rohner (1966) have estimated that more than two-thirds of the Kwakiutl materials were contributed by this indefatigable field "assistant."

John Beattie has described the crucial role that his Bunyoro assistants played in his second tour of field work in Uganda:

They acted as permanent informants, even though, as I remarked above, they often knew less to begin with about such aspects of Nyoro culture as sorcery, divination, and spirit mediumship than I did, from other informants and from the study of native court records. But they very quickly learned. On such topics as kinship, marriage, and family life they provided clear and direct information from the start. They helped me in making sense of difficult texts, and in interviewing and "softening up" reluctant or suspicious informants. They recorded statements (texts) dictated by illiterate informants, and they wrote long accounts (case histories) of incidents in their own lives or that they had been told about. They assisted in house-to-house surveys, and they made use of their own ties of kinship and neighborhood to follow up promising clues and lines of inquiry. The best of my few assistants were not just clerks or interpreters but apprentice social anthropologists, and without them my work would have been very much poorer and more superficial than it was. (Beattie, 1965:27.)

Anthropologists have often discovered in the course of fieldwork that their local assistants can be excellent tactical advisers, boon companions, and tireless collectors of information. Frequently these assistants become fascinated with finding out about their own patterns of culture through the systematic procedures of the anthropologist. (The lore of field work includes many tales, some of them probably apocryphal, about the native assistants' joy in discovering phonological and syntactical regularities in their native speech, or fascinating nuances of their kinship system.)

Hortense Powdermaker (1966) found an exceptionally able assistant named Phiri during her field research in the Copper Belt. "He became a kind of alter ego, and I can not imagine how the study would have been made without his help." She continues:

During the survey I knew he was the best interviewer, but his many other abilities became apparent when he began working more intensively with me. Equally important, he became truly *engaged*, identified with the project and with me [emphasis in the original].

Night and day, seven days a week he worked. Sometimes I suggested he take a day off, but he rarely did. (Powdermaker, 1966:261.)

In larger projects, involving field teams, the use of local assistants becomes, if possible, even more important to the success of the research. Multiperson projects are generally more "visible" in the local scene, and often have serious public-relations problems. Loyal and dedicated local assistants can smooth over the occasional rough edges of research encounters and keep project personnel informed of adverse local reactions and attitudes. More important, the local assistants can play a large role in keeping research discussions reality-oriented. The field team in concentrating on elements of the research design and in its weekly or twice-monthly research seminar discussions can have a tendency to become abstruse and theoretical. Such flights of theory and speculation will be useful if they can be related to the empirical "realities" of the local scene. Here the down-to-earth pragmatism of local assistants can be of great importance in asking such questions as: What does "family solidarity" mean really? What kinds of things make you say that these people are "inner directed"? What does "social stratification" mean?

Thus, local assistants are of great importance in bridging the gap between the abstracted, theoretical realm of social-sciences discourse and the everyday empirical realm of life in the research communities. Naturally they can't fulfill this function unless they are trained to do it; and it helps a great deal if they are treated in every way as apprentice social anthropologists (as Beattie suggests) rather than as simply employees or assistants.

The researcher needs to be alert to possible personality conflicts between his assistants and the people of the research communities, and he should also be highly aware of the particular social ties that assistants might have with segments of the local population. Some otherwise useful assistants might, for example, be unreliable in amassing information about their own kin groups, since they may be under pressure to "cover up" blemishes in the record.

When pretests of the interview schedule are being made (preferably in separate, "pretesting communities"), the anthropologist should accompany each of his field assistants in order to watch their styles of self-presentation and interaction with respondents. Also, where possible, the anthropologist himself (as well as each of his fellow fieldworkers) should administer some of the interview schedules, in order to get first-hand experience with the kinds of situations and data involved in the structured-interview process. The anthropologist who has conducted no interviews himself is in a poor position to discuss or argue with his assistants over the deletion, revision, or addition of particular items in the schedule.

Whether one's field assistants are recruited from universities in the "host country" or directly from the local population, anthropologists should keep in mind their obligation to train local persons for competence in the social sciences by interrelating field research with formal university programs. Some of the field workers "discovered" by anthropological teams have gone on to become highly competent, fully professional members of the scientific community. This same obligation to help field assistants toward professional training applies to research in our industrialized, urban centers—e.g., in projects dealing with city ghettos. A caution should be introduced, however. Careful assessment should be made of the local assistant's psychological durability, financial resources, and potential academic capability, in order to avoid the tragic consequences that may follow from arousing high hopes that are later crushed by the complex requirements of academic performance.

Communication Among Fieldworkers

In the usual one-man–one-community anthropological field project, the fieldworker generally finds himself more and more distant and alienated from the world of anthropology. This has some advantages, for he is then forced to immerse himself in the life of the research community. Under these circumstances he must cope with all variety of field problems on his own, relying on the (semimythological) lore of field work as imparted by his instructors. There is a high valuation placed on this individualistic mode of field work by anthropologists, and certainly some excellent and important research has resulted. On the other hand, we have no way of counting the casualties of the field, and many anthropologists who hardly count as casualties report periods of reduced efficacy in the field, some of it which is due to isolation from the stimulation of fellow researchers.

In multicommunity research there are often a number of fieldworkers in the region at one time. Each may be carrying on his special project in his own chosen community, but communication in the field is quite feasible. Fieldworkers can, and should, get together to compare notes about tactics of research, special insights, new research hypotheses, and so on. It is desirable that fieldworkers visit one another's research communities, in order to bring to light similarities and previously unnoticed differences among the local subpopulations.

Where several fieldworkers and a field director are in the field at the same time, frequent (usually weekly) meetings can provide a framework for exchange of theoretical ideas and concrete information. In this situation each fieldworker need not go through the entire process of trial-and-error learning on his own. Each can profit from the experiences of others in the project. No careful research has been done to test the efficacies of different styles of research organization, but it seems likely that sustained hard effort in field projects can be maintained at least as effectively by frequent interaction and exchange of information among the field team as it can by the pattern of prolonged isolation characteristic of one-man research.

Almost every fieldworker has periods when he loses perspective and feels that he is not getting anywhere. A typical complaint is, "I've been here for three months, and I still don't know a thing about the community." To these reactions, the presence of a substantial body of data in a survey interview provides some consolation, but a more important source of morale boosting is the frequent comparison of personal progress with the state of data collection of workers in other, not very distant communities. The field director of the research team should, of course, play an important part in morale maintenance, through individual conferences with the members of the field team, as well as through careful management of the weekly conferences or seminars.

Frequent research seminars in the field serve other useful functions as well. When field work is somewhat advanced, individual members of the field team can present working papers on the particular aspects of culture, social structure, or personality that are the foci of their research. The seminar presentation forces the fieldworker to make an inventory of his present state of data collection, and feedback from other members of the field team helps the individual to sharpen his conceptualizations of theoretical problems. In the absence of a team project, such sharpening of field materials through seminars usually occurs after a fieldworker returns to "home base," when it is too late to correct mistakes or to fill in data gaps.

Part of the rationale for multicommunity team projects in anthropological fieldwork is that the training stages of fieldwork (and later, "fully professional" research) should be more thoroughly integrated with the other side of anthropological study and work, which consists of conferences, seminars, and other modes of collaboration and communication. The structure of team projects can build some of these feedback mechanisms into the research situation itself. At the same time team projects make possible data collection on a large enough scale so that quantified comparisons and other more complex data manipulation can be carried out.

Team Research at Special Events

In any field project, there will be numerous special events—fiestas, weddings, markets, county fairs, or other special occasions—in which more effective coverage would be achieved if several researchers worked together. If one community of the region has a fiesta, for example, all or most of the fieldworkers can converge on the occasion, working under the leadership of the person who is most familiar with that community. His task, before the fiesta, is to develop some sort of "scenario," or program of events, which will make it possible to allocate specialized tasks of observation to different members of the team. One person may have responsibility for the parade, another the religious ceremonies, a third and fourth member of the team will "cover" the nearby market, and so on. Communications among the members of such a team should be carefully worked out, so that researchers do not become too obvious a foreign element in the local scene. Tactics of team research, once worked out, can be shifted from one community to another as occasions arise. The presence of several researchers in one community during complex events makes possible fuller over-all coverage, provides means of "validity checking" of important generalizations, and facilitates important quantified observations, such as counting the number of dancers in the powwow, the number of out-of-town cars, the number of special costumes among the visiting delegations, and so on. Fieldworkers are notorious for their differences in focus of observation. It would seem likely that any *one* fieldworker necessarily produces a one-sided, personalized view of a complex event. Such biases may be quite useful, if balanced by the presence of other fieldworkers in the same scene. Of course the lone fieldworker in a community can build up a special "team" of local assistants to cover special events. Frequently a "mix" of field researchers plus local assistants makes an excellent combination for study of complex festivals or other large-scale social action.

Interdisciplinary Research

In the past anthropologists generally tried to cover all aspects of social and cultural patterns in their ethnographic reporting. The well-rounded monograph contained linguistic, historical, and geographical data, as well as information on the local economic system, psychological characteristics, social organization, and intercommunity relations. Often the ethnographer was expected to give some consideration to data pertaining to soil science, botany, and zoology as well. The old-style anthropologist was truly a jack-of-all-trades.

But the problems posed and the types of information used in different disciplines have become more complex and sophisticated, and the all-round anthropologist can no longer claim in good conscience that he can do the entire job himself. Bringing in collaborators from other fields greatly increases the research competence of the team and ensures that essential data are gathered from the point of view of advanced methodologies appropriate to the area of inquiry. Thus, informant narratives about prices and costs are generally not sufficient for any serious economic analysis in a region, but economists collaborating with the anthropologists can specify the kinds of data that would provide a sound basis for certain types of theoretical work. The Culture and Ecology Project of Goldschmidt and associates in East Africa is an excellent example of a situation in which the contributions of a geographer (in the analysis of land use, rainfall, and soils) added a great deal to the research results (Goldschmidt *et al.*, 1965).

Agricultural economists and agronomists have carried out a great deal of research in so-called developing nations, and their analyses of technological procedures, as well as input-output analyses of local agricultural economics, can be important additions to the anthropologists' work. Since many anthropological analyses now deal with peoples and places on the margins of cash-crop economies, the agricultural economist's analysis can be an important adjunct to the study of adaptive strategies of individual farmers with reference to the "marketized" sector of local economies.

The statistician provides a different kind of expertise to the anthropological research project. He deals not in a specific area of data, but rather provides the criteria and rationale for determining the kinds and amounts of data that are needed for particular forms of numerical analysis. Thus, any well-organized research project needs to engage the services of a statistician before full details of research design are worked out. A most common complaint among statisticians is that social scientists ask for advice *after the data are collected*, when weaknesses in meeting the requirements of statistical procedures cannot be corrected.

COLLABORATION BETWEEN SOCIAL AND PHYSICAL ANTHROPOLOGY

In recent years the integration and interrelations of the different aspects of anthropology have encountered increasing strains; with some notable exceptions the primary research projects of the several subdisciplines have not involved close collaboration among physical and social anthropology, social anthropology and archaeology, or of these with linguistics. In some departments of anthropology this increasing specialization has been given de facto recognition in the graduate program, in that social anthropologists are not expected to acquaint themselves with the concepts and methods of the "new" physical anthropology, and vice versa.

There are, however, good reasons for both "sides" of anthropology (sociocultural and physical) to seek new ways of collaboration. While the older lines of physical anthropology were frequently concentrated on fossil remains plus other data concerning earlier human evolution, some newer interests include studying physiological adaptations to difficult environments, diseases and other pathologies, diet, motor patterns, and other data that involve close interaction of cultural and physical processes. Modern studies of ecological adaptation are greatly strengthened if both physiological and cultural data are included in the research design. Certainly the cultural anthropologist cannot afford to ignore data about illness and levels of physiological functioning in considering the patterning of food allocation, work habits, and other aspects of social organization.

At the same time, the studies that physical anthropologists pursue with respect to genetic (biologically inherited) patterns in human groups depend, to a considerable degree, on sociocultural data such as actual marriage patterns, estimated rates of extramarital liaisons, and other demographic data which the social anthropologist should be able to provide. Several of the hotly debated issues concerning acclimatization to heat, cold, and high altitude require sophisticated handling of interactions between sociocultural and physiological data. All of these studies argue for closer integration of the subdisciplines of anthropology.

Most research projects involving cooperation among physical anthropologists and sociocultural researchers have been methodologically weak because *the two kinds of data (physical and sociocultural) were not collected from the same individual members of the research populations*. Cultural descriptions of communities, no matter how thoroughly documented, cannot be fully integrated with genetic and physiological studies unless covariations of sociocultural and physical characteristics can be examined in terms of particular *individual* members of the communities studied.

PROBLEMS OF INTERDISCIPLINARY RESEARCH

It has been noted that interdisciplinary collaborative efforts have frequently involved serious problems of communication, with much frustration experienced by well-meaning (and puzzled) would-be collaborators. Team members from the different research fields have sometimes had very different theoretical conceptions of human behavior, so that interdisciplinary discussions became battles over whose theory is "right," instead of how the theoretical fields interrelate and support one another.

Interdisciplinary difficulties have been aggravated further by situations where no methodological agreement existed concerning the assessment of evidence. This problem was particularly characteristic of teamwork between psychoanalytic and anthropological investigators during the 1930s and 1940s. Each "side" held to an all-embracing theoretical paradigm concerning human behavior, which was generally supported by ad hoc logical argument plus ex cathedra recitation of theoretical dogma. No method of data gathering and analysis could be agreed on as suitable for critical testing of rival theories.

The more serious difficulties in interdisciplinary teamwork probably developed in a period when it was still possible for some social scientists to espouse exclusive single-factor explanations of human behavior. Thus, researchers with "economic explanations" of behavior at times disagreed strongly with the "configurationists," who in turn were in total disagreement with "psychological reductionists." Another interdisciplinary struggle involved "cultural" *vs.* "social" explanation.

More recently, however, the various social sciences appear to have grown more tolerant of each other's points of view, and at the same time investigators have become more knowledgeable about the methodological requirements for analysis and presentation of evidence. In a time when anecdotal illustrations could pass for evidence, rival theoreticians argued *ad infinitum* without the possibility of reaching a decision. When, on the other hand, a theoretical statement is tested by predicting a pattern of responses, or by systematically counting the cases for and against a proposition in a sample population, it is still impossible to "prove" a particular theoretical proposition, but it becomes feasible to select the more probable and apparently more useful among alternative paradigms of explanation.

Increased methodological rigor in field-work investigations has often resulted in data that are much more complex than had been predicted by earlier theoretical positions. Perhaps this mounting evidence concerning the complexity of human behavior has made all of us more humble concerning all-or-nothing theoretical positions.

Interdisciplinary projects can often continue fairly effectively in the face of serious theoretical difference among members of the team if "gentlemen's agreements" are made in the form of "agreements to disagree." Such gentlemen's agreements can help to ensure that field work will not be disrupted by the disagreements, and separate data analysis and separate publication can honestly reflect the alternatives of interpretation current in the research team.

One important aid to effective interdisciplinary collaboration is the preparation of a clear and methodologically rigorous research proposal. If the types of data to be collected are clearly set forth in the proposal, and the several responsibilities for their collection are unambiguous, the basic research proposal becomes a kind of "contract" that can be referred to by the team members in settling disputes. Once the data are collected and field work is complete, theoretical arguments can be productive in generating new ideas concerning data analysis.

Collaboration among different disciplines naturally proceeds most smoothly if each field of inquiry is respected by others as a legitimate informational and theoretical domain. Such areas of study as anthropology, sociology, economics, and psychology can generally be characterized in terms of somewhat different patterns of data collection, and these patterns can serve to structure main lines of collaboration. Caudill and Roberts (1960), Luszki (1960), and Le Clair (1960) have discussed the promise and pitfalls of interdisciplinary research.

Summary

Anthropological field work is much too complicated to be covered in a single chapter as I have attempted to do here. This is not said in order to perpetuate any sort of field-work mystique but simply to indicate that I have touched on a number of subjects very lightly and have omitted entirely some important aspects of field research. My intent has been to suggest a number of problem areas for discussion and to mention some of the literature and points of view that touch on these subjects.

Some of the needless mystery surrounding the field-work process will be dispelled as anthropologists add to the presently growing body of recollections and autobiographical statements about their individual field expeditions. Guidelines for the pursuit of the artistic, intuitive, social-interactional side of field research must be gained by each new recruit through reading this collected lore of the profession, to which must be added the accumulation of personal experience through field training sessions and apprenticeships in team projects.

On the operational, systematic data-collection side of field research there is much more in the way of standardized use of "instruments," modes of sampling, and logical structuring and interrelating of data that can be built into the working repertoire of anthropologists. There is, after all, a definable "kit of tools" by means of which anthropologists have usually collected their data. Each new cultural context may call for some modification of these basic tools, but these accommodations to the realities of field work can be made nicely if the researcher has a good grasp of the main prototypes.

Also, new research techniques are needed—particularly for those situations in which the fieldworker finds himself studying large populations in which cultural heterogeneity, rapid change, and multiplex communications with other social systems are the order of the day. In urban anthropology we find the fullest expression of these research problems.

Anthropological study of small, relatively homogeneous societies has usually been justified in part by the assumption that the gleanings from these efforts can be usefully transferred to more complex social scenes. Thus our anthropological literature abounds with theoretical propositions and concepts that originated in studies of bands and villages, but which now should be tested in towns, regions, and cities. But these theoretical materials often require more complicated methodological structuring if they are to be used in culturally and socially heterogeneous contexts.

I have suggested that team research involving multicommunity research designs is an increasingly important and productive part of the anthropological enterprise. The advantages of this kind of field work include, among other things simply the amassing of very much more data than single individuals can accomplish and, related to that, the possibility of careful collection of much more numerical data than has been usual in anthropological research. But these advantages are gained at a price. Valentine (1968) has argued, in essence, for one-man research even in the complex scene of urban problems, because of the very real advantages of rapport, "penetration," and personalization of the research process. The loss of these qualities must be balanced by the maximizing of gains that are only achievable in team research. If the possible methodological advantages of large-scale research are not maximized, then nothing is gained. The team members are simply getting in each other's way.

There is an advantage to the larger research projects that I have not yet mentioned. They have the time and other resources to experiment with new research techniques. If my analysis is correct that new research techniques and tools need to be developed, then a situation that maximizes experimentation earns a large plus on the balance sheet of advantage and disadvantage. Lone individual anthropologists often experiment with new techniques of data collection in the field, to be sure. But time is usually so short that the experimenter must often be content with a less than thorough weighing and matching of alternatives. He experiments, but he does not have time or resources for the necessary control cases.

Nothing in this discussion should be read to mean that all field research by single individuals is inferior. Far from it. The best, the most strikingly original research, will continue to be done by special individuals who bring the right combinations of abilities into the propitious research moment. The accumulation of more and more useful theoretical paradigms in the social sciences depends in part on these (few) highly innovative lone wolves of field work and also to a great extent on the patient amassing of data and testing of theory on a scale matched to the enormity of problems in modern society—made possible through cooperative research on a larger scale than has been the mode heretofore. The logic of the situation in anthropology appears to call for a "mix" not only in the qualitative and quantitative techniques and methods of field work, but in the scale of the research enterprises as well.

REFERENCES CITED

BARNES, J. A.
  1954. "Class and Committees in a Norwegian Island Parish." *Human Relations,* 7:39–58.
  1967. "Genealogies." In *The Craft of Social Anthropology,* ed. A. L. Epstein. London: Tavistock.

BEATTIE, JOHN
  1965. *Understanding an African Kingdom: Bunyoro.* New York: Holt, Rinehart and Winston. © 1965 by Holt, Rinehart and Winston, Inc. Reprinted by permission of the publisher.

BENNETT, JOHN W., and GUSTAV THAISS
  1967. "Sociocultural Anthropology and Survey Research." In *Survey Research in the Social Sciences,* ed. Charles Y. Clock. New York: Russell Sage Foundation.

BERREMAN, GERALD D.
  1962. *Behind Many Masks.* Ithaca: Society for Applied Anthropology, Monograph 4.
  1963. *Hindus of the Himalayas.* Berkeley and Los Angeles: University of California Press.

BOTT, ELIZABETH
  1957. *Family and Social Network.* London: Tavistock.

BOWEN, ELENORE
  1954. *Return to Laughter.* London: Gollancz.

BRIGGS, JEAN
  1968. "Utkuhiksalingmuit." Ph.D. dissertation. Harvard University.

CAUDILL, WILLIAM, and BERTRAM H. ROBERTS
  1960. "Pitfalls in the Organization of Interdisciplinary Research." In *Human Organization Research,* eds. Richard N. Adams and J. J. Preiss. Homewood, Ill.: Dorsey.

COLSON, ELIZABETH
  1954. "The Intensive Study of Small Sample Communities." In *Method and Perspective in Anthropology,* ed. R. F. Spencer. Minneapolis: University of Minnesota Press.

DIAMOND, STANLEY
1964. "Nigerian Discovery: The Politics of Field Work." In *Reflections on Community Studies,* eds. Vidich, Bensman, Stein. New York: Wiley.

EPSTEIN, A. L.
1967a. "The Case Method in the Field of Law." In *The Craft of Social Anthropology,* ed. A. L. Epstein. London: Tavistock Publications, Ltd.
1967b. *The Craft of Social Anthropology.* London: Tavistock Publications, Ltd.

FREILICH, MORRIS, ed.
1969. *Marginal Natives: Anthropologists at Work.* New York: Harper & Row.

GALLAHER, ART, JR.
1961. *Plainville Fifteen Years Later.* New York: Columbia University Press.

GERLACH, LUTHER
1964. "Socio-cultural Factors Affecting the Diet of the Northeast Coastal Bantu." *Journal of the American Dietetic Association,* 45:420–424.
n.d. Personal communication.

GOLDSCHMIDT, WALTER, et al.
1965. "Variation and Adaptability of Culture: A Symposium." *American Anthropologist,* 67:400–447.

HALPERN, JOEL
1958. *A Serbian Village.* New York: Columbia University Press.

HOLMBERG, ALLAN R.
1969. *Nomads of the Long Bow: The Siriono of Eastern Bolivia.* Garden City: The Natural History Press.

HOTCHKISS, JOHN C.
1967. "Children and Conduct in a Ladino Community of Chiapas, Mexico." *American Anthropologist,* 69:711–718.

HUGHES, CHARLES C., M. A. TREMBLAY, R. N. RAPPAPORT, and A. H. LEIGHTON
1960. *People of Cove and Woodlot.* New York: Basic Books.

JONGMANS, D. G., and P. GUTLAND, eds.
1967. *Anthropologists in the Field.* New York: Humanities Press.

KILBRIDE, PHILIP
n.d. Personal communication.

KÖBBEN, ANDRÉ J.
1967. "Participation and Quantification; Field Work Among the Djuka (Bush Negroes of Surinam)." In *Anthropologists in the Field,* eds. D. G. Jongmans and P. Gutkind. New York: Humanities Press.

LEACH, EDMUND
1967. "An Anthropologist's Reflections on a Social Survey." In *Anthropologists in the Field,* eds. D. G. Jongmans and P. Gutkind. New York: Humanities Press.

LeClair, Edward E., Jr.
1960. "Problems in Large-Scale Anthropological Research." In *Human Organization Research,* eds. Richard N. Adams and J. J. Preiss. Homewood, Ill.: Dorsey.

Leeds, Anthony and Andrew P. Vayda, eds.
1965. *Man, Culture and Animals: The Role of Animals in Human Ecological Adjustment.* Washington: American Association for the Advancement of Science.

Leighton, Alexander
1959. *My Name Is Legion.* New York: Basic Books.

Leighton, Dorothea, J. S. Harding, D. B. Macklin, L. M. Macmillan, and A. L. Leighton
1963. *The Character of Danger.* New York: Basic Books.

Leslie, Charles
1960. *Now We Are Civilized.* Detroit: Wayne State University Press.

Lewis, Oscar
1963. *Life in a Mexican Village: Tepoztlan Restudied.* Urbana: University of Illinois Press.

Little, Kenneth
1965. *West African Urbanization.* London: Cambridge University Press.

Lowie, Robert H.
1937. *The History of Ethnological Theory.* New York: Rinehart.

Luszki, Margaret B.
1960. "Team Research in Social Science: Major Consequences of a Growing Trend." In *Human Organization Research,* eds. Richard N. Adams and J. J. Preiss. Homewood, Ill.: Dorsey.

Mayer, Adrian
1966. "The Significance of Quasi-Groups in the Study of Complex Societies." In *The Social Anthropology of Complex Societies,* ed. M. Banton. A.S.A. Monograph 4. London: Tavistock Publications, Ltd.

Murdock, George P., *et al.*
1950. *Outline of Cultural Materials.* 4th Rev. ed. Behavior Science Outlines, 1. New Haven: Human Relations Area Files.

Nader, Laura
1964. *Talea and Juquila.* Berkeley and Los Angeles: University of California Publications in American Archaeology and Ethnology, 48.

Nash, Dennison
1963. "The Ethnologist as Stranger: An Essay in the Sociology of Knowledge." *Southwestern Journal of Anthropology,* 19:149–167.

Newman, Philip
1965. *Knowing the Gururumba.* New York: Holt, Rinehart and Winston.

PAINE, ROBERT
1957.   *Coast Lapp Society I.* Tromsö Museums Skrifter IV.
1965.   *Coast Lapp Society II.* Tromsö Museums Skrifter IV, 2.

PEATTIE, LISA
1968.   *The View from the Barrio.* Ann Arbor: University of Michigan Press.

PEHRSON, ROBERT
1957.   *The Bilateral Network of Social Relations in Könkämä Lapp Parish.* Bloomington: University Publications, Slavic and East European Series, No. 5.

PELTO, PERTTI J.
1962.   *Individualism in Skolt Lapp Society.* Kansatieteellinen Arkisto 16 (Finnish Antiquities Society), Helsinki.
1969.   "Research in Individualistic Societies." In *Marginal Natives,* ed. M. Freilich, New York: Harper & Row.

PHILLIPS, HERBERT P.
1966.   *Thai Peasant Personality.* Berkeley and Los Angeles: University of California Press.

POGGIE, JOHN J., JR.
1968.   "The Impact of Industrialization on a Mexican Intervillage Network." Ph.D. thesis, University of Minnesota.

POGGIE, JOHN J., JR., and FRANK C. MILLER
1969.   "Contact, Change and Industrialization in a Network of Mexican Villages." *Human Organization,* 28:190–198.

POWDERMAKER, HORTENSE
1966.   *Stranger and Friend.* New York: W. W. Norton.

RAPPAPORT, ROY A.
1967.   *Pigs for the Ancestors.* New Haven: Yale University Press.

REDFIELD, ROBERT
1941.   *Folk Cultures of the Yucatan.* Chicago: University of Chicago Press.

RIVERS, W. H. R.
1910.   "The Genealogical Method of Anthropological Inquiry." *Sociological Review,* 3:1–12.

ROHNER, RONALD
1966.   "Franz Boas, Ethnographer on the Northwest Coast." In *Pioneers in American Anthropology,* ed. June Helm. Seattle: University of Washington Press.

Royal Anthropological Institute
1951.   *Notes and Queries on Anthropology,* 6th ed. London: Routledge.

SARKAR, N. K., and S. J. TAMBIAH
1957.   *The Disintegrating Village.* Colombo, Ceylon.

SCHENSUL, STEPHEN
1969.   "Marginal Rural Peoples: Behavior and Cognitive Models Among Northern Minnesotans and Western Ugandans." Unpublished Ph.D. thesis, University of Minnesota.

SCHENSUL, STEPHEN, J. A. PAREDES, and P. J. PELTO
1968.   "The Twilight Zone of Poverty." *Human Organization,* 27:30–40.

SCHOFIELD, WILLIAM
1964. *Psychotherapy: The Purchase of Friendship.* Englewood Cliffs, N.J.: Prentice-Hall.

TURNBULL, COLIN
1962.   *The Forest People.* Garden City, New York: Doubleday.

VALENTINE, CHARLES
1968.   *Culture and Poverty.* Chicago: University of Chicago Press.

WAX, ROSALIE H.
1960a.   "Reciprocity in Field Work." In *Human Organization Research,* ed. Richard N. Adams and Jack J. Preiss. Homewood, Ill.: Dorsey.
1960b.   "Twelve Years Later: an Analysis of Field Experience." In *Human Organization Research,* ed. Richard N. Adams and Jack J. Preiss. Homewood, Ill.: Dorsey.

WHITE, LESLIE A.
1963.   *The Ethnography and Ethnology of Franz Boas.* Austin: Bulletin of the Texas Memorial Museum, 6.

WHITING, JOHN M., IRVIN L. CHILD, W. W. LAMBERT, and associates.
1968.   *Field Guide for the Study of Socialization.* New York: Wiley.

WHITTEN, NORMAN A., JR.
1965.   *Class, Kinship and Power in an Ecuadorian Town.* Stanford: Stanford University Press.

WILLIAMS, THOMAS R.
1967.   *Field Methods in the Study of Culture.* New York: Holt, Rinehart and Winston.

WINTROB, RONALD
1969.   "An Inward Focus: A Consideration of Psychological Stress in Field Work." In *Stress and Response to Fieldwork,* eds. F. Henry and S. Saberwal. New York: Holt, Rinehart and Winston.

Social Dancing Among the Mistassini Cree in Canada

9. Building Anthropological Theory: *Methods of Comparative Research*

Now that we have examined some of the main problems involved in gathering anthropological data, we can turn our attention to the development of theoretical generalizations—and to the building up of theoretical systems through cross-cultural comparative research. We should keep in mind, of course, that *intracultural* comparisons can be extremely useful first steps in the development of theoretical propositions, although generalizations based on research within a single cultural system require replication in other societal contexts before they can be accepted as "highly probable" statements about human behavior.

Useful theoretical statements come in all shapes and sizes. In the introductory chapter, I defined methodology as referring to the *logic-in-use* whereby the things and events of "the real world" are observed by investigators and translated into abstract, theoretical statements of varying levels of generality. In the example of field research among the Siriono by Allan Holmberg, I pointed out that the first two levels of abstraction in his field work involved generalizations particular to the Siriono (see p. 5, in Chapter 1). For example, Holmberg's generalizations include the observation that among the Siriono, "if a man is a good hunter, his status is apt to be high." Much of the material in this book is concerned with the problems of operationalizing such field-level concepts as "good hunter" and "high status" in ways that promote reliability and validity of basic descriptive statements.

Holmberg's work also suggested such cross-cultural theoretical statements as, for example, "Societies [with high food insecurity] will be characterized by a general backwardness of culture," and "Aggression will be expressed largely in terms of food." Such broadly stated propositions require, of necessity, verification through research models involving cross-cultural comparisons. These generalizations require at least the following operations:

1. Operational definition of the population of "societies with high food insecurity" in a manner permitting systematic comparison of these societies with others that contrast in this characteristic.
2. Operational definition of "general backwardness of culture."
3. Operational definition of "aggression expressed largely in terms of food."
4. Some systematic method of comparing a number of societies in order to ascertain the frequencies of cases for and against the proposed covariations of cultural patterns.

As we contemplate the nature of Holmberg's hypotheses, we are struck by the likelihood that food insecurity might best be regarded as a variable in terms of which societies could be ranked into a number of *degrees* of insecurity, rather than simply dichotomized into "Yes" and "No" cases. *A fortiori*, backwardness of culture and aggression expressed largely in terms of food could well be considered as continuous variables.

Cross-cultural testing of the suggested associations poses two important problems which have taxed the ingenuity of anthropological theorists. First, the definitions of terms (specification of observations) must be interculturally translatable. The concepts must "mean" comparable qualities in different cultural contexts. For example, backwardness of culture cannot be operationalized in terms of, "They build crude boats," or "Their graphic arts are not well developed," since the effects of different environments would render comparisons in these terms invalid. In fact, given the highly varied circumstances and physical habitats of different peoples, it is extremely difficult to suggest measures of these concepts that would be convincingly applicable to all societies.

A second, related problem posed by the requirements of cross-cultural theory testing is that the comparisons must frequently be made through systematic examination of published anthropological literature. Operationalizing the significant concepts must be done in terms of transformation rules whereby published data are systematically observed and measured, in order that different cultures may be ranked or otherwise compared in terms of the key variables. Not all cross-cultural comparisons involve analysis of published ethnographic literature, but it has certainly been assumed by practically all anthropologists that the basic descriptions of individual cultures that form a large part of our working libraries must be useful for comparative investigation of general hypotheses. Those anthropologists who have been struggling to build up systems of cross-cultural theory from the available ethnographic data have frequently been frustrated by the unevenness of these materials, but some of these problems can be overcome by careful methodological procedures, some of which will be discussed later in this chapter.

During the nineteenth century, a general cross-cultural, comparative methodology was developed which involved a relatively haphazard collecting of culture traits that were believed to covary with the progress of cultural evolution through the general stages of *savagery, barbarism,* and *civilization*. Assertions about these similarities of cultural patterning were not supported with compilations of cases "for" and "against" the theoretical statements, however.

An innovation of potentially far-reaching importance was introduced into nineteenth-century anthropological theory by Edward B. Tylor, when he set forth a statistical test of a hypothesis concerning the relationships between in-law avoidances and postmarital residence. We usually refer to Tylor's famous paper (1889:245–272) as the first statistically oriented paper in anthropology.

He stated:

I am . . . anxious to bring under discussion the method by which (these data) are here treated, how imperfectly I am well aware. The interpretations offered will have to be corrected, the tabulated materials improved in quantity and quality and the principles involved brought out more justly, yet at any rate it will remain clear that the rules of human conduct are amenable to classification in compact masses, so as to show by strict numerical treatment their relations to one another. It is only at this point that speculative explanation must begin, at once guided in its course strictly limited in its range by well-marked lines of fact to which it must conform. The key of the position is, as that veteran anthropologist, Professor Bastian, of the Berlin Museum, is never weary of repeating, that in statistical investigation the future of anthropology lies.

He added that

the treatment of social phenomena by numerical classification will, it must be added, react on the statistical material to which the method is applied. It is in classifying the records of tribes and nations that one becomes fully aware of their imperfect and even fragmentary state. The descriptions happily tend to correct one another's errors, but the great difficulty is blank want of information. (Tylor, 1889:269; page 25 in the reprinted version of Frank W. Moore, *Readings in Cross-Cultural Methodology*.)

André J. Köbben, in a review of the history of statistical method in social anthropology (1952), notes that Tylor's statistical analysis was partly foreshadowed in the writings of Herbert Spencer. Spencer, in his voluminous works, had amassed a large amount of cultural and other data from societies around the world in order to make frequency or probability inferences about human institutions.

After the Boasian attack on the theoretical and methodological framework of evolutionism (in the early decades of this century), cross-cultural comparisons became much more regionally oriented. Boas and his students insisted that the histories of particular cultural and social elements had to be known before they could be regarded as "the same culture trait." Therefore, much of the comparative work of the early twentieth century was carried on within the context of culture areas.

The historicalist school of anthropology produced a great many generalizing statements about human cultures, but their comparisons were often aimed at demonstrating *differences* in the processes of culture history. For example, some of the studies of the Plains Indian Sun Dance (cf. Bennett, 1944) were most concerned with demonstrating how and why this complex of cultural traits assumed different forms among different tribes. A more recent comparative study aimed at demonstrating differences is "Navaho and Zuñi Veterans" (Adair and Vogt, 1949).

The researchers demonstrated that although Navaho and Zuñi veterans could be regarded as roughly equivalent with respect to their military experience, the two groups were treated very differently on their return to their home communities. Zuñi veterans were received with great suspicion as possible carriers of dangerous and contaminating foreign ideas, while the Navahos were received much more openly, and their new information and ideas were accorded positive consideration. There was an increase in ceremonialism at Zuñi designed to counteract the disruptive effects of the returning veterans. Among the Navaho there was no such increase in "prophylactic" ceremonialism.

It should be kept in mind that whenever studies are undertaken to explain some kind of patterned difference between tribe A and tribe B, the logic of explanation involves the presence of some cross-culturally *uniform agent of causation;* otherwise the explanation of the differences between tribe A and tribe B has no meaning. The comparison of Navaho and Zuñi veterans by Adair and Vogt focuses most attention on differences between cultures, but the alert anthropological theoretician can restate this comparison in terms of covariation of cultural characteristics: "Communities of type X ("tight societies" with well-developed mechanisms for maintaining conformity) will react with hostility and prophylactic measures to the intrusion of an element Y (exposure of a portion of membership to a large dose of outside information and experience), as contrasted with more receptive tendencies in loosely-structured societies."

Although two-case cross-cultural comparisons have most often been used simply to illustrate differences between cultures, this research design has occasionally served to test and develop propositions about the uniform effects of definable causes. This is the methodological structure employed by S. F. Nadel in his well-known paper "Witchcraft in Four African Societies" (Nadel, 1952).

Nadel examined two paired comparisons involving the presence of particular patterns of witchcraft beliefs. In each case he was applying the classical research design of *the method of difference,* as described by John Stuart Mill (reprinted, 1930). In one paired comparison he presented evidence to show that the Nupe and the Gwari of Nigeria have similar social structure and culture in practically all respects except one. The significant difference is that, among the Nupe, women are important traders who often hold economic and social power over their husbands. This crucial difference in social organization, Nadel felt, accounts for the fact that the Nupe associate witchcraft with females and generally expect the attacks of witches to be directed at males.

The Gwari, on the other hand, have no such sexually biased beliefs about witches, since females in their social system do not have the economic and social power of the Nupe women. From this evidence Nadel argues that the patterning of witchcraft fears *is caused by* the tensions aroused by the special features of the female role found in the Nupe social system. The argument can be conceptualized in terms of Figure 11.

While Nadel's argument is well presented, closer examination reveals serious problems. As diagramed, the argument hinges on the claim that elements A and B (and all other culture traits) are truly the same in the two cases, and that *there are no other causal elements in the two societies that remain uncontrolled.* Careful reading of the descriptive statements given by Nadel make it clear that he has only quite general and incomplete information about the child-training practices, economic structures, and social organization of the Nupe and Gwari. His claim that other factors are held constant is not supported by extensive demonstration of equivalence in the two groups.

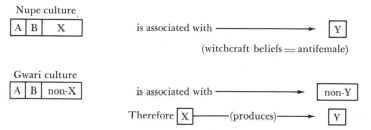

Nupe culture

| A | B | X |

is associated with ⟶ Y

(witchcraft beliefs = antifemale)

Gwari culture

| A | B | non-X |

is associated with ⟶ non-Y

Therefore X ⟶(produces)⟶ Y

FIGURE 11. **Logical Model of Nadel's Two-Culture Comparison**

As a matter of fact, demonstration of the equivalence of any two societies would be an enormously time-consuming task, considering the great complexity of human culture. Many anthropologists would insist, moreover, that the functional interrelationships among the elements of cultural and social systems make it impossible for two communities (or societies) to be the same except for one crucial difference. We would expect, on the contrary, that a significant difference in, e.g., female role, *must* be accompanied by many differences in such variables as socialization practices, male-female interactions, and a wide variety of other elements.

The propositions advanced by Nadel have strong face validity; they make theoretical sense; and they are supported by individual illustrative cases from other areas. But his claim that the theoretical propositions have been put to a rigorous scientific test cannot be accepted. Two-case comparisons thus appear to be a very weak basis for the demonstration of proposed causal relationships, particularly when the explanation is post hoc, as is true in the Nupe-Gwari case. We will examine a special kind of situation in which a two-case comparison can be more methodologically effective on page 303.

Statistical Cross-Cultural Comparisons

Because of the methodological problems inherent in studies involving only one or two societies, some researchers have moved to a method of cross-cultural comparison utilizing large numbers of societies as cases. This is the logical position, for example, of Murdock's *Social Structure,* mentioned in Chapter 7. The cross-cultural anthropologist reasons as follows:

1. In terms of some theoretical system, a causal relationship has been suggested between cultural elements X and Y.
2. If such a causal relationship exists, cultural elements X and Y should be found to covary in their occurrence among the world's cultures.
3. A first question to be resolved, therefore, is the empirical matter of the correlation between X and Y.
4. Answering the empirical question requires finding information about X and Y in some representative sample of the world's cultures.
5. If a sample of societies is selected, the covariation of X and Y can be examined statistically, in order to permit an inference concerning the relationships of X and Y in the total universe of human societies.
6. If X and Y are found to covary in human societies, this empirical information permits the theoretician to continue his belief in the usefulness of the explanatory system from which the relationship between X and Y was postulated.

As we noted earlier, Murdock decided, on the basis of over a hundred tests of covariation among elements of kinship terminology and social structure, that his general theory of social structure is a useful predictive paradigm for explaining one aspect of human sociocultural patterns.

Since the method of cross-cultural statistical comparison is, to some extent, a substitute for the two-case controlled comparison, we must immediately ask whether other factors are controlled more effectively in this paradigm than they were in the two-case analysis. Since only variables X and Y are examined, what happened to the other variables? The cross-culturalist's assumption is that extraneous variables have been controlled by the fact that they are "randomized out." While the presence of variables X and Y have been carefully controlled, extraneous variables have supposedly been free to vary at random; hence their effects have influenced the relationships of X and Y only insofar as they have perhaps introduced random errors into the cross-cultural observations. If random errors have occurred (and they always have), the strength of the relationship between X and Y has in all probability been *reduced* somewhat, so the researcher may assume that the "real" relationship between X and Y is *stronger* than his cross-cultural statistics demonstrate.

Of course, another theoretician can always claim that some other crucial variable is *not random* with regard to X and Y, and that the other variable Z accounts for the observed covariation of X and Y.

Such a "rival hypothesis" can be tested empirically by the same statistical procedure as that used to examine X and Y.

In order to examine the methodological structure of cross-cultural statistical comparisons in more detail and to analyze the logical problems of this approach, it will be useful to review one of these studies. *Child Training and Personality* (Whiting and Child, 1953) is one of the more notable applications of the cross-cultural method to propositions derived from culture-personality theory. John M. Whiting and Irvin L. Child modified some neo-Freudian hypotheses concerning the effects of socialization patterns in order to fit these propositions to a learning theory paradigm. The basic elements of the paradigm can be diagramed as follows:

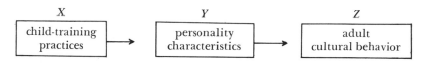

$$X \qquad\qquad Y \qquad\qquad Z$$

| child-training practices | → | personality characteristics | → | adult cultural behavior |

Thus, the theoretical system suggests that certain aspects of child-training practices (X) lead to patterned elements of personality (Y) (among persons so trained), and that these personality elements, in turn, lead to certain predictable patterns of adult culture Z. The researchers chose to test this theoretical system by looking for covariation between child-training variables and some predicted elements of adult culture. The intervening personality characteristics were not tested directly, but evidence of covariation between the X and the Z variables would be regarded as evidence of the existence of the interlinking Y variables.

As one of their theoretical propositions, Whiting and Child proposed that restrictiveness or punitiveness concerning oral socialization (the X variable) would induce oral anxiety in children, which would be carried over into adult life as a general anxiety about oral behavior (the Y variable). Such oral anxiety would be reflected in adult culture in the form of a tendency to give oral explanations for illness (Z variable). Beliefs about illness were selected as useful dependent variables in this study because it was felt that the true causes (bacteria, viruses, other infections, etc.) are generally not known by primitive peoples; hence the seeking of explanations is wide open to projections of personality needs.

THE SAMPLE

In most cross-cultural studies the units of analysis are individual cultures, each assumed to be internally homogeneous in terms of the relevant variables. Whiting and Child's first task, therefore, was to select a sample of societies within which they could examine the proposed relationships. As noted earlier, such a selection should be some kind of random sample if inferential statistical procedures are to be used; but this ideal is virtually impossible in cross-cultural studies. One reason for this weakness in cross-cultural research is that the investigators are limited to those societies for which the relevant data are in fact available. Thus, Whiting and Child report that the source material "consisted of extracts from ethnographic reports about the cultures of 75 different primitive societies which were selected and used in our study simply as being the 75 for which the necessary material was available" (Whiting and Child, 1953:48).

Most of the materials used by Whiting and Child were from the Cross Cultural File of the Institute for Human Relations, which was the forerunner of Murdock's Human Relations Area File. Not enough cases with adequate data were found in the Cross Cultural File, so that "in addition to the societies studied entirely or partly through use of the Cross Cultural File we sought additional societies for which especially full information was available about child training practices. We were able to add ten societies to the 65 obtained from the File" (Whiting and Child, 1953:49).

The problems posed by the far from ideal methods of sampling in cross-cultural research will be examined in the following pages.

OPERATIONALIZING THE VARIABLES

In the sample of ethnographic cases, Whiting and Child found descriptions of many aspects of child training, although the sources are quite variable in their thoroughness of coverage. To make any cross-cultural comparisons of these data, the researchers had to construct definitions of what constitutes high and low severity of oral socialization. Also, the investigators had to agree on an adequate operational definition of *oral explanations of illness,* as applied to the ethnographic reports available to them.

The problem of operationalization, in this case, is concerned with the question, "What rules of transformation or interpretation will be applied in converting the highly varied textual material of ethnographic reporting into ratings of presence or absence, or relative degrees of, the variables?" Also, "Who will make these transformations or judgments?"

DEFINITIONS OF CONCEPTS

In situations in which the operationalizing of concepts is accomplished by some type of content analysis of textual material (ethnographies, etc.) it is essential that the researchers specify very clearly the kinds of ethnographic statements that will be considered as evidence regarding particular theoretical concepts (variables). In

Chapter 3, on operationalism, I pointed out that an operational definition is, in most cases, some sort of sample from the total range of information implied in the theoretical concept. Thus, the definitions to be used in a particular piece of research should meet two criteria: First, they must be logically part of the universe of information intended by the theoretical concept; and second, they must be pragmatically useful in that information about them can be obtained.

Oral socialization, in Whiting and Child's research hypothesis, refers to the total universe of events (including verbal events) by means of which a child is taught the transition from infant to adult patterns of oral behavior. Presumably there are a great many occasions in a child's life when a parent (or some other adult) says something to him, or does something to him, that is intended to change his oral behavior. Verbal statements such as : "Don't eat that dirt!" "Finish your breakfast!" "Here's a piece of candy because you've been a good boy," "Get your finger out of your mouth," would seem to be part of the universe of meaning intended by the expression *oral socialization.*

In examining *severity* of oral socialization, Whiting and Child felt that severity of weaning constituted the most practical indicator of the variable, since it is information that is often reported in ethnographies. The investigators quoted a passage from Blackwood's description of Kurtatchi weaning practices as an illustration. The Kurtatchi were rated as having a very low degree of severity in oral socialization, based on this information:

Weaning is, in the normal course of affairs, a gradual process; other food, beginning with taro, which is given from birth, being gradually increased in quantity and variety. The child, according to the statement of the women, makes, of its own account, fewer and fewer demands upon its mother, who accedes to them till they cease. There would seem, accordingly, to be no shock to the child at weaning. (Blackwood, quoted by Whiting and Child, p. 72.)

The lenience of the Kurtatchi becomes more apparent if we compare them with the Kwakiutl:

Weaning was generally initiated at between two and three years of age, although it might be delayed even longer if the child were sickly. It was accomplished by increasing the amount of supplemental feeding and by punishing the child for suckling. (C. S. Ford, quoted by Whiting and Child, p. 72.)

These examples of data concerning *oral socialization anxiety* illustrate a very important point about content analysis; viz., that the concepts *severity, lenience, indulgence* (and a great many others) are best considered as relative statements, in terms of which the societies in a given sample can be ranked or rated in relation to one another. *No absolute criteria need be applied.* The Kwakiutl weaning practices as described above seem to be more severe than those of the Kurtatchi; on the other hand, they appear to be more lenient than those of some societies, since they were rated by Whiting and Child as falling in the median group (see Table 20).

TABLE 20.   **Relation Between Oral Socialization Anxiety and Oral Explanations of Illness**

	Societies with Oral Explanations Absent				*Societies with Oral Explanations Present*	
a	Societies above the median on oral socialization anxiety:			*b*	17 Marquesans	
					16 Dobuans	
					15 Baiga	
					15 Kwoma	
					15 Thongs	
					14 Alorese	
					14 Chagga	
					14 Navaho	
					13 Dahomeans	
					13 Lesu	
		③			13 Masal	⑰
					12 Lepcha	
					12 Maori	
					12 Pukapukans	
		13 Lapp*			12 Trobrianders	
		12 Chamorro			11 Kwakiutl	
		12 Samoans			11 Manus	
c	Societies below the median on oral socialization anxiety:	10 Arapesh		*d*	10 Chiricahua	
		10 Balinese			10 Comanche	
		10 Hopi			10 Siriono	
		10 Tanala			8 Bena	
		9 Paiute ⑬			8 Slave	⑥
		8 Chenchu			6 Kurtatchi	
		8 Teton				
		7 Flathead				
		7 Papago				
		7 Venda				
		7 Warrau				
		7 Wogeo				
		6 Ontong- Javanese				
					$t = 4.05$ $p < .0005$	

FROM Whiting and Child, 1953:156.
* The name of each society is preceded by its rating on oral socialization anxiety.

The second variable in Whiting and Child's hypotheses (the dependent variable in this case) is conceptually of a different order, at least in the work of these investigators. *Oral explanation of illness* was treated as a simple present-absent dichotomy. In terms of content analysis in the ethnographic material, the question is then posed for each society in the sample: "Are oral explanations of illness *present to any degree?*" The researchers provided the following operational description of the concept, in terms of which the ethnographic materials were to be examined:

1. Ingestion, i.e., eating or drinking, is the act of the patient which is believed responsible for illness; or food or poison is believed to be the material responsible for illness (but only classified here if the means involved entering by mouth). . . .
2. Verbal spells and incantations performed by other people are the material responsible for illness. This was selected as the one item which indicated concern about specifically oral activity in other people. We were led to include it by the psychoanalytic hypothesis that basic attitudes toward oral activity, acquired in connection with feeding and sucking in infancy, are generalized to the activity of the mouth in speaking. (Whiting and Child, 1953:150.)

To accomplish the transformation from ethnographic text to ratings, Whiting and Child selected three judges (research assistants) who were given the task of reading all the relevant ethnographic reports on child training for the 75 societies. Two of the judges were graduate students in psychology and the third was a logician. Each judge was instructed to rate the severity of oral socialization on a seven-point scale from "very severe" to "very lenient." The pooled ratings of the judges provided numerical scores with a possible range from 3 to 21 on each variable. For the variable, oral explanations of illness, on the other hand, each judge coded each society as "present" or "absent." (Similar procedures of ratings and judgments were employed with the large number of other child-training and adult-culture variables employed in this complex study.)

Use of more than one judge or rater makes it possible to assess the clarity and effectiveness of the detailed instructions concerning identification of variables. If the criteria for assigning particular labels or ratings to each ethnographic case are quite clear, we would expect that there would be a high degree of *reliability* (agreement) among the independent decisions of the judges. Whiting and Child report that in those cases for which the ethnographic data were relatively adequate their judges showed a median coefficient of correlation of .85; for those ethnographic cases in which the descriptions were scanty or unclear, the agreement of the judges was only .61.

Also, such measures of agreement (hence, reliability) among the judges can only have meaning if the judges worked in complete independence of one another. Many cross-cultural correlational studies are open to criticism because the ratings or judgments about variables were made by the principal researchers, with full awareness of the hypotheses being tested. In such cases there is no protection against "researcher bias" in the measurement operations. Whenever a researcher finds himself in the position of having to use his own ratings, the very least that he must do is to obtain at least one independent set of ratings (scores) on the same data so that reliability of the scoring procedure can be examined. It is apparent that Whiting and Child were well aware of the dangers of researcher bias and took adequate steps to guard against this "contaminating" factor.

STATISTICAL ANALYSIS

Having operationalized their key variables in the form of ratings by the three judges, Whiting and Child proceeded to examine the hypothesized relationships by means of the parametric t test. The data concerning oral socialization anxiety and oral explanations of illness are shown in Table 20. Inspection of the table suggests that societies above the median in oral socialization anxiety are, indeed, more likely to have oral explanations of illness, and vice versa. The probability of obtaining these results by chance is less than .0005, so the researchers can accept the hypothesis that the two variables are related in some way.

The association of variables portrayed in Table 20 is only one of a large number of relationships examined by Whiting and Child in this study. They found significant confirmation of some of their hypotheses concerning oral, dependence, and aggression socialization. Hypotheses concerning anal and sexual training were not supported by the data. Thus, parts of the specific content of their theoretical system had to be rejected, but the overall scheme was generally supported. They therefore felt justified in concluding that relationships of co-variation exist between elements of child training (variable X) and aspects of adult culture (variable Z), and that the demonstration of these relationships supports the idea that personality variables (variable Y) provide the linkages between the child-training and adult culture patterns. (It would be, of course, highly desirable to have direct evidence concerning variable Y.)

A great many questions have been raised about the logic and usefulness of cross-cultural statistical research of the type just described. Some of these questions and criticisms are concerned with serious weaknesses in this research strategy; others represent misunderstandings concerning the logic of scientific method.

1. *Do the statistical tests "prove" the researchers' theory?*

Simple correlations, no matter how statistically impressive, do not, of themselves, demonstrate anything about the *causes* of the observed patterns. In the example just reviewed, one could argue that the dependent variable (beliefs about illness) affects the practice of child training, rather than the reverse. On the other hand, it is perfectly possible that both child-training practices and beliefs about illness are influenced by some other, as yet unknown, set of factors.

The relationships do provide a network of circumstantial evidence which, together with other information, can be used to build up a system of explanations. The usefulness of such a system should be constantly tested by further analyses of the type described above, as well as by every other kind of independent probing of the theoretical network that the researchers can devise. Each successful statistical test of a particular hypothesis provides the investigators with a "go signal," saying that the theoretical model is working. Continued predictive success in the testing of hypotheses is circumstantial (but far from conclusive) testimony in favor of the theoretical model from which the hypotheses are derived.

John M. Roberts and Brian Sutton-Smith (1962) provide an excellent demonstration of the repeated testing of cross-cultural propositions. They refer to their strategy as *subsystem validation*. A series of hypotheses concerning types of games related to child-training variables were tested with the usual cross-cultural methods. The researchers then reasoned that the relationships between, e.g., obedience training and preference for games of strategy should also be testable *intraculturally,* for example in differences between males and females. They used the reported game preferences of nineteen hundred school children to test their theoretical propositions. Roberts and Sutton-Smith state:

> Although the above subsystem validation may not be fully convincing, it is promising enough to warrant further inquiry. It certainly suggests that cross-cultural findings may be used to predict intracultural variation. At the same time it enhances the confidence with which cross-cultural generalizations may be accepted. (Roberts and Sutton-Smith, 1962:178.)

2. *What about alternative theoretical explanations of the observed relationships?*

The psychological theory of Whiting and Child can be replaced by any other theoretical model that fits the observed information. In another context Frank Young has offered alternative explanations for the psychological theories of Whiting, Child, and associates. Young's proposed theoretical substitution involves what he refers to as a "sociogenic" theory as opposed to the "psychogenic" model described above (Young, 1965). When competing theoretical explanations are proposed, the social scientists concerned with the debate should devise a research situation in which the competing theoretical systems would predict *different* empirical results. Such a critical test would permit rejection of one or the other theoretical system. If no situation or set of data can be devised for which the competing theories would predict different results one must conclude that the two theoretical systems are not in fact different— they are different labels for (or focus on somewhat different aspects of) a single system. (In some cases theoretical systems are discussed at such a high level of abstraction that no operationally useful tests of the theory can be devised.)

3. *Why are there so many "exceptions" (e.g., in cells a and d in Table 20) if there "really is a relationship" between variables?*
   Many of the apparent exceptions in the statistical analysis may be errors. Errors may arise during the process of field work (ethnographer error), during the content analysis (coder or rater error), or somewhere in the data processing (typographical error). Almost everyone who has examined cross-cultural statistical tables closely has noted instances in which it seemed clear that the rating for particular societies seemed to be in error (usually in the case of a society in which one has done first-hand field work).

   Another important reason for exceptions is that single-factor explanations of behavior patterns cannot by themselves account for all of the great complexity of human culture. One may propose that child-training practices have some effect on adult culture patterns, including, e.g., explanations of illness, but it would seem foolhardy to expect that the child-training practices are the *only factor* influencing the nature of this aspect of culture. The fact that diffusion from tribe to tribe, the logico-aesthetic qualities of a people's religious beliefs, characteristics of locally available medicines, and many other variables might also affect beliefs about illness does not negate the relevance of child training as a contributing factor. Usually, therefore, exceptions in the statistical tables reflect the influence of other kinds of causal factors in operation. Sometimes these other factors will be so powerful as to obliterate completely the covariation one has predicted. More careful research design, controlling for some of the major "other variables," can correct for this problem.

   Thus, the logic of cross-cultural statistical analysis is based on the idea that, "other things being equal, controlled, or operating at random with regard to these observations," a particular relationship among variables is proposed for examination.

4. *If there are "errors" in the production of the data and the analysis from which cross-cultural statistics are compiled, how can we be sure that the errors did not cause spurious correlations?*

As already noted, the cross-cultural researcher assumes that most errors (especially typographical and coding errors) will be random. Random errors would have a tendency to obscure relationships, rather than to produce them, so the researcher assumes that the relationships he has found among cultural items are probably more powerful than his data reflect, as random errors (which are quasi-always present) work *against* demonstration of correlations.

But to leave it at that is begging the question. A more thoughtful approach to this important problem is provided by Naroll (1962), in his *Data Quality Control*. This is an important book, which is essential reading for cross-cultural researchers as well as for their critics. Naroll points out that in the type of correlational study we have examined above, a systematic bias on the part of either ethnographers or content analysts which affects *only one of the variables in question* will not lead to spurious correlations.

To see the logic of Naroll's argument we need to examine the possible effects of a systematic bias in one variable in Table 20. First, it is important to note that systematic bias by ethnographers in reporting weaning practices should theoretically have no effect, since the societies are ranked in relation to one another. Systematic bias toward reporting lenient weaning practices would simply reduce the range of variation in the rankings, without any change in the societies above and below the median. This is one of the distinct advantages of an ordinal scale in handling this kind of data. But suppose that field ethnographers for some reason had a tendency to report that most societies have oral explanations of illness, even when such is not the case. From examination of Table 20 we note that the systematic bias in reporting is four times as likely to cause a shift of cases from c to d as it is a shift from a to b. A bias in reporting in favor of oral explanations of illness is therefore most likely to add to the number of "misses" or exceptions, in cell d. A sufficient number of such biased statements should cause a marked diminution in the observed covariation of Table 20. The effects of the hypothesized bias are diagramed in Table 21.

Since the effects of biases in terms of one variable are most likely to *reduce* the possibilities of identifying covariations, the cross-cultural researcher should be even more concerned than his critics in locating, and controlling for, any such skewing of the raw data.

TABLE 21.   **Effects of Hypothetical 25 Percent Bias**

Oral Socialization Anxiety	Oral Explanation	
	ABSENT	PRESENT
above median	*a* $3 - 1 = 2$	*b* $17 + 1 = 18$
below median	*c* $13 - 3 = 10$	*d* $6 + 3 = 9$

Effects of 25% bias toward "present"

DATA ADAPTED FROM Whiting and Child, 1953:156.

Naroll states the strategy of data quality control as follows:

Field reports are classified by conditions of observation. Circumstances are selected that seem likely to affect the reliability of field reports and to produce either random error or systematic bias. Those reports gathered under supposedly more favorable conditions are (compared with) the "unfavorable reports."

Statistical tests are made to see if there is a statistically significant difference between favorable and unfavorable reports. Thus, for example, the investigator tests to see if favorable reports are more likely to report high rates of suicide than unfavorable reports. (Naroll, 1962:14.)

Naroll suggested that "unfavorable conditions of field reporting" might include the facts that the ethnographer did not live among the people he studied, the field research was too brief, the ethnographer was not fluent in the native language, the investigator was not a professionally trained ethnographer, and several other factors. In systematic statistical testing for the effects of these factors, Naroll uncovered a startling fact: Reporting of prevalence of witchcraft accusations and fears is correlated with the length of stay of the fieldworker. Evidently those anthropologists who stay longest in the field are the most likely to find out about the local attitudes on witchcraft, since this is an emotionally charged subject and belief in it is often denied or suppressed by informants. This finding should be taken as a very serious warning by all cross-cultural researchers.

Although Naroll did not find other serious informational biases caused by the factors listed, his sample was relatively small, and it would be important to make systematic tests for these same sources of possible distortion in any cross-cultural study.

Ronald Rohner (n.d.), in an extensive study of parental rejection and acceptance in socialization practices, included Naroll's variables in his data-quality-control strategy, and also inspected for the possible effects of (1) length of report (number of pages) devoted to the relevant aspect of culture, (2) characteristics of the ethnographer's informants, (3) nationality of ethnographer, (4) recency of field work, (5) the extent to which the ethnographer attempted to verify his observations and conclusions. The alert reader will notice that there are other possible sources of bias (how about amount of previous field-work experience of the ethnographer?) which can be statistically examined for their effects on particular bodies of data. When any such biases are found, the researcher can usually correct for them. One method of correcting for length of research stay (for example) is to test one's hypothesized relationships separately in the "long-field-work" and "short-field-work" halves of the sample.

5. *Aren't all cross-cultural statistics invalid because the samples are not strictly random?*

It is clear that truly random samples of societies are very difficult to attain in cross-cultural research. In the first place, it is not possible to define exactly the nature of the universe from which the samples are drawn. Furthermore, the availability of the data is very uneven, and the cross-cultural researchers must often construct "opportunistic samples" focusing on the societies for which the requisite data are known to be available. Estimates of the total number of human societies range from about three thousand upward, depending on the way in which particular researchers define what they include as a society. And the small percentage of societies that have been adequately covered ethnographically cannot be considered a random sample of the total human universe, however defined. In many cases, the sample that is finally adopted by the cross-cultural comparativist is that small group of societies for which relatively full data are available on the particular details which the investigator is concentrating on. In the Whiting and Child study, 75 societies were used as the basic sample, but we note that apparently there were only 39 cases for which reliable information was available for both the variables discussed.

How can the cross-cultural researcher justify using these "impure" samples? A statistical purist would, of course, insist that inferential statistics cannot be used in these works. But the cross-cultural researcher is hardly the only one who has problems in attaining "purity" in random sampling. It was noted above that the majority of public-opinion pollsters do not use strictly random samples. Practically all social surveys are subject to the unknown and non-random effects of the not-at-homes, refusals, wrong addresses, and numbers of other problems. All mail-in questionnaires are subject to the very serious effects of differential cooperation among the respondents. Nowhere in the social sciences except perhaps in certain laboratory situations can one find truly blameless random samples.

Given the harsh realities of sampling in the live world of people, the social scientist must often adopt the position that *some* statistical analysis is better than none at all. Often it may be useful to present correlation coefficients, without placing inordinate faith in the strict application of tests involving set levels of significance. On the other hand, it is always useful to know something about the probability that a particular array of statistics occurred simply by chance.

In defending these sampling procedures, the researcher may at times turn tables on his critics by asking for concrete evidence that his sample does, in fact, depart from randomness. Thus, Whiting and Child could argue that *to the best of their knowledge* their sample of societies is a random selection with regard to the relevant variables in their hypothesis testing. The researcher must, of course, keep searching for signs of bias in his sample, but the idea of non-randomness implies *some kind of causal agent* producing a bias in the relevant data to be examined. Practically all cases in which particular human samples have been effectively criticized (e.g., the *Literary Digest* poll of 1936) have involved known *causes* of bias to which specific spurious results could be attributed. In the absence of any known and demonstrable nonrandom effects, it seems useful for the cross-cultural researcher to continue working—with due caution and appropriate attempts to improve on sampling designs.

There is another argument that should be included. Frequently cross-cultural investigation is best regarded as exploratory. The results of any one statistical test should not be regarded as definitive, but should be supported by other studies with other samples. In exploratory research, it can be argued, considerable adventurousness and risk taking are necessary. In most cases the relationships suggested by cross-cultural research can be tested by other kinds of research designs; strong support of particular theoretical positions should involve systematic interrelating of cross-cultural co-variations with other kinds of supporting materials.

All of the cross-cultural research models discussed thus far have relied on some variant of *purposive* sampling in the selection of units for analysis. The sampling procedures used by Murdock, Whiting and Child, and a great many of their colleagues and followers have involved the purposive selection of societies to be as representative as possible of all the culture areas of the world. In the great majority of studies, the further refinement of the sample, down to those cases in which the needed data are available, is an essential step in the design.

Many recent studies have been designed to incorporate some portion of coded data from previous cross-cultural studies, thus necessitating use of *the same sample of societies* as that used in earlier studies. For example, Roberts and Sutton-Smith, in the study of games mentioned, used the list of child-training ratings for 111 societies prepared by Barry, Bacon, and Child (1952). They were able to find information about games for only 56 of these societies, however. Thus, the Roberts and Sutton-Smith sample can be described as the result of an intersection between the Barry, Bacon, and Child sample and a "game-information-available" sample. Studies based on the samples used in previous studies of other researchers have the virtue that, whatever the biases might be in the sampling procedure, they were not introduced by the present researcher in terms of his particular theoretical biases.

Naroll (1968) has constructed a more truly randomized method of selecting societies for his *Permanent Ethnographic Probability Sample*. The universe from which this sample is randomly drawn is that of "all recent primitive societies which we consider well enough known." A society is "well enough known"

if in standard ethnographic bibliographies we find a body of works by a man or woman who has spent at least a year in the field among the people of that society, makes some claim to know their language, and has published a fairly generalized description of their culture instead of keeping only to one or two narrow specialties. . . . A writer qualifies if his works devote a chapter or titled paper to each of 10 two-digit categories of the *Outline of Cultural Materials.* (Naroll, 1968:254.)

Although the original *PEPS* at Northwestern was an unstratified random sample, to avoid undue geographical clustering (see "Galton's problem," p. 296), Naroll now prefers a geographical stratification technique:

A tentative list of sampling units, such as Murdock's *Outline of World Cultures,* is stratified regionally. The number of tentative units in each region is noted. Within each region, tentative units are examined in turn in some randomly chosen order. The first tentative unit so examined in each stratum (region) which meets the explicit bibliographic criteria of the sample is chosen as the representative of that stratum. (Naroll, 1968: 257.)

Use of a true probability sample, such as the one proposed (and used) by Naroll, constitutes a distinct improvement in cross-cultural methodology. A main obstacle to wholesale adoption of this procedure has been cost, for the work of scanning the defined universe of the *Permanent Ethnographic Probability Sample* has required large expenditures of researcher time, and the relevant ethnographic literature is often difficult to obtain. Naroll has noted that studies using random samples from the total universe of reported cultures should include systematic checks for biases related to degree of thoroughness of ethnographic coverage. That is, the system as outlined is intentionally biased toward the *well-reported societies*. Data-quality-control methods can be used by individual researchers to see if this bias has an effect on the particular cultural data they are using.

6. *What about "Galton's problem"?*

When E. B. Tylor presented his famous statistical analysis of in-law avoidances and marital residence before the Royal Anthropological Institute in London (in the late nineteenth century), Sir Francis Galton raised a question which has continued to be one of the most important problems concerning cross-cultural statistical comparisons. According to the minutes of that discussion, Galton noted:

It (would be) extremely desirable for the sake of those who may wish to study the evidence for Dr. Tylor's conclusions, that full information should be given as to the degree in which the customs of the tribes and races which are paired together are independent. It might be, that some of the tribes have derived them from a common source, so that they were duplicate copies of the same original. Certainly in such an investigation as this, each of the observations ought, in the language of statisticians, to be carefully "weighted." It would give a useful idea of the distribution of the several customs and of their relative prevalence in the world, if a map were so marked by shadings and color as to present a picture of the geographical ranges. (Tylor, 1889, reprinted in 1961:23.)

Although it is probable that this so-called "Galton's problem" has been somewhat exaggerated, it is an important point for consideration. The various tribes and groups among Australian aborigines provide an excellent illustration of the problem. In many elements of social structure and other cultural traits the Australian groups resemble one another a good deal—in, for example, complex rules of prescribed marriages, initiation patterns, beliefs about supernaturals, subsistence techniques, and structuring of authority. Galton's question is whether these Australian groups can be considered separate tests of any hypothesis concerning co-variation of traits, or whether all of them should be considered a single "case" in a cross-cultural sample.

A strategy for handling this problem that has frequently been adopted is one suggested by Murdock. In his World Ethnographic Sample, Murdock divided the geographical regions of the world into an exhaustive series of culture areas and subareas. He then constructed his ethnographic sample in such a way as to include societies from each of the culture areas and subareas of the world. The particular societies included for any one subarea are, of course, those for which sufficient ethnographic data is available to warrant their listing.

With the World Ethnographic Sample as a basic listing of societies (or more recently the *Ethnographic Atlas,* also prepared by George P. Murdock, 1967) relative independence of cases can be assured by selecting only one or two societies from each of the geographical regions. If more than one society is chosen for each subarea, they may be chosen from different linguistic groups, or from noncontiguous localities. A number of other refinements in sampling procedures have also been suggested for handling this same problem.

Naroll and D'Andrade have set forth five different statistical solutions to Galton's problem. In one of the more interesting patterns (developed by Naroll) samples are selected from so-called "diffusion arcs." His "Cape arc" consists of all the cultures in the World Ethnographic Sample that are located along a track from Tierra del Fuego north across the Americas and west to Siberia across Asia to Africa and then to the Cape of Good Hope. About 114 societies are located along this track. His other diffusion arc starts with the Irish in Northeastern Europe and extends across Europe into Asia Minor, to India, to Southeast Asia, into Melanesia, and finally out into the South Pacific (Polynesia). A researcher using Naroll's diffusion-arc system would select his sample of cases from along the diffusion arcs, and then use a statistical test (suggested by Naroll) to check against undue geographical clustering among the cases. Of course several different methods could be used to select independent cases from Naroll's diffusion-arc lists.

The argument that the individual societies in cross-cultural samples must be "independent" of each other is based on the assumption that clusters of functionally unrelated cultural elements can sometimes diffuse together in a culture area, creating "spurious" correlations between the functionally unrelated cultural elements. One check against the possibility of such historical diffusion in functional and/or psychological cross-cultural investigations is to examine the postulated relationships separately for the major geographical areas of the world. This is, of course, possible only in cases where samples are large enough so that the geographical sub-samples have sufficient cases for statistical analysis. In a number of studies in which geographic subsamples have been separately examined, it has been shown that apparently worldwide statistical correlations often mask great regional variations. The correlations may be very strong in some areas, and practically nonexistent in other areas. Pursuing this argument, Philip Bock has demonstrated that love magic, sexual socialization anxiety, and elaborate menstrual taboos all tend to be found in the Americas, Africa, Melanesia, and much less in other world regions (Bock, 1967:213–216). This would argue that any studies involving correlations among those traits (e.g., Shirley and Romney, 1962; Young and Bacdayan, 1965) should control for geographic region in their statistical analyses. Murdock pointed this out as early as 1940:

A valid cross-cultural hypothesis should hold true in any area. If, however, some areas are discovered to yield negative coefficients, it must be concluded that the apparent statistical confirmation of the hypothesis is fictitious and accidental, and the hypothesis must either be rejected entirely or modified and tested again. (Murdock, 1940:369.)

Driver and Schuessler (1967) examined regional variations in their factor analysis of Murdock's World Ethnographic Sample. Examining the internal consistencies in their trait clusters, these authors found for example that *independent family, nuclear* or *polygynous,* and *patrilocal residence* correlate —.11 for the world, —.01 in North America, and —.51 around the Mediterranean (the difference between the latter two is significant at the .01 level). Here important historical differences appear to contribute to explaining these relationships. Also, they find that bride price and patrilineal descent yield a worldwide correlation at .41, but in North America it is only .03, while around the Mediterranean it is .60. Driver and Schuessler feel that the relationships between the bride price and patrilineal descent involve functional and structural "causes," but they are puzzled by the lack of correlation in North America. They suggest that "we must assume that in the New World patrilineal descent lagged behind changes in residence, which were more closely related to bride price. In the Old World no such lag took place, or patricentered social organization had more time to become stable" (Driver and Schuessler, 1967:343).

This case illustrates a second important point about geographical examination of cross-cultural statistical correlations. Comparisons of such interrelationships region by region bring to light differences which can lead to significant refinements of functional (and other) theoretical constructs. They can also lead to improvement of definitions of categories themselves. As we have suggested above, categorizations such as "patrilineal descent" and "bride price" may

be such gross measures that they must be refined into more carefully specified typologies or dimensions before relationships among
them can be made clear.

Driver's (1966) thorough statistical examination of kin avoidances in North America illustrates a further refinement of geographically controlled cross-cultural studies. Driver assembled data
on the varieties of avoidance patterns as related to marital residence
patterns and other kinship variables in a large number of North
American Indian tribes (Driver, 1966:131–182). He felt that this
exhaustive, geographically controlled study permitted sorting out
the effects of geographical-historical factors as against psychofunctional factors of the kin avoidances. He summed up his findings as
follows:

Probably all the psycho-functional "causes" of kin avoidances advocated
by Tylor, Fraser, Freud, Lowie, Murdock, and Stephens and D'Andrade
have had some influence on the origin, maintenance, and dispersal of these
behaviors. Even the most geographical-historical enthusiast needs a package
of psycho-functional "causes" to get the avoidance behavior started. Once
such behavior has become firmly established, however, it seems to diffuse by
intertribal marriage to peoples who lack some or even most of the "causes"
discovered so far. It also fails to occur among some peoples who possess
most of the "causes."

This study shows that essay-style descriptions collected even in great
bulk cannot produce valid generalizations about so complex a phenomenon. Tabulated or mapped data are also comparatively ineffective alone
and do not produce a general explanation. Cross-cultural correlations
based on fewer than 100 ethnic units may shed some light on psycho-
functional "causes," but reveal little of geographical-historical relationships. These methods combined, as I hope to have shown, yield a more
complete explanation. In addition, historical interpretation is considerably
sharpened by treating language families and culture areas as variables.
(Driver, 1966:147.)

One further note should be added here concerning the diffusion of
culture "traits." While some researchers, especially those of an earlier day, have taken the view that diffusion of cultural elements is a
counter-argument to "functional" explanations of co-variations, the
diffusionist must still explain *why* particular traits have diffused together and have persisted in their association. Most anthropologists
today would accept the proposition that functional relationships of
some kind exist whenever two cultural or social elements co-vary,
regardless of the effects of diffusion in accounting for their distribution among the cultures of the world. Thus, it is probably useful to
expect that *both* functional and diffusional factors would be involved in any patterns of co-variation among traits.

Causal Inferences from Correlational Data

I commented earlier that simple correlations among variables do not "prove" causation. In general, statements concerning causality even in experimental sciences involve inferences and assumptions which, strictly speaking, cannot be directly demonstrated experimentally (or mathematically). In all scientific work there is a logical gap between observations of relationships and the corresponding theoretical statements of causality. The logical gap is bridged by means of logical inferences which are given pragmatic supporting evidence whenever the scientist is successful in predicting events (e.g., in the testing of hypotheses; cf. Blalock, 1964).

The co-variations which social scientists observe in nonexperimental research (e.g., in cross-cultural statistical studies) are usually weaker bases for causal inferences than are laboratory experiments, but certain kinds of inferences may nonetheless be made from these data. For example, if one observes co-variations between some aspect of climate and a set of social variables, one may with some assurance make the inference that the social variables are *not* causes of the climatic variations.

Hubert M. Blalock, Jr. (1964), has examined the possibilities of making causal inferences from the patterning of multiple covariations. He takes for his example the testing of alternative causal models concerning division of labor, postnuptial residence, land tenure, and descent among North American Indians. Driver and Massey (1957) had tested the proposition that the variables as listed above represent a temporal ordering in causal terms. That is, that patterns of sexual division of labor produce particular residence patterns, which in turn will be followed by appropriate land-tenure patterns, and finally by a functionally appropriate system of descent. Thus the causal chain can be diagramed as in Figure 12.

FIGURE 12. **Causal Sequence of Culture Traits Postulated by Driver and Massey**
ADAPTED FROM Blalock, 1964.

Blalock proposed to compare the Driver-Massey model of causation with one proposed by David F. Aberle, who suggested that in addition to the causal chain as given in Figure 12, division of labor

(W) should be expected to have a direct relationship to the system of land tenure (Y). Thus Aberle's causal model can be diagramed as in Figure 13.

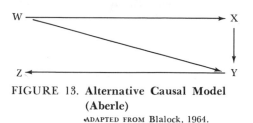

FIGURE 13. **Alternative Causal Model**
(Aberle)
ADAPTED FROM Blalock, 1964.

The logical basis for Blalock's tests of causal inference is quite simple. Since many other factors are presumably affecting the intercorrelations (e.g., differential time lag of culture change, effects of different ceremonial and belief systems, different soil fertilities and crops grown), he reasons that the correlations between any two *adjacent* variables in the "causal chain" should be higher than the correlations between variables that are more distant in the postulated sequence. The correlation between W and X should be higher than the correlation between, for example, W and Z. Applying the alternative causal models above, we note that Aberle's model (Figure 13) predicts a higher correlation between W and Y than does the Driver-Massey model (Figure 12). Table 22 shows the intercorrelations for the relevant matricentered traits among North American Indians as compiled by Driver and Massey.

TABLE 22. **Intercorrelations for Matricentered Traits of North American Indians**

	W	*X*	*Y*	*Z*
Matridominant division of labor	—	.49	.53	.39
Matrilocal residence	.49	—	.61	.51
Matricentered land tenure	.53	.61	—	.80
Matrilineal descent	.39	.51	.80	—

FROM Blalock, 1961:75.

Blalock's logical assumptions provide that the relationships between two distant variables (e.g., W and Y) should be equal to the product of the intervening correlations. Hence: Correlation WY =

Correlation WX × Correlation XY. Computation of the expected correlations for each of the relationships indicates that the observed relationships between WY and WZ are both higher than the Driver and Massey model predicts. (WZ should be .24, as a product of .49 times .61 times .80). The WZ correlation actually found (.39) fits better with the Aberle model, which predicts a correlation of .42 (.53 times .80).

Blalock notes explicitly that

we have *not* established the validity of Model II [Aberle's model]. We have merely eliminated Model I. As pointed out previously, there will ordinarily be several models that yield identical predictions. In particular, we cannot distinguish between Model I and the situation in which all arrows have been reversed, i.e., Z←—Y←—X←—W. (Blalock, 1964:76.)

Most frequently the anthropologist who wishes to test causal inferences in this manner is likely to find that he lacks sufficient data. Also, many of the causal models provided by anthropological theory are so diffuse and complex that the logical structuring necessary for predicting particular correlations cannot be determined. However, Blalock's work provides us with two excellent suggestions:

1. We need to examine cross-cultural covariations in terms of more complex patterns than the usual piecemeal two-variable style provides.
2. We need to refine theoretical models to the point where parts of them can be examined in logical terms analogous to the example given above.

Small Sample Studies, Controlled Comparisons, and "Natural Experiments"

THE SIX-CULTURES STUDY

Since one of the most frequent criticisms of cross-cultural studies is concerned with basic weaknesses of the primary ethnographic data, a logical improvement of research design could be achieved by intensive controlled collection of data from a sample of societies around the world for testing specific theoretical propositions. That was the research strategy in the Six Cultures Study of Whiting, Minturn, Lambert and associates (Minturn and Lambert, 1965). After careful preparation of questionnaires and other techniques of field observation, research teams were sent to communities in Mexico, Okinawa, the Philippines, India, East Africa, and New England. In each of the research sites the fieldworkers selected samples of children for intensive observations during play and other activities. The mothers of the sample children were interviewed and a number of other controlled observations were carried out. In addition, general ethnographic data, not only about socialization practices but other aspects of culture, were collected so that general ethnographies could be presented concerning the six cultures.

The data from the interviews with mothers were analyzed in a fairly complex statistical design involving factor analysis. The information from a total of 133 mothers was grouped (in a computerized process) into 10 factors including "warmth of mother," "mother's emotional stability," "responsibility training," and "aggression training." Having isolated these elements of mother behavior in the six cultures, antecedents of socialization practices were investigated in the residence patterns, household size and structure, extended kin groups, and patterning of sex roles. The researchers found that a number of the patterns of child training were significantly related to ecological variables involving family and household structuring. For example, they found that mothers tend to show more warmth and stability in socializing their children when there are a number of adults in the household (e.g., in extended families). A most significant finding in this research was the demonstration that *intracultural* variations appeared to be more important than cross-cultural variations in accounting for the totality of differences among the 133 mothers interviewed.

TABLE 23. **Maternal Instability *vs.* Number of Male Adults in Household**

Society*	Instability Rating	Number of Male Adults in Household	
		LOW	HIGH
Mexico	High	9	3
	Low	7	3
Philippines	High	10	2
	Low	7	4
Okinawa	High	10	1
	Low	7	6
India	High	6	5
	Low	4	9

Cumulative z score for the
four cases = 3.28
(chi square) $p < .01$ (two tailed)

ADAPTED FROM Minturn and Lambert, 1965:263.
* U.S. and East African samples not tested because they have no significant variations in number of male adults in household.

The design of the Six Cultures Study made possible an important methodological advantage, in that both intracultural and crosscultural relationships could be examined within the same research operation. Also, the generalization of research results was strengthened by showing the tendency for particular relationships to occur independently in the different cultures. Table 23 illustrates this feature of the research design.

The logic of the Six Culture Study did not place heavy emphasis on the representativeness of the six cultures as a sample from societies around the world. Rather, a main criterion for selection of the six cases appears to have been geographical separation, hence independence, of the cases. In a sense, the model provides a series of repeated tests of each hypothesis.

GEOGRAPHICALLY CONTROLLED COMPARISONS

American anthropologists have long had a tendency to prefer cross-cultural comparisons within defined geographical limits or culture areas. This tendency arose in part because of the theoretical importance of the concept of culture areas as an explanatory device, and it is further encouraged by the control of cultural detail and history that is possible if the researcher restricts his investigation to one territorially delimited segment of cultures. Fred Eggan (1954) has presented some of the theoretical arguments in support of this type of cross-cultural research.

An excellent example of geographically delimited comparisons is found in the Culture and Ecology Project carried out by Walter Goldschmidt and associates in East Africa. Their strategy was to locate a geographical area in which tribal groups were ecologically divided into pastoral and farming subgroups. To examine and to control for effects of general cultural variables they selected two cases of southern Nilotes and two cases of Bantu-speaking people. Table 24 presents the logical structure of this research.

Using this geographically restricted research design, Goldschmidt and associates were able to examine differences between pastoralists and farmers (I $vs.$ II), compared with differences across the four tribes (a_x $vs.$ b_x $vs.$ c_x $vs.$ d_x), as well as the differences across the two linguistic groups (ab $vs.$ cd). As a result of these two-way comparisons, the researchers felt that they had excellent evidence for the importance of ecological factors in accounting for differences among the subgroups. That is, in many characteristics, the farmers resembled each other *across* tribal boundaries, and differed systematically from their "tribal brethren," the pastoralists. Farmers in all the groups tended to be more hostile and suspicious, as well as "more indirect, abstract, given to fantasy, more anxious, less able to deal with their emotions, and less able to control their impulses. The herders, on the contrary, are direct, open, bound to reality, and their emotions, though constricted, are under control" (Edgerton, 1965:446).

TABLE 24. **Comparison Groups in Culture and Ecology Project (East Africa)**

		I *Pastoralists*	II *Farmers*
Kalenjian (Nilotes)	Sebei	a_1	a_2
	Pokot	b_1	b_2
Bantu	Kamba	c_1	c_2
	Hehe	d_1	d_2

ADAPTED FROM Goldschmidt *et al.*, 1965:400–447.

This research project, like the Six Cultures Project, includes within its logic a series of parallel tests of main propositions (each intratribal comparison between herders and farmers is logically independent of the others), though the several comparisons are not geographically independent as was the case in the Six Cultures Study.

NATURAL EXPERIMENTS

So-called "natural experiments" are usually systematic comparisons within specific geographical contexts. Morris Freilich (1963) has described the natural experiment as one in which "the researcher selects a situation for study where *change of a clear and dramatic nature* has occurred" (his italics). He suggests that this type of situation permits the investigator to make a strong case for assuming that the particular dramatic change can be regarded as the independent variable in a standard experimental design. It should be quickly pointed out, however, that standard experimental research structure is not achieved unless the investigator is able to find a second, comparable society or community in which the clear and dramatic change *has not occurred*. This control case is essential if the investigator is to show that the hypothesized effects are logically relatable to the dramatic change (independent variable). In the great majority of cases the control case is to be found in geographically adjacent communities, immediately outside the zone of "dramatic change."

The logical structure of the natural experiment should in most cases assume the same diagrammatic appearance as that employed by Nadel in comparing the Nupe and Gwari (Figure 11). (Also, a moment's reflection concerning this research model suggests to us that Goldschmidt and associates' Culture and Ecology Project corresponds in many respects to the requirements of a natural experiment. The ecological differences between the pastoralists and the farmers may be regarded as substituting for a "clear and dramatic change." However, a significant degree of additional control is provided whenever the time and nature of a clear and dramatic change can be specified.)

A study by Rodgers and Long (1968) provides a useful example of anthropological utilization of the natural experiment. In the course of their research in the Out Island Bahamas they found that within the past ten years a dramatic and theoretically important change had occurred in one of their research communities. Whereas most of the communities in the region are dependent on fishing (which takes the men out of the community for long periods of time), in one community (Murphy Town) recent economic development, including expanding local wage-labor opportunities, make it possible for most of the men to live at home with their families (Rodgers and Long, 1968:327–328).

The theoretical relevance of this natural experiment is that it sets up a possibility of testing the effects of "father absence" on personality development of young boys.

From the theoretical work of Whiting and associates (e.g., Whiting, Kluckhohn, and Anthony, 1958) and others, father absence of the sort found in most of the Out Island communities is postulated to cause "cross-sex identification" among boys, since appropriate male role models are largely absent from their daily experience. To test this idea, the investigators used a projective test involving shape preferences, adapted from the work of W. A. McElroy (1954). The nature of the figures is shown in Figure 14.

FIGURE 14. **Preference-for-Shapes Test: One Choice Pair**
ADAPTED FROM Rogers and Long, 1968.

The elements in their research design include the following:

1. The preference-for-shapes test should result in clear differentiation of boys and girls in that community in which the boys have opportunities to identify with adult males (Murphy Town).
2. The boys in a community where adult males are often absent should show "feminized" responses to the test—hence their responses will resemble those of the Murphy Town girls.
3. Adult males in the Out Islands become "initiated" to a man's role through participation in the fishing expeditions. Hence, their responses should resemble those of the Murphy Town boys, rather than those of their own male children.
4. If items 1, 2, and 3 are found to be true, the recent change (economic development) may be considered to be the cause of the observed patterns, since the communities are in other significant respects closely similar in culture and social structure.

The investigators chose the community of Crossing Rocks as the control community, since it manifested the typical Out Island pattern of father absence. The projective tests were administered by native assistants (two women in their early forties) who were thoroughly trained in order to ensure standardization of testing procedure. One particular pair of figures (see Figure 14) was found to differentiate most sharply between Murphy Town boys and girls. This choice pair was therefore selected to test the proposed differences between Crossing Rocks and Murphy Town. The results are shown in Table 25.

TABLE 25.   **Shape Preferences in the Out Island Bahamas**

	Curved Shape	Angular Shape	Totals
Murphy Town girls	24	12	36
boys (under 15 yrs.)	19	30	49
Crossing Rocks boys (under 15 yrs.)	15	5	20
Crossing Rocks men (16 and older)	5	20	25

ADAPTED FROM Rodgers and Long, 1968:329–330.
All differences are significant at $p < .01$ or better, using a chi-square test.

This utilization of a natural experiment has the logical form shown in Figure 15.

Since my earlier discussion dwells on serious methodological weaknesses in Nadel's two-case comparison, it is important to examine the ways in which this research by Rodgers and Long constitutes in any sense an improvement over previous research. The

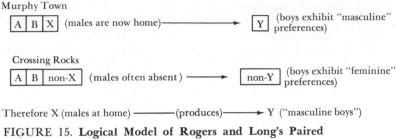

FIGURE 15. **Logical Model of Rogers and Long's Paired Comparison**

study appears to have the following advantages in the comparison:

1. Rodgers and Long set forth a hypothesis for testing, and specified *in advance* what data would be necessary to constitute support of the hypothesis. Nadel's arguments, on the other hand, appear to be post hoc explanation of research results.
2. Because their research model is based on testing a hypothesis about the influence of a *clear and dramatic change* (about which a specific prediction is made), Rodgers and Long are not forced to assume that the two cases are identical in all other respects. Similarity of the cases is, of course, highly desirable, but not as essential as was the case in Nadel's post hoc explanatory model. This case illustrates the crucial importance of theoretical systems as logical networks that provide reasons for concentrating attention on specific variables (and provide clear rules for discarding or revising particular hypotheses).
3. The variables are clearly specified (operationalized), and the data are tested statistically in order to rule out chance as an explanation of the observed relationships. Nadel, on the other hand, provided no information about frequencies of the witch-craft patterns he described.
4. The comparison of Crossing Rocks boys and men is an extremely significant additional piece in the overall research pattern, for it constitutes an *intracommunity* test of the validity of the research instrument.

There are, of course, a number of ways in which this natural experiment could be improved:

1. The evidence for the crucial dependent variable (cross-sex role identification) depends on a single instance of behavior which in itself is a relatively indirect measure. Preference for the curved shape in Figure 14 is not, in and of itself, cross-sex identification. Rather, it is postulated to be an indirect indicator of cross-sex tendencies. Following the argument in favor of multi-instrument

or multimethod research in Chapter 6, considerable strengthening of the case would follow from inclusion of several other kinds of measurements (including naturalistic observations) of this presumably very generalized behavior pattern.

2. Further description of the two communities, particularly with reference to their presumed similarities, would add credibility to the study.

3. In spite of the very considerable care taken to insure standardization of test administration, the possibility of contamination in the testing procedure cannot be ruled out (cf. page 128 concerning the subtlety of possible "administrator effects" in testing).

4. Further intracommunity testing of the theoretical propositions is distinctly possible, since there are significant variations in father absence within each of the communities.

5. Responses from a third community (e.g., another males-absent community), preferably collected by the same person who administered the tests in Murphy Town, would strengthen the network of supporting evidence.

It is, of course, a relatively easy task to point out shortcomings in even the most carefully designed research venture. The comments above are offered, therefore, not as a criticism of this specific piece of research but as guidelines for anthropologists who may find considerable usefulness in the natural-experiment model as exemplified by Rodgers and Long.

A chief weakness of the natural experiment as a basis for anthropological research lies in the fact that the independent variables (specific cultural changes) are far from being under the control of the researcher. The fieldworker must depend on luck to turn up useful instances of naturally occurring dramatic changes. Systematic exploration of a particular theoretical model cannot, therefore, depend on the vagaries of this type of experimentation. The problem is compounded by the fact that most cultural changes, whether due to specific community-development programs or the more diffuse effects of general "modernization," are not made up of clear-cut, isolable elements, but are complex networks of changes that simultaneously involve economic, political, religious, and other aspects of people's life ways.

FIELD EXPERIMENT

Since the natural experiment would be a fairly powerful research tool if anthropologists could find the appropriate dramatic cultural changes to match the needs of their theoretical systems, a natural and logical step would be for researchers purposefully to bring about the experimental conditions themselves. This is what is done in the "field experiment."

Allan Holmberg (1954) has described field experiments in which he markedly increased Siriono technological effectiveness by presenting the people with some steel axes and machetes. This experiment produced, he felt, a noticeable rise in in-group hostility.

One of the first effects of the increased production of wild honey, for example, was an increase in the supply of native beer and in the number and duration of drinking bouts. This in turn led to a more frequent expression of aggression, since drinking feasts are the principal occasions when both verbal and physical aggression are expressed among the men. . . . On one such occasion, in fact—and this was a direct result of the increased production of native beer—the aggressions expressed at a drinking bout of considerable intensity resulted in such a strong hostility among the members of two extended families that the unity of the band itself was threatened. Needless to say, this was an effect which I had not anticipated at the time the tools were introduced. (Holmberg, 1954:108.)

This example provides a very clear illustration of why anthropologists have been wary of carrying out field experiments. Any introduced changes that are large enough to be theoretically interesting are also likely to have relatively wide-reaching consequences beyond the prediction of the experimenter. Some of these consequences may be socially undesirable. For that reason many anthropologists have taken the position that field experimentation can practically never be justified on moral grounds.

But in a world in which extensive cultural changes are ubiquitous it is surely near-sighted of anthropologists to avoid any and all cultural innovation. By their very presence in their research communities all fieldworkers have introduced changes among their informants and hosts. Few anthropologists have had sufficient moral strictness to refuse aspirins and other medical help to the people of their research sites, even though such involvement in local activities almost certainly had consequences beyond the immediate expectations of the parties involved.

One solution to this problem about field experimentation is to introduce cultural items or situations which are already intermittently present in the community. Thus an experimenter might examine the effects on intrafamily behavior of the introduction of bicycles by given a few two-wheelers to families lacking these vehicles, in a community where some of the people already have bicycles. In fact, practically every human society exhibits considerable differentials in ownership of resources (and information). Thus, at least on an individual and household basis, there are possibilities for the introduction of experimental variables which are not totally new and untried in the population as a whole. Similar intracultural experimental possibilities are, of course, offered by the fact that individual villages and hamlets may vary a good deal in their rates of acquisition of new items from the wider world.

French (1953) has reviewed the possibilities of field experiments from the point of view of social psychologists carrying out research within the American cultural scene. The experimental manipulations he discusses include, for example, increasing the levels of social interactions in a housing project to test for changes in morale and changes in the structure of factory organization to test for effects on efficiency. Anthropologists are now deeply involved in study of various aspects of American culture, particularly in the realm of urban anthropology and study of "the culture of poverty"; it would appear that controlled experiments could be of great potential usefulness in some of this work.

Whether experiments are introduced by the anthropologist or provided by "natural happenings," their usefulness is strongly affected by the following considerations:

1. The testing of specific hypotheses derived *in advance* from a theoretical framework is a much stronger methodological model than one in which only post hoc explanations are provided of the experimental events.
2. Presence of a control group or case is essential in order to have a standard against which to measure the effects of the experimental variable.
3. The outcome of hypothesis testing remains in doubt if variables are not clearly defined in operational terms.
4. Where possible, researchers should use more than one type of instrument or method for observing the relevant variables.
5. In most cases some sort of quantification is very useful for measuring the strength of the experimental effects and for examining the statistical significance of the observed results.

Researchers in psychology, sociology, and related fields have learned about a number of pitfalls in experimental research design through long and sometimes painful experience. Any would be experimenter is well-advised to examine some of their methodological statements carefully before choosing a particular research structure. Campbell (1957) for example, has published a useful statement on "Factors Relevant to the Validity of Experiments in Social Settings."

Multiple Hypotheses: The Strategic Elimination of Alternatives

There are many ways in which provisional evidence can be amassed in support of a theoretical proposition. A statistical cross-cultural comparison, a regionally controlled comparison, a specialized "field experiment," or an intracultural comparison, can each in its separate way provide support for a theoretical statement. An effective theory-building strategy should combine all of these research modes. As suggested in Chapters 2 and 3, theoretical work is most effective when the goals of particular pieces of research are clearly spelled out, and when the steps of research are defined in a manner that permits replication. These are guidelines for the structuring of individual investigations, but what can be suggested concerning the most effective planning of *sequences* of investigations? How can the individual bits of theory construction be made solid and enduring —providing an increasingly elaborated frame of explanation for sectors of human behavior?

I have already suggested elements of a successful general research strategy in connection with several points taken up earlier. The investigatory attitude which seems to me the most promising is that particular style of theoretical eclecticism which has been labeled "the method of multiple working hypotheses" by the geographer T. C. Chamberlin (1890). Chamberlin opposed his methodological suggestion to that style most commonly encountered in many sciences—namely, that of deductive verification from a general theoretical framework. In simple terms, this latter research strategy usually involves an unstinting collection of *evidence in support of one's ruling theoretical position*. Anthropology is full of examples: of those who labored to pile up the evidence in favor of a theory of unilinear evolution; those who have collected instances of diffusion and borrowing to illustrate a nonevolutionist historicism; and all those tireless workers who have gathered up instances in support of the proposition that rituals and other social features reinforce and maintain social integration and solidarity. In psychology there are the workers in the vineyards of "cognitive dissonance theory" who have been ingenious in finding additional instances of situations in which the theoretical formulation can be made to apply; but the classic example of this particular research strategy is found in that very large output of Freudian psychoanalytic theory, in which, over the years, nearly every aspect of individual behavior and nearly every element of culture has in one way or another been subsumed within the extension of the Oedipus complex, castration anxiety, and other primal touchstones of the Freudian scenario.

Now, the point to all this is that these "ruling-theory" research paradigms generally involve an increasing ego involvement of the scientist with his personal theory, with increasing reluctance to entertain alternative forms of explanation. Not uncommonly, rules of evidence become lax, and cases which support the theory are accepted uncritically since their fit with the main theory makes them seem almost self-evident; hence there is no need for careful sifting of evidence. As Chamberlin put it:

A thousand applications of the supposed principle of levity to the explanation of ascending bodies brought no increase of evidence that it was the true theory of the phenomena, but it doubtless created the impression in the minds of the ancient physical philosophers that it did, for so many additional facts seemed to harmonize with it. (Chamberlin, 1897:841.)

Concerning the dangers of emotional involvement with one's pet theories (and a way to avoid such dangers) Chamberlin said:

The moment one has offered an original explanation for a phenomenon which seems satisfactory, that moment affection for his intellectual child springs into existence, and as the explanation grows into a definite theory his parental explanations cluster about his offspring and it grows more and more dear to him. While he persuades himself that he holds it still as tentative, it is none the less lovingly tentative and not impartially and indifferently tentative.

To avoid this grave danger, the method of multiple working hypotheses is urged. It differs from the simple working hypothesis in that it distributes the effort and divides the affections. . . . Each hypothesis suggests its own criteria, its own means of proof, its own method of developing the truth, and if a group of hypotheses encompass the subject on all sides, the total outcome of means and of methods is full and rich. (*Ibid.*, 843.)

Francis Bacon, more than three centuries ago, suggested this same research strategy:

The induction which is to be available for the discovery and demonstration of sciences and arts, must analyze nature by proper rejections and exclusions; and then, after a sufficient number of negatives, come to a conclusion on the affirmative instances. . . . [To man] it is granted only to proceed at first by negative, and at last to end in affirmatives after exclusion has been exhausted. (Bacon, reprinted 1960:99,151.)

John R. Platt has suggested that those sciences which appear to be making rapid progress at this time—e.g., molecular biology and high-energy physics—seem to be doing so because of their extensive employment of the strategy involving step-by-step elimination of alternative hypotheses. He feels that supposed differences in the kind of subject matter and relative tractability of various areas of research have been exaggerated, and that the areas of continuing progress are notable mainly for their methodological excellence. As he puts it:

Unfortunately, I think there are other areas of science today that are sick by comparison, because they have forgotten the necessity for alternative hypotheses and disproof. Each man has only one branch—or none—on the logical tree, and it twists at random without coming to the need for a crucial decision at any point. We can see from the external symptoms that there is something scientifically wrong. The Frozen Method. The Eternal Surveyor. The Never Finished. The Great Man with a Single Hypothesis. The Little Club of Dependents. The Vendetta. The All-encompassing Theory Which Can Never Be Falsified. (Platt, 1966:29.)

There are two important classes of alternative hypotheses which should be routinely examined by every anthropologist in the course of his investigations.

1. *Methodological Hypotheses.*

In any research it is imperative that the null hypothesis be considered: that the results of a particular set of observations (e.g., a co-occurrence of two cultural or social traits) happened because of sampling error.

A related alternative hypothesis is that the observed co-occurrence or pattern derives from nonrepresentativeness in sampling of cases: "He happened to find an exceptional society." A third possibility is that the observed pattern is caused by biases in the quality of the data themselves. A variant of this methodological question involves the possibility that the observed pattern is caused by biases in informants' *response styles* (e.g., on a questionnaire or psychological test), rather than by "true" cultural patterns.

Most of the studies we have looked at in this chapter involve the examination of some of these methodological alternatives, particularly the statistical hypothesis that the results obtained occurred because of chance errors in sampling. The data-quality-control methods of Naroll, Rohner, and others are concentrated attempts to test for a whole series of alternatives concerning biases of the ethnographer, biased effects of the field-work situation, and other sources of error in field-work observations.

2. *Theoretical Alternatives.*

When all of the "procedural hypotheses" have been considered, the anthropologist can move on to consider alternative theoretical formulations—the competing explanations variously labeled "psychological explanations," "social structural theory," "functionalism," "evolutionism," "economic determinism." Here a crucially important point must be emphasized: consideration of alternative hypotheses must be structured in a manner that permits the rejection of one or the other alternative. Rival theoretical positions, if they truly make a difference, must at some point *predict different results* under some specifiable condition. It is the job of the investigator to locate such critical differences in theoretical formulations and put them to the test. Blalock's statistical testing of two different explanations of the relationships among division of labor, land tenure, residence, and descent is an example of a situation in which the researcher was able to discard one alternative hypothesis in favor of the other. At the same time he admitted that other alternative formulations could be found which would require further testing and refinement of the data.

The statistical analysis by Driver of relationships between in-law avoidances and marriage among North American Indians is an example of a frequently encountered situation where rival theories each appear to contribute to the full explanation of the data. Thus, instead of discarding one or the other alternative, Driver suggested that the co-occurrence of the two trait clusters requires an explanation incorporating both psychofunctional and historical elements of theory. A next step in this kind of research situation is to design investigations that permit the measurement of the *relative strengths* of these two "causal factors" in a variety of circumstances.

In all of these efforts the anthropological investigator should be constantly watchful of opportunities for eliminating less-promising alternatives. The philosopher Karl Popper has argued strongly that we can never positively affirm or prove a theoretical proposition— we can only eliminate, for the moment, all the known alternative explanations. Unfortunately, anthropological research thus far has not succeeded in eliminating any except the more outlandishly improbable theoretical positions.

Methodology and the Culture of Anthropology

A principal weakness in much anthropological work is that investigation is not recycled. Most frequently the social scientist who has finished a neat piece of work publishes his conclusions and then moves on to another somewhat related area of research—to expand on the supposedly successful model of explanation, rather than submitting it to critical retesting. It is not difficult to see that there are important features in the general culture of the social sciences that encourage poor methodology. Pressures to publish—and to produce *new and novel* conceptualizations—encourage premature closure of investigation. And our social-science culture provides too few rewards for patient hesitation, recycling, and replication of research. Instead of hearing applause for a replication of observations, the anthropologist more often hears a scornful "That's already been done by ——, ten years ago."

One of the most pervasive features of anthropological culture is the general commitment to "holism." If this ideological commitment is translated always in terms of general "depictive integration" and other qualitative portrayals of cultural systems, serious obstacles are put in the path of methodological improvement; on the other hand, holism is just as easily translated into a multimethod, multihypothesis research style which fits well with the general strategy of investigation outlined above.

In some ways the most important area for immediate application of the "method of multiple working hypotheses" is that of anthropological data-gathering techniques. The inventory of anthropological research tools has been subjected to very little in the way of critical analysis. All of the techniques—interviewing key informants, survey techniques, projective tests, analysis of unobtrusive measures, participant observation—need to be compared one with another in order to eliminate techniques that are weak in reliability and validity, and to develop new tools of observation whose precision can make the testing of alternative hypotheses a more productive enterprise.

Throughout this discussion of anthropological research methods I have been suggesting, in agreement with Platt, that the apparent weaknesses of anthropological work derive much less from the inherent difficulties of our subject matter, and much more from persistently nonproductive features of our anthropological subculture. These nonproductive features are perpetuated through direct transmission within our programs of graduate instruction. They are also perpetuated by some very general tendencies in the institutional make-up of the social sciences. I have written this book with the hope of furthering a pattern of culture change which already seems to be gathering momentum. Possibly new methodological developments will arise that can bring about a real "revitalization movement."

REFERENCES CITED

ADAIR, JOHN, and EVON Z. VOGT
1949. "Navaho and Zuñi Veterans: A Study of Contrasting Modes of Culture Change." *American Anthropologist*, 51:547–561.

BACON, FRANCIS
1960. (First published in 1620.) *The New Organon and Related Writings*. Indianapolis: Bobbs-Merrill.

BARRY, H., M. K. BACON, and I. L. CHILD
1952. "Rater's Instructions for Analysis of Socialization Practices with Respect to Dependence and Independence." New Haven: Mimeographed.

BENNETT, JOHN W.
1944. "The Development of Ethnological Theories as Illustrated by Studies of the Plains Indian Sun Dance." *American Anthropologist,* 46: 162–181.

BLALOCK, HUBERT M., JR.
1964. "Causal Inferences in Non-experimental Research." Chapel Hill: University of North Carolina Press.

BOCK, PHILIP
1967. "Love Magic, Menstrual Taboos, and the Facts of Geography." *American Anthropologist,* 69:213–217.

CAMPBELL, DONALD T.
1957. "Factors Relevant to the Validity of Experiments in Social Settings." *Psychological Bulletin,* 54:297–312.

CHAMBERLIN, THOMAS C.
1890. "The Method of Multiple Working Hypotheses." *Science* (old series), 15:92–96.
1897. "The Method of Multiple Working Hypotheses." *Journal of Geology,* 5:837–848.

DRIVER, HAROLD
1966. "Geographical-Historical Versus Psycho-Functional Explanations of Kin Avoidances." *Current Anthropology,* 7:131–182.

DRIVER, HAROLD, and W. C. MASSEY
1957. *Comparative Studies of North American Indians.* Philadelphia: The American Philosophical Society.

DRIVER, HAROLD, and KARL F. SCHUESSLER
1967. "Correlational Analysis of Murdock's 1957 Ethnographic Sample." *American Anthropologist,* 69:322–352.

EDGERTON, ROBERT B.
1965. " 'Cultural' *vs.* 'Ecological' Factors in the Expression of Values, Attitudes, and Personality Characteristics." *American Anthropologist,* 67:422–447.

EGGAN, FRED
1954. "Social Anthropology and the Method of Controlled Comparison." *American Anthropologist,* 56:743–763.

FREILICH, MORRIS
1963. "The Natural Experiment, Ecology and Culture." *Southwestern Journal of Anthropology,* 19:21–39.

FRENCH, JOHN R. F., JR.
1953. "Experiments in Field Settings." In *Research Methods in the Behavioral Sciences,* eds. L. Festinger and D. Katz. New York: Holt, Rinehart and Winston.

GOLDSCHMIDT, W., *et al.*
1965. "Variation and Adaptability of Culture: A Symposium." *American Anthropologist,* 67:400–447. Reproduced by permission of the American Anthropological Association.

HOLMBERG, ALLAN
   1954. "Adventures in Culture Change." In *Method and Perspective in Anthropology*, ed. R. F. Spencer. Minneapolis: University of Minnesota Press: 103–116.
   1969. *Nomads of the Long Bow: The Siriono of Eastern Bolivia*. Garden City: The Natural History Press.

KÖBBEN, ANDRÉ J.
   1952. (Reprinted 1961.) "New Ways of Presenting an Old Idea: The Statistical Method in Social Anthropology." In *Readings in Cross-Cultural Methodology*, ed. F. W. Moore. New Haven: HRAF Press.

MCELROY, W. A.
   1954. "A Sex Difference in Preference for Shapes." *British Jorunal of Sociology*, 45:209–216.

MILL, JOHN S.
   1930. *A System of Logic*. New York: Longman's, 8th edition.

MINTURN, LEIGH, and W. W. LAMBERT
   1965. *Mothers of Six Cultures*. New York: Wiley.

MURDOCK, GEORGE P.
   1940. "The Cross-Cultural Survey." *American Sociological Review*, 5:369–370.
   1967. "Ethnographic Atlas." *Ethnology*, 6 (and other issues of this journal).
   1949. *Social Structure*. New York: Macmillan.

NADEL, S. F.
   1952. "Witchcraft in Four African Societies: An Essay in Comparison." *American Anthropologist*, 54:18–29.

NAROLL, RAOUL
   1962. *Data Quality Control: A New Research Technique*. Glencoe, Ill.: Free Press.
   1968. "Some Thoughts on Comparative Method in Cultural Anthropology." In *Methodology in Social Research*, ed. H. M. Blalock. New York: McGraw-Hill: 236–277.
   1961. "Two Solutions to Galton's Problem." In *Readings in Cross-Cultural Methodology*, ed. P. W. Moore. New Haven: HRAF Press: 217–242.
   1964. "A Fifth Solution to Galton's Problem." *American Anthropologist*, 66:863–867.

NAROLL, RAOUL, and ROY G. D'ANDRADE
   1963. "Two Further Solutions to Galton's Problem." *American Anthropologist*, 65:1953–1967.

PLATT, JOHN R.
   1966. *The Step to Man*. New York: Wiley.

ROBERTS, JOHN M., and BRIAN SUTTON-SMITH
   1962. "Child Training and Game Involvement." *Ethnology*, 1:167–185.

RODGERS, WILLIAM B., and JOHN M. LONG
1968. "Male Models and Sexual Identification. A Case from the Out Island Bahamas." *Human Organization,* 27:326–331.

ROHNER, RONALD
n.d.   Personal communication.

SHIRLEY, R. W., and A. K. ROMNEY
1962. "Love Magic and Socialization Anxiety." *American Anthropologist,* 64:1028–1031.

SIEGEL, SIDNEY
1956. *Nonparametric Statistics for the Behavioral Sciences.* New York: McGraw-Hill.

TYLOR, E. B.
1889. "On a Method of Investigating the Development of Institutions." Reprinted in 1961 in *Readings in Cross-Cultural Methodology,* ed. Frank W. Moore. New Haven: Human Relations Area Files: 1–28.

WHITING, JOHN M., and IRVIN CHILD
1953. *Child Training and Personality.* New Haven: Yale University Press.

WHITING, JOHN M., R. KLUCKHOHN, and A. ANTHONY
1958. "The Function of Male Initiation Ceremonies at Puberty." In *Readings in Social Psychology,* eds. E. Maccoby, T. Newcomb, and E. Hartley.

YOUNG, FRANK
1965. *Initiation Ceremonies: A Cross-Cultural Study of Status Dramatization.* Indianapolis: Bobbs-Merrill.

YOUNG, FRANK, and A. BACDAYAN
1962. "The Function of Male Initiation Ceremonies: A Cross-Cultural Test of an Alternative Hypothesis." With comment by John M. Whiting. *American Journal of Sociology,* 67:379–396.
1965. "Menstrual Taboos and Social Rigidity." *Ethnology,* 4:225–240.

Ritual Stick Fighting Among the People of the Nuba Hills, Sudan

Epilogue
Relevance, Ethics, and the Future of Anthropology

An important part of my creed as a social scientist is that on the grounds of absolute objectivity or on a posture of scientific detachment and indifference, a truly relevant and serious social science cannot ask to be taken seriously by a society desperately in need of moral and empirical guidance in human affairs. Nor can it support its claims to scientific purity or relevance by a preoccupation with methodology as an end and by innumerable articles in scientific journals devoted to escapist, even though quantifiable, trivia. I believe that to be taken seriously, to be viable, and to be relevant social science must dare to study the real problems of men and society, must use the real community, the market place, the arena of politics and power as its laboratories, and must confront and seek to understand the dynamics of social action and social change. The appropriate technology of serious and relevant social science would have as its prime goal helping society move toward humanity and justice with minimum irrationality, instability, and cruelty. If social science and social technology cannot help achieve these goals then they will be ignored or relegated to the level of irrelevance, while more serious men seek these goals through trial and error or through the crass exercise of power. (Kenneth B. Clark, *Dark Ghetto,* 1965: Introduction.)

So far in this book I have avoided discussing *which kinds* of research objectives should be pursued, since my main aim has been to examine the practical question of *how* research should be carried out. The methodological ideas that have grown up in the social sciences are applicable to a very broad range of theoretical and applied questions. Clearly, the methods of gathering useful information are generally the same whether one is pursuing a "completely theoretical" question with no immediate social significance, or, on the other hand, one's aim is to solve a pressing contemporary public issue.

In recent years social scientists have been the target of severe criticism of the sort that Kenneth Clark alludes to above—the increasingly noisy complaint that abstract theoretical concerns and preoccupation with methodological niceties have diverted social scientists from the "prime goal [of] helping society move toward humanity and justice. . . ." The evidence in support of this criticism is not hard to find. It has frequently been difficult for anthropologists to demonstrate that obtaining a collection of folk tales from still another poorly described primitive culture adds significantly to the problem-solving capacity of the discipline; for psychologists, the addition of one more variant to the pile of data on the maze-learning performance of rats or college sophomores is difficult to articulate with pressing contemporary social issues; and in sociology, abstract theoretical materials on "the integration of stable systems of social interaction" are often unconvincing as to their practical application, from the point of view of nonscientists.

On the other hand, anthropologists (and other scientists usually offer two main counter-arguments:

1. The freedom of the scientist to inquire into whatever most excites his interest and curiosity must be preserved, in order to maintain the broad freedoms of research and expression which have historically produced highly useful new knowledge.
2. Events in the physical sciences have demonstrated repeatedly that seemingly inconsequential discoveries are often essential ingredients of later technical developments of the utmost practicality and "relevance." This argument is usually expressed in the statement: "No one can predict in advance the potential future usefulness of a particular scientific discovery." (Examples supporting the argument usually include the apparent "impracticality" or "irrelevance" of early developments in atomic theory, Ben Frank-

lin's and others' experiments with electricity, James Watt's toy-ing with steam engines, and so on.)

The "freedom-of-investigation" argument is a rather convincing one, but it would be more convincing if social science research re-ports reflected a higher degree of truly exploratory and innovative research. Unfortunately, our social sciences journals and other pub-lications reflect a distressingly large amount of conforming and uni-maginative research. T. S. Kuhn has recently examined in some de-tail this conservative and noninnovative side of established scientific activity (Kuhn, 1962).

He notes that most scientists, social, physical, and biological, are not latter-year Franklins, Newtons, Darwins, and Pasteurs. They are, rather, the patient and plodding followers of one or another es-tablished "school" of theory, concerned less with blazing new and hitherto unexplored scientific pathways than with converting estab-lished theoretical positions into yet another publishable example of paradigmic progress.

In general, I feel that social scientists, like their fellow workers in other research disciplines, can if necessary demonstrate the potential practical relevance of a very wide range of seemingly obscure infor-mation. The whole past and never-to-be-relived history of human culture is an area of study from which able investigators can pro-duce practical evidence concerning basic patterns of human be-havior. Cross-cultural comparative studies have demonstrated the theoretical importance of descriptive data from the more exotic societies of mankind, and the resulting theoretical findings can have powerful application to the problems of our modern day.

But none of the arguments concerning the ultimate usefulness of any and all theoretical investigations can be entirely convincing to those many people—including legislators—who are insisting that so-cial sciences research money should be spent in the areas where the problems are. The fact is that none of the proponents of the practi-cal worth of the more obscure and theoretically abstract areas of re-search can claim that concentration directly on relevant and press-ing social issues is *less* likely to produce useful information for our publics and policy-makers. None of the arguments for a dissinter-ested social science can show that Kenneth Clark is on the wrong trail when he suggests that we "must dare to study the real prob-lems of men and society, must use the real community, the market place, the arena of politics and power as [our] laboratories." At some of our more awkward moments of defensiveness we tend to take our role models from the "hard sciences" of physics and chem-istry, but in this instance we might be better off to look at the example of the medical sciences; there a high level of concentration on "relevant" and immediate problems (such as seeking the eradication of various poxes, plagues, and pestilences of mankind) has demonstrated a very considerable balance sheet of scientific successes. Looking to the medical sciences and associated disciplines for a general research strategy, we might come to the conclusion that definition of research goals in terms of socially relevant problems has great potential profit.

Clark's statement of his credo is a plea against the posture of detachment and indifference. And, when it comes down to the question of which research projects will be—or should be—funded, he has a great deal of right in the matter. The claim to relevance of the social scientist who wants to study an abstract theoretical issue, unrelated to contemporary social problems, is frequently a handy alibi to mask his basic indifference to the social issues that publics and political bodies feel must be solved.

There are in the world of men uncountable numbers of theoretical problems to be solved, and only some of these are anywhere near the heart of the matter when it comes to the "urban crisis," the "crisis in our schools," "the American Dilemma" of race relations, the population explosion, and dozens of other problems that trouble us on the contemporary scene. There are millions of potential theoretical problems, but there are only some thousands of social scientists, and only some hundreds of these will have the wit and opportunity to make important inroads on the scientific questions they select for research. Where should the emphasis be?

Not all anthropologists (and other social scientists) need to rush headlong into the study of our American urban problems, however. First of all, neither Kenneth Clark nor anyone else has argued that all the relevant and pressing social issues are found in continental North America; scientific concerns should not be based on any nationalistic or provincialistic biases. The social problems of men everywhere—men adjusting to the now quite bewildering pace and patterns of "modernization," and "technologizing" of the world—are the fit subjects of our social science.

While we might be tempted to define "relevant research" in such a manner as to clearly exclude certain supposedly "irrelevant" categories of work now widely prevalent in our discipline, it is much more useful to suggest that certain highly visible social issues be listed which a majority of thoughtful people would regard as central to the prime goal of "helping society move toward humanity and justice with minimum irrationality, instability, and cruelty." Such a list of highly relevant questions for social sciences research could be drawn up by our professional associations, and project proposals directed to these prime targets could be given high financial and other priority.

There would appear to be two main ways in which "relevant research" could be programmed. Examples of both types may be found in current anthropological work. The first type of project is one in which a particular problem (or whole set of problems) *in a particular locale* is selected for study. Some contemporary examples include a number of on-going projects in urban ghettos; studies of mental health and social organization, such as the Leighton Stirling County project (and several others designed along similar lines); and studies of the effects of particular sociotechnological innovations, such as Elizabeth Colson's and Thayer Scudder's study of population dislocation and other effects of the Kariba Dam in Southeast Africa.

A second, and equally relevant, kind of research is that which aims at some one crucial social issue—e.g., human overpopulation or human aggression—which is studied through a series of investigations that may be carried out in a number of different locations.

The first alternative, above, typically involves examination of the systematic interrelationships of a great number of variables, perhaps broken down into several subsystems at various stages of the investigation; the second type of study tends on the whole to deal with a somewhat narrower slice of human behavior, but in a more "nomothetic" perspective.

RELEVANCE AND METHODOLOGICAL RIGOR

It is an accepted tenet of science that, to be useful, scientific statements must have high "truth value." Here we approach one of the sore points in the debate between social scientists and their critics. The partisans of "relevance" have often mistaken emotional commitment and persuasive philosophy for the stuff of scientific veracity. Their favorite social scientists are more often applauded for their polemics than for diligent testing of hypotheses. And some anthropologists have joined this argument, insisting that productive research depends on emotional involvement in the people whose problems are a focus of study.

Emotional commitment—even fanaticism—on the side of humanity and justice does not insure either scientific excellence or its opposite. Some highly productive scientists have carried out their research with serene detachment from the daily affairs of the world, but there are many examples of highly emotional, politically-motivated (some would even say bigoted) researchers who have contributed much to the growth of knowledge.

It is probable that much of the criticism that has been leveled at "irrelevant" social science is aroused by the fact that second-rate (or even worse) research materials abound in our journals. Some of the materials that are attacked as irrelevant or "intellectually sterile" are vulnerable because their theoretical underpinnings are confused or tautological; the supporting evidence is incomplete, unrepresentative, or conjectural, and the concluding generalizations unwarranted. Some social scientists whose work can thus be criticized are, in fact, devoting their attentions to relevant problems—only their methodologies betray them. In passing it can be suggested that much of the available data on "the culture of poverty," American race relations, and (at a more general level) relationships of political power to patterns of social stability and change are so methodologically questionable that they may be for practical usage irrelevant.

The kind of relevant social research that Kenneth Clark argues for in his introduction to *Dark Ghetto* has to involve hard-nosed and stubborn insistence on reliability and validity of information. It is revealing, in fact, to note that Clark's own writing about the black ghettos reflects a great amount of empirical data gathering. Most of us justify our science with the assumption that true information is a most powerful force for effective social adaptation. In fact, our version of human cultural history is generally made up of a chronicle of successful knowledge accumulation. Clearly, at this time we are woefully lacking in social knowledge about many aspects of our technosocial scene. To get that knowledge is in no wise easy, but there are ways of enhancing our knowledge-building performance. The ways that have been suggested here are, for the most part, fairly uncomplicated, time-tested, ideas which are current in the culture of general science. Application of these cultural patterns to the data-gathering process in anthropology (and the other social sciences) lags in part because of some problems in translating principles of naturalistic observation to what some people regard as the "nonnatural" domain of human activity; but the culture lag is also due to inhibiting factors in the social organization of our disciplines.

I am suggesting that relevant research in the social sciences should exhibit a blending of concern about current public issues with methodologically sound information-gathering and theory-testing procedures. In this connection it is important to make a clear separation between the domain of social symptomatology (about which the lay public may be quite well informed) and the more theoretical problems of identifying crucial underlying processes. Thus, social scientists rightly resist the suggestions of lay critics concerning causal factors, just as medical practitioners quite often disagree with their patients' "folk diagnoses," even though they take their statements of symptoms of distress quite seriously.

One important aspect of anthropological research operations that is often misunderstood by both our critics and some of our theory builders is the significance of basic descriptive information. Many crucial research areas are characterized by an overwhelming dearth of factual information concerning "what's really going on." The data on urban ghettos, for example, are thick with references to crime, delinquency, broken homes, and other pathological elements, but materials on many other significant aspects of day-to-day living are inadequate. Relevant research often requires that at the outset a high priority be placed on basic descriptive data—not just any old description, but careful delineation of representative arrays of facts concerning people's physical and psychological adaptations.

Social scientists frequently repeat a cliché to the effect that "mere description by itself is worthless; only when descriptive statements are relatable to theoretical propositions do they become useful knowledge." This kind of statement is frequently accompanied by another "axiom"—that to provide useful knowledge social scientists must be able to predict outcomes or consequences of actions.

These statements are particularly in error when it comes to practical applications of social information, for very often the predictions of consequences, or other forecasts, are made by administrators, planners, or other agencies (including reformers and revolutionaries), and not by social scientists. Their policy decisions, we may assume, are most effective when they are based on accurate descriptive data. Existential statements, such as: "Twenty-three percent of these people are malnourished (by some stated standard)" or "At any given time about one-third of the men are away from home, working at the plantations," are frequently of direct practical usefulness, provided such information is available at the time and place "where the action is."

It must be emphasized that research that is oriented toward the solution of particular social problems often involves a different strategy from the usual paradigms of theory building. The difference is clear when we examine the sequence of research projects of individual investigators. When a social scientist successfully completes a particular research venture, he often shifts his area of investigation (both conceptually and geographically) to some *theoretically* related domain. For example, successful conclusion of a study of role behavior in a hospital setting may lead the investigator to seek an expansion of his theoretical system through the application of the new-found theory to a different setting—perhaps to behavior in an industrial plant.

Problem-oriented research, on the other hand, involves the assumption that the successful bit of research concerning role behavior in hospitals brings to light *related research questions in the hospital setting*. This is because it is highly unlikely that a single research effort really solves any problems. More likely, it aids in the understanding of some one problem, concerning which a number of other, as yet unstudied, factors are also of importance.

To put the matter in somewhat homelier terms, if initial investigation tells us that one of the correlates of poor performance in the family automobile is the fact that it burns a lot of oil, a problem-solving research approach calls for further investigation into the concomitants of excessive oil consumption in *this* automobile. On the other hand, a theory-building approach, particularly as seen in the social sciences, would likely result in a comparative study of other automobiles, and perhaps other types of internal-combustion engines, with regard to oil-consumption characteristics. Seen in this light, certain of the paradigms of theory building that have become widespread in the social sciences have a fairly low probability of directly contributing to the practical issues about which our critics (and some of our financial backers) are deeply concerned. This is not to say that a comparative study of internal-combustion engines would be of no practical value; but we must be aware of the fact that our "clients" are often more concerned about this particular automobile, right now.

One of the most telling criticisms of social science research calls attention to our modes of reporting the results of our studies. How can it be argued that our social science research is generally relevant to the interested public when so much of it is buried away (in terms of language and place of publication) in materials that are of interest and usefulness only to fellow social scientists? The fact is that our reporting styles graphically reveal the nature of our "reference groups." Our language of research expression has grown up as an in-group argot, in terms of which fellow members of our particular subsociety understand and appreciate our contributions to the in-group-oriented body of knowledge. To be relevant, newly discovered information must be communicated. We need to develop new kinds of research-reporting channels (and language styles) that will maximize the flow of useful knowledge to the men and agencies of social action.

In anthropology the language of research reporting has very seldom taken into account the matter of communicating directly with the populations that are studied. Until recent times most of the people studied by anthropologists could neither read nor write, nor were they particularly concerned with knowing many details of the information the fieldworker collected. After all, the local "native" already knew all about his local culture. Now things are a bit different. The anthropologist is very likely to be studying some aspects of adaptation to recent sociocultural change (rather than trying to recapture details of the people's golden past), and the local people are increasingly aware that the data are of practical importance. Indian groups in the United States have been particularly vociferous in insisting that the anthropologist should report back to them with some sort of useful information—or what was he doing there anyway?

Therefore, one of the central ethical and practical problems that anthropologists must solve is that of feeding back relevant social information to the populations they have studied. To do this will require:

1. A research orientation that does, in fact, produce socially useful information.
2. Development of modes of communication—styles of retranslation—that can convey our scientific information to interested publics in a form that articulates with their local modes of talking about their social experience.

It may be that feedback relationships with local populations can become important elements in new strategies of theory testing.

I have not intended to suggest in this epilogue that all anthropologists must now redirect their research interests toward social issues that are currently at the top of the public's list of critical problems. But I do think that Kenneth Clark's statement, and many others like it, must be taken seriously by our profession; and that our departments and other organizations should carefully consider the matter of research priorities, as well as other aspects of our responsibilities and relationships to the social world of which we are all a part.

The questions raised by the whole matter of "relevance" are directly related to problems of research methodology because research must be methodologically sound before it can be relevant for anything.

REFERENCES CITED

CLARK, KENNETH B.
1965. *Dark Ghetto.* New York: Harper & Row.

KUHN, T. S.
1962. *The Structure of Scientific Revolutions.* Chicago: University of Chicago Press.

Irma Honigmann and Indian Informant in Inuvik, Northwest Territories

Appendixes

Appendix A
Notes on Research Design

Research design involves combining the essential elements of investigation into an effective problem-solving sequence. Thus, the plan of research is a statement that concentrates on the components which *must be present* in order for the objectives of the study to be realized. The trimmings, the tangential matters—all the behind-the-scenes details of "what really happens in research"—are left out in order to present an idealized "master plan."

Effective structuring of research designs is essential to productive scientific work, although the ablest scientists are those who are also masters of the unspecifiable interstitial skills that make up the art of scientific investigation. Creative development of new research ideas cannot be planned; effective exploitation of research serendipity often follows no preestablished sequences; and many other important aspects of the research enterprise are not included in our formal statements of research plans. Nonetheless, it is useful to review some main elements of structure that enhance the researcher's chances of achieving his knowledge-building objectives.

Formulation of a Research Problem

In anthropology we find a wide variety of research intentions, ranging from precisely defined testing of hypotheses (e.g., concerning covariations of a few cultural elements) to general explorations of one or another cultural domain, such as kinship or religious beliefs. Some of the main types of productive research goals in anthropological work are the following:

1. *Description of a selected cultural or social domain.*
   As already noted, this type of anthropological research objective has been accorded a rather low status in much recent methodological writing. However, examination of a wide range of research in other sciences indicates the probability that this type of research may be the modal style in some disciplines (though it is sometimes disguised by post hoc references to hypotheses, theoretical models, etc.). Examples of "straight descriptive" research in other areas of science include reports of newly discovered diseases, genetic anomalies, subspecies of animals, behavior of animals (e.g., microvolt electric signals emitted by fish; signaling behavior of bees); description of new fossil finds of significance for geology, paleontology, etc.; and findings about aspects of the general environment (and man-caused modifications of the environment) such as description of solar radiation measurements in unusual locations, amounts of Strontium 90 in ocean waters, and descriptions of plant assemblages in particular ecological contexts.
   In anthropological literature we often find studies that involve research questions such as: How do the ———— (tribe or other cultural group) conceptualize and categorize the plants and animals in their environment? What are main features of organization in the market system of ———— (town or region)? What is the role of animal husbandry among the ———— (tribe or society)? What kinds of mental illness are found among the ———— (tribe or society)? What are main elements in the relationships between males and females among the ———— (tribe or society)?

2. *Examination of co-variation of an element X with a trait Y with which it is thought to be causally linked.*
   This is probably the most common hypothesis-testing paradigm. Most of the research designs discussed in Chapter 9 (e.g., researches

of Whiting and Child, Rodgers and Long, etc.) are examples of this kind of study.

Examples:

Test of proposition that degree of acculturation is related to ———— (various) psychiatric characteristics.

Test of proposition that keeping of large domesticated animals is causally related to patrilineal systems of descent. Various hypotheses about relationships of particular kinship terminological systems and types of residence, descent, and marriage systems.

3. *Search for the "causes" of a phenomenon X.*

This type of research question is particularly prevalent (with good reason) in the medical sciences. Much of the history of medical science is a chronicling of discoveries of the specific agents responsible for yellow fever, heart disease, etc.

Examples in anthropology:

What are the causes of mental disorders among the ———— (tribe)? What accounts for the presence of transvestites in a number of cultural groups? Why do some groups have complex, painful male initiation rites? What factors account for cargo cults?

4. *Examination of the consequences or effects of particular events or cultural features.*

Whereas in 3 the focus is on a search for the "independent variables," examination of the "effects of" a cultural element specifies a prominent independent variable and seeks to identify the resulting dependent variables.

Examples:

What are the effects of relocating a village? What are the social and cultural effects of a technological innovation, e.g., development of a new agricultural practice? What are the effects of a new industrial plant?

5. *Complex research designs involving combinations of the above four types of goals.*

Anthropological research activities usually involve complex combinations of these basic research paradigms. In most cases, though, it is essential that the investigator sort out these basic analytic units and clarify his research design in terms of each such question as a quasi-independent research enterprise. Many research activities are hazy in conceptualization because they involve a combination of these basic questions and the researcher failed to segment his research work into manageable "subroutines." Often the anthropologist focuses on a particular social institution, e.g., initiation rites, and develops a series of research questions that include a mixture of all the types of paradigms listed above. He is treating initiation ceremonies at times as a dependent variable, and at times as an independent variable that has certain "effects on" other cultural and social patterns. No harm comes of such a mixture if the researcher is aware of the logical requirements of the different perspectives he adopts at different points in such a research project.

In Chapter 9, I discussed briefly Blalock's testing of alternative hypotheses concerning the relationships among division of labor, postmarital residence, land tenure, and descent system. Although this research problem can be broken down into examination of the covariations of each pair of cultural patterns, the logic of the research problem also included the "chaining" of the correlations among the four traits into a more complex system. Thus research problems of a simple correlational type are often the precursors of complex "systems" research.

6. *Research in complex "systems."*

When a researcher programs his research in such a manner that the interactions of several variables are observed simultaneously, we can refer to it as "systems research." Examination of covariations among pairs of variables is often a precursor to systems research problems, for it is often useless to set up a complex model of interactions among variables unless the relationships among some of the pairs have been established in at least a preliminary way.

Examples in anthropology:

All of the computer simulation studies mentioned in Appendix C are examples of systems research. In these research problems the investigators specified relationships among at least four or more variables, and it was assumed (at least in part) that the "true picture" of the relationships among the several elements (e.g., demographic characteristics, marriage rates, types of preferential marriage performances) could not be approximated unless all the contributing variables were present in the system.

Depending on *how* the researcher phrases his questions, a systems analysis *may* be similar in appearance to the type of research problem in which the investigator asks, "What causes X?" Thus, in the computer simulations by Kunstadter and associates and by Gilbert and Hammel, a particular variable (having to do with a preferred marriage pattern) had the appearance of being the dependent variable. But the structure of the computer simulation (as one type of system) makes it possible for the researchers to shift focus from one variable to another without any modification of the basic research structure.

Elements of a Model Research Plan [1]

The basic elements of a model research plan are the same in any good piece of anthropological investigation. However, in the several different kinds of research goals discussed above, the pieces are put together somewhat differently. The outline presented below is structured in terms of a "type 4" research goal—study of the effects of a particular event or innovation (independent variable).

MODEL FOR STUDY OF THE EFFECTS OF THE INTRODUCTION OF IRRIGATION AMONG THE ————.

    I. Introduction.
        a. Historical background: brief ethnographic sketch of the ————; situation prior to irrigation; chronology of events.
        b. Practical and theoretical significance.
        c. Brief summary of relevant studies and literature.

    II. Statement of specific research goals.
        a. Aspects of culture and social organization to be the focus of research (e.g., agricultural practices, land use, kin relations, etc.)
        b. Specific hypotheses (if any) to be tested.
        c. Definitions of terms.

    III. Specification of research operations.
        a. Description of intended research tools which will be the basis for operational definitions of key terms above.
        b. Mention of general descriptive procedures as well as quantifiable research operations.
        c. Mention of hypothesis-generating features of initial research phase.
        d. Description of "interfering variables" and how they will be controlled.

    IV. Research population and sampling procedure.
        a. Methods to be used in delimiting communities (or other populations) to be studied.
            If population is large, methods of selecting and studying representative sample should be specified here.
        b. Specification of control population—group *not* experiencing the effects of experimental variable (irrigation).

[1] The application forms provided by foundations and government agencies for research grant proposals vary in their make-up, so the ordering and arrangement of the items in this outline must be adjusted to the requirements of specific funding agencies. In any case, the model set forth here is to be regarded more as a guide for the anthropological researcher than a model for grant application.

V. Diagram of research design.

The researcher should set up his plan in the form of a diagram in order to visualize the logic of his operations. Such a diagram need not be included in a written grant application, though it is often useful for clarifying points of research strategy (Figure 16). This diagram calls attention to the fact that the researcher must provide the following information:

a. The prior situation in both experimental and control populations.

b. Clear evidence that irrigation was introduced into one group and not the other.

c. Observations on his dependent variables for both populations.

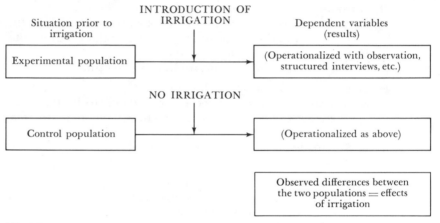

FIGURE 16. **Hypothetical Research Diagram**

VI. Analysis of results.

a. Types of statistical and/or other analysis to be used.

b. Statement of types of results that would lead to *rejection* of hypotheses listed above.

c. Facilities needed, e.g., calculator, computer, etc.

VII. Significance of the research (sometimes included in the Introduction).

a. Practical social implications, for development programs, etc.

b. Significance for anthropological theory.

c. Additional advantages, including professional training.

ADDITIONAL FEATURES OF A RESEARCH PROPOSAL
NOT PART OF ESSENTIAL DESIGN

VIII. Timetable (chronological sequence with estimated dates).

a. Travel (and preparations before entering field site).

  b. Initial period—rapport building, etc.
  c. Construction and development of research instruments.
  d. Pretesting of research tools and techniques.
  e. Selection of populations (samples).
  f. Collection of main data specified above in research diagram.
  g. Pre-analysis of data before leaving the field.
  h. Collection of further supporting data as time allows.
  i. Data analysis and writing.

IX. Personnel.
  a. Principal investigators.
  b. Assistants.
  c. Supporting persons in other fields.

X. Facilities available.
  a. In field area.
  b. Supporting informational sources.
  c. Data analysis and other assistance (computer center, statistical consultants, etc.).

XI. Budget.
  a. Personnel—salaries, wages, insurance, etc.
  b. Equipment—tape recorders, cameras, typewriters, etc.
  c. Supplies—paper, notebooks, film, tapes, etc.
  d. Travel—to the research site; internal travel during research.
  e. Computer and other data-processing facilities.
  f. Gifts for informants and other miscellaneous data-collection costs.
  g. Duplicating—maps, records, other archival materials.
  h. Shipping, mailing, etc.

As already mentioned, different types of research goals each require their particular ordering of essential design elements. For example, general descriptive study usually includes no hypothesis testing and ordinarily requires no control samples or populations. The operational definitions of terms often arise from the initial phase of research, rather than being delineated in advance. On the other hand, research designs involving advanced mathematical or statistical manipulation should be conceptualized in the form of equations and dummy statistical tables in order to clarify the types and relationships of the variables to be examined.

The creative field researcher will avoid strait-jacketing his data-gathering operations in unalterable research designs; at the same time, he remains fully aware that planless fact gathering usually results in a hodgepodge of incomplete (hence useless) materials.

cluding the assessment of the seriousness in breaches of these rules.

While Goodenough's scale of "setting one's self above another" is concerned with Trukese *ideal* behavior, it is often practical to develop scalograms concerning real behavior (or other attributes) of persons in order to rank them on a significant social dimension. Paul Kay (1964) has described consumer behavior in a sample of Tahitian households by means of a Guttman scale of durable goods. Table 27 presents an abbreviated version of his scale.

TABLE 27. **Scalogram of Durable Consumer Goods Ownership in Tahiti**

House-hold	Scale Type	Auto-mobile	Refrig-erator	Kerosene or Gas Stove	Two-Wheeled Motor Vehicle	Radio	Bicycle	Primus Stove
1	7	X	X	X	X	X	X	X
2		X	X	X	X	X	X	X
3	6		X	X	X	X	X	X
6			X	X	0	X	X	X
8	5			X	X	X	X	X
10				X	0	X	X	X
11	4		Ⓧ		X	X	X	X
13					X	X	X	X
17	3					X	X	X
24	2				Ⓧ		X	X
25							X	X
33							X	0
34	1							X
35								X
40	0	(household has none of the items)						0

$$\text{Rep.} = 1 - \frac{8}{320} = .98$$
(in original scale of 40 households)

ABRIDGED FROM Kay, 1964.

This scale of consumer goods represents the same logical pattern as that of Goodenough's scale presented in Table 25. The goods are ordered from left to right in terms of increasing frequency. The reverse direction would appear to be an ordering of their relative "scarcity value." The households are ranked from high to low in terms of their material possessions. The scale provides a very useful baseline of material-style-of-life in terms of which intracommunity comparisons can be made.

Unlike Goodenough's ideal scale of "setting oneself above another," we note that this pattern in Tahiti is not "perfect." In terms of the logic of the scale, Household 6 "should have" a two-wheeled motor vehicle; and Household 11 "should not have" a refrigerator, since they do not have the preceding item, kerosene or gas stove. Such errors in the scale are always to be expected in real human behavior, as contrasted with a set of rules for ideal behavior. However, it is important to know how many errors a scale can include without destroying its usefulness as a scale. Put in different terms, it can be argued that an array of items is not really a unidimensional scale if there are too many errors. Louis Guttman, the originator of this analytic technique, has suggested a way of deciding how many errors is too many to permit acceptance of a Guttman scale. He proposes a "coefficient of reproducibility" which is calculated from the formula $Rep = 1 - \dfrac{\text{number of errors}}{\text{number of entries}}$. Since Kay's scalogram involves information about eight items for 40 households, he has a total of 320 pieces of information. The total matrix of data shows 8 errors of the type discussed above. Hence his coefficient of reproducibility is .98. Guttman suggests that a reproducibility of .90 is sufficient for regarding a particular set of data as "scalable." Other measures of the adequacy of Guttman scales have been developed, notably a "coefficient of scalability" by Menzel (1953).

A number of social scientists have produced Guttman scales involving cross-cultural aggregates of data. Freeman and Winch (1957) developed a cross-cultural scale of social complexity; Carniero (1962) has examined propositions about general cultural evolution using Guttman scales; White (1967) has demonstrated that matrilineality and patrilineality can be usefully expressed as ranges of variation in scalogram form in place of the usual typological categories; and Frank and Ruth Young have used scalogram analysis in a number of studies concerning culture change and regional development. Young (1965) has also used this same technique in a cross-cultural study of initiation ceremonies.

Pauline Mahar (1960) has produced a very interesting scale of ritual pollution in terms of which Hindu castes are ranked in a village in Uttar Pradesh. From structured interviews with 18 respondents (representing 11 different castes) she was able to demonstrate a consistent cultural ranking. Table 28 gives the pattern of response for one respondent, a 40-year-old female of the Brahman caste. Mahar points out that the final version of the ritual pollution scale was not isomorphic with the responses of any one person in the

TABLE 28.   **Scale Picture of Responses Indicating Ritual Distance (Manbhi, Brahman Caste, Female, Aged 40) ***

Item	13	10	1	2	7	11	4	8	6	9	12	3	5	Score
CASTES														
Rajput	X	X	X	X	X	X	X	X	X	X				10
Merchants	X	X	X	X	X	X	X	X	X	X				10
Water-Carriers	X	X	X	X	X	X	X	X	X	X	0	X		10-11
Goldsmiths	X	X	X	X	X	X	X	X	X					9
Genealogists	X	X	X	X	X	X	X	X	X					9
Barbers	X	X	X	X	X	X	X	X						8
Goosaaii	X	X	X	X	X	X								6
Shepherds	X	X	X	X	X	X								6
Carpenters	X	X	X	X	X	X								6
Potters	X	X	X	X	0	X								5-6
Washermen	X	X	X	X	X									5
Grainparchers	X	X	X	X	X									5
K. B. Weavers	X	0	X	X										3-4
Joogiis	X	0	X	X										3-4
Mus. Rajputs	X	X	X											3
Oilpressers	X	X												2
Miraassii	X	0	X											1-2-3
Ch. Weavers														0
Shoemakers														0
Ag. laborers														0
Sweepers														0

Identification of above items:

** 13 Can touch our children
   10 Can accept dry, uncooked food
** 1 Can touch me
    2 Can sit on our cot
** 7 Can smoke bowl of pipe
   11 Can take water from his hand
** 4 Can touch our brass vessels
** 8 Can accept fried food from him
    6 Can smoke our pipe
** 9 Can accept boiled food from his hand
   12 Can touch our water vessel
    3 Can come on our cooking area
    5 Can touch our earthenware vessels.

ADAPTED FROM Mahar, 1960.
* Manbhi's own caste is omitted from the analysis here.
** Items used in final version of the scale.

community. That is, while the final over-all ranking is fairly consistent with all respondents' rankings, it can not be derived from any one individual's ranking.

We should be clear that the demonstration of a Guttman scalogram in a matrix of data does not provide unequivocal evidence that the scale measures or expresses the particular dimension claimed by the researcher. Any set of items in such a scale is open to interpretation as to the nature of the underlying dimension. The use of Guttman scales to infer chronological sequences (e.g., in the works of Carniero and, occasionally, by the Youngs) is especially open to question. Graves *et al.* (1969) have demonstrated that the items in a Guttman scale for a series of communities in Mexico (originally studied by Frank Young) did not appear in individual towns in the chronological progression implied by the scale. Apparently *some* new items spread very rapidly, once they make their appearance. Thus, for example in Kay's scalogram above, it is not safe to infer that the list of items demonstrates a chronological ordering of the appearance of those durable goods in Tahiti.

I have presented details about the use of Guttman scales at some length here for several reasons:

1. Scalograms provide an example of a general methodological strategy that has been relatively little used by anthropologists heretofore; namely, the ordering of cultural items into logically consistent sets whose internal patterning provide a *range of variation* rather than typological (nominal) categorizing of observations (persons, events, etc.)
2. The feature of rank ordering that emerges from this kind of analysis makes possible more powerful (and more convincing) statistical tools, such as rank-order correlations, the Mann-Whitney U test, and others.
3. The procedures involved in Guttman scaling of data—whether intracultural or cross-cultural—provide anthropologists with new tools for examining logical assumptions about essential dimensions of cultural systems.
4. Demonstration of Guttman-scaling effects can be used as a method for assessing the quality of data. Lozier (1967) used scalogram analysis to order responses concerning "politeness" in a cross-cultural study involving people from Lebanon, Colombia, Japan, and the United States. The fact that his subjects' responses could be scaled provides evidence that they understood the anthropologist's questions, and that the questions about politeness made sense to them. Further, the cross-cultural similarities in the scalograms strongly suggest that the concept of politeness is a single dimension with cross-cultural meaning, even though people of different cultural backgrounds weight elements in the general continuum of politeness differently.

REFERENCES CITED

CARNIERO, ROBERT L.
1962. "Scale Analysis as an Instrument for the Study of Cultural Evolution." *Southwestern Journal of Anthropology,* 18:149–169.

FREEMAN, LINTON C., and ROBERT F. WINCH
1957. "Societal Complexity: An Empirical Test of a Typology of Societies." *American Journal of Sociology,* 62:461–466.

GOODENOUGH, WARD
1963. "Some Applications of Guttman Scaling Analysis to Ethnography and Culture Theory." *Southwestern Journal of Anthropology,* 19:235–250.

GRAVES, THEODORE, NANCY B. GRAVES, and MICHAEL J. KOBRIN
1969. "Historical Inferences from Guttman Scales: The Return of Age-Area Magic?" *Current Anthropology,* 10:317–338.

GUTTMAN, LOUIS
1944. "A Basis for Scaling Qualitative Data." *American Sociological Review,* 9:139–150.

KAY, PAUL
1964. "A Guttman Scale Model of Tahitian Consumer Behavior." *Southwestern Journal of Anthropology,* 20:160–167.

LOZIER, JOHN D.
1967. "Perception of Politeness in Non-verbal Behavior." Unpublished M.A. thesis, University of Minnesota.

MAHAR, PAULINE
1960. "A Ritual Pollution Scale for Ranking Hindu Castes." *Sociometry,* 23:292–306. By permission of the author and the American Sociological Association.

MENZEL, HERBERT
1953. "A New Coefficient for Scalogram Analysis." *Public Opinion Quarterly,* 17:268–280.

WHITE, DOUGLAS R.
1967. "Concomitant Variation in Kinship Structures." Unpublished M.A. thesis, University of Minnesota.

YOUNG, FRANK W.
1965. *Initiation Ceremonies: A Cross-Cultural Study of Status Dramatization.* Indianapolis: Bobbs-Merrill.

YOUNG, FRANK W. and RUTH C. YOUNG
1960. "Social Integration and Change in Twenty-four Mexican Villages." *Economic Development and Cultural Change,* 8:366–377.
1962. "The Sequence and Direction of Community Growth: A Cross-Cultural Generalization." *Rural Sociology,* 27:374–386.

Appendix C
On Using Computers

As anthropologists become more and more accustomed to "counting things" and giving numerical statements concerning frequencies of behaviors, things, traits, and events, as well as computing expressions of the covariations among these cultural elements, the tasks of recording, storing, and analyzing these data become more and more complicated. Moreover, since we tend to be holistic in general orientation, we prefer to manipulate rather large numbers of different elements simultaneously. That is, none of us are particularly happy with the examination of individual cultural items, or pairs of items, torn out of the context of broad behavioral patterns to which they are related. Anthropological analysis most usually involves a multivariable strategy.

Beyond a certain point the tasks of storing and manipulating these data become so enormous that we tend to lose track of our materials, or our inventorying and managing of the data become overly cumbersome and time consuming. At some point in the growing complexity and perplexity of data handling we can save time and energy by turning to electronic computers for assistance.

Many people seem to react emotionally at the mention of computers. With some of our friends, the word "computer" brings an instant flush to the cheeks, a brightening of the eyes, slight dilation of the pupils, and a quickening of the pulse that signals excitement and enthusiasm. Other people we know tend to snort with contempt at suggestions of computerizing and thus "dehumanizing" the delicate art of data manipulation.

With large amounts of data in his hands, the anthropologist may find that even such simple operations as a tally of frequencies and percentages of traits or items can require hours and days of hand calculations, while the electronic computer can do the same job in a few seconds. The catch is, of course, that it may require hours and days of work to prepare the data in such a way that the computer can be utilized. Organizing, coding, key punching, and verifying the data is itself a long and tedious process, to which must be added the time-consuming task of preparing the instructions in terms of which the computer is to carry out the data analysis. And frequently we have to pay for the programming and the use of the computer.

If one is quite sure that a given set of procedures can be specified that will require only one pass through the data, then even fairly large bodies of materials can be hand processed, once and for all, without serious inefficiency compared to the investment of effort and time required to have the job done by computer. But in the vast majority of cases we need to go through our data in many different ways; we are constantly discovering new ways to look at our data, and most often the nature of later analytic procedures depends on what we find in our preliminary analysis. These repeated processes of looking through the data can often be done most efficiently by computer, even though the preparation of the materials requires a large initial investment of time and effort.

TYPES OF COMPUTER OPERATIONS

In this brief appendix I will not go into any detail about various computer operations, for that would require writing a book. However, it is useful to list some of the tasks for which anthropologists have found computerization useful.

DATA STORAGE

Large amounts of information, in the form of numerical codes or as words, phrases, or other nonnumerical symbols, can be stored on

IBM cards or magnetic tapes for quick retrieval by computer. Linguists, folklorists, and other language specialists store textual materials in forms that make it possible to retrieve (and count) the occurrences and contexts of individual words, types of words (in the form of noun and verb counts, etc.) and other shapes of textual elements. A great variety of content analytic methods can be employed with data stored in this form. Benjamin Colby's analysis of folklore materials, discussed in Chapter 5, is an example of this kind of usage.

Sebeok (1965) has described a complex storage and retrieval system used at Indiana University in connection with analysis of folklore. To facilitate retrieval of stored folklore data, Sebeok and associates have developed several different procedures, including a Co-occurrence Tally Program, Unit Inventory Program, Segmenting and Enumerating Routine, an Alphabetic Sort Routine, and several other automatic routines. For those of us most concerned about the "dehumanization" of the research process which overdependence on computer technology might bring, it is of some interest to note what Sebeok says about "browsing":

To affirm that the creative process is a human function is not to deny that a properly conceived mechanical system could enhance the process through simulation of browsing, both in non-directed and in directed fashion. In non-directed browsing the machine is instructed merely to draw units at random from an area circumscribed by an investigator who is guided by a suggestive clue he accidentally discovered in a previous drawing. In directed browsing, on the other hand, a specific area, exhaustively analyzed, must first of all be fed into the machine. A program of controlled associations enables the computer to locate items linked with the original area. Then the machine samples successively, to the extent instructed, from more and more remote areas. Such a method might, for instance, be used to identify significant tropes in poetic discourse. (Sebeok, 1965:271.)

Archaeologists, depending on the types of sites excavated, may be faced with problems of keeping track of anywhere from a few hundred artifacts and other materials to (more usually) thousands or hundreds of thousands of items. For each item certain key data about material, physical state and characteristics, where found, etc., must be recorded. I once heard an archaeologist state that it is just as easy for him to write up the information on seventy thousand potsherds by hand as it is to prepare the same materials for computerized processing. This is quite probable, but had he prepared those data for the computer he would have been able to do a great number of different kinds of analysis of the materials; and storage of the data in this form often makes recovery of particular items of information much easier.

Among social anthropologists it is probable that the majority of IBM card data decks consist of the stored data on a cross-cultural sample (e.g., Whiting and Child's 75 societies) or else the tabulations from a household survey such as the ones described by Colson, Beattie, and Köbben. It should be noted that simple frequency counts of particular items in an IBM data deck do not require access to a computer. Many simple operations of counting can be carried out using a counter-sorter.

STATISTICAL ANALYSIS

The computer utilization that is most familiar to most anthropologists is that of statistical analysis. While simple chi-square computations, Mann-Whitney U tests, and correlation coefficients (see Chapter 7) can easily be computed by hand for small numbers of cases, it is often more economical to computerize these operations when correlation matrices of 20 or more variables are involved. More complicated operations, such as factor analysis and multiple regression analysis, are practically always best carried out by computers.

In most university computer centers there are now available large libraries of "canned programs" for the statistical operations usually employed by social scientists. To use these standard programs the two main bodies of material which must be prepared are:

1. The data deck (IBM cards or magnetic tape) containing the coded research materials.
2. The set of control cards which instruct the computer concerning the essential features of this particular set of data, and identify the particular program that will be used.

As the processing of these materials has become more standardized, it is possible for an individual with relatively little knowledge of programming to communicate his wishes to the computer in the form of data deck and control cards, and to obtain a complex set of statistical operations with relatively little help from professional programmers and other specialists. However, special consultants are usually available at computer centers to guide the novice through that special sociotechnological world of electronic gadgetry.

COMPUTERIZED SIMULATIONS

Complex social actions such as warfare, exchange marriage systems, games, and economic transactions can sometimes be broken down into a manageable number of key operations (variables) which can be integrated into a simulation model for experimental purposes. When a sufficiently large set of variables has been identified, and relationships among them postulated, it is possible to construct physical models of a given system (e.g., a battlefield with troops, generals, supplies, fortifications, transport and communication systems, etc.) in order to experiment with different strategies and situations. One can "see what happens if the attacking army concentrates its main force on the left flank of the defenders," and so on.

When quantified relationships can be postulated among the variables, the matter of building a model can be carried out completely in mathematical terms. Instead of moving armies or supplies in a physical model, the experimenter calculates equations employing a series of rules governing the behavior of his variables under various conditions. Experimentation with such mathematical models very soon leads to enormously complicated and time-consuming mathematical work, beyond the time and energy available to the average anthropologist. This situation is ideal for computerization. Once the model has been accurately set up, the computer can run through a great number of sequences of experiments with the model, turning out solutions to various possible strategies, changes of operating rules, or modifications of situations.

Kunstadter, Buhler, Stephen, and Westoff (1963) carried out a computer simulation to "determine effects of variation in demographic variables such as population growth, birth rate, death rates, and age-specific marriage rates on the operation of an ideal pattern of preferential marriage." In this, as in all such computerized simulations, the specification of the variables (e.g., birth rates, death rates) and the rules for interaction of the variables depended on empirical data from well-studied populations. The investigator does not construct his model from "just any old" patterns of variables, but must find quantified descriptive data from which to build up the details of his model. If he has realistic values for parts of his model, and can state realistic rules of relationship between these known values and another, unquantified variable, he can try a number of different values for the unknown variable, to find out what range of values "works" in the model.

Kunstadter and associates found that "the proportion of ideal marriages is directly related to population growth, and to marriage rates, and that variability in proportion of ideal marriages is inversely related to population size" (Kunstadter *et al.*, 1963:518). Gilbert and Hammel (1966) used a computerized simulation in trying to answer the question "How much, and in what ways, is the rate of patrilateral parallel cousin (FBD) marriage influenced by the number of populations involved in the exchange of women, by their size, by their rules of postmarital residence, and by the degree of territorially endogamic preference?" (Gilbert and Hammel, 1966:73.) David Barry (1968) has used a computer simulation to study aspects of Chinese land tenure as related to family size, patterns of inheritance, and other factors.

Unlike the computer applications involved in simple storage and retrieval, counting and listing, and computations using standard statistical techniques, computerized simulation of necessity involves the development of elaborate sets of instructions in terms of which the computer is to carry out the simulation. These detailed instructions, called programs, must be written perfectly. That is, unlike humans, computers cannot tolerate any errors or gaps in their instructions. Thus, the most time consuming element in computer simulations, computerized "games," and other complicated operations is the writing of the program of instructions.

Special courses in computer programming are available at various levels, ranging from short-term familiarization courses to those complicated instructional sequences intended for computer science specialists. At the elementary level the computer language called FORTRAN is the most widely used symbol system in terms of which we can "tell the computer what to do." Probably all anthropologists who make occasional use of computer facilities should gain familiarity with the rudiments of FORTRAN.

THE CULTURE AND SOCIAL ORGANIZATION
OF COMPUTER USE

In any discussion about what can or can't be done with computers, or in debates pro and con concerning the suggestion to "computerize the whole operation," one main element should never be lost from sight. Successes and failures with computerization are best seen as reflections of social organization, cultural patterns, and personality. Of these, the crucial problem, in my experience, is the matter of social organization.

In one of my worst encounters with the computer (and most veterans of these campaigns can top this story) a rather large body of interview materials was coded and ready for key punching (transfer of data to IBM cards) in September 1967. Researchers, some of whom planned to finish term papers by Christmas, waited patiently for the advent of the electronic miracle of data processing. The first problems encountered were, of course, in the coding of the data. All the sheets of coded data had to be rechecked. Somehow the months rolled on as we checked through the coded materials, double checked the IBM cards, and then instructed our programmer concerning the specific blocks of data we needed to analyze. More weeks went by as the programmer occasionally checked back to inform us that his program apparently still had a few bugs in it, but would soon be running. At one point he informed us that several days had been lost because apparently someone at the computer center had dropped the data deck and mixed up the IBM cards (approximately 20 cards of data per household, for 500 households). The first signs of spring (which come pretty late in Minnesota) were in the air when we finally began to get listings of the data we wanted from this body of information.

In this example, and many others like it, we have found that the maintenance of structured communications with the various persons in the data-handling process—particularly the programmer—is a major element in successful management of computer utilization. Since we frequently need the services of well-trained programmers, we have to be able to communicate with them effectively, and for that we need to understand the rudiments, at least, of how computers "think" and how programmers, through FORTRAN and other computer languages, communicate with their electronic friends.

It is also clear that many, many problems in computerization arise through human errors in the coding and data-listing processes that occur before the data are punched onto IBM cards. In hand analysis these slip-ups are often overlooked and processing goes on; but the computer is less tolerant of error—missing information and information coded in nonexistent categories often bring the machines to a grinding halt. We need to keep our research assistants well-paid and happy, so that we can obtain precision in the pre-computer stages of data processing.

In spite of the great speed with which computers can process data —when *everything* is done correctly—utilization of these machines requires great patience. A program of data processing practically never makes it through the works on the first attempt. Repetition of the process of resubmitting data decks to the computer center is a humbling and thought-provoking process—which can be turned to advantage as we rethink our data logic and plan for a cleaner, more precise research operation the next time.

In addition to the immensely expanded range of data analysis made possible by the advent of the Age of Computers, another very large gain registered by anthropologists in the utilization of mechanical data-processing devices is the greatly increased precision with which we now regard our data. When we begin to use these precision tools in handling our data we are forced to define our units of analysis explicitly and to code our observations carefully. And we can't easily go slipping back to change an earlier categorization to fit with our current hypothesis, saying things like: "Those Siriono should *really* be classed as agricultural (since their kinship system doesn't fit our theory about hunters)."

There are many numerical operations that anthropologists should do by hand—out in the field or in their studies. And, up to a certain point, the well-equipped anthropologist should be ready at all times to do a computation or two, and to scan a block of data by hand, without having to rely on computers. When all of one's data are on IBM cards (or computer tapes) and every little analysis has to involve interaction with that social mazeway at the computer center, one experiences a truly helpless feeling. The researcher should never be completely dependent on the computers. He should have his data on hand in some noncomputerized form—so that data can be scanned and manipulated by hand.

When the anthropologist has the kinds of data storage and retrieval tasks, or series of statistical analyses, or other manipulations which can be economically handled by computers, the following points should be kept in mind:

1. Coding, key punching, and other preparation of data for computer processing must be done with great care and patience. Too often we underestimate the time and expense involved in these preparatory operations, thus reducing our efficiency in computer utilization.
2. Almost all computer centers provide consultants who will assist and advise in selecting the right computer operations in terms of the researcher's particular data needs. It is of great importance to consult the computer advisers and statistical specialists before data are coded. (Of course one should have extensive consultation with statistical advisers before data are collected.) Poorly organized data categories and codes can make computerized analysis very difficult and cumbersome.
3. Although the anthropologist does not usually expect to do his own programming of computer operations, it is extremely useful to develop familiarity with FORTRAN computer language, and to develop general understanding of the requirements, restrictions, and possibilities inherent in computer use. Communication with programmers and with other persons in the social organization of computer facilities are extremely difficult if we remain ignorant of their informal and formal cultural understandings.
4. The great speed with which statistical operations can be carried out, once the data are fully prepared, makes it possible for the researcher to run numbers of different kinds of analyses and data checks, rather than adhering to a few habitual routines. To maximize our data-processing capabilities, we should be continually on the lookout for new kinds of computer usages. Several easily-applied computer programs (such as factor analysis and multiple regression computations) have only recently become available.
5. The new "convert" to computer use should not set his hopes too high at first, and he should not be discouraged about those fre-

quent setbacks when programs must be resubmitted a number of times before they operate successfully. We *once* had a program that went through the first time it was submitted—a truly remarkable event.

6. If anthropology departments had adequate financing for all the facilities and services needed for optimum effectiveness of research, each department would have a staff programmer-and-computer adviser. Most departments cannot afford to employ such computer specialists, however, so the next best thing is to seek out a computer consultant who has an interest in the social sciences. Sometimes social scientists in other departments have developed special skills in computer utilization, which they are willing to share with anthropologists. These are the kinds of men with whom we need to develop interdisciplinary research projects. Another solution to the problem of developing special information about computer utilization is to attract mathematically-oriented students into anthropological study. It would be very much worth our while to provide special flexibility in our graduate training programs for those persons who want to combine anthropological interest with serious immersion in computer science.

7. The use of computers in data processing does not eliminate the "human factor" from our research. Rather, the computer must be used to do the drudgery that so often detracts from our human research effectiveness. Tedious routines of data scanning, counting, sorting, and calculating should be made as painless and economical of time as possible, so the anthropologist (and his research assistants) can concentrate attention on the important things of science.

But to make efficient use of this new electronic research assistant, we have to give a lot of attention, especially in these early years of exploration, to building up the social and cultural ties that are essential to interacting with the machines.

REFERENCES CITED

BARRY, DAVID
1968. "A Computer Simulation of the Chinese Peasant Land Tenure System." Unpublished M.A. thesis, University of Minnesota.

GILBERT, J. P. and E. A. HAMMEL
1966. "Computer Simulation and Analysis of Problems in Kinship and Social Structure." *American Anthropologist,* 68:70–93.

HYMES, DELL
1965. *The Use of Computers in Anthropology.* The Hague: Mouton and Co.

KUNSTADTER, PETER, and ROALD BUHLER, FREDERICK STEPHAN, CHARLES WESTOFF

1963.   "Demographic Variability and Preferential Marriage Patterns." *American Journal of Physical Anthropology,* 22:511–519.

SEBEOK, A. THOMAS

1965.   "The Computer as a Tool in Folklore Research." In *The Use of Computers in Anthropology,* ed. D. Hymes. The Hague: Mouton and Co.

Appendix D
Field Guide to North American Celebrations

Field observation of public celebrations is carried on mainly by participant observation and catch-as-catch-can interviewing. Fieldworkers should prepare themselves in advance of public celebrations with as much information as possible, so that observation of significant events will be effective. The fieldworker should make himself a list and schedule of most important events of the local celebrations. Official handbills and newspaper announcements are important sources of this information. In general the fieldworker should so schedule his activities that he is present in a wide variety of different events and places. During periods of time when nothing is happening, he should avoid lingering in one place. Fieldworkers may find it useful to partake of alcoholic beverages with informants, in public places where observations are important, or with friends or acquaintances; however, it should be remembered that overindulgence leads to lowered efficiency. The list of categories of observations is intended as a general guide and need not be followed rigidly. It is not necessarily complete; nor are all items applicable in each celebration.

I. Sponsoring or directing individuals and organizations.
   A. Main sponsoring organization(s)
   B. Sponsors of particular events: e.g., races, fireworks, dances.
   C. Master of ceremonies, announcers, other prominent figures.
      1. Is there one central figure?
      2. Out-of-town speaker?
      3. Town clown?
      4. Local queen or king?
   D. Publicity given to any or all of the central figures.

II. Official events—the program.
   A. Get handbills, fliers, newspaper announcements, and other printed information.
   B. Timing of official events, as compared with actual schedule. (Note deletions or additions.)
   C. Official participants.
   D. Actual participants: e.g., anybody can participate, but actually only the teenagers take part.)
   E. Check list of events.
      1. Dances: public, exhibition, contest.
      2. Ball games or other team contests (e.g., lacrosse, egg throwing).
      3. Individual contests, races, etc.
      4. Exhibited products (judging or prizes?).
      5. Raffles or games of chance (who sponsors?).
      6. Prizes?
      7. Speeches, honorary bestowals.
      8. Religious observances (prayers, etc.).
      9. Impromptu speeches.
     10. Recognition of visitors and mention of absent individuals.
     11. Expressions of patriotism and solidarity.
         a. Community solidarity expressed.
         b. National and state solidarity expressed.
         c. Recognition of subcommunities.
     12. Special picnics, luncheons, and beer busts.

Note: In all of these events, note hostile acts, audience reactions, hostility in essentially nonaggressive events, including intercommunity rivalry, as well as general level of enthusiasm for participants and spectators. If possible pick out the single most important event.

III. Concessions.
   A. Temporary concessions (popcorn stands and beer stands).
   B. Permanent businesses opened for this day.

    C. Transportation concessions (special busses, etc.).

    D. Ownership of concessions—individuals or groups.

IV. Private decorations, and decorations of public buildings. (Who was responsible for getting the public decorations up? Permanent fixtures used, like fairgrounds?) Dance circles?

V. Social Control.

    A. Police, special deputies, bouncers (armed? uniformed? local, state or county? prominent or inconspicuous? strict or relaxed?).

    B. Informal social controls. (control of children by adults, control of boisterous individuals by groups or individuals, gossiping about bad conduct, etc.)

VI. Spectators.

    A. General make-up of public (young people or old, families or single persons, gangs, couples, etc.)

    B. Out-of-town visitors, tourists, including distant visitors.

    C. Former local inhabitants returning for celebration.

    D. Any local people ignoring the celebration.

    E. Interactions of groups and individuals (Indian-White interaction; local people-tourists; conspicuous segregation of types of spectators).

VII. Dress.

    A. Different categories of spectators.

    B. Dress of participants.

    C. Funny hats, personal decorations, badges, ribbons, other unusual dress.

VIII. Unscheduled events (drinking parties, ball games, horse shoes, dancing).

IX. General impressions (Fun? Long-winded? Well organized or confused?).

If the fieldworker is a stranger in his community, he should note reactions of community members toward him and his family.

X. Other comments.

    A. Do informants make comparisons between this and previous celebrations?

    B. Many new events or additions?

    C. Have these celebrations been going on a long time in this community?

    D. Where do out-of-towners find lodging for the night?

    E. Announcements made of future celebrations or events?

    F. Weather.

XI. Make sketch map of the main areas of activity (and describe local scene, geography).

XII. Take many photographs.

Index of Names

359

Index of Subjects